Shirts, Shifts and Sheets
of Fine Linen

Also by Pam Inder and also published by Bloomsbury

*Busks, Basques and Brush-Braid: British dressmaking in the
18th and 19th centuries*

Shirts, Shifts and Sheets of Fine Linen

British seamstresses from the 17th to the 19th centuries

Pam Inder

BLOOMSBURY VISUAL ARTS
LONDON · NEW YORK · OXFORD · NEW DELHI · SYDNEY

BLOOMSBURY VISUAL ARTS

Bloomsbury Publishing Plc, 50 Bedford Square, London, WC1B 3DP, UK
Bloomsbury Publishing Inc, 1359 Broadway, New York, NY 10018, USA
Bloomsbury Publishing Ireland, 29 Earlsfort Terrace, Dublin 2, D02 AY28, Ireland

BLOOMSBURY, BLOOMSBURY VISUAL ARTS and the Diana logo are trademarks of
Bloomsbury Publishing Plc

First published in Great Britain 2024
Paperback edition published 2026
Copyright © Pam Inder, 2024

Cover image: Shirt, probably British, late 18th century.
(© Heritage Art/Heritage Images via Getty Images)

A catalogue record for this book is available from the British Library.

A catalog record for this book is available from the Library of Congress.

ISBN: HB: 978-1-3502-5296-7
        PB: 978-1-3502-5300-1
      ePDF: 978-1-3502-5297-4
     eBook: 978-1-3502-5298-1

Typeset by RefineCatch Limited, Bungay, Suffolk

For product safety related questions contact productsafety@bloomsbury.com.

To find out more about our authors and books visit www.bloomsbury.com
and sign up for our newsletters.

Contents

Illustrations

Colour Plates

Figures

Tables

Acknowledgements

I would like to thank the staff of all the record offices, archives, libraries and museums – too many to name individually – who have assisted me with my research. I would also like to thank my editors, Frances Arnold and Rebecca Hamilton, and my friends, Marion Aldis, Jenny Dyer, Michael and Christine Endacott, Jane May, Françoise Menestry, Jeff Morgan and Indira Nath for their various contributions, and, of course, my family for their support.

Introduction

Some twenty-odd years ago my son brought home a new girlfriend: 'Mum, K has some things that need mending.' I proffered my work basket. 'Er, I can't really sew', said K, looking embarrassed and clutching a little pile of bedraggled garments, a skirt with the hem half-down, a top with a detached frill, various items missing buttons and hooks and eyes. Forty minutes and several yards of black cotton later – K was a goth – the garments were intact. K was neither lazy nor stupid but her mother didn't sew and needlework had formed no part of her school curriculum.

Being unable to sew would have been incomprehensible to most women in the past. Even I learnt to do hemming and cross-stitch and run-and-fell seams in primary school, and at grammar school in the 1950s 'domestic science' started with the making of aprons and shoe-bags embroidered with our initials. By the age of fourteen I, and most of my classmates, were making at least some of our own clothes. We were, nonetheless, considerably less expert than most of our great – and several times great – grandmothers would have been. Museums are full of needlework samplers beautifully stitched, two hundred or more years ago, by little girls as young as seven or eight. Learning to sew was then a key part of a girl's education. In February 1796, for example, John Simcoe wrote to his daughter, Charlotte, who had made him a shirt: 'I have acknowledged my obligations to you for the *shirt* you sent me; your Mamma rather a better judge than I am, says it is most admirably worked & shews a great deal of proper Industry in you, my beloved Daughter. May God Almighty always bless you with a spirit above Idleness [*sic*].'[1] Charlotte was ten.

However, there were always women who disliked sewing, women who were not very good at it and, by the mid-nineteenth century if not before, there were some girls who, like K, had simply never had the opportunity to learn. Girls who started work as children and had little or no schooling did not learn to sew and so could not teach their own daughters. Several generations down the line, in many city slums sewing had become a lost art. In Birmingham in 1843, Sam

Page, a button-maker, told the Royal Commission on the Employment of Children and Young Persons in Trade and Manufacture (referred to hereafter as the Children's Employment Commission) that: 'It would be a great advantage to the family if the wife knew how to cut out, make and repair the linen',[2] but his wife was unable to do so, and a number of other Birmingham men made similar comments to the commissioners. It was the same in other places. In London, for example, sixteen-year-old Caroline Ormer, apprentice to a coffin-maker, said that neither she nor her mother could 'cut out and make any part of her things . . . it would have been an advantage if she had been taught such things'.[3]

Nonetheless, for many men, the woman doing needlework was a romantic, idealized figure; sewing was the perfect feminine activity, combining industry and genteel domesticity. Even the poor seamstress, stitching away hour after hour to support herself and her family, was seen as 'womanly' in a way that the, probably better-paid, factory worker, sullied by contact with the world of commerce, was not. But at the same time there was another, less flattering, belief about needlewomen that linked them inextricably with prostitution and low morals. Of course, impoverished women from all walks of life did, *in extremis*, resort to providing sex for money, but seamstresses were in reality no more likely to do so than anyone else. The idea may well have originated with the eighteenth-century writers of scurrilous plays like *The Intriguing Milliners and Attornies' Clerks* of 1738, and the slanderous comments made by R. Campbell in *The London Tradesman* of 1747 in which he implied that milliners and mantua-makers were little better than whores and urged parents not to apprentice their daughters to those trades. He did not mention seamstresses, but the needle trades tended to be seen as a homogenous whole. It was a persistent misconception that must have added another layer of misery to the lives of hard-working seamstresses. The ballad quoted below almost certainly dates from the second half of the nineteenth century, to judge by the wages quoted, and shows that the belief in the seamstress-prostitute was still current.

> You gentles of England, I pray give attention,
> Unto those few lines, I'm going to relate,
> Concerning the seamstress, I'm going to mention,
> Who long time has been, in a sad wretched state,
> Laboriously toiling, both night, noon, and morning,
> For a wretched subsistence, now mark what I say.
> She's quite unprotected, forlorn, and dejected
> For sixpence, or eightpence, or tenpence a day.

Come forward you nobles, and grant them assistance,
Give them employ, and a fair price them pay,
And then you will find, the poor hard-working seamstress,
From honour and virtue will not go astray.

> Roy Palmer, *A Ballad History of England* (London: Batsford, 1979)

'Fair seamstresses', 'the pretty seamstress', 'the poor seamstress', 'the seamstress in the garret', 'no better than she ought to be', 'shameless hussy'; the word 'seamstress' still conjures up a range of images, so before we proceed any further I must explain the scope and purpose of this work.

A great deal has been written about the history of dress but comparatively little about garment-makers. There are histories of well-known designers and couturiers, analyses of novels and paintings depicting needleworkers, and a good deal on the sweated industries that employed many nineteenth-century needlewomen, but information about the rank-and-file seamstress is scanty. This study is an attempt to address this deficiency and forms a companion volume to my earlier work, *Busks, Basques and Brush-Braid: British dressmaking in the 18th and 19th centuries.*[4]

In common parlance a 'seamstress' (or sempstress, or seamster, the words are interchangeable) simply means 'a woman who sews' and can be applied equally well to a wife darning her husband's socks, a gentlewoman doing embroidery, a servant mending the household linen, a dressmaker, or a female practitioner of any of the other trades that involved sewing, like milliners, the makers of needle-laces, or the 'seamers' who assembled machine-knitted garments and hosiery. In the periods under review, however, 'seamstress' was also a job title. Seamstresses also sometimes described themselves as 'needlewomen' or as makers of particular sorts of garment – 'shirtmaker', 'waistcoat hand', 'slop-worker' – all of which terms will be used, as appropriate, in this text.

To clarify: in the seventeenth century, and before, seamstresses were respected craftswomen. They worked in linen and made and mended undergarments, men's shirts, babywear, household linen and utilitarian items like aprons, caps and handkerchiefs, to order. Many of them also laundered fine linen, and many London seamstresses kept shops where they took orders and sold items they had made, alongside a whole range of fabrics, laces and haberdashery. Girls could pay a handsome premium to be apprenticed to a seamstress; a significant number of seamstresses left wills and clearly some of them had made a good living in the trade. However, as the seventeenth century became the eighteenth, the trade in ready-made garments increased, becoming far more important than dress historians used to believe. There is no modern term to describe the trade of the seamstress. In the seventeenth century it was called 'simistry', and I shall use a modernized version of this – 'seamstry' – even though it does not appear in dictionaries, rather than more cumbersome phrases like 'seamstress work' or 'the craft of the seamstress' to describe the trade my subjects followed.

It was another category of seamstresses who assembled ready-mades, joining together pieces already cut out for them to make whole garments or parts of them, and those garments were no longer always made of linen or cotton. Such seamstresses made sheets and table linen, and shirts and underwear, but they also made up dresses for ready-to-wear shops, men's 'slops' or work clothing, fancy waistcoats for more genteel customers and a host of other items. Unlike tailors and mantua-makers, their garments did not have to fit individual clients, they were generic items that could, if necessary, be altered after sale to better fit the buyer. These seamstresses did not have to know how to cut and fit, they simply had to be able to sew neatly – and fast. Some were employed by drapers or tailors to make items to order; others were at the bottom of a chain of entrepreneurs, producing goods ultimately bought up by a wholesaler, but not until a series of middlemen had made their own profit from the seamstress's work.

By the end of the eighteenth century there were probably more seamstresses assembling ready-made garments than there were women making bespoke shirts, shifts and household linen. Some such workers remained, but the mantua-makers, who in the eighteenth century took over the trade in making women's garments from the tailors, would also make up underwear and baby linen as requested. Some seamstresses were also employed, on a permanent or part-time basis, by wealthy households to make and repair body and household linen; servants advertising in the press in the latter years of the eighteenth century were often keen to stress their needlework skills.

As late as 1821 the local paper[5] recorded the death in Pembroke Street, Oxford, of seventy-year-old Mrs Frances Bradstreet 'who for many years carried on the business of a seamstress, and was much respected for her industry and integrity'. No doubt she did bespoke work for the well-to-do, and, given her age, her career would have begun back in the 1760s when seamstry was still a reasonably respectable occupation. It is unlikely that any of her younger colleagues would have received such an accolade. By the early nineteenth century the majority of seamstresses were working for wholesalers, often on government contracts for 'slop' clothing and uniforms, but it was not until the late 1830s that conditions really began to deteriorate, for reasons I shall explore in Chapter 5. Their plight came to public attention in the 1840s, and the poor, downtrodden seamstress became a trope. But, despite the publicity, conditions for seamstresses improved little, if at all, until well into the twentieth century, and they featured largely in the *Daily News*-sponsored Sweated Industries Exhibition of 1906.

There were a great many of them. According to the *Occupational Analysis of the Census* of 1841, in England and Wales that year there were 23,720 seamstresses over the age of twenty and 4,452 who were younger, forming the fourth largest category of women workers listed. To set that in context, the same document listed 106,238 dressmakers and 32,403 teachers – although domestic service remained by far the greatest employer of female labour, accounting for almost a million girls and women. The numbers of seamstresses only increased over time; by 1871 80,730 individuals were listed as seamstresses and shirtmakers. Unfortunately, the occupational analyses of later censuses were less specific and did not provide a separate category for seamstresses, so we cannot trace the increase in their numbers after 1871, but we do know that their numbers continued to expand, even as some parts of garment-making moved into factories. In Derry in Ireland in 1875, for example, there were between four thousand and five thousand women and girls employed in factories making Irish linen shirts, whereas in the countryside there were an estimated twelve thousand to fifteen thousand outworkers making shirts or parts of shirts for the same manufacturers.[6]

However, even contemporaries were confused about the various types and grades of needle workers. Dressmakers' employees are frequently described as seamstresses, and the 1843 Children's Employment Commission was often treated as a report on seamstresses, though in fact, the people interviewed were all dressmakers, working in workshops, not seamstresses who usually worked in their own homes and were thus outside the remit of the commissioners. Many of the paintings produced as a result of the report were, however, of seamstresses, women, usually on their own, stitching pristine white garments which made an artistically pleasing contrast to the drab, bare, poverty-stricken surroundings in which the women were placed. Thomas Hood's famous *Song of the Shirt* of 1844 was about a seamstress making shirts for a few pence a dozen.

Virginia Mordaunt, George Reynolds' victim-heroine in *The Seamstress: or, The White Slave of England* (1853), was used to illustrate the 'putting-out' system and the chain of people who profited from her work. Such hierarchies of entrepreneurs existed, but the garment Virginia made – a high-class, velvet evening dress costing eight guineas – would have been a bespoke item, made in a dressmaker's workshop.[7] Contrasting the privileged lives of the customers for such items with the hard lives of the women who made them became another trope and an illustration of this appears as the frontispiece of Reynolds' book.

Figure 0.1 Frontispiece from *The Seamstress: or, The White Slave of England* by G.M.W. Reynolds (1853). It shows a seamstress toiling at her needle on the left, and, on the right, young women going to a ball in the dresses she has made, the two scenes separated by the tools of the needlewoman's trade. Images showing similar contrasts were popular.

(Figure 0.1) There was considerable uncertainty amongst would-be reformers and authors about the trades they were trying to reform, and some of that uncertainty has persisted in more recent writing about the needle trades.

The twentieth century saw garment-making for the mass market move into the factories, though the women working the sewing machines in factories were still poorly paid for long hours of work. Only in recent years has the bespoke seamstress begun to make a comeback. Needlework is seldom taught in schools and fewer and fewer women know how to make and repair their own clothes; in recent years a trade in garment repairs and alterations has developed to help the Ks of this world, and programmes like *The Great British Sewing Bee* are sparking a revival of interest in garment-making and needlework generally.

This work will deal with the women who followed the profession of seamstress, in its various incarnations, and the items they made, from *c.* 1600 to the early twentieth century. They will be treated chronologically, which has necessitated taking some decisions which may appear capricious, about where pieces of information best fit. Would it, for example, have been better to treat all three examples of great households replacing their house linen together or in three separate chapters because they did so at different dates? Why are some examples of shirtmaking given in Chapter 1 and others in Chapter 4? I am aware there are inconsistencies and apologize in advance for any confusion they may cause, but I considered the issues carefully and arrived at what seemed at the time to be the most logical solutions.

*   *   *

At this point it might be useful to add some notes on money, measurement, places and terminology. Pre-decimal currency and measurements will be used throughout because these are what seamstresses would have known and are the values and measurements used in account books and on bills for the period under review; translating them into their modern equivalents would be both confusing and inaccurate.

'Old money' consisted of pounds (£), shillings (s.) and pence (d.). There were twenty shillings in a pound and twelve pence in a shilling; there were also halfpennies (½d.) and farthings (¼d.) and guineas (£1 1s.). Sometimes sums were rendered in shillings only, rather than pounds and shillings (e.g. 42s. rather than £2 2s.) or in pence only (e.g. 14d. rather than 1s. 2d.). Converting money to its present-day value is fairly meaningless because relative prices have changed so much; it is the differentials that are important.

Most British readers are still familiar with the Imperial measurement system of yards, feet and inches. There were three feet in a yard (91.44 cms) and twelve inches (12 × 2.54 cms) in a foot (30.48 cms). There were also ells, quarters and nails. The English ell was usually forty-five inches (a yard and a quarter or 114.3 cms), while the Scottish one was usually thirty-seven inches (93.98 cms), but it was a measure that could vary from district to district as well as from country to country. A quarter was a quarter of a yard or nine inches (22.86 cms) and a nail was two and a quarter inches (roughly 5.715 cms).

I am aware that I reference a large number of places in the text, some of them little more than villages; and I realize this may be confusing. I therefore include a map showing the nineteenth-century county boundaries and, where I reference a place in the text, I include its county, e.g. Horsted Keynes (Sussex), or city, e.g. Great Orford Street, Liverpool. Any place *not* so referenced will be in London, e.g. the East End.

As mentioned above, seamstresses were sometimes known as sempstresses or seamsters and sometimes they described themselves, or were described, as needlewomen. On bills they sometimes appear as 'shirtmakers' and in the census they often described themselves by their specialization, 'trouser-maker',

Figure 0.2 Map of England showing the county boundaries as they were in the 1850s.

'coat-maker', 'cap-maker', 'waistcoat hand' and so on. They were, however, not the same as dressmakers, mantua-makers or milliners, though even contemporaries did not always recognize the difference between the trades. I shall use the various terms in what, in the particular context, appear to be the most appropriate ways. I trust it will not prove unnecessarily confusing.

1

The 'art and mystery of simistry' in the seventeenth and eighteenth centuries

Cotton fabric became increasingly available in the eighteenth century, but up to that date seamstresses had worked in linen which was hard-wearing and could withstand the rigorous methods used by washerwomen. In fact, the general term 'linen' denotes the classes of goods seamstresses used to make; the terms 'body linen' and 'baby linen' are not commonly used today but we still speak of 'bed linen' and 'table linen', even though the items we mean are now likely to be made of cotton or synthetics.

Few of the items made by seventeenth- and eighteenth-century seamstresses survive. Searching in museum collections across the UK for linen items to examine for her study, *Sweet and Clean? Bodies and Clothes in Early Modern England,*[1] Susan North was only able to locate eleven shirts, eight smocks/shifts, three pairs of drawers, one night-smock, one nightshirt and one night shift from the period 1650–1800. This is largely because textiles, and particularly clothing, dating from before the middle of the eighteenth century are comparatively rare, and linen and cotton items are rarer still because they could be recycled in so many ways. The worn sections of shirts and shifts could be cut away and the better parts remade into children's clothes; even worn-out linen could be repurposed as bandages, cleaning cloths, babies' nappies or even sanitary napkins, the latter three all usually called 'clouts'. On 13 December 1619, for example, Lady Anne Sackville (usually known by her maiden name, Lady Anne Clifford) recorded: 'My Lord gave me 3 shirts to make clouts of.' Lady Anne was a countess, the wife of Richard Sackville, third Earl of Dorset, and then mistress of Knole House in Kent, and it is unlikely that she concerned herself with making cleaning rags for her servants to use, so it is probable that the 'clouts' were either nappies for a coming baby or sanitary wear for her own use.[2] (Colour plate I) Elizabeth Shackleton was a Lancashire gentlewoman who left a copious collection of diaries and papers. She recorded cutting up old sheets to make tea towels and worn-out tablecloths to make china cloths and dusters, while her 'pretty red and white linnen gown' became a cover for a chest of drawers.[3]

An additional problem is that women, both before and after marriage, made at least some of the linen used or worn in their households. Mothers, wives and sisters often made shirts for their menfolk and underwear for themselves, and mothers, nursemaids and female relations made clothes for babies and young children. A large household required prodigious amounts of linen, some of which might be made at home and some might be put out to seamstresses. Across the Atlantic in Philadelphia in 1798 Elizabeth Drinker recorded in her diary on 12 May, 'Sally Downing came after dinner to finish cutting out Shifts for Mary – she has 30 Shirts and Shifts now ready to work on.' Sally was Elizabeth's eldest, married, daughter and Mary was her younger daughter, who had married in 1796 and had just had her second child. The Drinkers were Quakers, industrious farmers and tradespeople, and were as self-sufficient as they could reasonably manage to be, but the sheer quantity of garments Mary was going to have to make up is telling.[4] Most of these garments were voluminous, made from geometrically shaped pieces with gathering to provide shaping. There were few manuals of instruction, most women must have learnt to make garments by watching and copying. 'J.F', the author of *The Merchant's Warehouse Laid Open: or, The Plain Dealing Linnen Draper*, an invaluable publication of 1696, did give lengthy and convoluted written instructions for cutting out shifts but provided no patterns. The writer began:

> I shall here give you such Instruction which if well observed and followed, you may thereby know how to Cut out a Shift out of two ells of Holland, as most People shall do out of two and a quarter.... If you will Cut out but one Shift ⅛ long, take two Ells of Holland, and slit it in three down the middle; let it be Ell wide or Yard wide . . . as the bigness of your body requires, and it is split through the middle, instead of taking a half bredth, and just the same length of the half bredth for the Body . . . and just the same length off of the half bredth, which take for the body of your Shift then take the remainder of one of the halfs and double it, then lay it a cross, and cut it foar Goars, then take the other remainder of the bredth and double it, and cut it in the middle, which is just a pair of Sleeves, then you want only four Gussets, which will come out of the hollow . . .

An anonymously-authored book, *Instructions for Cutting Out Apparel for the Poor*, appeared almost a century later, in 1789, and it, too, relied on text rather than diagrams. The author's descriptions were equally complicated, and a seamstress would have had to have had a pretty clear idea of what the end product was supposed to look like before she attempted to follow either set of instructions.

L'Art de la lingère of 1771 by François-Alexandre de Garsault gave fuller details of how items were made and some simple diagrams (Figure 1.1), but his book was in French and probably not widely available in the UK. Not until the early nineteenth century do books appear which contained what we would recognize as patterns, namely, *The Lady's Oeconomical Assistant: or, The Art of Cutting Out, and Making, the Most Useful Articles of Wearing Apparel, without Waste* of 1808 and *The Workwoman's Guide*, by 'A Lady', of 1838, but even the patterns in these books, useful though they were, would have had to have been scaled up for use. However, all the authors stressed the importance of cutting out several items at a time to economize on the use of material. Most linens were quite narrow, usually 29¼ inches (three quarters of a yard plus a nail) or thirty-six inches (a yard) wide, but widths could vary from batch to batch. As late as 1838 the author of *The Workwoman's Guide* advised readers to check the width of the fabric they were buying because: 'Much waste may arise from it being one nail too wide or too narrow.'[5]

Items seem to have been cut out with very narrow seam allowances, somewhere between a sixteenth and an eighth of an inch (two to four millimetres). Where possible, seamstresses joined pieces together using the selvedges of the fabric for greater durability, but where raw edges had to be joined together, or one raw edge joined to a selvedge, they used a type of felled seam. The *Workwoman's Guide* advised that cutting, folding and seaming should be done 'by a thread', in other words, measuring by counting the warp and weft threads and keeping cuts and seams perfectly aligned with the grain of the fabric, and this seems to have been the traditional practice. Stitching was also done according to the thread count, the finer the linen being stitched, the smaller the stitches. From an examination of surviving linens, Susan North estimated that on linens with a thread count of 100 there would be up to twenty-five stitches to the inch, while on linens with a thread count of sixty the number would be around thirteen.[6] Seamstry was a highly skilled craft requiring neatness, accuracy, manual dexterity, cool hands and good eyesight.

The cut of shirts and shifts and babywear changed little over time, though the size of the pieces varied. Seventeenth-century shirts, for example, had shoulder straps, but by the eighteenth century these had become yokes; women's shifts became shorter in the eighteenth century and had short sleeves rather than long. There is usually no reliable way of distinguishing the home-made garment from the professionally made as many women were consummate needlewomen. In this analysis of items by type, no attempt will be made to distinguish who made the items described, as the end products were much the same, regardless of their makers.

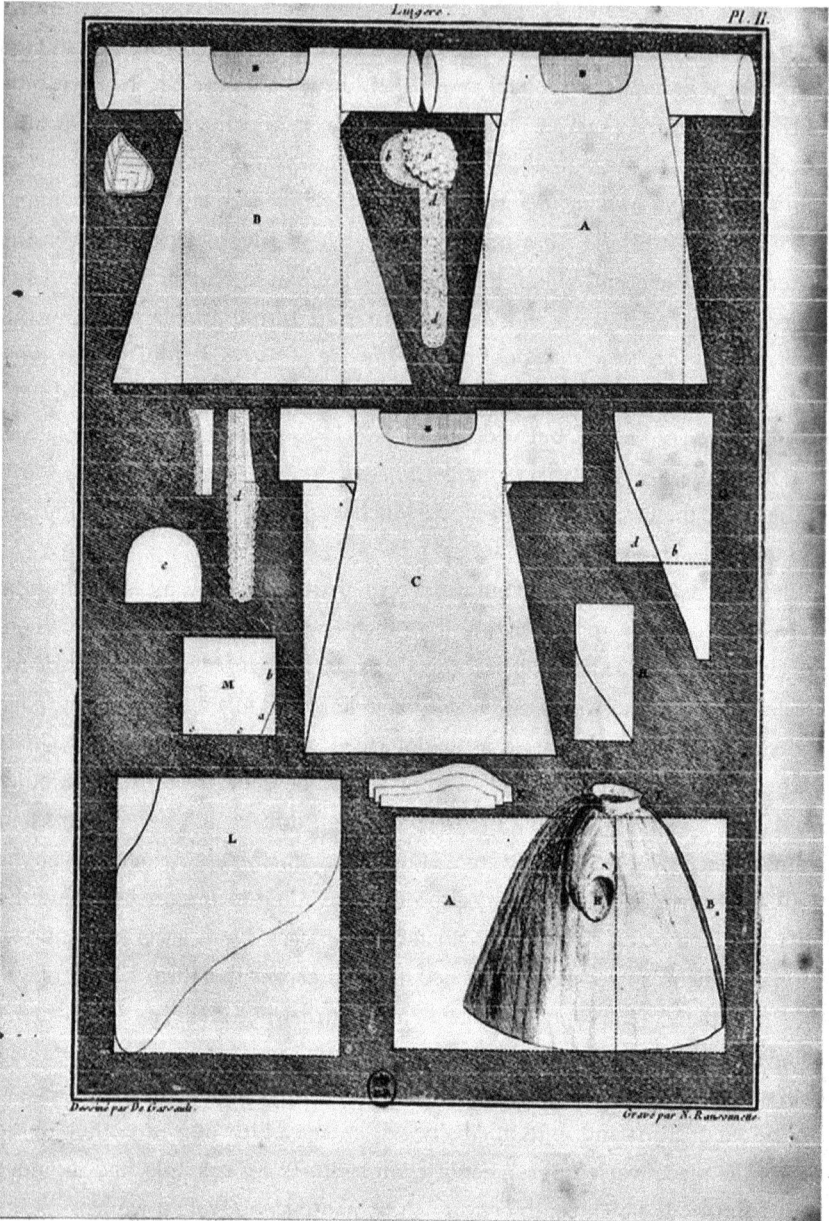

Figure 1.1 Diagram for cutting out shifts from *L'Art de la lingère* by François-Alexandre Pierre de Garsault (1771).

Shirts

There are few surviving examples of seventeenth-century shirts, for the reasons outlined above, and many of the extant ones were embroidered or decorated in some way which made them both special and less easy to re-use. There is, for example, a white linen shirt dating from *c.* 1585 to 1620 in the Warwickshire Museum collection; it is embroidered with a honeysuckle motif in red and has lace trimmed sleeves. Bath's Fashion Museum contains an unusually long shirt of similar date embroidered in black with birds, flowers and insects. There is another such shirt embroidered in red, green, gold and silver in the Museum of London and a blue embroidered one for a boy in the Victoria and Albert Museum. These shirts were long because they were the sole undergarment most men wore and they were intended to be tucked between the legs to protect the breeches.

The cut of shirts varied very little between 1600 and the mid-nineteenth century. They were made up of a series of squares and oblongs for front, back, sleeves, shoulder pieces or both sides of the yoke, underarm gussets and neck- and wrist-bands, joined together with seams made up of small, neat running- or back-stitches. Sleeves were gathered at the head to fit into the shoulder openings and into bands at the wrists, the back was gathered into the yoke, the front was slit partway down to form an opening and gathered either side into the yoke, and there was extra stitching at the base of the neck opening to strengthen it. (Figures 1.2 and 1.3) Workmen often simply left their shirts open at the front (Figure 1.4), but for formal wear there were various ways of decorating the neck, for example, bands, 'falling bands' (sometimes called 'falls'), neck-cloths, cravats or stocks. (See 'Neckwear' below.) Working men wore shirts of hemp, canvas, burlap (made from jute), dowlas, osnaburg or lockram (all types of coarse linen), but gentlemen's shirts were usually of fine linen, like Holland or Irish, though calico was thought to be warmer and *The Plain-Dealing Linen Draper* of 1696 recommended dimity for shirts and shifts as being both healthy and even warmer. Some men opted for flannel for the same reason. In 1685 John Locke wrote to a friend's wife thanking her for the 'flanen' shirts and ordering four more.[7] Flannel shirts and under-waistcoats became more popular in the eighteenth century, particularly for older men, though there was disagreement amongst medical men about the advisability of wearing wool next to the skin.

A spotless white linen shirt was the mark of a gentleman. Writing in 1701, Eustache le Noble, a French writer and playwright, opined, 'of what Age or Profession soever a Man be, his Linnen can never be too Clean; Nay 'tis the Cleanness of Linnen that will make an indifferent Suit pass.'[8] Le Noble had a

Figure 1.2 A man's shirt and drawers, 1775–1800. The shirt is British; the drawers are French.

chequered career; maybe he was speaking from experience. Some men had enormous quantities of shirts. For example, the Honourable William Monson of Burton in Lincolnshire had an inventory made of his clothing in 1747: he had fifty-nine 'ruffled' shirts, sixty-four plain ones and twenty-four 'little night shirts' – not to mention, forty-six neck-cloths, fifty-six stocks, 192 handkerchiefs, 186 caps of

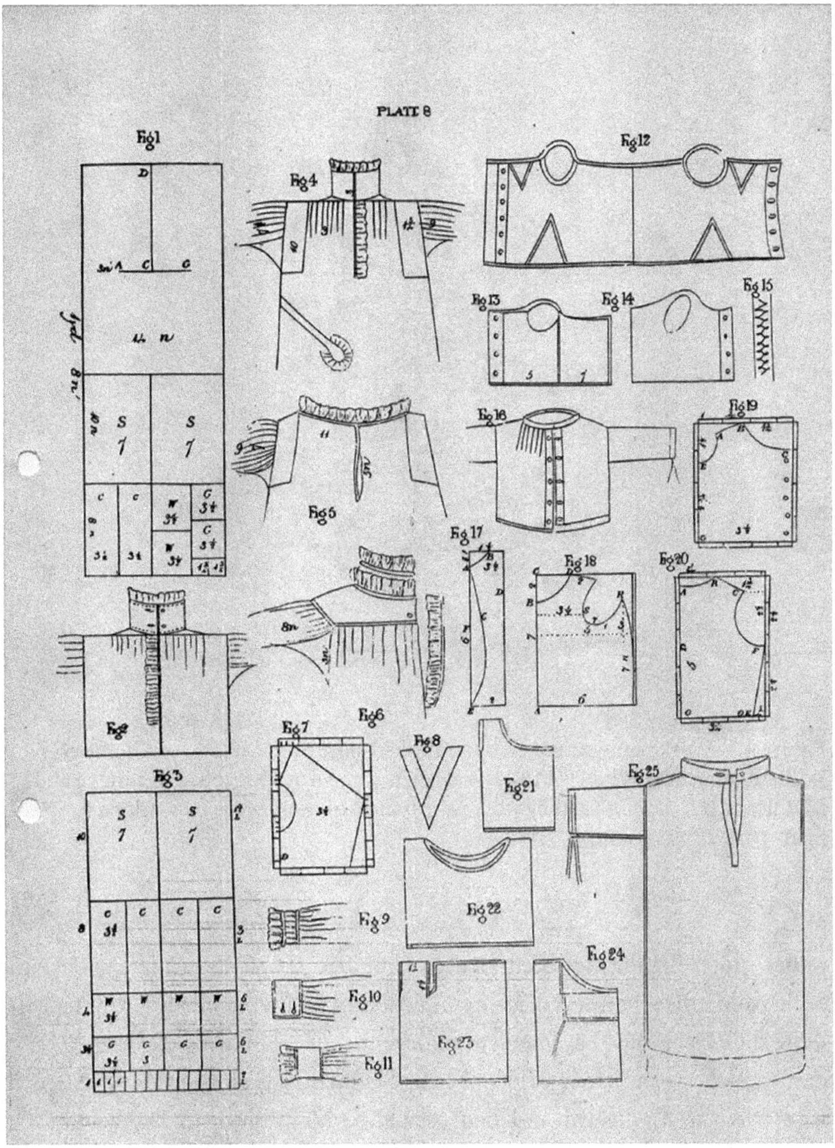

Figure 1.3 Page from *The Workwoman's Guide* by 'A Lady' (1838) showing how to cut out and assemble a shirt. Cutting out several shirts at the same time saved on fabric.

various sorts, seventy-three pairs of drawers and four 'flowerd Cotton Shaving Cloths'.[9] He had obviously kept a good many seamstresses in work over the years.

On the other hand, poor men had only two or three shirts; Poor Law records show that this was considered to be an acceptable minimum for working men who were not expected to be particularly clean or smart. The 'middling sort' had

Figure 1.4 Workman wearing an open-necked shirt from *Sketches of Characters* by
William Johnstone White (1818). His subjects came from Norfolk, Cambridge and
Middlesex, but the clothes they wore were typical of those worn by working people in
many parts of the country.

rather more: Bristol merchant George Lane had six shirts, while Devon vicar
Richard Matthew had seven, for example – though the fewer shirts you had, the
more difficult it must have been to achieve the ideal of having clean linen every
day.[10] Linen was a matter of pride. John Stedman was a Shropshire gentleman
who lived at Rindleford and had estates in Montford and Diddlebury. On
21 September 1761 he made a neat list of his 'Linnen Wearing Aparel' in a clear
sloping script. It consisted of '12 shirsts [sic], 8 Short Neck Cloths, 2 New Silk
Handkerchiefs, 2 Old Ditto, 2 New Pockett Handkerchiefs, 3 Old Ditto' and '4
Linnen Night-Caps'.[11] Perhaps it was the acquisition of the new handkerchiefs
that prompted him to check up on what he already owned or perhaps he was
simply a young man who was proud of his possessions.

Young James Boswell, living in London in 1762 and trying to make his way in
London society and gain a commission in the Guards, had an allowance of just

£200 a year from his father. He set himself a strict 'Scheme of Living' and allocated £50 a year for clothes. On top of this, he allowed £10 a year for stockings and shoes and 'I would have a suit of clean linens every day, which may be 4d. a day. I shall call it for the year £7.' This was presumably payment for washing and clear-starching. Boswell's careful account keeping was somewhat upset when he 'was reminded by Miss Terrie of a pair of lace ruffles that I had bespoke, which came to 16s.' Miss Terrie was his landlord's sister who did various needlework jobs for him and, when it came, he could ill afford the unexpected bill.[12]

Ruffles were the mark of a gentleman. Fanny Burney remembered that Dr Johnson, noted for his scruffy appearance and wigs singed at the front from bending too close to the candle, appeared for dinner one night at court in a shirt without ruffles. This eccentricity was unusual enough for her to record it in her memoirs.[13] For other people, wearing ruffles might suggest they had ideas above their station. On one occasion, John Macdonald, a footman and gentleman's gentleman who kept a diary in the 1750s and 1760s, failed to get a post he had applied for. He later spoke to the German servant who did get the job. The German told him that his employer 'spoke to me about you, and said you were more like a gentleman than a servant; now, I am plain-dressed and I have got the place.' Macdonald learnt his lesson and a few days later went after another job: 'I was dressed plain, without lace' – and was taken on.[14]

Even reprobates took a pride in their linen. George Hilton was a ne'er-do-well from a good family in Westmoreland. He sold the family estate, gambled, drank heavily, was cited in numerous lawsuits and on one occasion was involved in a fight in which a man lost his eye. Nonetheless, he wanted to *look* respectable. He recorded in his diary:

An account what it costs me in linen close per annum with all reperacions from Monday 2nd February 1701/2 Candlemasse Day

March 23rd 1701/2 For two large muslin crevates	4s. 0d.
March 31st 1702 for 10 Lenten handchuchers	15s. 4d.
For 3 more	4s. 6d.
October 27th 1702 for 3 new shirts	18s. 0d.
October the last 1702 for a piece of muslin for crevates	£1 1s. 10d.
The whole for linen for the yeare 1702 juste	£3 0s. 0d.[15]

Dress was a significant marker of social status. At one point, for reasons that are not entirely clear but certainly involved getting cut-price service from prostitutes, James Boswell disguised himself as a labourer. This involved wearing a grubby shirt which he interpreted as one he had already worn twice.[16] In

Smollett's novel of 1771, *The Expedition of Humphry Clinker*, it is clear how much people relied on clothes, including a clean shirt, as evidence of respectability. Humphrey is taken on as a temporary coachman by a family on their travels after a coaching accident and shocks them by his dirty appearance and split breeches. The following day, having received payment and rescued some of his clothes from the pawnshop:

> as our aunt stept into the coach, she observed, with some marks of satisfaction, that the postilion, who rode next to her, was not a shabby wretch like the ragamuffin who had them into Marlborough. Indeed, the difference was very conspicuous: this was a smart fellow, with a narrow-brimmed hat, with gold cording, a cut bob, a decent blue jacket, leather-breeches, *and a clean linen shirt, puffed above the waist-band* [my emphasis].[17]

Some months later the indispensable Mr Clinker was found to be the illegitimate son of Sir Matthew Bramble, the head of the family of travellers, and had become engaged to 'our aunt's' servant, Win Jenkins; he 'is now out of livery and wears ruffles', his fiancée wrote proudly.[18]

Shirts were worn next to the skin, but in cold weather two might be worn for extra warmth. On 19 September 1666 Pepys noted: 'This day I put on two shirts, the first time this year.' Almost a hundred years later, in 1763, one cold winter's day James Boswell wrapped himself in two shirts and two pairs of stockings before braving the London streets.[19] Conversely, in hot weather, men might choose to wear 'half-shirts': for example, on 28 June 1664, Pepys 'this day put on a half shirt first this summer it being very hot'. According to Susan North,[20] working from the 1684 inventory of John Wynnstay who equated 'halfe shurts' with 'day Shurts', they were short shirts to be worn with breeches; however, this does not really explain why Pepys only chose to wear them in hot weather.

Shirts were also worn in bed. Poor men no doubt slept in the shirts they had worn during the day but the well-to-do had purpose-made nightshirts, cut like their day shirts but longer. Other men chose to sleep naked. There is an account in *Humphry Clinker* of such an individual, who, believing the house to be on fire (though it was actually a practical joke), put on his day shirt to climb down a ladder from his bedroom window:

> The rueful aspect of the lieutenant in his shirt, with a quilted night-cap fastened under his chin, and his long lank limbs and posteriors exposed to the wind, made a very picturesque appearance, when illumined by the links and torches which the servants held up to light him in his descent.[21]

Smocks

While men of all classes wore types of shirt, the amount of material used varied according to the owner's purse and status, and countrymen might wear 'round frocks' (smocks) rather than shirts. These were not necessarily the heavily smocked and embroidered garments that appear in many illustrations of idyllic country scenes and which have garnered a mythology all their own; everyday cotton or linen smocks could be bought ready-made and were undecorated. In Tonbridge in 1721, for example, Thomas Webb stocked 'ladd's frocks' valued at 4s. 6d. each and men's valued at fifteen shillings.[22] That was expensive. In 1688 in Derbyshire, Edward Munday gave Jarvas Woodroffe, probably one of his workers, '5s. 0d. to buy him a frock'.[23]

Thomas Turner kept a shop in East Hoathley near Brighton (Sussex) and sold everything the villagers might conceivably need, including clothing. On Monday, 17 November 1757 he wrote in his diary: 'At home all day.... Cut out 10 round

Figure 1.5 Working people from *Sketches of Characters* by William Johnstone White (1818). The man at the back is wearing a simple smock, probably very similar to those sold by Thomas Turner in East Hoathley, with a handkerchief knotted round his neck.

frocks'. The following day he delivered them to a local girl, Elizabeth Mepham, 'with thread and buttons' to be made up, and on Sunday, 6 December he 'Paid Eliz Mepham 5s. for making 10 round frocks'.[24] These were stock items, not bespoke.

They were also worn in other parts of the country. In 1817 young Joseph Moss, an apprentice stockinger in Lambley in Nottinghamshire, managed to save enough money to buy a new 'smockfrock'. It probably cost him about six shillings. He saved the money by working overtime; at that date apprentices in the stocking trade had to complete a set amount of work for their master but could work for themselves and sell their own goods when that quota was completed. According to the terms of his indenture, Joseph's master should have provided him with clothes, but times were hard and his master was mean. Thirty years later, when he wrote his memoirs, Joseph was still proud of this purchase.[25]

Smocks, often recorded as 'frocks', were not solely the preserve of the poorer classes. Thomas Babington, a Leicester gentleman, kept an account book in the last decades of the seventeenth century and, though he certainly bought and wore shirts and cravats, he also seems to have worn frocks. For example, in 1695 he recorded buying 8⅜ yards of Holland for three shifts for his niece 'and a frock for me' for £1 12s. 0d.[26] Samuel Jeake, a respectable Sussex businessman who normally dressed in suits and shirts, spent 5s. 6¼d. on a linen 'frock' in 1676, possibly to wear when doing menial work in his warehouse.[27] Thomas Brown, a Derbyshire farmer and landowner, kept an account book in the early years of the nineteenth century. In February 1808 he paid a Miss Smedley 17s. 6½d. for (fabric for) shirts, plus 1s. 5d. for thread and 2s. 2d. for making up, but the previous October he had bought two 'stock frocks' for 10s. 7d. and 12s. 6d., probably ready-made as he usually itemized the cost of fabric and making up separately.[28]

Neckwear

By the early part of the seventeenth century the ruffs that were so characteristic of the Tudor period had fallen out of favour and been replaced by the cravat, a wide strip of linen loosely knotted and with the ends hanging loose at the front, or the 'falling band', essentially a wide collar. In *The Fayre Maid of the Exchange* of 1607 (the eponymous heroine is a seamstress with a shop in London's Royal Exchange), Frank Golding, in love with the 'fayre maid' and somewhat surprised by his own feelings, puns, 'Shall I fall to falling bands and be a ruff-an no longer?'[29] implying that, due to his love for the seller of linen, he might begin to wear the new style of neckwear.

Figure 1.6 Man wearing a lace-trimmed 'falling band', German School, 1655–95.

By the 1620s the 'band' and 'falling band' (or 'fall'), which were types of separate collars attached to the shirt by ties ('band strings') or tacking stitches, had become popular and remained so for much of the century. Bands could be small and plain, but others were large and made of lace or lace trimmed, reaching across the shoulders. They were available ready-made. In the provincial Norfolk town of Great Yarmouth in 1628, for example, John Uttinges senior had twenty-two 'falling bands laced' and twenty-seven 'bands for men' in his shop when his stock was inventoried. The falling bands were valued at 14s. 8d. (or eightpence each) and the plain ones were valued at 6s. 9d. (threepence each),[30] though they might have retailed for more.

Bands, cravats and neck-cloths could also be made of lace. On 19 October 1662, Samuel Pepys wrote in his diary: 'Put on my first new lace-band; and so neat it is, that I am resolved my great expence [*sic*] shall be lace-bands'[31] (Figure 1.7). As the century wore on bands became less extravagant, and simple bands, essentially two oblongs of cloth on a tape, reminiscent of the neckwear worn today by members of the legal profession, were also worn. Versions of the band continued to be worn into the eighteenth century, though cravats and neck-cloths which could be folded or knotted in a variety of ways were more common. They were sometimes replaced by the 'stock', a pre-pleated and folded item which fastened at the back of the neck with ties or buckles and simplified the whole business of arranging one's neckwear.

Figure 1.7 Samuel Pepys, attributed to John Riley, *c.* 1690. He wears a lace cravat or 'band'.

Neckwear was an important accessory for men, as the tie is today, and a spotless white collar or cravat of fine fabric was the mark of a gentleman. Like Pepys, many spent a good deal of money on neckwear. For example, in the 1670s in Leicestershire, Thomas Babington spent seven shillings on two muslin cravats, nine shillings on a cravat and cuffs and 2s. 4d. on a 'yd of muslin for Tom's bands' in 1680.[32] Tom was his young son.

Neckwear was equally important for women. Women's ruffs, like men's, were replaced by 'bands' or other neckwear in the early seventeenth century. 'Whisks' were elaborate collars, the successors to the starched ruffs of the previous century, standing out at the back and sometimes stiffened with cardboard, flattering, but restrictive and uncomfortable to wear. Partlets were little tops that went over the head and under the neck of the dress to fill in the top of low-cut bodices, the forerunners of the 'habit shirts' of the early nineteenth century. Gorgets, named after the piece of armour that protected the neck and throat, were similar. Poor women wore 'cross cloths' a linen cloth that wrapped round the shoulders, crossing over at the front and tied or fastened with pins at the back, almost entirely obscuring the bodice beneath. By the eighteenth century neck-handkerchiefs or 'fichus' were generally worn, squares of fine fabric folded in half diagonally, and these could be plain, but many were frilled or lace-trimmed or embroidered, usually white on white, and were often of muslin or fine lawn. (See Figures 1.12 and 10.1.)

Sleeves

It was also important that the part of the shirt or shift that showed at the wrist was pristine. Both genders often wore detachable ruffles or 'sleeve frills' made of finer material than the shirt or shift itself, tacked or pinned to the sleeves of the main garment. Accounts like those of Thomas Babington in Leicestershire in the seventeenth century (see Chapter 2) and Elizabeth Jervis in Staffordshire in the eighteenth (see Chapter 4) record the purchase of fine linen and muslin for making cuffs or ruffles or even sometimes whole sleeves. For women, ruffles, a neck-handkerchief or fichu, a cap and sometimes an apron, trimmed with matching lace or embroidered with the same design, formed what they called a 'sute'. Elizabeth Shackleton, a Lancashire gentlewoman, listed a 'sute of linen' that she had embroidered herself in her 1769 inventory of clothing.[33] Frances Smith, a respectable middle-class lady who lived in Richmond in North Yorkshire, was proud of the ruffles she embroidered. On 26 March 1765, for example, it rained all day and Frances spent her time 'drawing [a design on] a pair of Ruffles to work'.[34] Bought ones could be very expensive. In 1751 Lady Frances North spent a whole twelve guineas on a 'Dresden' apron, a pair of ruffles and a tucker.[35]

Like bands, sleeves could be bought ready-made. John Uttinges in Great Yarmouth had seven pairs of 'wrought sleeves' in stock in 1628, valued at 8½d. a pair.[36] They were relatively cheap compared to those sold by Henry Mitchell in Lincoln in 1679, who had 'lacest' cuffs at 7s. 6d. for three pairs or eight shillings for two, lawn cuffs for 2s. 6d. and plain ones at one shilling and three shillings.[37] As we shall see in Chapter 2, Henry Mitchell seems to have catered for very well-to-do customers.

Shifts

The female version of the shirt was the shift: before 1700 this was often called a 'smock'; after 1800 it was usually known as a 'chemise'. Changing one's underwear was sometimes referred to as 'shifting'. Like shirts, shifts were made from geometric shapes but unlike shirts they were not made with a yoke, the front and back pieces were oblongs, sometimes slightly tapered, gathered into a band at the neck, and triangular gores were usually added at the sides of the skirts for fullness. Sleeves were often long and sometimes gathered into a band at the wrist, with a square folded crosswise as a gusset under the arm. Amongst the numerous papers left by Elizabeth Shackleton is a little memo, probably a reminder to herself. It reads: 'December ye 8th 1749 fourteen yards makes me six shifts good quarter-and-half long the gores cut in three. Two ells makes six pairs of sleeves. The last I had was Scotch Holland bought of Mr Hamilton at 4 shillings per yard and the sleeves at 6s. 6d.'[38]

Like shirts, some of the few surviving early shifts are embroidered, the former possessions of wealthy women. Decorated shifts were a mark of status. On 21 May 1662 Samuel Pepys 'went with wife to White Hall' and saw 'the finest smocks and linen petticoats of my Lady Castlemaine's, laced with rich lace at the bottom, that ever I saw'. Lady Castlemaine was one of the king's mistresses and Pepys had something of a crush on her. Embroidery on shirts and shifts was not done by the seamstress, however, it was the province of specialist embroiderers.

While the shift was an undergarment, it was all-concealing enough for decency and there are numerous portraits of ladies in their shifts and little else. (Colour plate II) Women doing penance in church for some perceived sin often appeared just wearing their shifts and, like shirts, shifts were also worn as nightwear.

References in literature to 'nightgowns' mean something quite different, a loose type of dress. Countrywomen might wear a coloured skirt or 'petticoat' over their shift, and a corset or 'body' above the waist, leaving the shift showing almost like a blouse. As women's fashions changed in the eighteenth century, shifts became less visible, though they were still worn, and their sleeves became shorter.

The number and quality of shifts a woman owned depended on her wealth and social status. In Samuel Richardson's novel *Pamela: or, Virtue Rewarded* of 1740, Pamela is given her late mistress's clothing by her widowed master, Mr B. She wrote to her parents:

> He has given me a suit of my late lady's clothes, and half a dozen of her shifts, and six fine handkerchiefs, and three of her cambric aprons and four holland ones. The clothes are fine silk, too rich and good for me to be sure. I wish it was no affront to him to make money of them, and send it to you; it would do me more good.

However, when it becomes clear that Mr B.'s intentions were less than honourable, Pamela decided to go home to her parents' village and equipped herself with clothing more appropriate to her status as 'Goody Andrews' daughter'. This included:

> two flannel petticoats, not so good as my swanskin and fine linen ones, but what will keep me warm, if any neighbour should get me to milk, as sometimes I used to do formerly; ... I got some Scots cloth and made me at mornings and nights when nobody saw me two shifts; I have enough left for two shirts and two shifts for you, my dear father and mother.[39]

Apparently two shifts, one to wash against the other, was deemed appropriate for a village girl in the same way that two shirts were thought to be adequate for a working man. In the 1760s, Molly Williams, a farmer's daughter in Gloucestershire, had just two new shifts when she lost the bundle containing her trousseau by the side of the road.[40]

Wealthy women had far more. Mrs B. had had at least six. Elizabeth Shackleton, the Lancashire gentlewoman diarist, made an inventory of her clothes when she moved house in 1769 and listed fifteen shifts, along with five under-petticoats, while in 1747, the inventory of Mary Churchill, Duchess of Montague, listed no fewer than twelve trimmed shifts and thirteen plain ones.[41] However, de Garsault, in his *L'Art de la lingère*, suggested that a young woman should have seventy-two chemises in her trousseau![42]

A lady called Jane Treadwell died in Stamford in Lincolnshire in 1772. An inventory of her 'Wareing Apparel' was taken in 1773 and included thirteen gowns – though seven of them were described as 'old'. She also had two 'dimothy' under-petticoats (7s. 0d.), two flannel under-petticoats (5s. 0d.), seven shifts and eight pairs of sleeves (£1 8s. 0d.), five 'old' shifts (10s. 0d.) and eleven caps (19s. 0d.) and numerous 'handles' (handkerchiefs).[43] We know very little else about Mrs Treadwell, but we can deduce she was quite well-to-do and had provided her seamstress with plenty of work.

The shift remained the basic female undergarment, worn next to the skin, under the corset, throughout the nineteenth century, although as the century progressed, more and more items of underwear were added on top.

Drawers

While drawers were less generally worn in the seventeenth and eighteenth centuries than shirts and shifts, they did exist and were worn by both men and women. Some men wore detachable linings in their breeches which served the same purpose; for example, the Reverend Giles Moore in Sussex recorded several such pairs of linen 'loynings' in his 'Journal'.[44] Gregory King included 'Drawers or Linings' in his lists of clothing, though he claimed there were only half as many bought as there were breeches, and estimated their cost at 1s. 3d. to 1s. 5d. in 1688.[45] In 1620, however, Lord Howard of Naworth in Cumbria had spent two shillings on 'linen for linings' and eightpence for making them up (along with footing a pair of stockings which appeared, un-itemized, on the same bill). He also spent 12s. 8d. on buying a pair of ready-made linen drawers and fivepence on having two more pairs made.[46] Perhaps having tried the new-fangled garments he found them more comfortable than linings. They were certainly more convenient because linings had to be unpicked and sewn back in each time they were washed. It may be that Lord Howard's drawers were made by a seamstress, the low price would suggest this was possibly the case, but, as we shall see, it seems that most pairs of men's drawers were made by tailors rather than seamstresses.

Images of felons in seventeenth-century broadsheets often show them clad only in their drawers, knee-length linen long johns, tied at the waist with a drawstring. Defoe tells us that in 1665 he saw a man so maddened by fear of the plague that he 'run about Naked, except a pair of drawers about his Waste'.[47] Samuel Pepys also wore some form of under-breeches. On a number of occasions, he mentions sleeping in his drawers when he was away from home, for example, during the Great Fire while staying at a friend's house: 'Sept 1666. So here I went the first time into a naked bed, only my drawers on.' On an earlier occasion (26

July 1664), having discussed the fact that his wife had been unable to conceive, he was given some surprisingly modern advice about keeping his nether regions cool by wearing 'cool holland drawers' – although his friends' other suggestions of drinking sage juice, or rum and sugar, and avoiding late suppers probably belong in the category of old wives' tales. Despite the advice, the Pepys never had children.

Randle Holme wrote the *Academy of Armory* between 1649 and 1688. Book One dealt exclusively with heraldry as the title implies, but the remaining books were a kind of encyclopaedia, listing all sorts of eclectic facts, including the terms used, and products produced, by various tradesmen. He describes men's drawers as 'Linnen Breeches worn under the Breeches which are tied about the Waist and either under or over the Knee' and lists them as tailors' work, not seamstresses'.[48]

There is a pair of eighteenth-century linen under-breeches, said to be French, in the Victoria and Albert Museum[49] which are cut like normal breeches and are thought to be tailor-made. (See Figure 1.2.) In 1743 in Kent Sir Edward Filmer paid 'Rives the tailor' 4s. 6d. for making him three pairs of drawers.[50] In 1776 Sir Willoughby Dixie of Bosworth Park in Leicestershire paid his bill from William Fell, a tailor in St Martin's Lane, Leicester. It included 9s. 6d. for two pairs of linen drawers and eleven shillings for two pairs of dimity drawers, albeit a small fraction of the £37 0s. 3¾d. he had spent on clothes from that particular tailor over the previous two years.[51] Sir Willoughby was a comparatively young man, he was thirty-four in 1776, so wearing drawers was not necessarily the preserve of older men as some accounts suggest, though they may well have been popular with older men who felt the cold. The collection of clothing worn by Thomas Coutts the banker (1735–1822) was loaned to the Victoria and Albert Museum in 1908 and contained twenty-five pairs of flannel drawers (and ten flannel vests), which suggests that, at least in his later years, Coutts regularly wore drawers. The surviving ones are simply cut, like breeches but with a simple front opening and ribbon ties at the knee.[52]

We know even less about women's drawers than we do about men's. Pepys famously checked to see whether his wife was wearing drawers when she visited Pembleton, her dancing master, with whom Samuel thought she might be having an affair. On 15 May 1663 he wrote: 'But I am ashamed to think what a course I did take by lying to see whether my wife did wear drawers today as she used to do', and again, on 4 June 1663: 'I did so watch to see my wife put on drawers, which poor soul, she did, and yet I could not get off my suspicions.' Other wealthy women wore drawers too. Lady Grisell Baillie at Mellerstain in the Scottish Lowlands mentions linen for drawers quite frequently; for example, she acquired twelve ells of Holland in 1731, six for drawers for her husband and six for drawers for herself.[53] The Duchess of Montague's 1747 inventory listed eight pairs, four of dimity and four of Holland, a comparatively small number given that she had twenty-five shifts.[54]

A further analysis of the prevalence of wearing drawers comes from the Old Bailey records. Throughout the seventeenth and eighteenth centuries thefts of clothing were common; washerwomen, shopkeepers, tailors and mantua-makers were often targeted, but stealing from private houses was not uncommon. Drawers are sometimes listed amongst the items stolen, though they appear far less frequently than shirts and shifts and it is often not clear whether they belonged to men or women as cases were usually brought in the name of the man of the house, even when many of the items stolen clearly belonged to women. Between 1697 and 1819 just forty-one thefts of drawers are recorded out of the several hundred clothing thefts that came before the Old Bailey in that period. The earliest was in 1697 when Robert Oliver was accused of stealing a pair of dimity drawers worth 2s. 6d. belonging to Henry Bradley's wife. The case was dismissed when it transpired that Mrs Bradley had *given* Oliver the drawers in return for 'his kindness'.[55] One can only speculate!

Unfortunately, no pairs of women's drawers survive from the seventeenth and eighteenth centuries, probably because they became stained and were discarded or cut up; we therefore do not really know what they looked like and we cannot be sure whether drawers for women were made by seamstresses or tailors at that point. However, in 1808, when the *Ladies' Oeconomical Assistant* was published, the author did include instructions for making drawers for small children and, by 1838, when *The Workwoman's Guide* came out, the author clearly expected her 'workwoman' to be making drawers for both men and women as she included instructions for both.[56] However, as late as 1802, the Overseers of the Poor in Sandhurst in Kent paid a *tailor*, Thomas Horton, four shillings for making a pair of long flannel drawers for a pauper in their charge, even though they employed the seamstresses working for Edward Wenman's shop to make up shifts and shirts for other members of the village poor.[57]

Children's Clothes

Seamstresses made clothes for babies and toddlers and childbed linen for their mothers. For much of history babies were swaddled for their first few months of life and, apart from shirts and caps, layettes consisted largely of

Figure 1.8 Ivory statuettes of swaddled babies by Johan Christian von Lucke, 1753–55. They are sixteen centimetres long.

swaddling bands and wrappers of various sorts (Figure 1.8). After a week or two the baby's arms would be left free and decorative sleeves might be worn. However, by the mid-eighteenth century the practice was falling out of favour; the physician, William Cadogan, wrote an article condemning swaddling (*Essay upon Nursing*) in 1748, though the most famous exponent of leaving babies free to stretch their limbs was Jean-Jacques Rousseau (*Émile, ou de l'éducation*, 1762).

There were fashions in babywear, even when babies were swaddled. In 1718, Sarah Long in Totteridge (now part of Barnet in North London) wrote to her mother about preparations for the baby she was expecting that December and it sounds very much as if it was her first child. Much of the letter was devoted to hiring a nanny, a wet nurse and a nurse to be with her when she gave birth, but a longish section also relates to changing attitudes to dressing babies:

> Mrs Cannon told me that most people of fashion make a laced sute [this probably means lace trimmed] for the child or fine cambric edge with fine edging for the

christening sute just as they used to make them formerly with pinners and neckcloath ruffled as the point sute is made, but she says if I won't have such a sute if I have only the other sort of cap and neckcloath which she described to be the same of those I have already by me which you saw when you was hear, I must have a rich white satten mantle to dress the child in besides that which I have for it is only to wrap loos about it. I have not bought anything yet nor washed up those things I have by me for I have expected my sister Harvey every day but she is not come for I thought to gett her to recommend somebody to me that would do that well for I don't know of any one myself.[58]

The baby clothes Sarah needed to wash were probably second-hand things she had been given, but what is interesting is that she was looking for a seamstress/ washerwoman to prepare new things for the child rather than making them herself. Within a generation, there would be numerous baby linen warehouses to supply women like young Mrs Long.

For example, in October 1743, a Shropshire lady, Susanna Maria Hill,[59] visited 'At the Naked Boy', the shop of James and Isabella Thompson in the Strand. James was a linen draper and Isabella sold babies' and children's clothes, cradles and Moses baskets, fabrics, underwear and 'every Thing that is necessary for Ladies in their Lying-in'. (Figure 1.9) James and Isabella[60] had married in 1729 and, prior to moving to the Naked Boy, Isabella had had a shop in the Royal Exchange, though whether she had established it before or after her marriage is not clear. Mrs Hill bought '2 setts of Dutch coats' at 7s. 6d. each, two flannel coats at 2s. 9d. apiece, a pair of stockings for 1s. 9d., a pair of satin shoes for 1s. 8d. and two linsey coats at 4s. 6d. The purchases were for her two daughters, Maria born in 1742 and Susanna born in 1743. Baby clothes were available outside London, too. For example, the inventory of Mary Woollett, who kept a millinery shop in the little seaside town of Rye (East Sussex), was taken in 1742 and amongst the remnants of fabrics, trimmings and sundries was a 'parcel of childbed linen'.[61]

In *L'Art de la lingère*, François-Alexandre de Garsault described what a seamstress was expected to prepare for a wealthy French mother and her new baby. Despite the fact that Garsault was very much a figure of the Enlightenment, he does not seem to have conformed to contemporary ideas of allowing babies to kick and move about; the layette he describes was for a swaddled child. For completeness sake he included the full range of items a new mother was thought to need, though he is careful to make it clear that the seamstress was only responsible for the items made of cotton and linen; the woollen and satin items

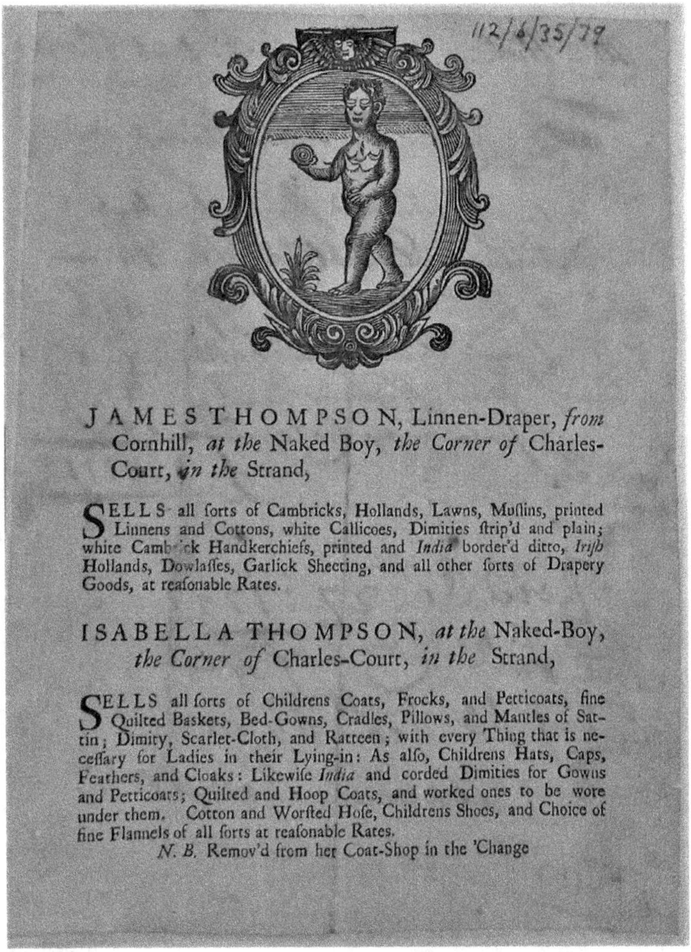

Figure 1.9 Advertisement for James and Isabella Thompson 'At the Naked Boy', 1740s, listing some of the fabrics James sold and Isabella's stock of babywear.

would be made elsewhere.[62] The list is reproduced here in full, in translation and with some explanatory notes:

For the mother

Six breast cloths – these were large binders with strings to tie at the back, round the neck and below the breasts

Twelve 'pods' (*gousses*) for milk – these were to suppress the mother's milk and seem to have been fabric nipple pads

Two night chemises

Six pairs of sleeves *en amadis*, four of muslin, two of lace – 'en amadis' was a style
associated with the chivalric tale of Amadis de Gaulle, popular at the time,
and consisted of tight-fitting sleeves buttoned at the wrist

Twelve flat undersheets

Twelve folded undersheets

Six bellybands

Two muslin negligées

Seventy-two *chauffoirs* (sanitary towels)

Six nightshirts 'en amadis avec ou sans coqueluchons' – a 'coqueluchon' was a
type of cowl or hood, usually associated with monks' habits

A big bed cover (*couvre-pied*)

A smaller one for the chaise longue on which the mother might recline to receive
visitors.

(Women were expected to rest for at least a month after giving birth. Mrs Drinker
was scandalised when her daughter, Nancy Skyrin, went for a three-mile drive
with her husband in their wagon and 'dined downstairs!' just twelve days after
giving birth in August 1801. 'Nothing like this was ever done by me', she wrote
disapprovingly.[63])

For the child

Head:

Forty-eight caps

Two headpieces (*têtières*) – these were only worn for a couple of weeks because
it was thought necessary to hold a newborn's head in shape

Twenty-four woollen bonnet liners of three sizes – de Garsault explains the
plethora of liners by saying that soft muslin or something similar was needed
to protect the baby's skin from chafing by coarse fabrics

Twenty-four night caps, in three sizes, in muslin or lace (*cornettes*)

Six muslin neckerchiefs

Six woollen bonnets

Body:

Seventy-two nappies

Twelve swaddling bands – de Garsault suggested these should be three ells long
and an eighth of an ell wide. (The ell was a unit of measurement based on
double the length of the forearm and outstretched hand and the standard
length varied from country to country. In England it was usually 45 inches or
1.143 metres, in France it was 54 inches or 1.372 metres – so the baby was to
be wrapped in what were effectively four-metre-long bandages, criss-crossed
around its body and legs.)

Eighteen fustian swaddling cloths – these were probably what were called 'beds' in English, i.e. large wrappers. (The baby would be swaddled, then wrapped in a series of layers – wool, over muslin liners, and finally a decorative outer cover – probably one of the decorated muslin wrappers or the satin one.)

Six liners for the woollen cloths

Two trimmed muslin cloths

Two liners for the muslin cloths

A white satin cover

Twenty-four shirts, in three sizes

Twelve bibs, in two sizes, in muslin or lace – these were decorative rather than useful and continued to be worn by toddlers to keep the fronts of their dresses clean

Thirty-six handkerchiefs for wiping the baby's face and keeping it clean

Six big white swaddling cloths in *drap de Dreux*

Four cloths in 'espagnolette' – *espagnolette* was a woollen fabric, Spanish in origin but later made in France

A decorated white satin cover – this might well have been used at the christening

Six shirts in *espagnolette*

Two sets of matching items (*parures*) each consisting of:

Two caps

Two round bonnets

Four bibs

Two big muslin shawls (*coeffes*)

Two bias-cut neck cloths (*biaies*)

Six pairs of thread mittens

The cradle

A cradle

A cover

A liner

A mattress

Two mattresses stuffed with hay

A straw mat

Six pairs of sheets

Two woollen blankets

Two feather pillows

Twelve pillowcases

De Garsault's quantities are very extravagant. It is unlikely that many mothers, even wealthy French ones, had anything like the quantity of items he suggested;

FRONT OF THE FOUNDLING HOSPITAL. (*See page 356.*)

Figure 1.10 The Foundling Hospital from *Old and New London: A Narrative of Its People and Its Places* by Walter Thornbury (1873).

however, even babies from poor households were dressed in far more layers of clothing than we would think appropriate today.

The London Foundling Hospital opened in 1741 for the children of mothers who, for whatever reason – usually the stigma of having an illegitimate child or the sheer impossibility of supporting one – were unable to care for their own babies. (Figure 1.10) The hospital kept meticulous records, including listing the garments the child was wearing on admission. Foundling number 15329, a little boy about three weeks old, was admitted on 29 January 1760, wearing:

Ribbon	[a decorative top knot on the outer cap]
cap	Holland cambric border
bonnet	
biggin	Irish trimmed ditto [a plain under-cap]
forehead-cloth	Ditto [like the *têtière* – a triangular head cloth]
head-cloth	[ditto]
long-stay	[a binder, usually quilted, rather like a corset]
bibb	
gown	Purpill and white flowerd cotting
frock	
uppercoat and stay	

petticoat	
bodice-coat	
robe	
barrow	[a long sleeveless garment, usually of flannel]
mantle	
sleeves	
blanket	White flannel overcast with pinck wossted
neckcloth	
handkerchief	
cloak	
roller	Sheloone bond with white ribing
	[like a swaddling band – Shalloon was wool twill]
bed	[a wrapper]
waistcoat	Dammask
shirt	Irish trimmed with musling
clout	Irish rag [a nappy]
pilch	[a triangular cloth that pinned over the nappy to hold it in place]
stockings	
shoes	

Little 15329 was well and warmly dressed, and like most of the babies admitted he was not fully swaddled, though he was wrapped in a roller and blanket. His sleeves were separate items and would have been pinned to his other garments.[64] Over time, separate sleeves became less common, and babies' gowns and bodices were made with integral sleeves. The hospital conformed to contemporary views of childcare as Dr Cadogan was one of its advisers. Hospital issue consisted of caps and biggins, clouts and pilches, shirts and linen sleeves, shoes, stockings, bodice-coats, outer coats and stays, with the blanket remaining as an outer wrap. The swaddling 'rollers' were not thought necessary, and bodice-coats, coats and separate sleeves were used rather than gowns. Wet nurses taking in foundling hospital babies were allocated four each of biggins, caps, neckcloths, linen stays and shirts and a dozen clouts per baby; these were returned to the hospital and replaced with larger ones as the infant grew.

De Garsault's description depicts one end of the babywear spectrum; the Foundling Hospital garments are at the other. Babies in more middle-class homes no doubt wore something resembling one or the other type of outfit, depending on how 'modern' their mothers were and on what was left over from their older siblings. However, of one thing we can be certain, creating a layette involved a great deal of work for mother or seamstress, and the arrival of shops specializing in providing 'childbed linen' to clothe both mother and baby must have been a boon.

As the child grew, the seamstress would provide dresses, petticoats and the 'shirts' that were worn as vests and cut like a woman's chemise. Garments for the children of the well-to-do were fairly simply cut, but the decoration on them could be very elaborate. Mrs Papendiek, whose husband was a court musician and who knew Queen Charlotte well, described what was expected of the seamstress appointed in 1763 to look after the Prince of Wales. Mrs Chapman was nurse to the royal child and her daughter, Miss Chapman, 'was appointed sempstress to the young Prince, which appointment was continued to the succeeding eight children. Their frocks were of cambric, the tucks and hems being hem-stitched with Valenciennes lace tuckers and cuffs for the evening; plain for the morning. This place was no sinecure.'[65]

Figure 1.11 George III, Queen Charlotte and their six eldest children by Johann Zoffany, 1769–70. The older children wear small versions of adult dress, though Princess Elizabeth's dress does incorporate leading strings. The two youngest wear silken versions of the type of dresses Mrs Papendiek says Miss Chapman made for them.

Figure 1.12 Portrait of Mrs Papendiek and her son, Frederick, by Thomas Lawrence, 1789.

Children of both genders in less rarefied households wore plainer versions of such dresses, made of cotton rather than cambric, and any trimmings were likely to be of cutwork or embroidery rather than Valenciennes lace, but tucked decoration which could be let out or down as the child grew was always popular.

Mrs Papendiek also wrote about making dresses for her eldest daughter, Charlotte, in 1763. Charlotte had just been weaned so was probably a little under a year old: 'We made her two white dresses and two coloured ones, with the skirts full and three tucks and a hem; the bodies plain, cut cross-ways, and the sleeves plain, with a cuff turned up. These, with converting of underclothing, nurse, T, and a workwoman finished off in a week.'[66]

These were toddlers' clothes. By the time the seventeenth- or eighteenth-century child was three or four they would have been dressed in miniature versions of adult garments, and these would have been made by the tailor or mantua-maker who dressed their parents, so only their shirts and shifts would have continued to be seamstress-made.

Household Linen

Seamstresses made and repaired all the household linen, sheets, pillowcases, tablecloths, napkins, towels (which were made of absorbent linen or huckaback as there was no equivalent for modern terry-towelling) and a whole range of cloths for various purposes.

In June 1835 Joseph M'Cleland, a linen manufacturer from County Armagh in Ireland, held a sale at Theatre Buildings in Shrewsbury (Shropshire). No doubt he held such sales all over the country but it so happens that the flier for this one survives.[67] The sale consisted of 'The largest and Best and CHEAPEST Stock of Linens ever offered in this Town.' He was selling a range of types of linen, Scottish, Irish and Russian, diaper and damask woven table linens, lawns, cambric handkerchiefs, huckabacks and towellings and some exceptionally wide sheeting 'FROM ONE TO THREE YARDS WIDE, WOVEN WITHOUT SEAM'. Doilies and napkins were available to match the tablecloths, but perhaps the offering that best describes the aspirations of his buyers was 'FAMILY COATS OF ARMS AND CRESTS WOVEN TO ORDER ON SETS OF TABLE LINEN.' It is highly unlikely that members of the aristocracy who actually had coats-of-arms and crests would have deigned to go to a public sale of cut-price linens, this offer was for middle-class families with pretensions of grandeur.

Even in the seventeenth century the display of table linen was a matter of prestige. On 22 January 1669 Samuel Pepys wrote: 'Mightily pleased with the fellow that came to lay the cloth and fold the napkins; which I liked so well that I am resolved to give him 40s to teach my wife to do it.' Wealthy households had enormous quantities of linen. In July 1676 an inventory was prepared of the possessions of the Finch family, earls of Nottingham and Winchilsea, at Burley-on-the-Hill in Rutland.[68] It is beautifully written, in a purpose-made, blue, leather-covered book tooled in gold, with ties of embossed ribbon which are now perished and weathered to a grubby grey colour. Under 'Linnen', the items are described by fabric – damask, 'dyaper', 'flackson', huckaback and canvas – and the marks on them in red or blue silk or eyelet holes are carefully recorded. In total, the house at Burley contained ten 'great' tablecloths, one of which was five yards long, nine little tablecloths, fourteen 'sideboard cloths' and no fewer than 420 napkins to match the various sets of cloths. Moreover, that was without counting the number of cloths assigned to the steward and the servants; the steward's cloths were of diaper but the servants' were of 'whited canvas'.

Burley also contained sixty-two damask towels and thirteen dozen diaper ones and there were at least nineteen 'chamber sideboard cloths' and a dozen 'packing cloths', whatever those might have been. There were 140 pairs of sheets but, if the inventory is to be believed, just twenty-five pairs of pillowberes. The size of the sheets was also recorded, some were three breadths wide, some two, and some one and a half.

In the eighteenth century even the accounts of middle-class households list large quantities of linen. For example, in 1794, Richard Hall, a London hosier and haberdasher who had a shop at one end of London Bridge, had an inventory made of his household possessions. It listed under 'Linen' fourteen 'Diaper' tablecloths of which two were small and four were designated 'Breakfast Table Cloths', ten pairs of sheets (variously described as 'Lancashire' and 'Russian') and two odd ones, eight pairs of pillowcases, forty-nine towels of various types and materials, another 'Breakfast' cloth, two pudding cloths, a cotton counterpane and 'a sett of blue check bed Curtains'.[69]

At about the same time, Elizabeth Penrose, wife of the vicar of St Gluvias in Cornwall, made a list of her own household linen. She owned one large tablecloth, valued at £1 10s., fifteen smaller ones ranging in value from a penny to 1s. 3d., three sets of table napkins, a cotton quilt and a cotton counterpane, four pairs of Holland sheets and nine pairs of 'common' sheets, total value £3 15s.[70] If she owned towels – and she must have done – she chose not to list them. There are numerous similar inventories.

Replacing linen was an expensive business. Less than two weeks before her death, Lady Anne Clifford decided to upgrade the household linen at Brougham Castle, one of the three northern estates she owned. By this point she was twice widowed and, after a long legal battle, had taken possession of the family estates in Westmoreland and Craven which her misogynistic father had left to a male relative. On 10 March 1676 she wrote:

> And this morning I saw not only A Strickland payd for the weekbook in my
> chamber, but I also saw G Goodgion payd for 249 yards of Linnen cloth that he
> bought for mee at Penrith, designed for 20 pares of Sheets and som Pillowveres

for the use of my house. And after dinner I gave away severall old Sheets which were divided amongst my servants.

Fabric widths were relatively narrow, so each of the new sheets would probably have taken at least two breadths. If they were an average length of two and a half yards, then each would have taken five yards; and forty sheets (twenty pairs) would therefore have used 200 of the 249 yards. The remainder would have been made into 'pillowveres' or pillowcases. A few days later Lady Anne wrote, 'And this afternoon did Margaret Montgomery of Penrith, the Seamstress come hither so I had her in my chamber and kist her and talked with her, and shee came to make up the 20 pares of Sheets and Pillowveres.'[71] We should not read too much into the fact that Anne 'kist' her seamstress, that was the way she treated all women guests, though it is unlikely that she would have greeted her kitchen maids or the wives of labourers on her estates that way. Margaret Montgomerie was not her social equal, but she was an honourable craftswoman and entitled to be treated with respect.

Almost 150 years later Anne's estates had come into the possession of the earls of Thanet. Anne's daughter, Margaret Sackville, married John Tufton,

Figure 1.13 Appleby Castle from *A Series of Picturesque Views of the Seats of the Noblemen and Gentlemen of Great Britain and Ireland* by F.O. Morris (1840).

second Earl of Thanet, and their grandson, Anne's great-grandson, the eleventh (and last) Earl, Henry Tufton, succeeded to the title in 1775. In 1843, for reasons that are not entirely clear, he had an inventory made of the linen in Appleby Castle, another northern property that had been Anne's. It was made by Jane Heelis, wife of John Heelis, who described himself as a 'clerk' to the census enumerators in 1841, but who seems to have taken over from his brother, Thomas, as steward of the castle. That year, he, Jane, another John Heelis (a solicitor who was their son or nephew), and a female servant were the castle's sole inhabitants.

Jane and John were both in their seventies, and she had obviously known the castle and its contents well for many years, because her inventory is extremely detailed and informative. She listed the linen, the closets in which it was stored, the various qualities of sheets – 'fine old', 'backroom', 'course' [sic] and 'garret' – and the various marks on items (many bore a 'T' and a coronet, all were numbered). There were large tablecloths, servants' hall tablecloths, breakfast cloths, some of damask, some of huckaback, some of diaper, some listed as 'strong', and endless napkins. Where sets were incomplete numbers of items were listed as 'wanting'. There were towels, 'dressing fringed drawer covers', 'fringed table covers', 'fish covers', 'glass covers', 'hall cloths', 'doyles' and 'bedroom napkins'. Many items were described as 'fine' or 'fine old' and a number of items were 'bought in 1792 the first time the earl came to Appleby Castle', though some sheets were acquired 'many years earlier' and were 'nearly worn out'. A few items had been acquired by one Lady Thanet in 1816, and some – namely, nine small damask breakfast cloths (part of a set of twelve, three of which were at Skipton Castle, another part of the estate), nine new servants' hall cloths, six unused breakfast cloths for the steward, seventy-six unused dinner cloths, and ninety-six old diaper cloths for the kitchen – had all been 'made by Mrs Heelis'. 'Mrs Heelis' might have been Jane herself but is more likely to have been her sister-in-law, wife of the former steward.

In total, in 1843 Appleby Castle contained: forty new pairs of sheets; fifty-six pairs of 'fine old' ones; twenty-two pairs of backroom and garret sheets; six worn out 'little considered' ones; 'twenty-and-a-half dozen' towels of various qualities and sizes; thirty-eight dozen table napkins; 351 tablecloths for a range of purposes; forty-one breakfast cloths; and an endless array of cloths and covers of various sorts.[72]

The inventory covers six sides of neatly written foolscap. As stately homes go, Appleby was neither exceptionally large nor very prestigious. This inventory is worth quoting because of the range of detail it contains, but no doubt in the nineteenth century grander houses could boast even longer and more complex lists of linen. Such households had provided plenty of work for the jobbing seamstress.

Conclusion

While little material evidence of seamstress work survives from the period pre-1800, there is a wealth of written evidence in the form of account books and inventories, bills, letters and diaries to tell us what linen people owned and bought, what they paid for it, where they acquired it, who made it for them and how much they valued it. We learn that even in the seventeenth century it was possible to buy many items ready-made, though it would seem that the highest quality linens were usually made to order.

Almost everyone owned some examples of seamstry. Poor men had their shirts or smocks; poor women had their shifts; pauper mothers and babies were supplied with childbed linen, even if it came in the form of a parish 'baby box', the items in which had to be returned, washed and ironed, at the end of a month. Even the Poor Law officials recognized that the very poor were entitled to at least one change of undergarments; they might not be able to have clean linen every day like their betters, but clean linen once a week was a reasonable expectation. By contrast, a wealthy bride would have had several dozen shifts in her trousseau, along with caps and neckwear, sleeves and aprons, and her husband would have had a stock of fine shirts, neckwear and sleeve ruffles. Well-to-do households had closets and chests full of sheets and towels, tablecloths and napkins, as well as quantities of cloths and covers for a range of purposes.

Linen was an important marker of social status. A clean white shirt or shift and pristine collars and cuffs signified their wearer's aspirations to gentility, or at least respectability, and acted as a foil for their more colourful garments. Even servants were expected to reflect the position of the people they served; ruffles might suggest they had ideas above their station, as John Macdonald discovered to his cost, but a grubby shirt suggested slovenliness. In a society bound by rules of etiquette, linen played its part; only the most eccentric individuals, like Dr Johnson, could defy convention by not wearing sleeve frills at a formal dinner, for example.

Children's wear also reflected their families' status. A layette of fine linen for a swaddled baby, or white dresses for toddlers, showed off the family's wealth and implied that they could afford sufficient changes of clothes to keep their children looking clean and smart all the time – and also that they had enough servants to do the necessary laundry and ironing. Fine linen sheets ensured that the family and any guests had a comfortable night and showed off rich bedspreads to advantage; fine white tablecloths acted as a backdrop to silver dishes and cutlery, gleaming glassware and dinner services of fine china. Sheets and tablecloths of inferior materials were provided for the servants according to their rank, but they were all items that could be washed, thus ensuring a degree of cleanliness for everyone. Linen of all sorts was a matter of pride and had significant value; in most inventories it was listed in detail in a separate section.

Most women could sew and some saw making their husbands' shirts, their own and their children's underclothes and linen for their households as a major part of their wifely duties, but a large household generated a great deal of needlework and most housewives who could afford to do so farmed out at least some of the work of making and mending to seamstresses. Well into the eighteenth century the seamstress was a respected craftswoman, able to earn a respectable living and, if she was lucky, to save for her old age.

2

'Well-handed needlewomen'

In 1636 the overseers of the poor in Bewcastle, an isolated rural parish in northern Cumberland (now part of Cumbria), sent a petition to the local Justices of the Peace. (Colour plate III) There was a blind man in their parish by the name of John Armstrong and the overseers had been supporting him for some time, to the tune of 1s. 6d. a week, which they were struggling to afford. John was fit and strong and the overseers were sure that he could find work if he really wanted to. However, the detail that clinched the matter as far as they were concerned was that John's wife was:

> a very well-handed needlewoman who as a schoolmistress or otherwise by her work is able to earn 5s. 0d. a week or upward and when your petitioners' said parish (which is a very poor one) cannot find her business of that kind she usually goes abroad into other parishes for five or six months together where she can get a school or simistry work: by which means they may live very comfortably without any productive assistance.[1]

What is interesting in this context is the way being a schoolmistress and being a seamstress were equated, and just how much Mrs Armstrong was able to earn. Presumably as a schoolmistress she taught mostly needlework, but it is not impossible that she taught basic reading and writing as well.

In 1636 the Elizabethan Poor Law of 1601 was still relatively new. It mandated parishes to appoint overseers of the poor whose job it was to raise a tax on the wealthier members of the community and use it to support those people in their parishes who were unable to support themselves. Not surprisingly, the Poor Law was very unpopular with those parishioners required to pay the Poor Rate and attempts like this to keep payments to a minimum were not uncommon.

Economic Background

Despite the mid-century traumas of the Civil War, the regicide, the Restoration and a plague that killed almost a quarter of London's population within eighteen months followed by a fire which left the city unrecognizable, by the end of the seventeenth century England was an increasingly prosperous nation. Nonetheless, longstanding problems which hampered trade persisted. There was, for example, a shortage of coinage, and many of the coins in circulation had been clipped and their value reduced. The system of making payments by notes of hand and bills of exchange was cumbersome and open to abuse. However, by the 1690s and early 1700s an infrastructure that supported business was gradually established. The Bank of England was founded in 1694, and in 1696 the Recoinage Act was passed whereby the government undertook to replace all the clipped coins in circulation with new ones. This process was completed by 1699, at great expense, and the new coins had milled edges to deter clippers of the future.

The first English newspapers, carrying business news and advertisements, as well as political and international news, were published in the early 1700s. The Sun Fire Assurance Company was established in 1710 and the Royal Exchange Assurance Company in 1720, though for many years both only offered insurance against destruction by fire. The Royal Exchange itself had been destroyed by the

Figure 2.1 *The Old Royal Exchange*, London, by Wenceslaus Hollar, *c.* 1647.

Great Fire and was rebuilt in the mid-1670s as the 'New Exchange'. Both before and after the fire it functioned as a stock exchange, a place where merchants from Britain and abroad transacted business and exchanged news, and as a shopping mall, frequented by fashionable shoppers anxious to see and be seen. It was, as one contemporary put it, 'The glory of the world in a moment'.[2] On the first-floor galleries city seamstresses had their shops, took orders and sold ready-made goods and linens, and, though theirs' was an old-established trade, they, like other tradespeople, benefited from the new developments designed to encourage trade.

Earnings and Prices

There is comparatively little information about wages and prices to enable us to set Mrs Armstrong's putative earnings in context. The evidence suggests a seventeenth-century agricultural labourer was lucky to earn sevenpence to tenpence a day,[3] though city workers could earn more. For example, the daily rate for a building labourer in London rose from 1s. 6d. in 1600 to 2s. 8d. in 1700, partly due to the need to rebuild the fire-ravaged city.[4] However, a lot of women's work was unskilled or semi-skilled and a payment of around fourpence a day in 1600, rising to sixpence or sevenpence a day in 1700 was the norm.[5] A live-in female servant might earn up to five pounds a year plus her board and lodging, though many got less; for example, Sir Daniel Fleming in Lancashire paid his kitchen maid just twenty-two shillings a year, in two instalments over the period 1690 to 1691.[6] Mrs Armstrong's five shillings a week (or £13 a year) was therefore a very respectable wage in the seventeenth-century countryside, when the rent on a village cottage was cheap at a little over a pound a year.[7] The price of foodstuffs, the other key item of expenditure for most people, was more problematic, and varied widely according to the season and the harvest. A 4lb loaf varied in price between threepence in 1633 and tenpence in 1661, for example, though it averaged out at about sixpence, and one loaf would feed a family of two adults and three or four children for a day.[8]

Royal employees were obviously a category apart, but between 1660 and 1685 the royal seamstress received £20 a year, not so very much more than Mrs Armstrong's £13, though the king's seamstress was allowed another £50 a year for 'necessaries'. By 1689, the royal seamstress and the royal clear-starcher between them were paid an annual £81 12s. 11½d. plus one 'mess of mutton', one loaf of bread, one gallon of beer, candles, faggots and (in winter) charcoal. That increased to £200 in 1690, plus another £200 because of the 'very great Expense and charge in washing Our points and Laces'.[9] We do not know what she was paid earlier in the century but the royal seamstress was clearly a person of some standing. In 1626 Sir Henry Mildmay, Master of the Jewels, received a warrant to deliver thirty-one ounces of gilt plate to Mrs Julian Elliott, then the king's seamstress, as a New Year's gift.[10]

Gregory King, the engraver and surveyor, turned herald, turned commissioner of taxes, wrote a compendious economic treatise, *Natural and Political Observations and Conclusions upon the State and Condition of England*, in 1696.[11] It contains estimates of the population and wealth of England and Wales in the year 1688. It describes the demographic profile of the population in terms of age, gender, marital status, numbers of children, and classification as 'Rulers' or 'Ruled'. King also calculated the income of the various social classes, ranging from seven pounds a year for the poorest pauper to £3,200 a year for the wealthiest aristocrat. He did not separate out women's wages, indeed he does not seem to have considered them to have been economically active, but he did gauge – or guess – the wages of 'artisans' to be around £15 a year. He has been much criticized; it is generally reckoned that many of his figures were underestimates and that he was at his least accurate when dealing with the poorer sections of society – although, applied to the specific case of Mrs John Armstrong, his calculation was not so very far out. The Bewcastle petition remains one of very few indications we have of what a seventeenth-century country seamstress was able to earn per week, though of course we cannot be sure that the overseers did not exaggerate Mrs Armstrong's potential earnings to reinforce their argument.

Obviously, the earnings of most ordinary seamstresses, like Mrs Armstrong, depended on how many commissions they were given and the value of the goods they made also depended on the cost of the fabric they worked with, which was often, but not always, supplied by the customer. Estimating seamstresses' earnings is therefore not straightforward. Gregory King's treatise estimated the cost of living and provided tables showing the cost of foodstuffs and of individual items of clothing. Both shirts and shifts in the 1680s cost, he believed, 2s. 6d.[12] However, his estimates were on the low side.

A few accounts of the actual cost of shirts and shifts in the seventeenth century do survive in shop inventories. Hester Kinge's 1664 probate inventory, for example, valued the ten shifts she had in her London shop at three shillings each, but it is quite possible that she was selling them for rather more than that.[13] Probate inventories of shop goods tend to reflect the cost price rather than the retail price. On the other hand, Hester, or her apprentice or journeywoman, might well have made the shirts herself, so a retail price of three shillings might actually have given her a respectable profit – though there were certainly other shops that charged more.

In London in May 1682 Thomas Marshall placed his younger brother, George, as apprentice to a Mr Banks (trade unknown) for a premium of 8s. 6d. Between them, Thomas and Mr Banks spent £15 on kitting George out, £1 10s. of which bought him six shirts at five shillings each, along with two hats, two suits, nine pairs of shoes and a five-shilling bible.[14] The probate inventory of Henry Mitchell in Lincoln was made in 1679 and some of his shirts were valued at a pound each while separate sleeves were an enormous ten shillings a pair. One can only assume that Henry was catering for very well-to-do customers and that he employed seamstresses, who, it is to be hoped, shared his profits.[15] By contrast, in Kent in 1668 George Johnson's stock shirts were valued at 1s. 4d. apiece,[16] while John Smith of Randwick in Gloucestershire had five shirts valued at three shillings each in stock in 1691.[17] Shop inventories like these list quite small numbers of made items, frequently fewer than a dozen of each type, which suggests that, like Thomas Turner in East Hoathley a century later (see Chapter 1, 'Smocks'), a single seamstress or tailor directly employed by the shopkeeper, or a member of his/her family, could supply as much stock as was needed.

Poor Law records are another useful indicator of costs. A trawl through the overseers' account books of many parishes yields details of clothing costs. To quote a few examples from London parishes: in March 1691 the parish of St Botolph's, Aldgate supplied a gown, two shifts and a pair of stockings, total cost twelve shillings, for 'Mad Mary', one of their regular claimants;[18] that same month they also spent three shillings on a shift for Ann Rachael and the same sum on a shirt for John Collins;[19] in November 1694 Goody Tarver's two shifts cost them six shillings and two for 'Patman's child' were five shillings.[20] There are numerous other examples and three shillings for an adult's shift or shirt and rather less for a child's seems to have been the norm across the capital.

Children fared rather better for parish clothing than did their parents. Children put out to nurse by the parish of St Clement Danes were supplied with shoes, pincloths (pinafores), gowns, shirts, stockings, hats, shifts, coats, breeches, waistcoats, aprons, caps, buckles and clouts, but the 'Parish Clothing Books with Names of Children at Nurse' did not itemize costs for individual items of clothing.[21] To modern eyes, waistcoats and breeches and shoes with buckles all sound like very grown-up clothing for babies still being breast-fed. In 1697 the overseers of St Dionis Backchurch paid a Mrs Roberts 17s. 6d. for 'linnen for a found Child',[22] while the following year 'Linnen for ye five children sent to nurse' came to a substantial £3 15s.;[23] again, we cannot be sure which items this covered or how many of them were being provided, although, as we saw in the previous chapter, in the mid-eighteenth century the Foundling Hospital supplied its wet nurses with a dozen nappies per baby and four each of the other main garments it required and this may well have been the standard allocation elsewhere too.

London parishes dealt with enormous numbers of paupers and the sums spent on clothing alone must have been prodigious. Nonetheless, provincial parishes also had poor people to clothe, although, in fact, many parishes simply supplied paupers with cash, not actual garments. Three random examples are given below:

(i)   Between the 1630s and the 1670s the overseers of the parish of St Mary the Great[24] in Cambridge supported large numbers of paupers, mostly by weekly payments or help in paying rent, but from time to time their account book lists 'Extraordinary disbursements' which sometimes include purchases of clothing. In 1649, for example, two shirts cost them seven shillings, which suggests the person making the shirts received between one and two shillings. In 1650, kitting out one of their clients with two shirts, two pairs of stockings and two pairs of shoes cost 19s. 8d., which again suggests the maker of the shirts was being fairly well-paid. Two years later, three child's shifts cost 4s. 4d. but, as there is no indication of the age of the child, we cannot estimate how much of that was the cost of the fabric. Similarly, in 1659 'child's shifts' – which probably means two – cost four shillings. Prices changed over time. In 1667 John Barnes' two shirts cost just 5s. 6d. which may reflect the fact that fabric prices dropped as the century progressed.

St Mary's overseers seem sometimes to have employed paupers in their care to make up items: for example, in 1660 Goodwife Watts was given four shillings for making shirts for the two Lowsdon boys; in 1670 Widow Dickson was paid 2s. 5d. for making a shift for 'Machum's child'; and in 1672 Goody Garrett got two shillings for making a coat for one of the Ableson children. It is not clear whether the overseers supplied the fabric for these items but it seems likely that they did as they were buying material in quantity at bulk prices. The Ableson family (sometimes recorded as Ablingson) were regular recipients of aid. Another child from the family had a shift for 1s. 8d. in 1667, while two of his or her sisters had shifts costing 2s. 8d., and a year later the overseers spent a whole eleven shillings on 'linen for the Ableson children'.

(ii) At Worth in West Sussex[25] in 1644 the overseers paid three shillings for a smock, sixpence for a band and three shillings for 'apparel for a child'. By 1693 three pairs of children's shifts cost them 3s. 8d., 3s. and 2s. 4d., respectively, and were made from linen costing two shillings a yard, while (petti)'coates' cost one shilling and two shillings. At those prices the seamstress can only have been paid a few pence per garment.

The Worth overseers' year's outlay in 1693 with their supplier, James Coleman, was as follows:

> Camfield's child 2 coats 7s. 6d., 2 shirts and 2 back clouts, 2 'bedds', a waistcoat and a cap 4s. 10d.
> Vests, britches, drawers and 2 shirts 12s. 8d.
> Humphry, a vest, a coat and 2 shirts and hatt 12s. 0d.
> Barbara Blake 2 shifts 3s. 0d.
> Widow Tingley 2 shifts 5s. 6d.
> Elizabeth Longley 2 shifts 6s. 6d.
> Mary Winn a gowne and coat 12s., 2 shifts 5s. 0d.
> Widow Blake a hatt and lining 2s. 1d., 2 shifts 6s. 6d., bodice, stomacher, manto and petticoat £1 3s. 8d.

Camfield's child seems to have been a baby as it was provided with 'back clouts' and 'bedds'. The difference in the price of the various shifts presumably reflects the difference between child, teenager, adult and small adult. James Coleman seems to have been a tailor-cum-draper but it is likely he employed a seamstress to make up the shirts and shifts. Many country seamstresses derived much of their income from working for the local overseers or for shopkeepers employed by them.

(iii) In the latter part of the seventeenth century the overseers of the poor in Shrewsbury made various payments for clothing paupers who wound up in the town out of what they termed the 'vagabond money'.[26] For example, Anne Roberts was provided with a shift, price 3s. 2d., and a gown, made from 5½ yards of 'stript linsey' which cost 4s. 7d. The cost of making it was 1s. 3d. William Hannover and his son were clothed from the same fund; William had a waistcoat and breeches costing 9s. 6d. and his son, who presumably was rather smaller than his father, had a coat and breeches for 7s. 6d. and a shirt for 3s. 2d., the same price as Anne Roberts' shift. Assuming the shirt and shift were made from the cheapest calico available, the fabric for both would have cost in the region of 2s. 2d. so the seamstress who made them would have received a fairly generous payment of around a shilling for each garment.

Another useful source of information about prices comes from the proceedings of various courts. The Essex Quarter Sessions' records[27] are particularly complete for the seventeenth century and, as in other counties, dealing with thefts of clothing formed a large part of the courts' business, and valuations were often given for the items stolen. By definition, few of these items were brand new, so age and condition must have affected the calculations of value but, nonetheless, they provide a useful way of estimating the cost of replacing garments. In seventeenth-century Essex, of the 123 thefts which involved shirts and where the value of the stolen items was recorded, fifty-two stolen shirts were valued at under a shilling, thirty-four were valued at between a shilling and 2s. 6d., twenty-seven were valued at between 2s. 6d. and five shillings, while ten were estimated to be worth more than five shillings. Of these, the most valuable were the three taken by Thomas Pollen of Walthamstow which were said to be worth fifteen shillings apiece; one belonged to William Threele, 'gentleman', while the owners of the other two could not be traced. Thomas Pollen obviously had an eye for quality and he was punished for it by being branded. The punishments meted out to thieves seem capricious to modern eyes. Most convicted clothing thieves were whipped or branded, but John Bulleyton of Ashdon, a labourer, who in 1632 stole two shirts worth twelvepence, a pair of breeches also worth twelvepence, a jerkin worth sixpence and three yards of woollen cloth valued at ten shillings – a comparatively modest haul – was sentenced to *hang*.

Fabric Costs

All types of cloth were expensive, and thieves sometimes went to extraordinary lengths to acquire it. Defoe, for example, records how plague corpses might be stripped of their fine linen shrouds for profit: 'It was reported by way of a Scandal upon the Buriers, that if any Corpse was delivered to them, decently wound up ... in a Winding Sheet Ty'd over the Head and Feet ... which was generally of good Linen ... that the Buriers were so wicked as to strip them in the Cart and carry them quite naked to the Grounds.'[28] Reckless as well as wicked!

Fabrics came in a range of qualities and widths, and prices varied from place to place and purchaser to purchaser, as Table 2.1, culled from a range of sources and examples, shows.

Table 2.1 Fabric prices per yard in the late seventeenth century

Type of fabric	1640–60	1660–80	1680–1700
'Blew' cotton		16d.–20d.	12d.
Buckram			8d.
Calico	8d.	1s. 9d.–2s. 3d.	
Callamanco	3s. 8d.		1s. 6d.
Cambric		3s. 8d.–4s. 6d.	
Canvas		1s.	
Cheesecloth			6d.
Diaper		9d.	8d.
Dimity	1s.	9d.	10d.
Dowlas			7½d.–10d.
Flannel	2s. 9d.		9½d.–1s. 3d.
Garlicks*			6d.–1s. 2d.
Hempen cloth	2s. 10d.		
Holland	3s.	2s.–8s. 3d.	9½d., 1s. 2d. (broad)
Kersey		3s. 6d.–4s.	10d. (coarse)
Lawn		4s.	12d. (coarse)
Linen	1s. 11d.; 2s. 6d.; 2s. 9½d.	6½d.–10d. (printed); 1s. 7d.–1s. 10d.	
Linsey wolsey		1s. 1½d.	
Muslin		3s.–10s. 1d.	1s. 8d. (coarse)

* Linen from Pomeranian Silesia.

Case Studies

Reverend Giles Moore

Reverend Giles Moore was rector of Horsted Keynes in Sussex from 1655 to his death in 1679.[29] He kept a 'Journal', more properly an account book, in which he made a meticulous record of his income and expenditure. He bought Holland at three shillings an ell (or 2s. 5d. a yard), black calamanco for his cassocks at 3s. 8d. a yard, dimity at one shilling, calico at eightpence, flannel for winter shirts for 2s. 9d., and 'hempen cloth' for around 2s. 10d. a yard. Fourteen ells of 'flaxen cloth' at 2s. 7½d. an ell (or about 2s. 1d. a yard) made the family a pair of sheets, a tablecloth and two petticoats for his wife or niece. In 1659 four ells of 'coarse cloth' at a shilling an ell (about tenpence a yard) made three tablecloths, some towels and an 'ash cloth', while 'coarse cloth' worth 10s. 6d. made two pairs of sheets and two aprons.

Some of the cloth was hand-woven locally and was supplied, and the items were made up, by his parishioners, Goodwife Seaman, Goodwife Buckwell, Goodwife Cornford, Goodwife Vinall, Sarah Winter and Widow Wetter. Prices varied slightly from purchase to purchase, for example, the two ells of Holland that made a pair of pillowberes for the household in 1658 cost 3s. 11d. an ell, while that bought in Brighton in 1664 and made into handkerchiefs was 3s. 5d. an ell. The rector bought some household linen ready-made at considerable expense; in 1662 John Osbourne in Lindfield supplied two pairs of sheets marked with Moore's cipher, 'GMS', for eighteen shillings. Giles Moore shopped in London, but he also bought at the door from pedlars and chapmen. In 1660 he bought two ells of Holland from a pedlar at the bargain price of five shillings an ell. In 1676 he bought an ell of 'bag Holland' from 'Patrick the Scotchman' and later the same year he bought two pairs of stockings for five shillings from 'a Scotch Youth at the Door'. His wife and niece also bought fabrics and accessories at local fairs.

Unusually, we also know a good deal about what Reverend Moore paid for having items made up. His tailor, Richard Harland, charged between three shillings and 4s. 6d. for making up cassocks, and from the number Giles Moore had made it looks as though he wore a cassock most of the time, not just in church. In 1662 Mrs Harland, the tailor's wife, was paid 1s. 6d. apiece for making three shirts, plus twopence 'supra' (a tip, probably because he didn't have the right change; coin was in short supply in the mid-seventeenth century); in 1664 she earned 19s. 8d. from him for an unspecified amount of work; in 1665 she was paid 2s. 6d. for making bands and cuffs (threepence a pair for bands, twopence a pair for cuffs); and a year later she made and marked four handkerchiefs at eightpence each.

Some of his parishioners also made items for him. In 1666 Elizabeth Pocock was paid a shilling for making more bands and cuffs, while Goodwife Wickham was paid 1s. 10d. for the same service a year later, though we do not know how many items they each made. On other occasions the rector bought his bands and cuffs ready-made, as he did in London in 1657 when he spent 10s. 8d. on bands and band-strings. He also sometimes tells us how much fabric items took; six ells and two feet of 'Douglas', costing 14s. 6d. in 1656, made him two voluminous shirts, and in 1663 one ell of Holland made three caps, two handkerchiefs and 'several pares' of cuffs.

Thomas Babington

Thomas Babington of Rothley Temple in Leicestershire, MP for Leicester in 1685 and 1689, kept an account book between 1674 and 1698.[30] He recorded numerous purchases of fabric to make 'frocks', shirts, cravats, bands and cuffs for himself, for his brother, for 'Tom', 'Bill', and his young nephew, and shifts and petticoats and aprons for his niece. Thomas paid two shillings and 2s. 2d. a yard for 'Holland' in 1680, but only 1s. 2d. a yard for thirty-four yards in 1695 and a similar sum per yard for 8⅜ yards in 1691. We do not know what the thirty-four yards were for but he tells us that the second amount was for three shifts for his niece and a 'frock' for himself, thus each garment would have taken approximately two yards of material. He paid 2s. 10d. a yard for rather better-quality Holland in 1695 for some shirts and shifts, and shortly after that he bought four ells and a yard (six yards) for £1 16s. 6d. 'to make 8 prs of sleeves'. Each of the sixteen sleeves therefore took 13½ inches of fabric so they were probably either full sleeves or double frills, intended for show and made of finer material than the shirt or shift to which they were attached. Though he does not describe it as such, this would have been superfine Holland, and it was pricey at six shillings a yard. He paid the same for 2¾ yards of Holland for a shift for his niece in 1691, probably to wear 'for best' as most of her other shifts were made of cheaper fabric.

He also bought muslin for a range of prices per yard – 3s., 4s. 8d., 4s. 10d., 6s. 6d., 8s., 10s. 1d. – 'strip't calico for frocks' at 1s. 9d., 'strip't dimity for p.coat' at one shilling, painted calico at 2s. 3d. for an apron, and twenty yards of 'flaxon cloth' from his tailor's wife, Mrs Wagstaff, at 1s. 7d. a yard. He does not record any prices for making up, and probably that was done at home by his womenfolk and servants, but in 1791 there is a reference to paying 'Mrs Wagstaff's bill' of £1 11s. 6d. Given that she also sold linen, did Mrs Wagstaff supplement her tailor husband's income by making up shirts for his customers and under linen for their wives? It seems entirely possible; other tailors' wives sometimes worked as seamstresses. Richard Harland provided tailoring for the clergyman, Giles Moore, in Sussex, and his wife made linen clothing for the household. As we saw, in March 1663 Moore paid her 1s. 6d. for making him three shirts and in November 1665 he paid her 1s. 8d. for making three more and marking some caps. As a bachelor in London in the 1670s, Edward Clarke, MP for Taunton, had lodged with a tailor named Jewell. Mrs Jewell subsequently made undergarments for the Clarke children, for example, in 1696 she was paid a pound for buying material and making three shirts for 'Ward', Edward's eldest son, then aged about sixteen.[31]

Lady Grisell Baillie

Lady Grisell Baillie,[32] née Hume, was a Scottish gentlewoman, quite well-known in her day as a song writer, and in 1692 she married George Baillie, her childhood sweetheart. They lived at Mellerstain House in the Scottish Borders, some eight miles north of Kelso. Today it is known as one of Robert Adam's greatest masterpieces but Lady Grisell would not recognize it. She and her husband began the work of extending the house in 1725, but the house as we know it today was not completed until 1778, long after the deaths of Grisell and George Baillie.

Lady Grisell kept detailed accounts of her household expenditure from the time of her marriage to her death in 1746. She had two daughters, Grizel and Rachel, and a son, Robert – 'My Robin' – who died in 1696 at the age of two. Her early accounts are kept in Scots money which is somewhat confusing for modern readers. In the 1690s £1 (Scots) was the equivalent of 1s. 8d. (sterling) and a Scots shilling was roughly the equivalent of an English penny-halfpenny, hence the apparently enormous sums she spent. After the Act of Union of 1707 the Scots were required to use English money, though they retained their copper coinage and many of their names for coins, like 'bawbee' for sixpence, and so Grisell Baillie's later accounts are in sterling. A further complication is that she often bought fabric by the ell; if she shopped in Scotland an ell was a fraction over a yard, if she shopped in England it was a yard and a quarter. Lady Grisell's accounts have to be approached with a calculator and a clear head!

She bought large quantities of fabric for making shirts and shifts, for example: she spent £33 6s. (Scots) on 'linent' for shirts and shifts in 1693 and £29 (Scots) on 'holland from Holland' in 1695; she bought fifty ells of linen for shifts for £50 (Scots) in June 1702 and another 20 ells that November for £12 (Scots), along with 'shirt Holland' worth £42 (Scots). In October 1707 she settled a series of debts with a linen draper, Francis Newton: £62 16s. (Scots) for twenty-one ells of shirt Holland; 10½ ells of muslin for 'sutes' which came to £34 6s. 6d. (Scots); 11¼ ells of 'fin cambrick for rufils' costing £52 14s. 6d. (Scots); and striped muslins worth £114 (Scots) that she took to London to have made up. In 1710 she bought forty ells of linen for shifts and aprons at around two shillings (sterling) an ell. By 1717 she was buying quantities of 'Indian quilting', presumably for petticoats, along with cambric, lawn and calico.

She bought some ready-made goods and also paid to have various items made: for example, in November 1694 and May 1695 she paid £1 16s. (Scots) for making gowns for 'Grise' and in November 1695 she also spent £2 3s. (Scots) on a 'frok to Gris' – Grizel was then aged about three. These were toddler's clothes and would have been seamstress-made. In January and February 1696 she bought two batches of 'linin for little cloathes' at £1 16s. (Scots) and £1 6s. (Scots), respectively, and later that month, after her son's death, she wrote sadly that 'For my childs dead linin' she had spent £17 8s. (Scots). In June another gown for 'Grisie' cost £4 2s. (Scots) and that July she spent £5 7s. 6d. (Scots) on 'shirts' – the terms 'shift' and 'shirt' for the basic female undergarment seem to be interchangeable in the account book – for the two girls. In 1702 she bought 'strip flanen coats' for the girls, presumably ready-made, and she spent £15 19s. (Scots) on calico for the 'bairenses gowns' – Grizel was nine by then and Rachel six – and paid £15 1s. (Scots) for 'Rachy's calico nightgown from Mr Hogg' in November.

As we have seen from her account with Francis Newton, she spent a considerable amount on frills and accessories of fine cambric or muslin. For example, she spent £5 8s. (Scots) on striped muslin for cravats and 'slives' in 1693. In February 1696 she paid £14 16s. (Scots) for a muslin cravat, presumably ready-made and for her husband, and bought several batches of muslin to make more cravats. Similar entries occur throughout the accounts. Entries for 'Lace to shirt hands' (probably 'bands') occur frequently, for example, in Edinburgh on 23 January 1702 she spent £7 10s. Scots for 2¼ ells of it.

Some items she seems to have made herself but, as we saw with her children's clothes, some were made for her or bought ready-made. A 'white satin paticoat from Lisie Rainalds' cost £24 (Scots) in November 1702, for example, and in April 1707 she paid someone £1 12s. (Scots) for 'mending the bairens dust-gouns' and later that month she paid for someone to line Rachel's collars and she also paid Grisell Robinson £3 12s. (Scots) for 'sowing'. That September she paid a seamstress for making twenty-four 'shirts' at 3s. (Scots) apiece. In July 1710, by which time her accounts are in sterling, she paid Grisie Lumb 3½d. apiece for sewing shirts. 'Grisell' in its various forms was obviously a common name in the area. In 1717 Lady Grisell spent 6s. 8d. (sterling) on a seamstress 'Sowing 4 shifts'; the seamstress received 1s. 8d. for each one and so did considerably better than her colleague had seven years before.

Young Grizel Baillie married in 1710 and her mother spent a good deal of money on her, some of it with seamstresses. Sewing a Holland 'coat' (probably petticoat) for her cost £2 12s. 6d. She had a 'head sute of fine laces' for £10 9s. 9d. and ruffles for £5 8s. Her best night clothes and ruffles cost £3 12s., and there were more fancy 'head sutes' (headdresses) for her and her sister.

Rachel married in 1717 and £4 1s. 6d. was spent on cambric night clothes and ruffles for her, all of which were probably ready-made. Her first child was born in 1718 and it seems Lady Baillie paid most of the costs, which included £74 4s.

3d. 'For child Bed Linins and everything she wanted' – remember we are now working in sterling – and £4 11s. 6d. for 'coats and froks' from Mrs Child, who was either a seamstress or kept a baby linen shop.

In some ways the accounts are frustrating in that Lady Grisell seldom tells us how many garments the fabric she bought made, and she very rarely tells us who made them. On the other hand, there are some fascinating insights. For example, we know drawers were not generally worn at this period, but it is cold in the Scottish Lowlands and Lady Grisell frequently bought fabric to make drawers and 'linings' for herself, her husband and daughters, though we do not know whether she made them herself or paid someone to do it for her. Similarly, we know that she took snuff as she frequently mentions buying snuff handkerchiefs; maybe her husband did too, but certainly some of the handkerchiefs are listed as being hers. In 1717, for example, she bought four 'snuf' handkerchiefs at 1s. 4d. each. Taking snuff was a dirty habit and handkerchiefs quickly became stained and unusable.

There is a great deal more to be gleaned from these clothing accounts. However, for the purpose of this work, what is clear is that at Mellerstain House they employed seamstresses for at least some, if not all, of the work of making up the family's wearing linen, and that Lady Grisell and her husband and daughters had considerable quantities of it.

Sir John Talbot

Prices could be considerably higher than average depending on where you shopped. For example, in 1675, Sir John Talbot of Lacock Abbey in Wiltshire spent £23 3s. 6d. with Margaret Shaw, a linen draper on Ludgate Hill, from whom he bought twenty-nine ells of Holland for £8 14s., another twenty-one ells of a rather better quality Holland for £7 17s. 6d. and twelve ells of 'fine' Holland for £6 12s.[33] As an English ell was 1¼ yards, the fabrics worked out at roughly 4s. 9d., 6s. and 8s. 9d. a yard, respectively. A shirt took at least two yards of material, so if Sir John Talbot had any of his finest Holland made into shirts the fabric for each one would have cost at least 17s. 6d. in fabric alone.

The Job of the Seamstress

City seamstresses were more than just needlewomen. Mary Jones was apprenticed to Frances Carey in the early 1660s and her contract of employment – not an indenture – was drawn up by a family friend, Robert Blaney. He was concerned, rightly as it transpired, that Frances might not be able to provide Mary with a proper training as her business was quite newly established, and the contract was explicit about what was expected of her: 'Provided that she the said Frances kept open shopp & continued in th'art of a sempstresse and to wash and starch Linnen and to sell wares in ye shop'. Like many seamstresses, Frances sold fabrics, laces and trimmings, as well as ready-made goods, and 'got up' linen, by means of washing, bleaching and starching, as well as actually making goods to order.[34]

Mrs Wagstaff, the tailor's wife, in Leicestershire seems to have worked in a similar way; and in seventeenth-century London seamstresses were often shopkeepers and laundresses of fine linen as well as needlewomen. In June 1675 Sir John Talbot – or more probably, Barbara, his second wife – ran up a bill of £55 1s. 6d. with Margaret Shaw, 'simpstress' in the New Exchange in London. She had made up some handkerchiefs and aprons, but also sold them considerable quantities of lace, fine linen and 'Colberteen', a type of French lace.[35] (Figure 2.2) The Talbot's servant, Thomas Dingley, paid off the first £15 of the bill that July, but we do not know how long Margaret had to wait for the remainder; the gentry were notoriously tardy in paying their bills as many retailers found to their cost. Barbara Talbot was a fashionable lady and a big spender. An account for 1674 to 1675 shows that between them in that period, she and her husband spent £178 on clothes and fabric, which included the payments to Margaret Smith and Margaret Shaw and £9 3s. 7d. to 'Mrs Deborah', milliner.

Hester Kinge, in the parish of St Giles, Cripplegate, died in 1664. She was a widow and had kept what sounds like quite a well-appointed shop; there was a glass showcase and no fewer than four looking-glasses. She sold handkerchiefs, caps, socks, cravats, shifts, aprons, half-shirts, hoods and cuffs, and had 'a parcel of linen which was hanging out of the shop for show', all valued at £38 19s. 3d. It included the ten 'shiftes' valued at £1 10s. and three half-shirts, three quoifs, twelve pinners, nine whisks, three neck-handkerchiefs and some odds and ends of linen, valued together at £3 0s. 4d. Mary Harper also had a shop in the same district and sold bone lace, haberdashery items and linen 'made and unmade'. Her shop goods, including the shop fittings, were listed for probate in 1792 and valued at £31 16s.[36] Similarly, Elizabeth Barker on Gray's Inn Lane sold thread, tapes, cotton, needles, worsted, linen and lace, along with caps, tippets, cravats and other small made goods. An inventory was taken of her goods when she died in 1790 and she, too, was working on quite a small scale; her entire estate was valued at £23 7s. 9d.[37] None of these women described themselves as seamstresses but it seems likely that they made some or all of the items they sold. Many other seamstress/linen sellers – like Margaret Shaw – had shops in

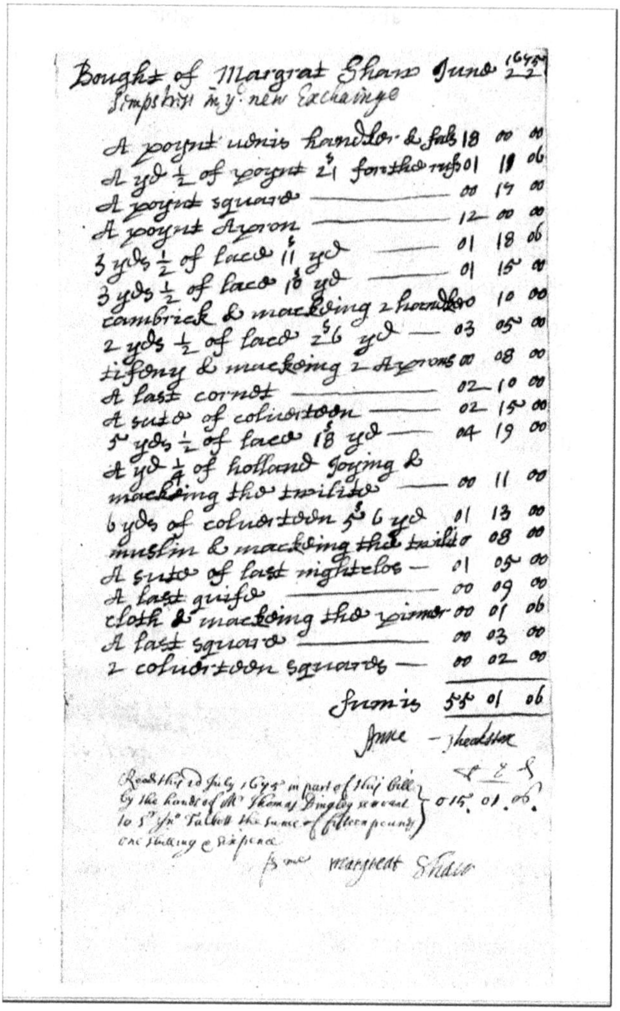

Figure 2.2 Bill from Margaret Shaw, 'simpstress in ye New Exchange', June 1645.

the Exchange, both before it was burnt down in 1666 and in the rebuilt New Exchange of the 1670s. Laura Gowing lists some of them in her book on women and work in seventeenth-century London, *Ingenious Trade* – Herbert and Katherine Allen, Mary Barton, Rachel Erskine, Martha Hunlock, Hester Pinney, Frances Spillett and numerous others.[38]

In the St Pancras area of London, Barbara Kay died in 1707. She too had kept a shop, and the goods she sold are listed in her inventory. She sold fabrics – cambric, Holland and muslin – and some made goods like stockings and gloves which were presumably bought in, but she was described as a 'spinster and sempstress' so we can be reasonably sure she did personally make some goods to order from the fabrics she sold. At the time of her death, she was owed £12 in unpaid debts and her estate was valued at £49 0s. 6d.[39] Many of these women were able businesswoman and most were literate; female literacy in London stood at 48 per cent in the 1690s[40] and in order to run a successful business literacy and numeracy were almost essential. Indeed, some seamstress apprenticeship indentures specified that the apprentice was to be taught to write.

The fact that seamstresses were often also shopkeepers, and that some of them sold luxury goods to wealthy customers, may account for the considerable sums some seamstresses seem to have amassed. In 1694, for example, John and Martha Greenwood of Hirst in Wadsworth in the West Riding of Yorkshire, agreed to pay 'Grace Greenwood of Burlees in Wadsworth, seamstress', an annuity of six pounds a year, from £120 she had deposited with them.[41] This is an example of individuals acting as bankers, in this case for someone who was probably a kinswoman, but what is interesting is that Grace had been able to amass £120 in the first place in the relatively mundane profession of seamstry.

Apprentices

Seamstry was seen as a promising enough career for parents, parishes and patrons to put up substantial apprentice premiums for young girls to learn the trade. Unfortunately, comparatively few seventeenth-century apprenticeship indentures survive for girls, particularly from the first half of the century; for example, the *Registers of Apprentices of the City of Gloucester 1595–1700* record just one girl, Alice Drinkwater, whose late father was described as a 'yeoman'. She was apprenticed in 1615 to Elizabeth Purlewent, spinster, for seven years, with a premium of just five shillings, to learn to be a seamstress.[42] There were always fewer girl apprentices than boys and, though indentures become more common after 1650, many girls were apprenticed informally, to relatives and family friends, and many did not serve a full term.

Interestingly, by the middle of the century, apprenticeship was attracting the daughters of the clergy and the lesser gentry, well-to-do families who nonetheless wanted or needed their children to be independent, and who saw a guild apprenticeship as a way of giving a girl a trade and, through the freedom of the city that she would be granted on completion of her term, the opportunity to set up in business on her own account if she failed to marry or was widowed.

Families across the country sent their girls to London to learn from women they knew, or knew of, through their social networks. A majority of these girls were apprenticed to the needle trades where they would learn or hone skills that would be useful to them as wives and mothers – needlework, cutting out patterns and getting up linen – but, perhaps the most useful transferable skill they would learn was to sell and keep shop. This was a more complex process than it might appear as much seventeenth-century, and, indeed, eighteenth-century, trade relied on credit. Goods might change hands with only a fraction of the price being paid and the girl behind the counter had to be a good enough judge of character, or have a good enough memory for faces, to know which customers could be trusted to pay their bills and which could not. No doubt country shopkeepers faced similar issues but they usually knew their customers; in the city with its numerous visitors, well-dressed and plausible-sounding, it was a genuine problem.

Apprenticeship premiums for girls from respectable backgrounds could be surprisingly high – £20, £30, £40, even £50[43] – reflecting their potential future earnings. Elsewhere the sums paid varied enormously. In Bristol in 1688 Joan Little apprenticed her fatherless niece, Mary Keene, and undertook to pay three pounds a year for seven years,[44] while two years later, just over a hundred miles north in Shrewsbury, the premium paid for Hannah Johnson, described in an unconventional indenture scribbled on a slip of paper, was just £2 10s. for an unspecified period.[45] In 1711, Elizabeth Simpson, a yeoman's daughter from Prees in north Shropshire, was apprenticed to Elizabeth, wife of Allen Higginson, a tailor, to learn to be a seamstress. No money seems to have changed hands, but part of the deal was that Alan was to teach Elizabeth to write, something he was well equipped to do as he signed the indenture in a beautiful copperplate script.[46]

Of course, many things could go wrong, and many of the apprenticeships we know about were the ones that came to court, prosecuted by girls like Christiana Hutchins who in 1673 accused her mistress of ill-treatment and failure to teach,[47] or by mistresses like Apollonia Maddox who accused her apprentice, Frances Angell,[48] of being lazy and insolent, or Mary Johnson, who accused her apprentice of theft.[49] Girls as young as nine or ten could be apprenticed while they were still children and needed mothering as well as teaching; however, the majority of apprentices were bound between the ages of fourteen and sixteen. Nonetheless, they were still young and living away from home with a strange family, so it is hardly surprising that relationships sometimes broke down and, as harsh discipline and physical punishments were the norm in schools and homes, masters and mistresses saw nothing wrong in meting out severe punishments to recalcitrant apprentices. Also, many of the mistresses who took girl apprentices had started work in the first half of the century and had not themselves served an apprenticeship so they did not know quite what was expected of them as mistresses. They had acquired their 'freedom' or right to trade through their fathers or husbands but, as women, their right to participate in the activities and discussions of the guilds and learn what was expected of them in relation to their apprentices was limited. However, by the 1680s and 1690s around 250 girls a year gained their freedom through guild apprenticeships; their apprentices were likely to benefit from a more informed and professional training than they themselves had had.

By no means all apprentices came from wealthy backgrounds, however. Many apprentices were paid for by parishes or charities. Between 1695 and 1725, for example, Christ's Hospital apprenticed 124 girls to various trades paying a £5 premium each time. Twenty-one of these girls were apprenticed to seamstresses. They also placed sixteen girls with mantua-makers, and two apiece with milliners, 'plainworkers' and quilters, three with 'child's coat makers' and three with the makers of blackwork, so for thirty years almost half of the girls in their care went into the needle trades.[50] Hereford City apprenticed nine poor girls to seamstry between 1662 and 1732, but after that date they seem to have recognized that the trade did not offer the opportunities it once had, and sent their pauper girls off to learn the new(ish) trade of mantua-making instead.[51] Nonetheless, despite the declining profits and status associated with the trade, into the early nineteenth century some parishes and charities were still apprenticing girls to seamstresses.

Wills

Between 1600 and 1730 some thirty-two former seamstresses left wills. A few, like Mary Blacklock in Manchester,[52] Anne Horner in Titchfield[53] and Anne Pidder in Sherborne,[54] just left goods and chattels, and some, like Mary Cherry in Westminster in 1654[55] or Christian Porter in Corsham in 1691[56] left comparatively small sums (roughly eleven pounds and seven pounds, respectively), but sixteen of them, half, left in excess of thirty pounds and of those, nine left over £100, either in cash or in bills and bonds.

As we have seen, by the mid-seventeenth century seamstry was attracting girls from gentry families, and some of the seamstresses who left substantial sums in their wills had undoubtedly inherited some of their wealth. The Honourable Anne Mohun of Boconnoc in Cornwall, who left £2,200 in 1676, was a gentlewoman who had inherited most of her money from her father. Nonetheless, she described herself as a 'seamster'.[57] There were other seamstresses who also seem to have been well-connected, for example, Sarah Court in Salisbury died in 1686 and her uncle and two of her sisters' husbands are variously described as 'Esq.' and 'gent.' in her will. She left £100 apiece to her four sisters and an estate in Taunton Deane worth £300.[58] In Norfolk in 1688 Ann Bale left £50 in cash bequests and a messuage with yards and buildings to her aunt.[59] Property was likely to have been inherited so these women probably also came from relatively prosperous families. In Cornwall in 1690 Mary Phillippe of Poughill left £182 10s., which included six pounds to the parish poor and bequests to her mother's servants (plural), which suggests she too came from a well-to-do family.[60]

Others may well have made their money by their own efforts. In 1657 Margaret Wilcox of Colyton in Devon left £90 in bequests to her nephews and nieces and small bequests to the poor of two parishes.[61] In Cumbria in 1666, Frances Atkinson left £106 in fourteen separate legacies, which varied in size from £20 to her unmarried sister to ten shillings apiece to five cousins, and £1 10s., which was to be distributed to the mourners at her funeral.[62] In Sussex in 1694, Elizabeth Jordan left £106 in bequests to her family. Interestingly, she left sums of £10 and £20 to her cousins and their children, but just ten shillings apiece to her two sisters and the same amount to the parish poor. We cannot know whether that meant there was bad feeling in the family or whether the sisters were already well provided for.[63] In fact, many of the testatrixes left money to the poor; they obviously felt they should share their good fortune in having succeeded in their careers. Joan Read in Lyme Regis died in 1714. In her inventory her goods and chattels were valued at £19 17s. (bed and bedding, £4 10s.; clothes, £8 9s. 6d.) but her 'bills and bonds' were valued at £246 7s. 6d.[64]

Conclusion

Of course, there must have been many women who were much less successful than the testatrixes listed above but in the seventeenth century, for some women at least, seamstry could be a reasonably lucrative profession at a time when there were few opportunities for women and their wages were always lower than men's. However, it is very difficult to ascertain just how lucrative it really was as prices varied so widely and information about payments to seamstresses is limited. Ready-made shirts could be valued at just 1s. 4d. like those in George Johnson's shop in Kent in 1668, or at as much as one pound like those in Henry Mitchell's drapery business in Lincoln in 1671. Presumably the wages of the women who made them varied equally widely. Bespoke payments could be just as inequitable: in 1670s Cambridge Widow Dickson was paid 2s. 5d. for making a pauper's shift, for example; while in 1710 in the Lowlands of Scotland Lady Grisell Baillie paid her seamstress just 3½d. for making a shirt for her daughter. Shirts stolen in seventeenth-century Essex varied in value from twopence to fifteen shillings, but all the thefts were deemed worthy of reporting; the purchase of a new shirt to replace a stolen one involved a considerable outlay of effort and money.

Fabric prices were high throughout the seventeenth century and the cost of the material used to make an item almost always exceeded the wage paid to the worker who made it. Coarse linens and hempen cloth might only cost a few pence a yard, but fine Holland could cost eight shillings or more. Fabrics came in narrow widths and bore names which are unfamiliar to us today, but the seamstress had to know what they were and what properties they had. That knowledge, together with knowledge about how to cut out and make basic garments following traditional techniques, was handed down from mother to daughter or mistress to apprentice; there were virtually no instruction manuals. As a result, the style of seamstress-made garments like shirts and shifts changed little in three centuries. Making them required little in the way of originality, but a good deal in the way of skill in stitching garments that could withstand repeated washing and ironing.

By the mid-seventeenth century, seamstry was seen as a respectable enough trade to attract girls from good families as apprentices. No doubt the fact that the skills they would acquire would benefit them as wives and mothers as well as enabling them to earn a living if the need arose was part of the appeal. Formal apprenticeships for girls were still relatively uncommon at this date and numerous problems arose, many of which reached the courts. Mistresses, who had not themselves served apprenticeships, and had little real contact with the guilds to which they nominally belonged, were not always good teachers or responsible employers. Nonetheless, by the latter years of the century 200-300 girls a year served their terms and gained the freedom to trade as seamstresses and, through them, over time, the trade became more professional.

These young women might work for shops and many became shopkeepers themselves, selling fabrics and trimmings and made goods, and washing and 'doing up' linen, as well as taking orders for bespoke work. Other seamstresses worked for families, moving from household to household to make and mend, while others, rather lower down the social scale, took in work from the Poor Law officials, ensuring that their local paupers were decently clad and that local teenagers went into service or into apprenticeships looking respectable.

However she worked, the seventeenth-century seamstress was a craftswoman, providing a valuable and valued service, though how much she earned varied widely. Even by the end of the seventeenth century not all needlewomen worked in the bespoke trade and there were already numerous women working for wholesalers and slop-sellers. Their earnings were probably on a par with country seamstresses working for the Poor Law officials but, as we shall see, over time their situation would deteriorate markedly.

The development of ready-to-wear

As Beverly Lemire has shown in her *Dress, Culture and Commerce*,[1] the need to clothe large numbers of soldiers and sailors, respectably and quickly, during the various conflicts of the seventeenth century, provided a spur to clothiers to supply quantities of ready-made garments at short notice, and encouraged the creation – or expansion – of networks of garment-makers and middlemen. This, she argues, would not have been possible had such networks not already been in existence, though the numerous complaints about the quality of clothing supplied to the troops during the Civil War, about breeches that were too narrow, coats with sleeves that barely reached the elbow, shirts 'so short dyverse of them would nott hide their pryvities', suggest that those networks were stretched to their limits.[2]

This was hardly surprising. One Civil War contract specified that 2,000 shirts were to be supplied within two weeks, and a further 2,000 within the following fortnight, and, although contracts usually stated that shirts should be made of around 3⅓ yards of fabric (usually a coarse linen like dowlas, lockram or osnaburg), the sheer numbers and pressure of time must have meant that corners were cut and proper checking was impossible. Nonetheless, contracting to the army could be profitable; the 4,000 shirts, however inadequate they were, were paid for at the rate of between 2s. 6d. and 3s. 8d. apiece.[3] The disadvantage was that slop-sellers often had to wait months, if not years, for the army to pay up, and smaller dealers often went bankrupt while waiting. For example, in his PhD study Miles Lambert found evidence of four Nantwich (Cheshire) tailors who supplied coats at a cost of £26,399 for local soldiers in 1643. They did not receive payment until August 1647.[4] Their businesses seem to have survived, but many did not.

Up until the English Civil War there was no military uniform as such, though richer colonels, like the Marquis of Newcastle, provided uniforms for their men at their own expense. The Marquis's troops were known as the 'Whitecoats' for obvious reasons, while King Charles's own Lifeguard of Foot were uniformed in red. For the most part, however, men turned out for war in their ordinary clothes, over which they wore whatever armour they had or was provided – and a sword-belt if they were lucky enough to have a sword. Then in 1645 the Long Parliament raised the 'New Model Army' for permanent service and the troops were dressed in a uniform of full-skirted red coats over grey breeches, with white stockings, and shoes with buckles. Regimental facings of various colours were chosen by the individual commanders. (Figure 3.1) Over time the shape of the garments changed, but the colours and insignia remained until twentieth-century warfare rendered the wearing of scarlet coats impossibly dangerous.

There were numerous army suppliers; and it will be instructive to examine one of them in detail. Large collections of documents relating to regimental contracts with Joseph Ashley in London survive in Northamptonshire Record Office and Westminster Archives and make an interesting case study.

Figure 3.1 Soldiers of the Coldstream Guards in the uniform of the mid-seventeenth century, sketch made *c.* 1900.

Joseph Ashley

Joseph Ashley of the parish of St Clement Danes described himself as a 'draper' and a very large part of his trade between 1691 and 1706, if not all of it, was supplying the army in England and Ireland. In 1691 he was trading from 'White Lyom, backside of St Clement Danes', though it seems he and his family lived in a 'newly-built house in Holywell Street'.[5] He was a married man and between 1684 and 1699 he and his first wife had seven children; she died in or about 1700 and Joseph remarried in 1702 and had two more children.[6] He also seems to have taken responsibility for the affairs of his widowed sister, Mary Gravenor.[7] In addition to his business, it appears that he owned and rented out a number of properties, lent money, and had investments in the East India, South Sea and Royal Africa trading companies[8] and, not unusually for a man of this period with numerous business interests, he was frequently involved in litigation with people to whom he owed money and others who were in debt to him. Joseph's business affairs are complex and fascinating, but a detailed description of them is beyond the scope of this chapter.

Suffice it to say that with the need to clothe a standing army came the opportunity for profit, and Joseph Ashley took full advantage of it. From 1691 he supplied uniform for, among others, the Coldstream Guards under General Lord John Cutts and the Queen's (later the Queen's Royal) Regiment under Brigadier Seymour.[9] He provided garments in bulk quantities, along with things like hats, shoes with buckles, swords, bayonets, belts and cartridge-boxes, most of which were certainly not drapery goods, so he must have been acting as an agent for other manufacturers. Indeed, we know that in 1697 he paid £990 to William Humfry of London, ironmonger, and that in 1699 he had dealings with John Hawgood of St Martin's in the Fields, 'sword cutler'.[10]

In March 1695,[11] to look at just one contract in detail, Joseph undertook to provide:

	Per item	Total
720 musketeers' and corporals' red coats with blue facings and blue kersey breeches	£2 3s. 6d. a set	£1,566
216 sets for pikemen	£2 4s. 0d. a set	£475 4s.
936 blue kersey waistcoats trimmed with broad and narrow lace	13s. 6d.	£631 16s.
936 shoes with buckles	4s. 10d.	£226. 4s.

	Per item	Total
936 hats laced with broad worsted lace	7s. 0d.	£327 12s.
1,326 shirts	4s. 6d.	£298 7s.
1,326 neckcloths	1s. 2d.	£77 7s.
1,326 pairs of white stockings	2s. 6d.	£165 15s.
720 boxes for powder and cartridges	16s. 0d.	£576
216 pikemen's belts of Russian leather covered in blue cloth	6s. 3d.	£67 10s.
936 pairs of gloves	1s. 3d.	£58 10s.
140 'surtute' coats of 'whole thick Kerry faced with blew bays with loops and large clasps'	£1 0s. 6d.	£143 10s.
170 swords	5s. 0d.	£42 10s.
156 each of grenadiers' coats with blue kersey breeches	£2 5s. 6d.	£354 18s.
156 large blue kersey waistcoats	15s. 6d.	£120 18s.
156 grenadiers' caps	12s. 0d.	£93 12s.
156 pouches and cartridge boxes with brass plates and cyphers and slings	16s. 0d.	£124 16s.
156 shoes with buckles	4s. 6d.	£37 14s.
156 pairs of gloves	1s. 3d.	£9 15s.
234 shirts	4s. 6d.	£52 13s.
234 neckcloths	1s. 2d.	£13 13s.
234 pairs of stockings	2s. 6d.	£29 5s.
30 'hangers'	8s. 0d.	£12
30 'byonets'	2s. 4d.	£3 10s.
6 sergeants' caps of crimson cloth embroidered with silver	16s. 0d.	£4 16s.
Total		£5,513 15s. 0d.

There are numerous other equally detailed and lucrative accounts. There is, for example, another (undated) bill for £5,307 10s. 8d. to General Cutts for roughly the same types and quantities of items as the regiment had in 1695, and another of similar date for £7,364 0s. 11½d. In 1700 he supplied clothing worth £2,997 9s. 0d. to General Cutts, and prices had risen. A set of coat, waistcoat and breeches for a private was now £3 13s., his shirt was 5s. 6d., rather than 4s. 6d., as were his shoes, and his gloves cost 1s. 8d., as opposed to the 1s. 3d. they had cost five years earlier. Sergeants' shirts were now a whopping 10s. 6d. A further bill of 1702 for £3,551 5s. costed Holland shirts at six shillings and muslin neckcloths at three shillings. Presumably they were for officers, though the bill does not say so.

There are also two bills of 1701 and 1702 to Colonel, later Brigadier, William Seymour of the Queen's Regiment for £1,533 0s. 4d. for clothing 679 men and £2,497 10s. 8d. for 694 men, and an account to the Honourable Colonel Frederick Hamilton in 1696 for £2,314 10s. 6d. for kitting out 747 men of various ranks. It seems that these surviving documents represent a mere fraction of his trade.

Joseph Ashley must have had an enormous number of seamstresses and slop-tailors in his employ. To take the 1695 order for the Coldstream Guards as an example, the seamstresses alone had to supply 1,560 shirts and 1,560 neck-cloths. If one woman could make one shirt and one neck-cloth in a day (journalist Henry Mayhew's nineteenth-century interviewees suggest that would have been just about possible)[12] and she worked a six-day week, the shirts and neck-cloths alone would have taken 260 woman-weeks of work. The Ashley contracts do not specify a timescale, but presumably the items would have been needed relatively quickly – for ease of reckoning let us assume within four weeks – which would require him to have had around sixty-five seamstresses working on that part of the order alone, and four or five times that number of tailors.

Ashley was turning over thousands of pounds a year, but we have no knowledge of how much his seamstresses were paid for making the Holland shirts that he sold for 10s. 6d. or the coarse ones that he sold for 4s. 6d., or of how much he paid his tailors. Nor do we know whether all the coats, waistcoats, breeches and caps were indeed made by slop-tailors or whether some of the lighter jobs like cap-making were already being farmed out to women. We do not know whether all the tailors and seamstresses worked directly to Mr Ashley or whether he employed middlemen; nor do we know what profit margin he made on the items supplied to him by the hat-makers, shoemakers, swordsmiths and the rest who enabled him to deliver these comprehensive orders. The documents pose as many questions as they answer. However, what is clear is that Joseph Ashley became a very wealthy man and was able to buy himself into the gentry.

In 1703 he purchased a stately home, Ashby St Ledgers Manor House in Northamptonshire. He must have been accepted and respected for in 1708 he was appointed Lord Lieutenant of the county.[13] He seems to have spent his later years in Northamptonshire and he purchased a substantial amount of property there. Joseph died in 1740 leaving a will that runs to thirty-one pages, mostly disposing of this property: 'My Messuages, Cottages, Closes, Tythes, Lands, Tenements and every of their Appurtenances in the Parishes of Long Buckby, Welton, Hellidon and Broughton in the County of Northamptonshire and Catthorpe in the County of Leicestershire', with further properties in the parish of Ashby St Ledgers bequeathed separately. Joseph wanted his estate to stay intact. His eldest son, Isaac, and his children, 'in order of seniority', were first in line to inherit this estate, followed by his sons, John, Moses and Solomon, and their progeny, followed by Joseph's three nephews. Eight hundred pounds was bequeathed to his granddaughter, and the sons who did not inherit property received fairly small allocations of goods and £6,000 apiece to be paid by Isaac.[14] Documents relating to several later lawsuits suggest that Isaac did not fulfil this obligation. There is no mention in the will of any property in London or of the business there; presumably he had disposed of it before 1740. Joseph Ashley intended to end his life as a country gentleman, not as a draper.

Other Suppliers

There were many men like Joseph Ashley supplying the army and navy, some taking orders for thousands of items, others, like the Nantwich tailors mentioned above, supplying hundreds or dozens. For example, in 1712, the stock of Joseph Ashton, a tailor in Gosport, Hampshire, was listed for probate. It contained twenty-five pairs of 'plush' breeches, eight 'pee jackets', thirty-one 'under wastcoats' and eighteen pairs of linen drawers, plus shirts, stockings and handkerchiefs. In this case there were also outstanding debts of £857 for slop-clothing, owed by 'Sailors belonging to her Ma'tys Shipps of Warr'. Ashton was a manufacturing tailor who had undertaken what he believed would be a lucrative naval contract, alongside running a shop supplying civilians,[15] and he must have employed significant numbers of seamstresses and slop-tailors to execute it.

However, some other slop-sellers' returns make Joseph Ashton's £857 look like small change and dwarf even Joseph Ashley's profits. During the War of the Spanish Succession (1701–14) there were tens of thousands of British troops in Spain, fighting alongside their Dutch, Prussian and Austrian allies, in an ultimately unsuccessful campaign to place Archduke Charles Habsburg of Austria on the Spanish throne rather than Philip, Duke of Anjou, grandson of Louis XIV of France. There were vast profits to be made. For example, Churchill and Harnage in London made £24,571 19s. 6d. from army contracts in 1705 and £17,061 18s. in 1706.[16] In 1707 Charles Robinson (address unknown) supplied the army with 10,000 shirts and neck-cloths at a cost of three shillings a shirt and one shilling a cravat (£2,000 in total), all made up into bales of between 500 and 1,500 items for ease of transport and delivered to the 'stores at Barcelona'.[17] Contractors had to be masters of logistics as well as entrepreneurs. Robinson charged less than Joseph Ashley. The army did not pay a standard price; each contract was negotiated separately by the commander.

There was good money to be made from the army, so long as the contractor could survive the often ruinously long wait for payment. How much of that money filtered through to the seamstresses and slop-tailors who actually made the goods is, however, open to question.

Naval Supplies

Like the army, the navy also required ever-increasing quantities of slop clothing. In fact, the word 'slop' was naval slang, and it was the navy, not the army, that created the so-called 'slop' system. In the seventeenth and eighteenth centuries 'slops' and 'slop clothing' were recognized terms, used in captains' correspondence with the Admiralty. The term did not acquire its negative connotations until the mid- to late nineteenth century when it was more widely used in a civilian context.

Britain's navy was in a sorry state in 1689, as Samuel Pepys tells us. It had 134 ships, of which almost half were in need of repair, and employed around 16,000 men at any one time, although, as men were employed for one voyage at a time, there was a considerable turnover of personnel. Under William III the 1690s saw a great upsurge in shipbuilding; between 1690 and 1700 some seventy-three ships were built or ordered, eleven were substantially rebuilt and a number of vessels were captured and incorporated into the service.[18] This all necessitated an increase in manpower; by 1695 the number of men had risen to 48,000 and voluntary recruitment could not produce the manpower required, so large numbers of men were 'impressed' – pressganged – into service. These men often arrived with just the clothes they stood up in, hence the need for large quantities of slop clothing. In February 1695, for example, Captain John Lytcott of the *Rupert Prize* at Portsmouth (the name tells us it was a captured ship) wrote that he would soon be taking impressed men on board and needed slops and beds for them.[19]

Slop-sellers received orders for large quantities of clothing but, like the army, the Admiralty was slow to settle its debts. To quote just one example, Thomas Beckford, a major supplier, was paid £3,000 in 1668 for 'clothes issued to Mariners'; however, by 1674 the Admiralty owed him an enormous £18,000 for more clothes issued but not paid for.[20]

A very rare set of early naval slop clothing survives in the Museum of London, probably dating from sometime in the early seventeenth century.[21] Ordinary seamen from the Elizabethan period onwards wore garments like these. The set consists of a tunic with a small collar and full three-quarter-length sleeves gathered into cuffs, and a pair of baggy, wide, mid-calf-length breeches, all made of brown, heavy-duty linen. The breeches have been much patched and mended – probably by the owner himself – and the tunic is stained with tar from hauling ropes. The tunic might have been worn over a shirt. (Figure 3.2) Sailors' breeches were loose to allow for freedom of movement and were not always gathered at the knee as these are: a pair of knee-length, wide, slop breeches of heavy-duty, blue-and-white, striped cotton is featured on textile consultant Meg Andrews' website, for example.[22] 'Strip'd breeches' like these are mentioned in a contract made by the Commissioners of the Admiralty with a Mr Richard Harnage in

Figure 3.2 Very rare set of sailor's slops made of strong linen, much patched and mended, probably by the owner himself, believed to be early seventeenth century.

1706, quite highly priced at 3s. 3d. apiece.[23] He was probably the partner in the firm of Churchill and Harnage, mentioned above as army suppliers.

Slop clothing was provided through the navy but it was not free, the cost was deducted from the men's wages and, if it was too expensive, they would have been unable to pay for it.[24] There was no official uniform for ratings until 1857 but, because most of their clothing came from the same sources, there was a degree of uniformity in how sailors were dressed. A typical stock of slops was listed in 1675 as an 'Accompt of Clothes now resting on board the *Speedwell*.[25] It comprised:

12 cotton waistcoats at 3s.0d.	£1 16s. 0d.
12 prs cotton drawers at 3s. 0d.	£1 16s. 0d.
36 'blew shirts' at 4s. 6d.	£8 2s. 0d.
24 prs woollen hose at 3s. 0d.	£3 12s. 0d.
12 prs coloured dimity drawers at 4s. 6d.	£2 14s. 0d.
12 'blew' jackets at 3s. 0d.	£1 16s. 0d.
12 prs blew drawers at 3s. 0d.	£1 16s. 0d.
24 prs plain shoes at 3s. 6d.	£4 4s. 0d.
10 kersey waistcoats at 9s. 0d.	£4 10s. 0d.
24 prs French falls at 4s. 6d.	£5 8s. 0d.
3 cloath coats at £1	£3 0s. 0d.
10 red capps at 1s. 1d.	10s. 10d.
6 serge waistcoats at 10s. 0d.	£3 0s. 0d.
6 white dimity waistcoats at 5s. 6d.	£1 15s. 0d.
12 neckcloaths at 1s. 4d.	16s. 0d.
Total	£42 19s. 10d.

As this account shows, by the later seventeenth century smocks like the one in the Museum of London were being replaced by a short coat and waistcoat over a shirt and long trousers, but these were still loose fitting to allow for easy movement; sailors led active lives, hauling ropes, climbing the rigging, shifting cargo. The navy ordered slops in quantity, very much on a one-or-two-sizes-fit-all basis, and the seamstress or tailor making the items up would have received the pieces cut out and ready to assemble. Nonetheless, these were quite complex garments.

There were official slop-sellers but captains were allowed to purchase essential slops elsewhere at their own discretion. The majority of slop-sellers were in London but, as Miles Lambert has shown,[26] firms set up in other places as well, particularly in ports like Liverpool. There are literally hundreds of documents in the Public Record Office relating to the supply of slops between *c.* 1670 and the early 1700s – clothing in stock, clothing received, clothing needed, the logistics of delivering it and complaints about late, over-priced or inadequate supplies. In September 1693, for example, Captain John Beverley aboard the *Falmouth*, off Spithead, complained that, though he had received a consignment of slops, he still needed watch-gowns, cloth coats, Monmouth caps and red caps – in other words, essential warm clothing.[27] The lack of watch-gowns (or watch-coats – the long, warm, heavy-duty garments worn by lookouts) was a recurring theme in captains' complaints; presumably they were expensive and complex to make.

The slop-sellers also supplied hammocks and bedding and, when these supplies failed, sailors could be left with nowhere to sleep. In February 1691, for example, Captain Charles Skelton of the *Coronation*, at Gillingham (near Chatham in Kent), repeated an urgent request for clothing and bedding, claiming half his men were 'in danger of death' from the cold.[28] A similar complaint came from Captain Richard Kirby aboard the *Southampton* off Hoylake (the Wirral peninsula) whose men were falling sick because of the lack of warm clothing and bedding; while in September 1698 on the *Dunkirk* Captain Charles Adamson, who had been allocated men from a series of different navy vessels, asked permission to clothe them from his ship's slop stores as if they were his own crew because they were so ill-clad they were too cold to work.[29]

On the other hand, there were endless complaints from slop-sellers about late payments, unfair monopolies, captains who sought to undercut them by buying slops in places like Ireland and Barbados where prices were lower, and unreasonable demands. For example, in October 1693, Thomas Beckford made a complaint about Mr Burton, purser on the *Monke*, who had returned a batch of slops to him which were so damaged as to be unsaleable. The *Monke* was requesting a further consignment but Beckford refused to supply them because he did not trust the purser.[30]

Keeping the thousands of men aboard British naval vessels in different parts of the world adequately clothed must have been a logistical nightmare.

Civilian Slops

In 1668 seven men – known, rather confusingly, as the 'Oxford Milliners' – were indicted at the petty sessions in Oxford accused by the tailors' guild of contravening the Elizabethan Statute of Artificers of 1563 by selling ready-to-wear clothing. The men defended themselves by claiming their trade 'hath not been in use above thirty yeares ... and they doe not make coates or the things they sell but buy them ready made of the Taylors whose Trade it is to make garments.' The following year nine more men were indicted by the tailors' guild for the same offence, and tailors' guilds in other cities, like Chester and Salisbury, had similar issues with the sellers of ready-to-wear.[31] The guilds also struggled with travelling salesmen who sold clothing at fairs, men like Samuel Dalling (d. 1699) who regularly visited fairs across the south of England from Bristol in the west to Maidstone in the east, as well as having a shop in London. In his last six months of trading, he made in excess of £600, roughly half of it from sales of ready-made clothing at fairs.[32]

In fact, the trade in ready-made garments has a long history and dated back for many more than the thirty years claimed by the Oxford milliners. The area around London's Birchin Lane was known for garment-sellers as early as the 1580s, and there were numerous complaints at that time about the traders' aggressive selling techniques.[33] Much of what they sold was second-hand, but some was almost certainly ready-made.

Retailing ready-to-wear clothing to civilian customers was fairly straightforward compared to fulfilling contracts with the army and navy. Many of these civilian clothiers, also often known as 'slop-sellers', seem to have traded in the central London parish of St Giles, Cripplegate. For example, James Fish died there in 1665 and his probate inventory listed the goods he sold as petticoats, waistcoats, coats, suits, doublets, hose, breeches, trousers and hats.[34] Edward Jarvas was his neighbour and close contemporary and his probate inventory of 1666 shows he too sold a range of garments including cloaks, gowns, doublets, waistcoats and linen.[35] Henry Francklin traded in the same area and the list of his stock in 1672 included remnants of various fabrics, parcels of blue and green aprons, hoods, scarves, mantles, shirts and shifts.[36] Henry Howard's extensive stock of clothing and shop goods were valued at over £200 in 1700.[37] Unlike the shop-keeping seamstresses whose inventories were discussed in the last chapter, these men were selling a wide range of ready-made garments, some of which must have been bought in from other suppliers, including seamstresses.

There were numerous sellers of ready-made goods in the provinces as well as in London. In Sussex in the 1660s and 1670s, for example, Walter Deane in Rudgewick and Michael Woodgate in Horsham were both selling ready-made clothing alongside drapery and haberdashery;[38] and at least one Oxford 'milliner' in the 1670s stocked ready-made linens in the form of morning gowns, shirts, drawers, trousers, frocks, petticoats and children's coats.[39] Ready-made clothing was not necessarily cheap. Henry Mitchell, the Lincoln haberdasher, had shirts in stock valued at 4s. 6d., eight shillings and one pound in 1679.[40] Robert Amsden had a shop in Canterbury and sold clothes for women and girls. His inventory, taken in 1703, listed gowns of damask, silk, worsted and serge costing from three shillings for 'smale girls gowns' to 5s. 6d. for gowns for older girls, and six shillings for 'riding gowns', seven shillings for serge and worsted gowns and eight shillings for damask mantuas, while petticoats ranged in price from two shillings to 5s. 6d. He also stocked men's and boys' smocks, coats, waistcoats and breeches. However, he did not carry large numbers of any of the items, in most cases fewer than a dozen items.[41]

At Sittingbourne in Kent John Wood sold waistcoats, coats, breeches, gowns, petticoats and mantuas. Most interestingly from our point of view, when his inventory was taken in 1704, he had in stock 'twelve boyes' dimity frocks, seven men's frocks, six canvas frocks and four pairs of canvas drawers', the work of one or more unknown seamstresses.[42] In Reading, Berkshire County Record Office holds the bankruptcy schedule of an unnamed draper, dated 1708. It would seem he worked for a relatively down-market clientele; all the people who owed him money were listed by name and the majority of them owed less than a pound, some as little as sixpence. Over half his stock was ready-made clothing: 152 coats, 109 frocks, 129 waistcoats, ninety-four pairs of breeches, eighty-seven gowns, fifty-one shirts and nine shifts, all of various qualities and sizes for both adults and children.[43]

Exports

By the early seventeenth century ready-to-wear garments were being shipped in bulk to the New World and the West Indies to clothe both slaves and settlers, which bears out Lemire's assertion that systems of mass manufacture and sale were already well-established. For example, in 1626–27, Richard Perry, a merchant, sent a consignment of woollen clothes to Virginia on board the *Anne*, but in 1628 he was still struggling to get payment for them. First, the ship's master to whom he had entrusted the goods died and his place was taken by Robert Lowe, who had never met Perry, then, on the return voyage the ship was taken by a French man-o'-war and all the account books were lost so there was no record of the consignment.[44] A notebook also survives of the cargo sent to Barbados on the *Abraham* in 1636 and it listed quantities of ready-made clothing for both men and women as well as hose, fabric, ribbons, silver lace, small household goods, shot and wine.[45]

In August 1643 a case came before the Mayor's Court in London. James Oyles, a London merchant, sought compensation for a consignment of goods bound for 'Middleborough'[46] aboard the *Anne of London*, in charge of the master, William Ellington. Like the *Anne*, the ship had been captured by a French man-o'-war and taken to Boulogne, and the goods, consisting of bed 'furniture', table linen and women's clothes, were lost.[47]

In Derbyshire, Edward Mundy's account book details his dealings with Barbados in the 1680s and 1690s. He imported sugar and spices and shipped out hampers of shoes and clothing, presumably for the workers and slaves on the plantations in which he had an interest. In 1682, as we have seen, he had William Wagstaffe, his tailor, make up dozens of 'French falls' at 3s. 4d. a dozen and source three dozen pairs of shoes, all for export, and in 1685 he laid out £70 in 'apparel' to send to Barbados. Nonetheless, his trade with the West Indies made up only a tiny fraction of his business interests.[48]

Within fifty years, the trade in ready-made garments for export was well-established. Miles Lambert cites advertisements in American newspapers of the 1740s for slops from Liverpool, Leith and other northern cities.[49] He also quotes an advertisement for slops to be sold at auction in 1767 from a ship originally bound for West Africa – quantities of double-breasted jackets, osnaburg frocks and trousers, check shirts, frocks and trousers, drawers and worsted caps[50] – and that was just one cargo.

Conclusion

What is important about the ready-made clothing trade is that all the garments were ready-made by *someone*, or rather, by numerous someones. Networks of suppliers may well have been in existence before the middle of the seventeenth century, as Beverly Lemire suggests, but it was the military and naval contracts of the mid-century that caused them to develop as they did. Supplying the army and navy made men like Joseph Ashley rich and enabled big London firms like Churchill and Harnage to turn over tens of thousands of pounds a year, but late and unreliable payments drove many smaller firms to bankruptcy. However, once systems of mass production were in existence, they were unstoppable and it was only a matter of time before they began to produce goods for the civilian market. While this may have been somewhat less lucrative than supplying the military, it posed far fewer problems in terms of delivery and deadlines.

Certainly, by the late seventeenth century if not before, the London Tailors' Guild divided its members into 'cutting' tailors who made bespoke garments and 'salesman' tailors who sold ready-to-wear goods made up off the premises.[51]

Some of these garments were kept in stock for sale or alteration for respectable customers and poorer-quality items went to slop-sellers who sold to working men. The ready-made trade employed numerous middlemen who subcontracted to workers, tailors making jackets and trousers, gowns and bodices, knitters making woollen caps and hosiery, and seamstresses making shirts and linen garments. As the trade expanded, tailors ignored their guilds and put work out to women, so seamstresses no longer just made goods of linen and cotton, they sewed slop coats and trousers, women's bodices and skirts, anything the market demanded.

There must have been a great many of these women but we know very little about them; they were at the bottom of the hierarchy of garment-makers and were no doubt paid accordingly, only records of their employers tell us they existed. For example, in 1661 in Frome Selwood in Somerset an inventory was made of the goods and chattels of Robert Smith the Younger and it included goods worth £80 listed in the 'acc^{nt} Book of Clothes under manufacture sent this day to London'.[52] Similarly, Herbert and Katherine Allen had a shop in the Exchange in London. Their inventory was taken in 1668 and the final entry, almost an afterthought, was 'Holland and Cambrick in the hands of workwomen to make up' valued at £51 12s. (out of a total estate worth £2,301).[53] Assuming – for ease of calculation – that the fabrics listed in both these accounts were valued at 2s. 6d. a yard, Robert Smith was having 640 yards of fabric made up and Herbert Allen had put out 412 yards to workwomen. Given that both shirts and shifts took approximately two yards of material, Herbert Allen would have had around 200 shirts or shifts to sell when the work was completed. We do not know what fabric Robert Smith had sent to London or what it was to be made into, but 640 yards would have made a lot of garments. Of course, we do not know how many workwomen these men employed or how quickly those women were expected to work, nor do we know how often they sent out such quantities of material to be made up. Did Robert Smith ship fabric to London for making up annually or monthly or more often? How many batches of fabric did Herbert Allen put out to his workwomen in a year? Were middlemen involved? What was everyone paid? Not until the next century do we begin to find answers.

4

'Linnen drapery at reasonable rates':
1720–1820

By 1720 Great Britain, which from 1707 included England, Wales and Scotland, was a wealthy nation with colonies in North America and the West Indies, trading posts in the East Indies and coastal China, control of large parts of the Indian sub-continent through the East India Company, and a series of forts along the West coast of Africa from which slaves were shipped across the Atlantic in huge numbers. Daniel Defoe dubbed Britain 'the greatest trading nation in the world', although it has to be said that much of that trade was carried on at rates that were disadvantageous to the countries with which she traded. There were occasional mishaps, the most notable being the 'South Sea Bubble' of 1720, the world's first major financial crash. Fortunes were lost, but confidence in trade soon revived.

By the end of the century Britain had become the world's first industrial nation. Developments in the production of iron simplified the creation of machines, and this was initially most noticeable in the production of textile-making machinery. Traditional home-based industries like weaving in Devon were supplanted by factory production in Manchester and the West Riding of Yorkshire. Networks of canals were built to transport raw materials and manufactured goods. The population grew from around 5.5 million in 1700 to nearly 10.5 million at the time of the census in 1811. Country people flocked to the towns in search of work and cities like Manchester and Birmingham became noted for their slums. Alongside the miserable conditions of the working poor, traders, factory owners and entrepreneurs grew rich and created a new social class with money to spend, in parallel with an increasingly aspirational section of the working class. There was a growing market for goods and services. As Lorna Weatherill has shown in *Consumer Behaviour and Material Culture in Britain, 1660-1760*,[1] between 1680 and 1720 more and more people, particularly in the towns, acquired more and more material possessions; and, although her study does not deal in detail with clothing, it seems reasonable to assume that the people buying clocks and curtains, looking-glasses and tableware, in greater quantities than ever before, were probably also buying an increasing number of clothes.

Certainly, far more records for purchases of clothing in the eighteenth century survive than do for the seventeenth. Unfortunately, there are more records for tailors and mantua-makers than there are for seamstresses, partly because seamstresses' charges were often so low that they were not always deemed worthy of recording separately, and partly because many seamstresses worked through drapers and did not submit bills of their own.

Fabric Prices

Fabric remained an expensive commodity and, though most prices were on the whole lower than they had been in the seventeenth century, the cost of material was always much higher than the cost of making it up. However, prices varied widely from place to place and from purchase to purchase and bills do not necessarily give enough details, like width and quality and whether there was a reduction for bulk purchase, to make accurate price comparisons possible. Supplies also seem sometimes to have been quite limited, possibly because weavers were struggling to keep up with increasing demand. Quite often, when a draper could not supply a sufficient quantity of the fabric the purchaser required, he would make up the amount with a batch of something similar at a slightly different price; for example, in 1741, Marsh and Meredith, linen drapers in London's Haymarket, sold Mrs Hill 7¾ yards of 'child's linen' (a fine, soft linen for babywear) at 3s. 6d. a yard and another fourteen yards at 2s. 6d. a yard.[2]

Small town drapers might carry a wide range of goods but only have quite small quantities of each. For example, John Friskney, a linen draper in Bolingbroke in Lincolnshire, died in 1720 owning goods and stock valued at £152 1s. 10d. He sold various fabrics but his inventory lists most of them as 'pieces'; the only ones he had in any quantity were 'bag Holland' (a type of linen), of which he had twenty yards valued at 3s. 6d. a yard, and thirty-five yards of 'cloth' – probably wool or a wool mix – valued at a shilling a yard.[3]

Most of the fabrics used by the bespoke seamstress in the eighteenth century were of linen or cotton, though occasionally she used flannel (a soft woollen fabric), calamanco (also wool) or 'hempen cloth' (like linen but much coarser). *The Plain Dealing Linen Draper* of 1696 listed fifteen sorts of linen (checked linen, two types of dimity, dowlas, several types of Irish linen, linen from

Lancashire in three widths, 'garlits', 'gulix', 'hammils', two widths of Holland, bleached and unbleached osnaburgs, and Silesian lawn) and nine types of calico (bafts, birompots, dimities, dungarees, gingham, izarees, long cloth, morees and percallis).[4] However, many of those terms do not seem to have been in common use and do not appear in Table 4.1.

As this list shows, the terms used for different types of textile can be extremely confusing for the modern reader. They confused contemporaries too. On 27 February 1664 Pepys records having a dispute with the East India Company as to whether 'callico be linen or no', as that would have affected how much import duty was due. The company claimed, rightly, that it was cotton. Different terms were used in different parts of the country and by different retailers, and not all seamstresses would have understood all the names and descriptions. Nonetheless, in order to understand the various bills and accounts that will appear later in the text, it is necessary to have a working knowledge of fabric terminology.

'Holland' and 'Irish' were both types of good quality linen and the names describe the origin of the fabric, or at least referred to linen of the quality originally produced in those countries. Cambric was also a linen textile and was originally made around Cambrai in France, but by the eighteenth century it simply meant a fine, expensive, quality linen textile. 'Osnaburg', misspelled in a variety of inventive ways, was a type of coarse linen, probably initially imported from Osnabrück in north-west Germany but subsequently made in Scotland. 'Garlits' or 'gulix', sometimes written 'garlicks', was a coarse linen from Silesian Pomerania (in central Europe, now part of Poland and Germany) and 'hammils' was similarly a coarse hempen or linen fabric. Dowlas, like osnaburg, was a coarse linen cloth used for coarse sheeting, workwear and linings.

'Hempen cloth' was made from hemp (*cannabis sativa*) fibre, one of the earliest fibres to be used by man; it was processed like linen but produced a much coarser thread. Hempen cloth was also called 'canvas' from the name 'cannabis'. Hessian, made from jute, was similar, and 'borelaps', now known as 'burlap', was also made from jute, even though *The Plain Dealing Linen Draper* listed it as linen. Linen, hemp and jute were all 'bast' fibres, made from part of the stem of the plant and retted (rotted down) in water. While today we think of hessian and canvas as being akin to sacking, in the seventeenth and eighteenth centuries workmen wore both fabrics as shirts, so presumably they were less abrasive than the textiles we know today.

Terms like 'huckaback', 'diaper' and 'damask' referred to types of weave rather than the fibre from which a fabric was made, and all three textiles could be made of either cotton or linen or any other material. Huckaback was a loose, open weave material that was absorbent and was therefore suitable for towels; diaper and damask were patterned weaves, usually used for table linen.

There were also numerous names for cotton. Calico came originally from Calicut (now Kozhikode, Kerala) in India and was a plain woven fabric made from unbleached cotton that had not been fully processed so that scraps of cotton husk got incorporated in the weave. Heavy duties were levied on imports of foreign goods, including textiles, and for a time after 1700 imports of Indian goods were banned altogether. Gingham, which often appeared on eighteenth-century bills simply as 'check', is still familiar to us today. Its origins are obscure; some believe it originated in Malaya as *genggang*, others that it came from the French town of Guingamp, but either way, the white-and-coloured fabric, originally striped rather than checked, seems to have arrived in Britain from Holland in the seventeenth century. It was the textile mills of Manchester that turned it into the check fabric we know today. 'Jean' is another fabric name that is still familiar, although we usually call it denim, a heavy-duty, warp-faced cotton fabric, originally from Nîmes in France.

Muslin, a fine, open-weave textile, is at the other end of the spectrum of cotton cloths. It gets its name from Mosul, in Iraq where it originated but, by the eighteenth century, gossamer-fine muslins were being woven in Bengal from delicate hand-spun yarns; these were sometimes called 'Jaconet muslin', a corruption of the Hindi word, *Jagganath*, meaning 'lord of the universe', and could be astronomically expensive. 'Dimity' was a lightweight cotton fabric with a woven pattern, often of sprigs or stripes, the name again refers to the weave; in fact, dimities were originally made in silk or wool. It was considered to be a very feminine fabric, suitable for girls and children. Lawn was used in similar ways; it was a lightweight, sheer cotton cloth, also sometimes called 'batiste' or 'nainsook'.

Flannel, still available today, is a soft fabric made from loosely-woven wool, and was much used for baby clothes and underwear. 'Calamanco' was a more closely woven wool which had been given a surface sheen by 'calendaring' (rolling between hot rollers), while 'camlet' or 'camblet' was a silk-and-wool textile. It was originally made of camel hair and silk, hence the name, but by the eighteenth century it was a warm fabric for cheap dresses and petticoats.

The following table gives a range of actual prices paid by various purchasers at different dates and in different places, culled from a variety of sources. Inevitably many of the purchasers were well-to-do, and a majority of the bills referenced relate to purchases in London, but the table also includes purchases made in provincial centres as far apart as Cumbria and Hampshire, and purchases made by overseers of the poor to clothe paupers. For example, in 1798 John

Table 4.1 Fabric prices per yard, 1700–1820

	Early 1700s	1740s–1750s	1760s–1780s	1790s–1820
Boreslap (burlap)	8d.			
Calamanco	2s. 8d.–2s. 10d.		2s. 8d.–5s.	
Calico	1s.–5s.; 7s. (good quality); 9s. (thick); 10d. (cut-price)	4s. 6d.–6s. (superfine)	1s. 4½d.–6s.; 2s. 10½d. (chintz calico); 5s. 6d.; 4d. (cut-price)	10d.–5s. 9d.; 2s. (ell wide); 2s. 3d. (printed)
Camblet	2s. 8d.	1s. 2½d.	14s.	10d.–10s.
Cambric	1s. 4d.–15s. 6d.; 10s (average)	3s. 9d.–7s. 9d. (thick)	8s.–14s.	7s. 6d.–12s. 6d. (fine)
Canvas	2d.–2s. (fine)		4d.	7d.–1s. 1d.
Diaper			1s. 3d.	15s.
Dimity	1s. 3d.–1s. 8d.	1s. 4d.–2s.	2s. 8d.–3s. 10d.	1s. 8d.
Dowlas		7d.–8d.	1s. 2d.	1s. 3d.–1s. 8d.
Flannel	1s. 6d.–3s.	6d.–1s. 10d.	1s. 2d.–3s.	6d.–1s. 10d.; 10d. (coarse); 6s. 6d. (Welsh)
Gingham/ 'check'	1s.		1s.–2s. 6d.; 1s. 8d. (furniture)	4d.–2s. 6d.
Hempen cloth	4d.–4½d.		1s.–1s. 4d.	1s.
Holland	2s.–10s. 9d.; 17s. 6d. (for the Mundy children's best shirts, in Lincolnshire)[6]	1s. 6d. (broad)	5s. 2½d.–5s. 9½d.; 7s. 6d. (sheeting)	9d.
Huckaback	6½d.		11d.	
Irish	9d.	3s.–4s. 6d.	1s.–6s. 6d.; 4s.–5s. (sheeting)	2s. 6d.–19s.
Wide Irish			2s. 8d.–3s. 4d.	3s.–3s. 6d.
Jean				1s. 4d.
Lawn	4s. 6d.–10s. 6d.	8s. 6d.	2s.–8s. 6d.	2s.–12s.
Linen	1s. 4d.–3s.; 1s. 6d. ('shifte linen')	2s. 6d.	1s. 2½d.–1s. 4d. (striped)	1s. 6d.

(Continued)

Table 4.1 (Continued)

	Early 1700s	1740s–1750s	1760s–1780s	1790s–1820
Coarse linen	6d.			5d.
'Child's' linen		2s. 6d.–3s. 6d.		
Home-made linen			4s. 6d.	
Patterned linen	2s.	2s. 8d.	11s. 6d.	
Muslin	2s.–10s.; 9s. (thick)	4s. 6d.–10s.	1s. 9d.–9s. 6d.; 12s. (ell broad); 13s. (book)	3s. 6d.–8s.; 63s. (fine openwork); 18s. (fine worked)
Jaconet muslin				6s.–35s.
Osnaburg	9d.–6d.			
Sheeting			10d.–1s. 5d.	1s. 5d.

Diggens, linen draper, supplied the trustees of Robert Ray's Charity in Odiham, which existed for 'the benefit of the poor of Odiham and Hartley Witney' in Hampshire, with forty-two ells of dowlas at a cost of £3 6s. 6d.[5] It would have been used for shirts and shifts and cost 1s. 7d. an ell or about 1s. 4d. a yard; it is the cheapest dowlas listed in the table above for the 1790s.

What Table 4.1 really serves to illustrate is just how widely prices varied and how meaningless it would be to try to come up with averages; what is important, however, is that it shows how expensive many fabrics were. It took courage and confidence to take scissors and needle to a length of fabric that cost considerably more than the wage that would be paid for making the finished article.

Apprentices

Throughout the eighteenth century, girls continued to be apprenticed to seamstry, though fewer now came from well-to-do backgrounds. The Bedford charity paid for upwards of eighty girls to become seamstresses between the 1760s and the 1790s,[7] while the Barnstaple charity apprenticed eleven girls to seamstresses in the 1730s and 1740s.[8] After that date they seem to have realised that seamstry had become a much less attractive career. Nonetheless, they set Elizabeth Leworthy to the trade in 1777; and four more of their girls were unfortunate enough to be sent to seamstress mistresses between 1801 and 1810, at a time when the bespoke trade was very much in decline.[7] Charities usually had a fixed sum they paid for apprentices, often more for boys than for girls. In Bedford, that sum for girls was £15: a down payment of £10 and a further £5 at the end of the apprenticeship. In Barnstaple, the charity paid £4 down and £4 when the term was completed. In seventeenth-century Hereford, mistresses were paid a paltry shilling a year to feed, clothe and train their apprentices, but by the 1730s that had become a down payment of £3 and a bond of £20 redeemable at the end of the apprenticeship.[9]

Throughout the eighteenth century the Manchester Cathedral charity seems to have paid eight pounds a time to apprentice girls to the needle trades.[10] On the Isle of Wight in 1738 Mary Mounsher was apprenticed by her parish to Alice Knoll for £7 7s. for seven years.[11] Almost fifty years later, in 1786 in Cambridge, Mary Scafe's parish paid just six pounds to apprentice her to Katherine Boys.[12] The overseers in the parish of Great Staughton in Huntingdonshire were more generous, and more cautious, than most. Between 1723 and 1738 they apprenticed seven girls to seamstresses, in each case making a down payment and a series of further payments in stages; the overseers wanted to make sure that mistresses had incentives in the form of future payments to continue to look after the girls in their care. The premiums varied widely, from the £21 paid for Elisabeth Adams in 1723[13] to the mere two guineas paid for Sarah Sabey in 1728.[14] It was not that the parish got meaner over time – in 1733 they paid William Grant twelve pounds for his wife to train Ann Gregory[15] – but different mistresses seem to have had different requirements and may well have offered different standards of training.

Most indentures do not give the ages of the girls being apprenticed and usually simply stipulate that the apprenticeship should run until the girl married or reached the age of twenty-one. Traditionally, apprenticeships were for seven years, entered into when the young person was about fourteen and covering the period until they reached their majority, but, quite often, girls were apprenticed later and served shorter terms. However, in some cases it seems parishes and parents were anxious simply to get children out of the way. In Cumbria in 1787, little Sarah Sisson from Penrith was just nine when she was sent to learn 'simistry' with Dorothy Nicholson nine miles away at Sharrow on Lake Ullswater. The apprenticeship was to run for twelve years, until Sarah was twenty-one. Her mother had recently remarried and it very much looks as if her new husband, William Graham, did not want responsibility for a stepdaughter and had persuaded the feoffees of Barton Grammar School to put up the £5 premium Ms Nicholson required.[16]

In 1754 Ann Taylor of Hitchin in Hertfordshire was sent to London to learn seamstry in Bloomsbury under the tutelage of Elinor Matthews. It seems that a London seamstress taking on a provincial girl could command a high price,

Elinor was to have an £8 down payment and £3 a year for four years, a total of £20 if Ann saw out her term.[17] Records show that the family of another young London apprentice, Margarett Plaine, had paid £35 to have her trained by Alicia Rutland in Westminster. Not content with this, Alicia had managed to steal some jewellery left to Margarett by her mother; the case came to court in 1732.[18] It would seem, from the premium they were able to raise, and the diamond jewellery that Margarett had had stolen, that the Plaines were quite well-to-do; further evidence that up to the mid-eighteenth century at least, being a seamstress was an occupation for respectable women. However, that was not the whole story; there were seamstresses working at the other end of the clothing spectrum, too.

The Various Categories of Seamstresses

Seamstresses were employed in a variety of ways. Firstly, and most profitably, was being self-employed and doing bespoke work for individual clients. Such women would build up a customer base and would often do work for the same families over a period of years. Often they would move from house to house, staying a week or two at a time to make and mend, sleeping in the servants' quarters and eating in the servants' hall, so their board and lodging formed part of their wages and reduced their own overheads.

These women were often literate, they made out their own bills and wrote letters to their customers. For instance, in August 1756 Susan Massey wrote to 'Peter Shakerley Esq at Somerford' (Cheshire) about some shirts: 'if those Last Shirts dos not fit Please to send an exact width'. In November she wrote again about some shirts she had made but had not been able to send because she did not know where he was: 'I never hear or knew at so^t plaice to Send them.' She had also done some mending for him: 'ye old fine Shirts I fear will not do much … though have dun as much as possible.' She does not mention numbers of shirts or prices, but a little sum in the margin of one of the letters suggests he owed her £3 8s. 9d., quite a considerable amount for a mid-eighteenth-century working woman to have to wait for.[19]

Other seamstresses were employed on the eighteenth-century equivalent of zero hours' contracts by linen drapers who offered garment-making services. Probably the earliest example of this comes in 1721 in a bill, dated 11 March, and written in a clear looping hand on a small scrap of paper. It was from John Dollin in Bedfordshire for six ells (or 7½ yards) of Holland at £1 7s. and the making of two shirts at a cost of 1s. 6d. each. The bill is signed by Ann Dollin, probably John's wife, daughter or sister and the person who may well have made the shirts, but unfortunately we do not know the name of the purchaser or even the location of the Dollins' business.[20] Shirts at this date were longer and more voluminous than they were later in the century, so it is quite likely that each of the shirts took three ells of the Holland.

While a seamstress employed by a draper could easily lose her source of income when trade was poor, not all employers were indifferent to the welfare of their staff. For example, a letter from Mr Burden, a Shropshire draper, dated October 1822 to Mr Hodsdon in Ludlow, presumably a parish official, pleaded the case of a 'Mrs Bullock who has for some years been in my employ as a seamstress but on account of a serious complaint in her hand is unable to work half her time and is frequently in great distress.' He continued: 'I understand her pay from the parish has been withheld the last 2 months which I cannot but lament', and urged that her benefit be reinstated as soon as possible. It seems he had also gone to the trouble of obtaining 'a little relief' for her from a local benevolent association but it was insufficient for her to live on.[21] Evidence of this nature is rare; perhaps Mrs Bullock had been an exceptionally good seamstress or Mr Burden was an unusually compassionate employer, or perhaps there were other employers who showed similar concern for their workpeople but left no record of it.

These two categories of seamstresses working in the bespoke trade are the ones most fully documented in existing bills and account books but, at the bottom of the pile, there were also seamstresses who worked for middlemen or wholesalers. They are shadowy figures in that, although we know they existed, we know very little about them. These were the women who made ready-made shirts, slops, waistcoats and gowns, and it is obvious from the low prices for which many of these retailed that their makers must have been paid very little indeed. While, as was suggested in the last chapter, some shopkeepers carrying small stocks of ready-made goods may have employed seamstresses direct, as shops grew larger and kept larger ranges of goods, wholesalers must have become increasingly important.

Local newspapers were in their infancy in the early 1700s, but advertisements for ready-made garments could be seen in, for example, the *Ipswich Journal*, the *Stamford Mercury* and the *Newcastle Courant* as early as the 1720s. Many drapers carried stocks of ready-made goods, some new, some second-hand. Pedlars or 'chapmen' carried goods like pins and needles, ribbons, haberdashery, fabric 'pieces' (offcuts large enough to make a shirt, shift or some babywear) and some small made items like sleeves and bands, stockings and handkerchiefs to villages and isolated farms, so even dwellers in rural locations had access to some ready-

DAWES

Elizabeth Dawes
MILLINER,
at the LAMB in the Long Walk near CHRIST's Hospital
LONDON.
Sells

Flowerd Silk & Gaufe Capuchins	Quilted & Dimity Bed-Gowns	Mechlin Lace
Velvet & Silk Cloaks	Women's & Childrens Waistcoats	Bath Lace
Cloath & Duffil Cloaks	Children's Stays	English Lace
Satten & Silk Quilted Coats	Children's Coats & Frocks	Black Lace
Callico & Ruffel Quilted Coats	Children's Flannel Coats	Stripd & Plain Muslin
Callimanco & Stuff Quilted Coats	Small Shoes & Stockings	Cambrick & Lawns
Whalebone & Cane Hoops	Children's Velvet & Silk Caps	Workt Handker. Aprons & Bord
Duffil & Flannel under Coats	White & Black Feathers	Readymade Linnen
Dimity Upper & Under Coats	Ladies Riding Caps	Fans Muffs & Tippets
ALSO	Mens Night Gowns & Jocky Caps	Ribbons Flowers & Muffatees
Child-bed Linnen	Damask & Diaper Night Caps	Silk & Thread Fringes
Quilted Satten Baskets	Quilted & Dimity Caps	Paris net Cyprus & Gaufe
Pincushions Rolers & Chin Line	Black Velvet & Silk Hoods	Black & Colour Velvets
Blankets & Mantles	Black Silk & Velvet Bonnets	Black Silk & Allamodes
Satten & Dimity Robes	Silk & Gaufe Handkerchiefs	Cardinals &c.

1757

1757 see back

Figure 4.1 Trade card of Elizabeth Dawes, milliner, 1757, listing the items she sold which included childbed linen, children's clothes, caps, bonnets, handkerchiefs and ready-made linen.

made goods. Many chapmen also had stalls or shops in town and carried a range of fabrics and larger items in addition to the portable wares they hawked door to door.[22] Finally, there were seamstresses who worked as servants. Some were employed specifically as needlewomen but, for most, needlework for the household was just one part of their duties.

Shirts

The best documented examples of seamstress work are men's shirts and Table 4.2 gives some idea of the range of prices for which these sold. Unless otherwise stated, the prices given include the cost of materials and sundries like buttons and tapes.

It is worth noting that making a shirt was no light undertaking. An article in the *Falkirk Herald* as late as 1846[23] estimated that there were 20,682 stitches in an average shirt.

As this shows, the price of shirts varied enormously according to the quality the buyer could afford and the skill or reputation of the maker. The survival of documents is patchy and they are often not as informative as we should like. While numerous bills survive for men's shirts, many do not distinguish between the cost of fabric and the cost of making. For example, in 1730 John Benson of Hawkshead in Cumbria recorded in his account book that he had spent the enormous sum of £18 on two dozen calico shirts 'not yet touched'.[30] The shirts therefore cost fifteen shillings each. Calico was a comparatively cheap material, though no doubt Mr Benson bought the best quality available. We know that he was a wealthy man; his account book shows that in the 1720s and 1730s his annual income from stocks, loans, rents etc. was between £10,000 and £12,000. However, without knowing what he spent on fabric, we cannot make any valid evaluation as to how much his seamstress earned for making his expensive shirts.

In the same district, but very much at the other end of the price spectrum, the overseers of the poor of Hawkshead St Michael paid 3s. 7d. for a pauper's shirt in 1785.[31] Again, we do not know how much they paid for fabric, though we can deduce that it was unlikely to be much over a shilling a yard, giving the seamstress a profit of no more than 1s. 6d., although, as we shall see below, that was very considerably more than some parishes paid their needlewomen.

Prices of other seamstress-made items varied just as widely as those for shirts. The next section will be sub-divided by type of seamstress, not by what they made, and will consist of case studies. This seemed the clearest way of managing a wealth of disparate information from a range of sources, even if it reads in a rather disjointed way.

Case Studies

A. Bespoke

(i) Lady Arabella Watson was the third daughter of Lewis Watson, first Earl of Rockingham and in 1714 she married Sir Robert Furnese, second Baronet of

Table 4.2 Shirt prices

Source	1700–20	1720–40	1740–60	1760–80	1780–1800
Joseph Ashley's army contracts	4s. 6d.–10s. 6d.				
Lady Grisell Baillie	3½d. (making only); 1s. 9d. (girl's shift)				
John Benson (Cumbria)		15s.			
Robert Blunt, shirtmaker (London)					30s.–34s.
C. Churchill, draper (London?)		4s. 6d.			
Churchill and Harnage, army contractors	3s.				
The Hon. Robert Clive					3s. (making only)
Crowland parish (Lincs.)					4d. (making only); 2s. (total)
Rev. Dr Davenport (Worcs.)				3s. 6d. (making only)	
His sons				1s. 4d. (making only)	
John Dollin, draper (Beds.)	13s. 6d. (fabric); 1s. 6d. (making)				
Dublin draper (unknown)					5s. plus
Third Earl of Egremont					3s. 2½d. (plain); 4s. 6d. (ruffled); 9d. apiece for buttons and marking

(Continued)

Second Earl of Guildford (or Frances North, his wife)			2s. 1d.; 3s. 3d. for making	He also spent large sums: £9 6s.; £2 3s. with 'P. Barrington'; and £2 7s. 7½d. with 'S.Greenall';	and £8 6s. with 'J.Goodchild' for unspecified numbers of shirts in the 1760s
Hawkshead parish (Cumbria)					3s. 7d.
George Hilton	3s.				
Swynfen Jervis			2s. 4d. (making only)		
Mary Lemoine to John Archard[24]				4s. 1d. (including fabric)	
Sam Lowe (Notts)[25]	2s. 2d. (making); 3s. 1d. (fabric)				
John Macgie (Downham Market, chapman)[26]		1s. 6d. (boy's ready-made)			
Catherine Morley (Dublin)				4s. 4d.–21s. 9d. (ready-made)	
Over parish (Cambs)		1s.–1s. 4d. (childs)	1s. 9d.–2s. 1½d. (making)	2s. 7d.	
Prater, supplying Shropshire militia[27]					6s. (and stocks at 9d.)
Reading draper (bankruptcy)				2s. 6d. (ready-made)	
Edward Sackley, draper, Rochester[28]	1s. 3½d. (ready-made 'coarse')				
Swepstone parish, Leics.				3s. 11d –4s. 1d.	
Thomas Webb, draper, Tonbridge[29]	1s. 8d. (ready-made)				

(Most of the makers/buyers of shirts are referenced below or elsewhere in the text. Those that are not, are referenced in endnotes.)

Waldershare in Kent. From then until her death in 1727 she kept an account book of her personal expenditure.[32] Lady Arabella was wealthy and well connected and she had a position to keep up; her husband was a senior Whig politician. Arabella spent lavishly on clothes, including paying seamstresses and buying material for them to make up.

For example, in 1721 she paid Mrs Beger £19 15s. for Holland for a dozen shifts and an ell of it for a 'combing cloth' and she also bought six pounds-worth of 'heads, ruffles and tuckers' (presumably ready-made) from her. Like many shopkeepers, Mrs Beger supplemented her takings by raffling off stock. She held a 'raffel' in 1720 which Lady Arabella attended though she does not seem to have won anything. Two years later, her ladyship spent £1 5s. on a piece of cambric for 'night clothes', possibly for her children. In 1724, Holland for ten night shifts for her own use set her back £10 9s., so the fabric alone cost nearly a guinea a shift; and three years later she bought another 29½ yards for another dozen night shifts at the rather cheaper price of £9 9s., so each of that batch of shifts took around 2½ yards of material at a cost of about 6s. 3d. In 1726 she spent seventeen shillings on a length of 'fine cambrick' and £1 16s. on 4¾ yards of calico, while fourteen yards of flannel for seven petticoats for her maids cost £1 3s. She spent three guineas on linen to make frocks for her god-daughters, £2 15s. on cambric for pocket handkerchiefs and £1 7s. on three yards of what she called 'thick calico'. It seems unlikely that a lady of Arabella's status would have made her own night shifts or clothes for her children. The accounts are not entirely clear but it looks as if Mrs Beger, or her employees, did some of the making up.

As well as the ruffles and tuckers Arabella also bought other ready-made items, presumably made up by seeamstresses employed by drapers or wholesalers: quilted caps for herself or her children at three shillings and 4s. 6d. each, a flannel petticoat for 3s. 6d., an expensive embroidered handkerchief for £1 4s., two 'work'd under petticoats' at nine shillings each, two quilted white calico petticoats at £2 each, an embroidered linen apron for £1 5s., another for £2 and a red 'working apron' for eight shillings.

She also acquired numerous other quilted petticoats. As well as the ones mentioned above, she bought a silk one for £3 10s. in July 1714, around the time of her marriage, and a black silk one the same year for £2 3s. Four years later she bought another at the same price and paid £1 9s. for having a bespoke one quilted and lined. She also paid a Mrs Greene £2 17s. for making, quilting and lining two under-petticoats. Waldershare House must have been a draughty place.

Clearly, Lady Arabella patronized seamstresses, both directly and through the shops she visited, but it is difficult to ascertain how much they would have earned.

(ii) Elizabeth Parker married Swynfen Jervis of Meaford in Staffordshire in 1727.[33] He was a solicitor, and in 1747 was appointed Solicitor to the Admiralty and Treasurer and Auditor of the Seamen's Hospital in Greenwich. The Greenwich post gave him the use of apartments in Greenwich College, and for a time the Jervises and their five children lived there, though they returned to Meaford at regular intervals and finally went back there to live in 1757. Elizabeth kept careful records of her expenditure on clothes for herself and her children, and of occasional purchases for her husband.

There are comparatively few payments to seamstresses, so it seems likely that Elizabeth and her servants made most of the family's underwear at home; she bought quantities of Holland, nankeen, 'double threaded calico', 'dimithy', linen, lawn and 'muslain'. In 1754 she 'Pd at Meaford making nightgown 3s. 6d.' and in 1767, by which time she was living back at Meaford full time, she paid William Vernon five shillings for making two more nightgowns. Presumably William was a shopkeeper who employed needlewomen to make up bespoke articles. In 1759, again at Meaford, she paid a shilling for having two shifts made and two shillings for four pairs of shift sleeves. Those were the only payments for women's underclothing in the whole of the period covered by the account books (1746–79) yet Elizabeth had three daughters so between them they must have had numerous day and night shifts, petticoats and (probably) drawers.

In 1756 she spent £1 4s. on 'Making 12 shirts for husband & son' and in 1762 she paid 3s. 3d. for making her son's 'frock' and mending a pair of breeches for her husband. She also bought nankeen worth 7s. 6d. for W. Jervis in 1755, 'Scotts Holland for Jack Jervis' at £1 10s. in 1747, 'Holland for Will Jervis shirt sleeves 6 ells' in 1748, and also for £1 10s, 'Irish cloth to line Mr Jervis breeches' for 1s. 4d. and 1½ yards of muslin for his ruffles for 13s. 6d. in 1749. 'W.' and 'Will' seem to have been her son, William, 'Jack' was her son, John, while her husband was described by the respectful honorific 'Mr'. He seems to have worn breeches with linings that could be removed for washing, rather than drawers, and no doubt he owned more shirts and ruffles than are listed but paid for them himself.

Seamstresses did not do particularly well out of the Jervis family.

(iii) In the 1730s and 1740s the family of the Reverend Dr William Davenport, Rector of Bredon and Salwarpe in Worcestershire, had a considerable amount of needlework done.[34] In 1736, for example, Mrs Davenport had a new tucker and ruffles for 3s. 6d., and numerous handkerchiefs, single ones for seven pence each and double ones for one shilling and 1s. 4d. She had three new shifts 'Shired and Triming' for 3s. 6d., and several others repaired: 'Mending 6 Shifts 5s. 0d', '5

Shifts sewing in ye sleeves and mending 5s. 0d.' It also looks as though she had her seamstress, who we know was Mary Cave, finish off various projects she had started: 'crowning 4 caps 2s. 0d.', 'finishing a neckcloth 3d.', 'finishing a sute of mobs 6d.' By 1742 she was patronizing another seamstress, Anne Hippwood, who submitted a bill, in her own hand so she was obviously literate, for four shifts (10s. 0d.) and a 'shirt for William' (the Davenport's son), with an additional two shillings for thread and buttons. Clearly costs were rising.

Mary Berrington also did work for the family. In 1776 she made Dr Davenport five shirts at 3s. 6d. each and later that year she charged him 14s. 10d. and 6s. 11d. for shirt making (numbers of items unspecified). She would have had to pay a few pence for thread and supply her own needles, but most of that money was hers to keep. In 1777 she was again making shirts, thirteen of them for £2 4s., several shifts for 8s. 3d. and boys' shirts at eight shillings for six.

The Davenports' accounts of their expenditure with seamstresses are unusually detailed and informative, and Mary Berrington was seen as a valued employee. She was sufficiently close to the family to be given a Christmas box of five shillings in December 1776.

(iv) In 1764–5 in Rutland the Earl of Gainsborough set about renewing the household linen at Exton Hall.[35] (Figure 4.2) He spent a total of £192 12s. 7d. on fabric; £97 10s. 10½d. of it with Mr Huntley of Huntley, Brown and Bacon, linen drapers in London, 'to cloth for sheets' and 18s. 11d. for thread to make them. It was nowhere near enough and he went on to buy twenty-five yards of hempen cloth from Susannah Henry in Rutland at sixteen pence a yard and a further forty-eight yards from Samuel Brown of 'Stokersden' (Stockerston, just over the county boundary in Leicestershire) at fifteen pence, some more at fourteen pence and another four guineas'-worth (so probably about sixty-seven yards) from George Toons in Oakham, Rutland. The hempen cloth was probably for servants' sheets. He bought an unspecified quantity of 'yard wide huckaback' at sixteen pence a yard, also from Samuel Brown. Huckaback was absorbent and was usually used for towels, and these would have been larger than average ones. Most eighteenth-century fabrics were narrow – plus or minus twenty inches – hence the stress on the huckaback being a 'yard wide'. He bought forty-one yards of linen cloth from John Brearley at 1s. 2½d. a yard, and an enormous 268¾ yards of 'flaxen cloth' from Mrs Clarke for £28 15s. 9d. It seems likely that these purchases were local, though we only have the names, not the addresses, of these latter two suppliers. Mrs Clarke's cloth made sixteen pairs of sheets 2½ breadths wide, five bolster cloths and six pairs of pillowcases.

Figure 4.2 Exton Hall, Rutland, seat of the Earls of Gainsborough, from *A Series of Picturesque Views of the Seats of the Noblemen and Gentlemen of Great Britain and Ireland* by F.O. Morris (1840).

All this material had to be made up, and the Earls, or more probably his housekeeper, employed six local seamstresses to do it; they were Martha Winterton, Anne Fancourt, Betty Gunn, Elizabeth Stephenson, Anne Rudham and Bridget Prangnell. They were paid next to nothing; in total, making up these yards and yards of fabric cost the Earl just £9 7s. 11½d. It would seem the women were all self-employed and they all submitted their bills separately and piecemeal; most were for less than a pound a time.[36] It would be tedious to list all the prices but they related to the quality of the fabrics being sewn rather than the amount of work involved; for example, making a pair of Holland sheets earned the seamstress two shillings, a pair of Irish linen ones 1s. 6d., but Anne Rudham was paid only four pence a pair for making hempen ones. As noted in Chapter 1, the fineness of the stitching was expected to relate to the fineness of the fabric, hence the disparity in payment, although Anne Rudham does seem to have been particularly unlucky. Sheets were made up of several breadths – some of the bills specify two and a half – so making one sheet involved one or often two long felled seams as well as four long hems, regardless of fabric.

Tablecloths cost sixpence apiece and table napkins, each with four edges to hem, were paid for at a rate of between one and two shillings a dozen. Betty Gunn was paid 1s. 5d. for making eight linen pillowcases and a penny a time for marking them, while Martha Winterton earned 9½d. apiece for making 'bolster drawers' plus a penny each for marking. 'Marking' usually meant embroidering a monogram and number rather than using ink. We do not know how long the seamstresses were employed by the Earl, though the bills kept coming in for over a year, but they must have done other work as well for they certainly could not have lived on the pittance he paid them.

The Earl also paid 19s. 8d. for having two scarlet quilted bedspreads made by James Springthorpe. James supplied the fabric and thread but, no doubt, the people he employed to make the bedspreads were women quilters.

It does look as if the Earl was particularly parsimonious in the sums he paid his seamstresses. By contrast, on 18 August 1734, the Goughs of Perry Hall in Birmingham paid Ann Coldery, seamstress, 15s. 9d. for making 'towels, sheets, etc.'[37] We do not know how many items she made, or how long she took, but only two of the Earl's seamstresses earned more for work spread out over many months.

(v) George Wyndham,[38] then the Honourable Lord Cockermouth, was at school over 1762 and 1763. Between August 1762 and December 1763 his mother, Alicia Wyndham, Countess of Egremont, paid a shilling to an unknown seamstress for mending three pairs of his drawers, sixpence for mending his coat and eightpence for mending a pair of breeches. This was on top of the £17 15s. 9d. the family paid for his thirty-seven weeks of board and lodgings, his allowance of £1 17s., and the 11s. 4d. paid to 'Mrs Morel' for mending his linen and cleaning his shoes. In 1763, on the death of his father, twelve-year-old George became the third Earl of Egremont and succeeded to the estates of Petworth House in Sussex and Orchard Wyndham in Somerset.

George's younger brother, the Honourable Percy Wyndham, aged six, was also away at school in 1763 and cost his mother £15 for a half-year's board and tuition. He got through five pairs of shoes at three shillings a pair and incurred costs of five shillings for having his linen mended. Meanwhile, that same year, Alicia gave birth to her last child, William Frederick, and spent a good deal on babywear: £3 18s. on six fine dimity robes, £1 8s. on four sets of 'robe blankets', two satin-bound robes and large quantities of fine flannel at three shillings a yard, white sarsnet at 3s. 3d. and dimity at 2s. 6d. These accounts are quite unusual in that comparatively few accounts for the purchase and mending of children's clothes survive.

Within a few years the third Earl was in charge of his own money – and he was a very big spender. Some of his money went on items for Petworth. In July 1779, for example, he paid Thomas Chippendale £764 19s. for upholstery work. He bought quantities of pottery and porcelain from Spode and Wedgwood, and was a liberal patron of artists, notably John Constable and J.M.W. Turner, who virtually lived at Petworth from 1820 onwards. However, George Wyndham also spent a great deal of money on himself. In 1791/2, for example, he paid an incredible £273 14s. to his perfumier, almost double the amount he spent on wine in the same year.

In 1779 he spent £76 16s. on hosiery and an enormous £95 14s. 3½d. with Stilbing and Co., linen drapers. It seems likely that some of this fabric was for household linen, but some of it also went to his seamstress, Mrs Mary Carnaby, who made him three dozen ruffled 'shertes' at 4s. 6d. apiece, plus 18s. for 'buttons and marking' and 12s. for washing. She was also paid £1s 10s. for marking three dozen silk stockings.

Over 1785 to 1786, aged thirty-four, the third Earl got through £3,493 19s. 11d. This included £104 16s. 5d. with his tailor, £29 8s. 6d. with his hosier, nineteen guineas on shoes, £39 9s. 6d. on perfume, £45 7s. 10d. with his apothecary and £11 9s. 6d. on a gross of tennis balls. He spent £40 9s. 3d. with William Wilks, linen draper on Piccadilly, and £37 10s. 9½d. with another London linen draper by the name of Smith. Some of it was for bed linen, fine Holland sheeting at 7s. 6d. a yard, fine Irish linen at five shillings a yard and ordinary Irish linen at four shillings. He paid William Wilks 3s. 6d. for making and marking a pair of sheets and 1s. 6d. for pillowcases, so presumably Wilks employed seamstresses. However, Mary Carnaby remained the Earl's shirtmaker of choice and he gave her some of Wilks' linen to be made into seven plain shirts for £1 1s. (three shillings each) and twenty-four fine ruffled ones for £5 8s. 6d., or roughly 4s. 6d. each. She was paid £7 10s. by him for shirts earlier in the year and made him another batch a year later.

However, the Earl also employed another seamstress, Hannah Kerr, wife of his 'bitt maker' (the man who made bits for his horses). He first seems to have used her as a washerwoman in 1786/7 when she charged him five shillings for washing seventeen shirts, nine shillings for twenty-three more, a shilling for washing a dozen cravats, a penny for a pair of socks, twopence for washing six pieces of flannel and 2s. 9d. for the much trickier job of laundering a pair of silk stockings. By the 1790s, however, she was doing needlework for him, in particular marking and 'looping' dozens of pairs of stockings at between 1s. 2d. and two shillings a pair. Embroidering the earl's cipher – probably a coronet above a 'W' – on the stretchy welts of expensive knitted silk stockings was a fiddly task, though stitching on the loops by which the stockings could be pulled up over the knee without the risk of laddering was probably easier.

Mrs Carnaby and Mrs Kerr were both based in London; back home at Petworth the Earl's sewing would have been done by his servants, his mother, sister or one of his numerous mistresses. George O'Brien Wyndham (he added O'Brien to his name in 1774 when he inherited estates in Ireland from an uncle) had a colourful family life. (Figure 4.3) He had at least fifteen mistresses who between them produced an estimated forty-three illegitimate children, many of whom lived with their mothers and father at Petworth. He eventually married one the mistresses, Elizabeth Ilive, in 1801, although the marriage did not last long. She had already borne him seven children; the eighth, a girl named

Figure 4.3 George O'Brien Wyndham, third Earl of Egremont, engraved by H. Cook after T. Phillips, *c.* 1800.

Elizabeth after her mother, was born in wedlock and would have been her father's heir, but she died in infancy in 1803, and the Petworth estate passed to a nephew, George Francis Wyndham.

(vi) Mrs Mary Owens worked for the Honourable Robert Clive (a younger son of Clive of India) in Shropshire in the 1790s, probably as housekeeper, but her responsibilities included his clothing.[39] In December 1790 she ordered fifteen cambric handkerchiefs 'made and worked' for five shillings, eleven muslin ones for 3s. 8d. and twelve shirts 'full trimmed' for £1 16s. She also purchased four dozen shirt buttons for three shillings, 'thread for making' for another three shillings, and paid one shilling for marking. In 1791 she ordered two dozen more shirts for Robert Clive, at a cost of £3 12s., and arranged to have new sleeves put in six of his old ones for a shilling a shirt. In 1792 she ordered twelve more shirts for £1 16s., so each of the four dozen new shirts cost three shillings. We cannot be certain that these were ordered direct from a seamstress, but the next entry in the account book in 1790 was 'Paid Mr Wilkes for cambric as per bill £2 7s. 3d.', which suggests she was buying fabric separately – along with buttons and thread – to supply a seamstress. Between 1790 and 1792 she bought many yards of 'fine wide Irish cloth' from Thomas J. Howe, linen draper, and his prices varied from 3s. 3d. to 3s. 6d. a yard over the two-year period. We do not know where he traded, but 'Mr Wilkes' may well be the William Wilks in London patronized by the Earl of Egremont.

We do not know who made up Robert Clive's shirts, but at three shillings a time the seamstress or seamstresses commissioned by Mrs Owens were making a respectable profit, given that even the fanciest of shirts would not have taken more than two days to make.

(vii) Arabella Calley lived at Burderop House in Chiseldon, Wiltshire (now part of Swindon).[40] She was a wealthy widow – her husband had died in 1768 – and she had an annuity of £500 a year. She lived comfortably but not extravagantly, visiting Bath and London most years, and spending more money on her four children than she did on herself. For a time, she employed a Mrs Norris to do small mending jobs for her, for example, she paid her 1s. 8d. in 1770 for 'mending aprons and laces' and 1s. 2d. in 1777 for mending an apron.

In 1781 Arabella made the acquaintance of Elizabeth Prynne, a seamstress, and over the next eight years she made regular small payments to her. The payments are not usually itemized, although sometimes they are simply captioned 'for work' or 'in full' when a debt had accrued. Mrs Calley also employed other people alongside Miss Prynne to do seamstress work. In 1787

Table 4.3 Payments to Elizabeth Prynne

1782	1783	1784	1785
Working and turning a cloak 4s. 8d.; Work 2s. 2d.	Work 3s.	Making cap 4s.; In full 5s. 4d.; Work 4s. 4d.	£1 8s. 1d.; Work 5s. 6d.; Making cap 8s. 6d.

1786	1787	1788	1789
Work 11s. 1d.	Work 6s. 9½d.; Work 7s.	In full £1 12s.; Work 4s.8d	Work 3s. 6d.; Work 2s. 2d.; Work 1s. 7½d.

Sarah Thomas was paid 14s. 6d. for 'making shifts' – we do not know how many – and in 1788 Mrs Parslie earned 5s. 8d. for making caps, but Arabella's favourite cap-maker, who made the dressiest ones, was Miss Mayo, a society milliner in Bath.

Like many seamstresses, Elizabeth Prynne seems to have visited Burderop at regular intervals to make and mend, staying overnight while she worked and then moving on to one of her other customers. We have no way of knowing whether she had a home of her own or whether she was continually on the move, but she could not have lived on what she earned at Burderop.

(viii) Mary Hardy was the wife of a farmer, maltster and brewer and they lived at Coltishall, near the little market town of Holt in Norfolk.[41] They employed nine men in the business and had one, sometimes two, maidservants. They were respectable, middle-class people but not members of the gentry. Between 1773 and her death in 1809, Mary kept a diary. The family patronized the local tailor and mantua-makers in Holt and also gave work to Lydia Youngman, a seamstress. Lydia did a range of jobs for them. In December 1788, for example, we find her at Coltishall helping to quilt a 'coat' (petticoat) for the Hardy's daughter, Mary Anne, and in September 1791 she was there again 'helping' to make shirts for William Hardy. In other words, she and Mary Hardy were working together on needlework projects, though Lydia was being paid (but we do not know how much) for her contribution. Lydia was the wife of a local millwright and Mary obviously saw her as a friend, if not necessarily a social equal; on 27 September 1790, for example, she recorded that she walked to Holt, had two gowns fitted at the dressmaker's and then drank tea with Lydia.

Mary later employed another seamstress, Ann Fryer. Some of the jobs that Ann undertook do not necessarily fit within our picture of a seamstress; it seems a jobbing needlewoman had to turn her hand to almost anything. For example, on 27 April 1803 Mary's diary entry reads: 'Ann Fryer at work ½ a Day upon the Carpet and ½ a Day for me.' Like Lydia, Ann was treated as a friend, and was invited to meals with the Hardys.

Ann and Lydia both had husbands and did not have to live on the proceeds of their work. Their earnings would have enabled their families to live a little more comfortably, and there can be no doubt that they were grateful for the commissions that came their way, but they were not dependent on them.

B. Poor People's Clothing Made to Order

Most surviving accounts relate to wealthy families, or at least to respectable middle-class ones. To learn what the poorest and least prestigious seamstresses were paid, we have to turn to records other than bills and personal account books.

Those kept by the overseers of the poor are particularly informative. As we have seen, the Elizabethan Poor Law of 1601 decreed that parishes were responsible for those parishioners – the old, the sick, widows with small children, the disabled or mentally ill – who were unable to support themselves. Each parish had to appoint overseers of the poor whose duty it was to levy a tax on the wealthier members of the community which would then be used to support the needy. The numbers of overseers varied according to the size of the parish.

This tax, known as the 'Poor Rate', was deeply unpopular and the system, although it appeared good in principle, did not always work well in practice. Some parishes, for example, particularly in industrial towns, had a preponderance of poor people and few who were wealthy enough to contribute to the Poor Rate. Where there were difficulties in raising an adequate Poor Rate, parishes provided cash, or concentrated on providing food and fuel and rather than clothes, so only a few surviving overseers' accounts tell us about payments to seamstresses.

The overseers were, however, expected to look after the paupers in their care and those that could afford to supplied garments or, sometimes in the case of female paupers, fabric for the recipients to make up themselves. The garments supplied were made from cheap, but usually durable, materials and were made up by a local seamstress who was paid the minimum rate for her work. The accounts are therefore a useful source for the lower end of the scale of needlewomen's wages. The ones given below are a random sample from different parts of the country:

(i)   At Over in Cambridgeshire the Overseers' Accounts date back to the 1730s and 1740s.[42] In 1734, for example, they paid 2s. 4d. for two shirts for 'Boules' child', five shillings for two shifts for Widow Rocket, 2s. 8d. for two shirts for 'Couper's boy', two shillings for two for 'Hopkins' child' and a shilling for a child's blanket . 'Child' seems to have denoted someone fairly young, while 'boy' suggests a lad of working age, so at least over the age of seven.

Unusually, they often differentiate between making, and supplying the fabric and making, which is useful when it comes to assessing seamstresses' earnings. In 1736, for example, they paid 1s. 6d and two shillings for making gowns, and in 1737 making Ellen Johnson's shift cost eightpence while making a petticoat and a shift cost one shilling. Quilting two petticoats for Martha and Mary Hunt in 1741 cost 5s. 6d. (*The London Tradesman* suggests quilters were comparatively well paid) and making an apron cost 1s. 4d., while 'E. Hilton', who must have been a seamstress, earned £1 18s. 8d. for 'mending and making clothes for poor children'. Other garment prices are recorded as supplying and making; five shillings for two shifts and 4s. 3d. for two shirts was paid to Mary Hall, presumably another local seamstress, in 1741, for example.

(ii)   The 'Clothing Book 1786–93' for Ashford workhouse in Kent[43] listed the prices paid for bulk purchases of fabric and goods; 'check' at seven- to twentypence a yard, shirting at fifteenpence, striped linen at sixteenpence, sheeting at ten- to fourteenpence, long lawn at around two shillings, gown linsey at 1s. 6d. and 1s. 4¾d. and 'kersey linsey' at 2s. 3d., dowlas at fourteenpence, flannel at tenpence and worsted at twentypence, ready-made tan aprons at seventeenpence and cotton handkerchiefs at a penny each. Tailors were paid 3s. 6d. to five shillings for making up a suit, one shilling for breeches and 1s. 6d. for waistcoats. Mary Viner was employed at the workhouse for nine days in 1792 to make gowns for the girls and was paid 6s. 9d. (or ninepence a day) and presumably also had her meals. Kitting out Hannah Horton to go into service in 1789 cost £2 2s.; while providing Mary Slaughter's two boys with 'round frocks' cost 7s. 6d. (3s. 6d. and 4s. 0d.) of which the seamstress would have got at least two shillings. Ashford seems to have treated its employees fairly generously.

(iii)   At Boughton Monchelsea in Kent,[44] between 1805 and 1820, the overseers provided round frocks, shirts, breeches, waistcoats, gowns, petticoats, stockings, hats and shoes and ensured that the paupers in their parish had what they described as a 'change', in other words, at least one spare set of respectable clothing. This clothing was doled out as needed, some people got a full set, others just got a jacket or a pair of shoes or two shillings or 2s. 6d. towards the purchase of a hat or shoes. Women often got fabric to make their own clothes. In addition, the overseers kept a list of the thirty-two families who received 'Parochial Relief weekly'; of these nearly all had large numbers of children and were in receipt of quantities of clothing as the children grew or needed new outfits when they were apprenticed or went into service. The parish must have employed needlewomen, and the quantities of goods they needed probably kept the women quite fully employed, but we can only guess at what they earned.

(iv)   In 1794 the overseers of the poor in the parish of Crowland[45] in Lincolnshire employed Mrs Esbil (Isabel) Ashley as a seamstress. That year she made six shirts for '3 prentis boys' for two shillings and six shifts for '3 prentis girls' for 1s. 6d.; parishes sending out children as apprentices were responsible for seeing they arrived respectably clothed. She also made six caps for one shilling, six flannel 'undercoats' (presumably under-petticoats) for one shilling, six 'scearts' (probably skirts/petticoats) for two shillings, six 'heaporns' (meaning unknown) for one shilling and six handkerchiefs for sixpence. These may also have been for the apprentices but could equally well have been for other local paupers. Finally, she made up eight 'pare sheets' for two shillings, presumably also for poor families in the parish. The parish supplied the fabric she used.

Esbil Ashley earned just fourpence for a shirt, three pence for a shift, two pence for a cap, a penny for a handkerchief and three pence for a sheet but, living in the wilds of Lincolnshire, she had little bargaining power and had to take what she was offered. She could not have lived on what the parish paid her; it may be that she took in other work from private clients, or had a husband bringing in a regular wage.

(v)   In May 1795 the overseers of the poor in the parish of Rockbourne[46] in Hampshire paid Rachel Muschet, the seamstress, £1 15s. to provide Mrs Joanna Fiford with a complete set of new clothes, consisting of two shifts (1s. 6d.), three aprons (4s. 9d.), three handkerchiefs (3s. 8d.), two pairs of stockings (2s. 6d.), five caps (4s.), a gown (7s.), a pair of stays (3s. 6d.), two pairs of shoes (5s.), a hat (2s. 6d.) and a bed gown (5s. 3d.). Looking at the figures, it seems likely that Rachel provided the fabric as well as making up the garments and sourcing the shoes, stays, stockings and hat from specialist makers. The overseers also gave Mrs Fiford 1s. 6d. in cash. Exactly why she was so much in need of clothing is not clear, particularly as the overseers were able to recoup £1 15s. of their £2 1s. 2d. outlay from her brother. Had he been unaware of his sister's plight up to that point? Moreover, just what had happened to her to render her so destitute? We shall never know.

(vi)   Some parishes were more generous than others and this seems to have been the case at Swepstone, a small village four miles south-east of Ashby-de-la-Zouche in Leicestershire.[47] It had a population of 412 in 1811, a significant number of whom were in receipt of poor relief. In many places that meant a weekly payment of 1s. 6d. to 2s. 6d., but in Swepstone in the late eighteenth century many families were receiving in excess of three shillings, and some as much as six shillings, according to the overseers' accounts. In addition, many families received loads of coal in the winter, usually valued at between six and eight shillings; there had been coal mining near Ashby since Roman times and by the 1780s deep mines were being sunk, so coal was readily available and probably fairly cheap. The overseers also hired a thatcher to repair leaking cottage roofs, provided coffins for the dead at around twelve to fourteen shillings apiece, issued sheets and bed 'tick' to the living and paid around a pound a time for a woman's 'lying-in'.

They were equally liberal when it came to clothing. They occasionally provided one-off garments, like a shirt for Ross Merricks for 4s. 1d. in 1780 and another for 3s. 11d. three years later, a pair of breeches for 6s. 6d. in 1792, a shift for Ann Bailey at 1s. 2d. in 1795, two shirts for Daniel Taylor for 5s. 10½d. in 1802 and a shift and flannel petticoat at 5s. 1d. for Mary Vesty in 1814. For the most part, however, they seem to have concentrated on outfitting pauper children, probably when they were apprenticed or went into service. The clothes they provided were not itemized but, from the prices they paid, it looks like they were providing complete sets of clothing. They spent sixteen shillings on 'Jn Cooper's child' in 1782, plus another 13s. 8d. on two pairs of breeches and two shirts for him later that year, for example. Clothing 'Dand's boy' cost £1 14s. 6d. in 1790, though 'Heape's girl' only merited expenditure of 1s. 8d. at the same time. In 1791 'Bolton's girl' got stockings and handkerchiefs costing 3s. 3d. but, a year later, Henry Kirby, the tailor and fabric supplier, was paid £1 19s. 9d. for clothing two boys, a guinea for equipping 'Smith's boys' in 1795 and £2 10s. 2d. for providing clothing for two more lads in 1799. They spent 12s. 6d. on 'Smith's girl' in 1806, a pound on 'Pegg's daughter' in 1813 and ten shillings on clothes for young Miss Jones in 1814.

Josh Bailey had been the overseers' supplier of choice in 1790 but by 1792 they were patronizing Henry Kirby. Either these men or the overseers themselves must have paid seamstresses to make up the shirts, shifts, handkerchiefs and petticoats. Unfortunately, we do not know their names or how much they were paid, but they were almost certainly better remunerated than our next needlewoman.

(vii) An account book for the years 1799–1813 survives for a seamstress who made and mended clothes for the Foundling Hospital in London.[48] Admittedly these were children's clothes, but her usual charges were three pence for a coat and two pence for a pair of breeches, sometimes with a reduction of a penny or two if she had a large order. She also did mending at a penny a garment. She had plenty of work – growing children are hard on their clothes – but can barely have made a living.

C. Seamstresses Working for Drapers

(i) In May 1740 Mr C. Churchill charged Mrs Hill, wife of Thomas Hill of Tern in Shropshire, for work his firm had done for her husband.[49] We do not know where Churchill worked, but the Hills did much of their clothes shopping in London. Churchill's bill included making and trimming twelve shirts at 4s. 6d. each, making, washing and trimming night caps (number unspecified) and washing a shirt, all for 8s. 6d., making and washing twelve stocks for ten shillings and providing four large silk handkerchiefs for one pound. Like many drapers, it would seem Mr Churchill employed both seamstresses and washerwomen, though whether he paid them as much for their work as he charged his customers is open to question.

(ii) In the 1760s and 1770s Mrs Ives in Oxford had a range of small items made by M. and E. Nicholas and Co., linen drapers;[50] she paid sixpence, nine pence and ten pence for everyday caps, eight shillings for two more decorative ones and one shilling for a ruffle. The firm also did washing and 'dressing'; for example, in 1774, she paid 3s. 3d. for having a cap 'washed and dressed'. Unusually, we know the names of at least two of the seamstresses the firm employed; they were Mrs Wright and S. Stevens. They submitted their bills in person and seem to have been paid direct rather than through the firm.

Mary Ives was an alderman's widow but she was not a wealthy woman. We know from her account book that she lived in a rented property for which she paid just nine pounds a year. She seems to have lived alone and bought her food in small quantities – four pence-worth of oysters, a ¼lb of bohea tea for 1s. 6d., a single beefsteak for sixpence. She spent comparatively little on clothes. Her main expenditure seems to have been on alcohol which she bought in considerable quantities, including rum at 10s. 6d. a gallon, a cask of wine for £1 16s. 9d. and two more gallons of wine for six shillings!

(iii) Robert Blunt at the Golden Ball in Charing Cross (London) had a linen warehouse and advertised shirt- and shift-making services in the 1780s and 1790s. A trade card of 1785 in the Lennox-Boyd collection described the work his firm produced: 'SHIRTS and SHIFTS Made in the neatest manner of fine Holland or Irish Cloth Plain or Ruffled. Ladies' fine Dimity flounced Coats, the Needlework elegantly performed. Household and all other Linen for Family or Gentlemen going Abroad ready-made and contracted for on the lowest Terms for ready Money only.'

Between 1789 and 1791 the firm supplied Sir John Nelthorpe of Brigg in Lincolnshire with numerous fine ruffled shirts at the extremely high price of thirty shillings each. By 1794 the price had risen. That year Sir John paid £10 4s. for '6 Veryfine [*sic*] Ruffled Shirts' at thirty-four shillings each.[51] Presumably Blunts kept a staff of highly-trained needlewomen whose skill justified the prices they charged.

Robert Blunt's business made him a wealthy man, entitled to vote in Westminster elections by reason of the property he owned, and when he died in 1788 he left substantial annuities to his two eldest sons, £1,000 to his unmarried daughter to match the marriage portion he had given her married sister, and £500 apiece to his four younger children.[52] His wife, Sarah, was left in charge of the business until Robert, the eldest son, was twenty-one, so she was actually running the business when Sir John bought his shirts.

(iv) There were firms that specialized in particular types of needlework. For example, Miss Wyndham of Petworth Hall, sister of the third Earl, patronized the Moravian Establishment at 2 Lower Grosvenor Street in London.[53] It supplied baby robes, caps, women's day and evening dresses and accessories 'beautifully made if required'; it also sold patterns, lace and fans, and cleaned and repaired Moravian work 'in a superior way'. Miss Wyndham spent £24 12s. 6d. there in 1823. The bill is not fully itemized but included a habit-shirt costing two guineas and two caps at three guineas each.

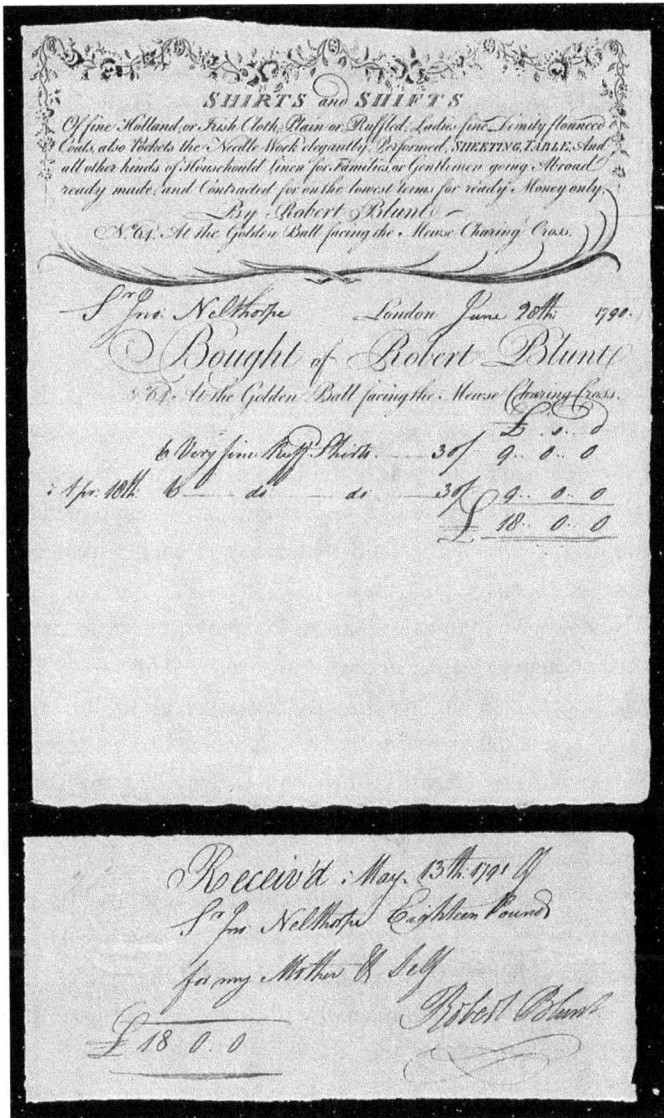

Figure 4.4 Bill for shirts bought by Sir John Nelthorpe from Robert Blunt in June 1790.

She also patronized Challinor's Fancy Muslin and Lawn Warehouse, also in London, where she bought three dressing gowns at thirty-five shillings each and a dozen French cambric handkerchiefs at six shillings apiece. Both firms must have employed skilled seamstresses and charged highly for their work. There were many other similar establishments.

D. Slop-Workers

These will be discussed in more detail in the next chapter. However, it is clear that by the mid-eighteenth century if not before, there was a growing civilian market for ready-made goods, which presupposes that by then most towns had large cohorts of seamstresses making slops.

E. Seamstresses as Servants

A few seamstresses had full-time employment as servants. The royal family continued to have seamstresses on their staff, listed as 'menial bedchamber servants' along with the laundresses and clear-starchers. Under Queen Anne the royal seamstress earned £150 a year, but in 1714 the post was combined with that of the royal clear-starcher. In 1727 Margaret Purcell was appointed to the joint role of laundress, clear-starcher and seamstress at £400 a year for life and remained in her lucrative post until 1755. Thereafter the value of the role declined.[54] No doubt Mrs Purcell had a staff to do the actual work, but they were not important enough to feature in the list of royal servants.

Other big houses also employed seamstresses; we know, for example, that there was at least one designated seamstress at a time on the staff at Petworth House in Sussex in the nineteenth century, and it seems likely that the post dated back at least a hundred years, though at that stage the holder was listed simply as one of the maidservants.

Mistresses advertising for servants in the eighteenth century also stressed the need for them to be able to sew. For example, a lady who advertised for an 'Upper Maid Servant' in the *Bury and Norwich Post* on 11 February 1789 required the candidate to be 'a good needlewoman who understands getting up small linen', (as well as being good at pickling and preserving!). Servants recognized this. The 'Woman of Good Character and Family' who advertised for a place as a chambermaid through the *Salisbury and Winchester Journal* on 8 June 1767 was 'a Good Plain Needlewoman' and could 'iron and get up linen well'. There were numerous such advertisements from both mistresses and would-be servants.

Elizabeth Shackleton (1726–81), the Lancashire gentlewoman, makes a good case study in this context. We know a good deal about her because she kept copious diaries, letters, financial accounts and other paperwork.[55] Like Mary Hardy in Norfolk, she worked alongside the women she employed to do sewing but, in Elizabeth's case, they usually seem to have been servants in full-time employment with her. One of them was Lucy Smith, who made a whole range of 'sutes' (matching sets of fichus and sleeve frills, sometimes with matching caps and aprons) of worked muslin, single aprons and caps, and shirts for Elizabeth's three sons. She was certainly with the Shackletons from the late 1760s, but most of the references to her doing needlework come after 1770. By 1777 we know she was being paid six pounds a year, but she also sometimes received extra payments for sewing: for example, in March 1773 she was given 1s. 6d. for 'getting up' six aprons and in February 1775 she was paid 2s. 6d. for making a fancy apron of muslin, silk and lace. Elizabeth also gave her presents of clothing and fabric; these included black figured satin and lace for a cloak, muslin for an apron, a handkerchief and a pair of double ruffles in April 1767, a pair of red leather gloves in October 1773, two 'best' aprons and a book muslin handkerchief in March 1779.

An unfortunately named teenager, Nanny Nutter, also worked for the Shackletons for a number of years. Elizabeth took an unusual interest in her and put up with a great deal from Nanny who seems to have been less than grateful for all the unwonted (and apparently unwanted) attention and eventually ran away. However, while she was in post, Nanny sewed, footing stockings, making shirts, making garments for Elizabeth to bestow on the local poor and stitching the endless caps and fancy aprons with which the middle-aged Mrs Shackleton revamped her outfits. Ladies wore caps indoors and out, night and day, but Elizabeth Shackleton seems to have been obsessed with them. When she moved house in 1769 she made a list of her clothing and, at that point, she had no fewer than fifty caps of various types. However, clearly that wasn't enough as year after year she had new ones made.

Elizabeth's three sons seem to have got through large numbers of shirts. In April 1770 she recorded providing Thomas and Robert with eight shirts apiece and John with nine, and shirtmaking occupied a considerable amount of her and her servants' time. Nonetheless, other people were also brought in to help. In March 1775, 'Molly Hartley came to make shirts' and, in August 1777, Molly Bennet was given numerous shirts to 'remake'; it is not clear whether this actually means to repair, or whether she had made them badly in the first place and was having to redo them. Molly – or Mary – Hartley reappears as 'the quilter from Colne', repairing a green quilted petticoat in August 1777, and being paid three shillings for quilting a calamanco petticoat in April 1779. Elizabeth also employed other women, notably Peggy Parkinson and Margaret Fielden, to make her dresses and petticoats.

Elizabeth Shackleton liked clothes and had sufficient money to indulge herself, keeping her wardrobe in good repair required the services of an army of needlewomen, paid and unpaid, employed and hired. She was probably fairly typical of women of her class and generation, but she is highly unusual in the amount of information she left behind.

Conclusion

Eighteenth-century Britain was a superpower, the head of a vast trading empire and the world's first industrialized nation. More and more people had money to spend and the demand for goods and services expanded rapidly. Body linen and household linen remained markers of social status and demand for seamstress-made goods, both bespoke and ready-made, increased, though the status of the seamstresses who made them began to decline.

An ever-widening range of fabrics was available, many of them imported, including fine Indian muslins and cottons, and raw cotton from America to be spun and woven in the Manchester cotton mills. Seamstresses making traditional goods were now as likely to be working in cotton as in linen, and the fabrics they used came in narrow widths and had a bewildering variety of exotic names. Fabric was slightly cheaper than it had been in the previous century but, nonetheless, needlewomen were paid considerably less than the cost of the materials on which they worked, although the quality of a seamstress's stitching was expected to relate to the quality of the material which she sewed. For example, in the mid-1760s some of the fine Holland the Earl of Gainsborough bought for his best sheets cost 2s. 1d. a yard and each sheet would have taken at least five yards; the seamstress who made them up was paid two shillings a *pair*, less than a tenth of the value of the fabric entrusted to her.

Working in the bespoke trade as a seamstress, either on one's own account or through an upmarket draper, could provide a modest living and records of work undertaken for well-to-do families survive in considerable numbers – although it is clear that the prices customers paid still varied widely, as did their relationships with the women they employed. For example, Mary Hardy in Norfolk saw her seamstresses as friends, if not as equals, the Davenports in Worcestershire saw their seamstress as a valued servant to whom they gave a present at Christmas, the Earl of Gainsborough – or his housekeeper – exploited his seamstresses shamelessly and paid them as little as he could get away with. Seamstresses working for Poor Law officials (at the bottom end of the bespoke trade) usually earned a few pence per garment, eight pence for a shift in 1730s Over or four pence for a shirt in 1790s Crowland, for example; while gentlemen's shirts, like those ordered for Swynfen Jarvis in the 1750s and for the Earl of

Egremont and the Honourable Robert Clive in the 1780s and 1790s usually cost between two shillings and 4s. 6d. apiece. However, though the stitches might vary in size, the difference between the amount of work that went into a gentleman's shirt and that of a pauper was not so very great. Records of seamstresses working for shops are few and far between and we can only guess, or hope, that shopkeepers like Robert Blunt paid the women who made his thirty-shilling shirts a fair price. It seems that independent seamstresses' earnings were dictated by a combination of luck and geography.

Being a competent needlewoman was also helpful in procuring a good place as a servant, and servants advertising for work and mistresses advertising for servants in the latter part of the century all stressed the importance of needlework skills. However, as the century progressed increasing numbers of women went into the slop trade or worked for wholesalers and many of them struggled to make an adequate living, especially if they were their family's sole breadwinner. Their situation would only get worse in the following century.

Slops and slop-sellers in the eighteenth and nineteenth centuries

An article in the *Northern Whig* of 20 June 1846 blamed army contractors for the development of the entire sweating system in the clothing trades, though it was vague about the date when this had begun:

> Having taken their [the army clothiers'] orders at a low figure, they [the tailors] had to get the articles made cheaply; they could not even afford to find their work-people house-room; and, instead of receiving them at a stipend, under their own roofs, they 'put the work out' at so much per garment. At first, such wages were remunerative; but clever competitors took the work at lower contracts, which they were able to do, by grinding down the seamsters and seamstresses. Under this system, a new class of jobbers sprung up, in the persons of sub-contractors or middlemen, who took large quantities of work from the army clothiers, and undertook to get it done at a still lower price. These men went about, from garret to garret, from hovel to hovel, hawking about the work, at the lowest possible remuneration. If one would not sew at their price, another would, rather than face starvation, or go into the workhouse, till these men – known in various localities as 'undertakers', 'grinders', or by the less elegant appellation of 'sweaters' – succeeded in reducing the price of such labour to its present low ebb....
>
> It was soon seen that if military clothing can be made upon these starvation terms, other garments could also be produced at similar cost, provided a sufficient number could be made at the same time, and a market insured for them. Vast clothing establishments were commenced, grinders were set to work, and now the patronisers of cheap clothing may have the satisfaction of knowing, that they are worked for at the rate, in many instances, of something under sixpence a dozen.

Judging from the quantities of ready-made goods produced for the armed forces, for civilian slop-sellers and for export, by 1700 there must already have been large numbers of slop-workers in Britain and their numbers only increased as the century progressed. We can therefore probably date the development of the sweating system to the early eighteenth century rather than the nineteenth, though it was not until the 1840s that wages reached starvation levels and sweating was recognized as a social problem.

The Prevalence of Slop-Working

The army and navy remained major customers for slop clothing throughout the eighteenth century. The Seven Years' War against France (1756–63) and the American War of Independence (1775–83) saw renewed demands for military clothing and, once again, there were vast profits to be made. Between September 1760 and September 1762, for instance, Charles James supplied goods costing almost £45,000 to troops fighting the French. Twenty years later during the American War, between 1780 and 1782, James Wadham shipped some 613,000 shirts, frocks and trousers to government storehouses on the other side of the Atlantic and earned himself over £79,000.[1] Government contracts remained attractive to small suppliers and they jumped onto the government gravy train whenever the opportunity arose. In or around 1770, for example, an unknown linen draper in Reading went bankrupt owing £45,999 5s. 4d.[2] He was owed £174 2s. 2d. by 'the Ship Sumer', which suggests that he had sold some slop clothing to the navy. Like many other dealers, most of his customers were civilians, but an order from a ship's captain had seemed too good to refuse.

The civilian market for ready-made clothing was also buoyant. As we have seen, by the late seventeenth century some dealers were already carrying large quantities of ready-to-wear garments and by the first half of the eighteenth century, advertisements for ready-made clothes begin to appear in local newspapers where these had been established. For example, in March 1721 the *Ipswich Journal* carried several advertisements for the closing-down sale of John May, woollen draper in Ipswich, who had stocks of 'ready made cloaths at reasonable rates'. In July 1729 Mr Joseph Curry in Newcastle reminded readers of the *Newcastle Courant* that, alongside the leather 'dress'd in oyl' that he sold by the pound, he also had a stock of ready-made breeches and gloves. In 1739 in the little town of Spalding in Lincolnshire, Ann Atkinson announced that she had recently returned from London with new fabrics, short cloaks, mantelets of velvet and cloth, velvet pelerines, hoops, and stays for women and children,[3] while in May of the same year at Margate in Kent, the executors of the late Stephen Bennett, 'taylor and draper', who had had a shop near the pier, were selling off 'Stockings, Caps, ready-made Cloaths, and many other Things too tedious to mention.'[4] The fact that these dealers, and many others, chose to advertise in the press implies that their hoped-for customers were literate newspaper readers, respectable people with some education and money. The market for ready-to-wear was expanding.

By the second half of the eighteenth century such advertisements, particularly for men's shirts, were commonplace. For example, the *Manchester Mercury* of 29 February 1752 carried an advertisement for William Clarke's 'Linnen Warehouse' on Deansgate selling 'an assortment of linen drapery goods.'[5] *Saunders's News-Letter* in Dublin, Ireland on 26 November 1779 ran an advertisement for:

READY MADE SHIRTS, STOCKS &c. &c. Ruffled and plain Shirts, from 4s. 4d. to 22s. 9d. Children's Shirts of all Sizes and Prices, Cravats, Stocks of all Sorts, Ladies Riding Habit Shirts, Sheets, Table Cloths, &c., &c. All the above will be engaged to be the best in, or if not approved of after bought, will be taken back and the Money returned.

Twenty years later, on 12 March 1799[6] in the same newspaper, Catherine Morley of 4 Henry Street, Dublin, informed her friends that she had 'laid in a large and fashionable assortment of plain white linen' which she had bought for 'ready money' and so could sell 'on the most reasonable terms'. She was also 'induced to become more extensive in the sale of ready-made shirts, and will be constantly supplied with them at various prices, from 5s. English[7] to 20s. each ... no house in the city can deal on better terms'. There must have been teams of seamstresses in Dublin working for these two suppliers alone. Ms Morley also claimed: 'Several dozen of shirts fit for the army, always ready.' The government bandwagon was always too lucrative to ignore.

In Oxford in 1789 D. Parr '(From PICCADILLY, LONDON)' advertised[8] a wide range of 'linen drapery' which included:

... cottons, calicoes, muslins and ginghams, long lawns, cambrics, dowlas and 'Housewife Cloths', tucked aprons from 2s. 9d. to 8s. 0d., India Muslin Neckcloths from 10d. to 5s. 0d., muslin handkerchiefs at 10d. to 10s. 6d., shawls, quilted petticoats at 6s. 0d. to 16s. 0d., all sorts of hosiery, and shirts from 3s. 0d. to any Price ...

Meanwhile 'Gentlemen' could be 'accommodated with ready-made linens of all sorts', presumably more shirts, nightshirts and neckwear, again made by seamstresses employed directly by Parr or through a middleman. In Canterbury in the same year, the local newspaper carried an advertisement for Chalks 'near the Butter Market',[9] offering an even wider range of fabrics, along with haberdashery, worsted, thread and cotton hosiery, men's, women's and children's gloves, ready-made shirts, children's blankets, gowns and caps, scarlet cloaks and stays, aprons and pockets, cotton, silk and 'sousee' handkerchiefs. The fabrics Chalks sold included Hambro Roughs, Russia Ducks and Drabs, York 'Huccabacks', 'Wigan and Home made Checks' and brown Hollands, with cheap 'Corded Dimities at between 12d. and 3s. a yard'. They seem to have been catering for a more down-market customer base than Parr in Oxford – which probably means Chalks' seamstresses and/or middlemen were being paid at the lowest rates.

There were hundreds of such advertisements nationwide; and there would also have been many similar firms which did not advertise in the press. At this point it is important to explain that there was no real distinction between 'ready-made' garments and 'slops' from the point of view of the makers, although as the prices imply, the quality of ready-made goods varied widely. The description 'ready-made' suggested respectability; 'slops' were mostly for working people, though not until the later nineteenth century did the term really begin to acquire a pejorative meaning. The goods or slops sold were all made by armies of seamstresses in towns and in the countryside. In September 1800, for example, one slop-seller claimed that he and his partner employed between 1,000 and 1,200 needlewomen to make shirts. He could not be more precise about the numbers because he 'could not state the number within five hundred; we employ a great number of parishes, and how many of the poor are employed upon our work it is impossible for me to tell'.[10] Clearly, he was having needlework done via the Poor Law officials of various parishes who were acting as his middlemen and possibly making a profit themselves.

Even before 1800 there were dozens of slop-sellers in London and elsewhere, supplying civilians as well as the navy and the army. Some of them were tailors, selling ready-made clothing from stock as well as doing bespoke work, others were linen drapers or even milliners. Lambert cites the example of Mary Halsall who advertised in the *Liverpool Chronicle* in July 1757. She was a milliner and linen draper, but her stock included 'Slops for Seamen'.[11] Between 1781 and 1800, 205 slop-sellers insured themselves with the Royal Sun Alliance Company; the majority were in the London area, many in Woolwich and Wapping to take advantage of the naval trade, others in Portsmouth and Gosport for the same reason, but others traded in different parts of London, at Blandford and Poole in Dorset, at Fowey in Cornwall, at Hastings in Sussex and in Newcastle-upon-Tyne. Most were men, but thirty-three, roughly a sixth of the cohort, were women. There can be no doubt there were many other men and women who traded uninsured.

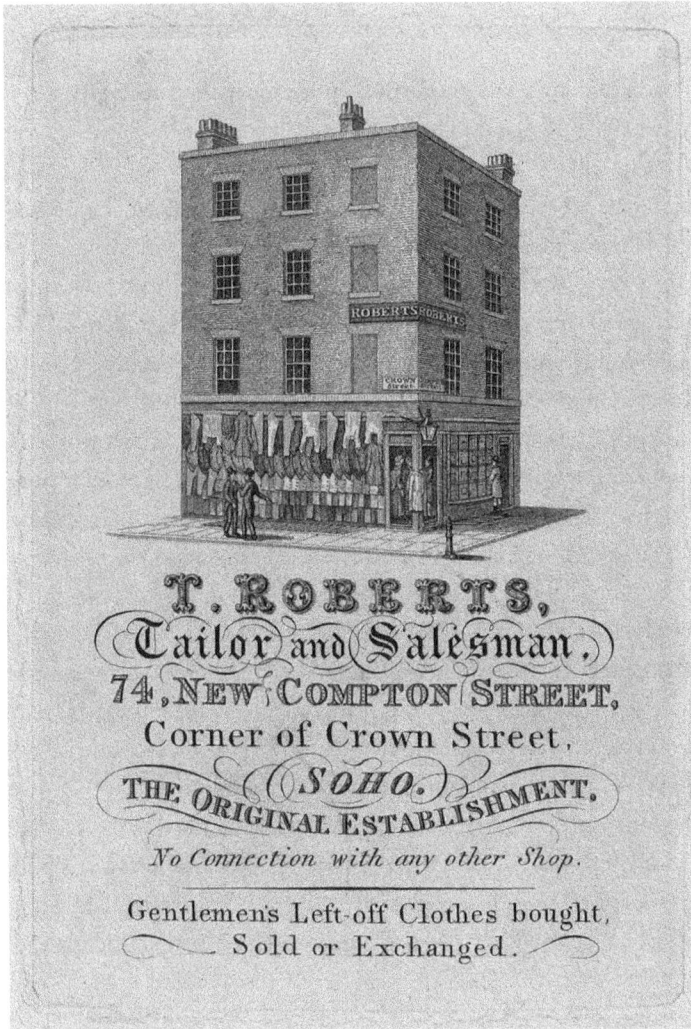

Figure 5.1 Trade card for Thomas Roberts, tailor, second-hand clothes dealer and slop-seller.

Slop-Workers

By the early nineteenth century, therefore, there were increasing numbers of garment-makers working from home, in competition with the craft tailors who worked in workshops under the aegis of a master craftsmen and, crucially, were paid an hourly rate rather than by the piece. These craft tailors were men and styled themselves 'flints' and their trade as 'honourable', as opposed to the slop-workers in sweat-shops whose trade was deemed 'dishonourable' and who were referred to as 'dungs'. In 1824 'flints' outnumbered 'dungs' four to one, but twenty-five years later the proportions were more than reversed. Increasingly, too, slop-workers were women who either helped their husbands or worked on their own account.[12]

Women slop-workers were seen as even more disreputable than 'dungs', partly because the tailors' guilds had always been hostile to women garment-makers. In 1702, for example, the guilds in York, Oxford, Salisbury and Norwich petitioned parliament 'to suppress the women mantua-makers'. Mantuas were a type of loose dress that became popular in the mid-1670s. They were relatively easy to make and a number of seamstresses set themselves up as 'mantua-makers'. The tailors resented this because up to the late seventeenth century, making women's dresses had been tailoring work and they feared a large proportion of their trade would disappear into the hands of women. Many tailors' guilds prosecuted women mantua-makers for infringing their trade; the Chester guild was especially hostile and instituted at least forty-three investigations into women making women's dresses between 1698 and 1725. The Scottish guilds came up with a more pragmatic system of 'tollerations', essentially extracting protection money from mantua-makers in return for letting them carry on their trade in peace; their opposition was more long-lasting and not until a ruling in the Court of Session in 1763 did this practice come to an end north of the border.[13]

By the nineteenth century hostility to women making dresses for women was a thing of the past, but the tailors had a new grievance. Tailoring was poorly paid and the tailors had staged a series of strikes in 1827, 1830 and 1834 for shorter hours and higher wages. In 1834 they also agitated for piecework and home-working to be banned. This would effectively have barred many women slop-makers from working. The strikes failed and the men blamed the women slop-workers as strike-breakers, with some justification because some employers had actually taken women on while the men were out on strike. Times had changed and, whatever the striking tailors in the 'honourable' part of the trade might have wished, there was a growing market for slops. Large numbers of working- and lower middle-class men wanted to dress decently, indeed, in many cases, like that of clerks, their employers required them to look respectable at work. Such workers could not afford bespoke suits; ready-made clothing, however shoddily made and badly finished it was, was at least affordable.

For obvious reasons, comparatively few examples of cheap clothing survive, but part of the purpose of this chapter is to look at some of the types of goods made by slop-workers. Slop-work was not necessarily the preserve of women, indeed, in the earlier part of the period under review the majority of slop-workers were probably male tailors, although there certainly were some women. For example, Elizabeth Sanderson, in her book, *Women and Work in Eighteenth-Century Edinburgh*, cites the mid-eighteenth-century case of the wife of a soldier, Alexander Little, who made linen slop shirts that were then sold on by James Black.[14] By the early nineteenth century, however, if not before, there were more women than men in the trade.

Examples of Ready-made Clothing

Military Slops

As we have seen, the army and navy continued to patronize slop-sellers throughout the eighteenth century in much the same way as they had in the seventeenth but towards the end of the century, things began to change as both tried to streamline and centralize their systems of provision. In July 1781 numerous newspapers reported that: 'The Navy Slop Office, established under Lord Winchelsea's Administration, has produced to Government since its Institution a clear Profit of 70,000L [£] besides paying all Expenses of Management, Officers, etc.'[15] Clearly, the new system was cost-effective.

The efficiency of the new naval slop system inspired the army. In 1782 the press reported that:

> the enquiry now carrying on by General Barré for the better clothing of the Army on the same System with the Navy Slop-Office, it has appeared that beside the Prevention of all possible Fraud from the private Workman, whether Contractor, Clothier or Taylor, the Average Saving to the Public will, on a War Establishment, amount from 12 to 20,000L [£] a Year.[16]

The fate of the army slop-makers was sealed: if working for Joseph Ashley and his ilk had been poorly paid, things were about to get a whole lot worse.

Pictures of soldiers usually show them smartly clad in scarlet tunics, customized with facings and insignia denoting the regiment to which they belonged, and dark trousers, often with a stripe down the side seams. Furthermore, most surviving portraits are of officers, and officers paid for their own clothing which usually looked smart because it was made-to-measure by their own tailors, but the troops, like sailors, were supplied with 'slops', and their tunics and breeches were often ill-fitting. We are mostly dependent on paintings and illustrations to show us what ordinary soldiers looked like, and these images were not necessarily very realistic, at least not so far as the fit of their clothes was concerned.

The records of two young men from the Midlands in the first half of the nineteenth century illustrate this distinction. In the 1830s William Mellish Chambers[17] from Hodsock Priory in Nottinghamshire was a young lieutenant in the Rifle Brigade and he spent a good deal on his uniform. In 1834, for example, a London tailor, Burghart on Clifford Street, supplied him with a 'rifle green' frock coat for £5 12s. and a pair of regimental trousers for £4; in 1836 a pair of braided 'rifle green' buckskin trousers cost him £3 14s.; and in 1837 he spent £15 7s. with John Jones in Regent Street on a range of items, including 'A Superfine Green Regimental Pelisse richly trimmed'. The same year he spent a further £41 3s. 6d. with Spardings, the army outfitters in New Bond Street.

By contrast, in 1841 eighteen-year-old Frederick Green[18] from Weedon in Northamptonshire joined the 54th Regiment of Infantry and received a 'bounty' of £3 17s. 6d. The army retained £3 15s. of this for his clothes and necessary items like his mess tin, cutlery and knapsack. His uniform consisted of two pairs of white linen trousers, a pair of short boots, a fatigue jacket, three pairs of socks, three shirts, a black stock and a pair of braces, all from the stores and none of it made-to-measure.

The seamstresses and tailors who made garments for the army slop-sellers assembled them, but the regimental details would probably have been added later, by the men themselves or by their wives and girlfriends. Throughout the eighteenth century the traditional distinction between male tailors, who worked in wool, and seamstresses, who worked in cotton, linen and lighter fabrics, had usually been preserved, but by the mid-nineteenth century seamstresses were doing a lot of what would previously have been seen as tailors' work, including making uniforms or parts of them.

Dresses

Women's dresses were available ready-made by 1700: for example, we see an advertisement in *The Spectator* of 1711[19] for a gown shop that had moved from Exchange Alley to Cornhill and its dresses being advertised as costing from thirty-seven shillings to six guineas. They were not unique. Even a comparatively downmarket draper in Reading had ninety-four gowns in stock when he went bankrupt in 1708, along with numerous men's 'frocks', waistcoats, breeches and coats.[20] In his case, he served a fairly working-class clientele, but well-to-do ladies who normally had their dresses made to measure also occasionally bought ready-made ones: for example, in 1740, Mrs Frances Shakerley in Cheshire bought an Irish poplin gown for £1 0s. 2d.;[21] in 1782, Mary Hardy in

Norfolk bought a chintz gown for £1 14s.;[22] while in York, Miss Woodhouse, a fashionable lady who spent a great deal on dress, bought two ready-to-wear gowns in 1787, a 'Canterbury muslin' for £1 8s. and a chintz 'common gown' for a guinea.[23]

Such gowns were produced in quantity, the 1711 *Spectator* advertisement, for example, promised that fifty new gowns, in a range of sizes, would be arriving in Cornhill the following week. A wholesaler's order book survives in Manchester Local History Library and covers the period 1773–9.[24] Unfortunately, the name of the wholesaler is unknown and many of his customers are untraceable. He sold gowns in ones and twos to some customers, and in twenties, fifties and hundreds to others; for example, in August 1775 he sold Richard Lomax a single

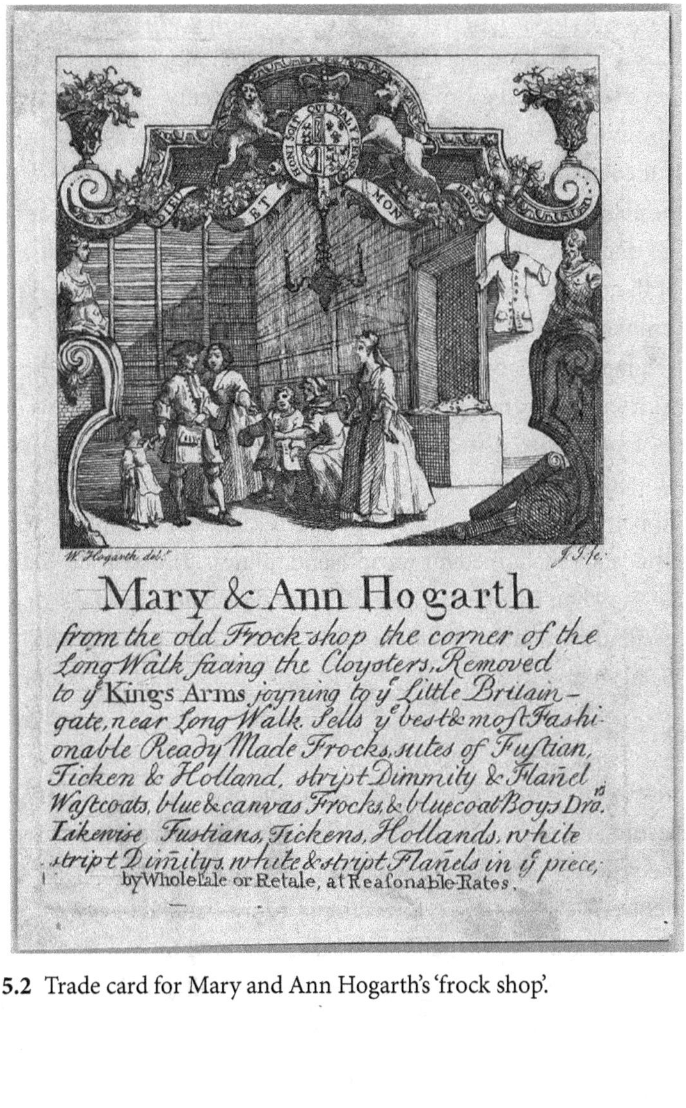

Figure 5.2 Trade card for Mary and Ann Hogarth's 'frock shop'.

cotton gown for 8s. 6d., while in September 1777, J. and E. Kenworthy bought a hundred 'moree' gowns at seventeen shillings each. They were good customers, as were Kettle and Mandeville in London, who bought batches of twenty to thirty dresses a month, and Bentley and Boardman, hosiers in Liverpool, who bought in much smaller quantities – two or three items at a time – several times a month. The wholesaler sent goods as far afield as Donegal and he sold various other items of clothing and fabrics, as well as cheese, beer, rum and port – in fact, sales of gowns accounted for less than ten per cent of his trade.

His gowns came in 'moree' (a type of calico), rich moree, common moree, silk and cotton mix and plain cotton, and he also sold 'Irish wrappers' at between two and seven shillings apiece. Sometimes the colour – pink, maroon, blue-and-white, purple, green or 'drab' – is specified. Given that the book's owner was selling wholesale, his prices were quite high. Cotton gowns cost between 7s. 6d. to 8s. 6d., silk and cotton ones around sixteen shillings, common morees were usually seventeen shillings, morees nineteen to twenty-one shillings and rich morees twenty-two shillings or more or more. It was a lucrative business. The record is incomplete in that numerous papers have been pasted into the book, hiding the accounts, but for 1776 the record is fairly full and that year he turned over more than £14,500 of which just over £2,000 was from the sale of dresses. No doubt there were many such wholesalers around the country and they must all have employed hundreds, if not thousands, of seamstresses.

Most eighteenth-century dresses were what we now call 'open robes', rather like full-skirted coats. The open bodice front was often filled in with a decorated triangle of fabric called a 'stomacher' and these could be purchased ready-made from milliners and drapers. The skirts of the dress were open to display a decorated petticoat or 'coat'. This might match the dress or contrast with it, and many petticoats were quilted for warmth and fullness. The style allowed for quite a lot of leeway when it came to fit, useful in the days before formal sizing systems were in use and particularly helpful in the case of ready-made gowns.

Petticoats

The decorative petticoats that went under open robes were also mass-produced, and the fashion for them lasted from the late seventeenth century through to the 1780s. The sellers were usually men, but they often employed women to make the garments. As early as 1722, for example, Mary Pattenden of East Grinstead was apprenticed to a London petticoat-maker.[25] In 1781 there were four 'petticoat manufacturers' in the Manchester area alone: William Alexander, Edward

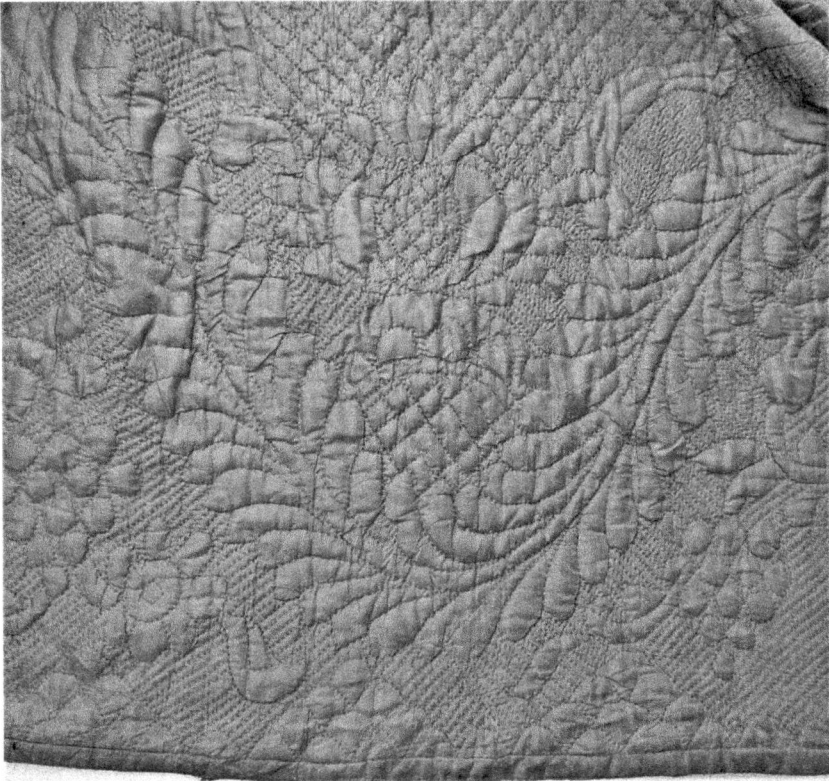

Figure 5.3 Detail of a woman's quilted petticoat (1730–50) of shot blue-and-pink taffeta, the shape of which was altered in the nineteenth century.

Blakely and Thomas Connelly in Salford and Francis O'Brien in Oldfield Lane;[26] and the Sun Fire Office Insurance registers record five London-based petticoat-makers in the 1777–86 period. No doubt there were many others.

Petticoats lent themselves to mass production. They were full, slit at the sides so the wearers could reach into the pockets they wore underneath their skirts, and fastened front and back with tapes so one size fitted most women unless they were unusually tall or short. Beverly Lemire has made a study of three dozen quilted petticoats in the Royal Ontario Museum in Toronto and in the Museum of London in the UK.[27] Most were made of coloured silk or satin padded with wool and backed with a linen or wool fabric. The quilting was usually a simple diamond, lattice or scallop pattern, sometimes with more complex motifs like flowers on the lower, more visible, third, and the hem, top and side pocket openings were bound with tape or ribbon. The stitching was a basic running-stitch. Lemire concluded that the work, though showy, was not particularly carefully executed and suggested that most petticoats were probably made on quilting frames by a number of women working together.

According to *The Book of Trades* of 1747 for quiltwork women earned between one and two shillings a day which was quite a respectable wage. Some manufacturers offered new patterns 'never before quilted' and 'superior work', though whether their petticoats matched their advertising is impossible to ascertain.[28] Of course, some women, like Lady Arabella Farnese, Elizabeth Shackleton and Mary Hardy, had their quilting done to order, as we saw in Chapter 3.

Ready-made, quilted silk petticoats were expensive, usually retailing at between eighteen shillings and £3 10s., though plain 'stuff' petticoats, few of which survive, sold at around six shillings. Shops carried large quantities of petticoats: in 1693 Thomas Walker, in London, for example, had 458 petticoats in stock (along with 434 mantuas, 120 gowns and numerous suits and waistcoats);[29] south of the river in Southwark in 1699 Samuel Dalling had over 240.[30]

Trousers and Breeches

Throughout the eighteenth century men wore breeches, buckled at the knee over stockings, and with a buttoned fall-front. For dress wear, wealthy men had breeches of silk or velvet, but for day wear breeches were usually of leather, wool, linen, cotton or mixed fabrics. Working men in certain trades might have thick leather breeches which were exceptionally hard-wearing and offered extra protection and 'leather breeches-maker' was a recognized trade, while 'breeches-maker' was a branch of tailoring. Sometimes tailors made matching sets of coat, waistcoat and breeches, or just coat and breeches, and these were known as 'suits of dittos'.

Portraits often show breeches as close-fitting, almost skin-tight, but such examples were almost certainly tailor-made to the customers' requirements. For ordinary wear, breeches were looser and more comfortable, baggy at the seat, with the waist adjustable at the back by means of straps and buckles, like waistcoats. Across the country, numerous tradesmen described themselves as breeches-makers; the records of the Sun Fire Office Insurance Company list at least 150 in the latter years of the eighteenth century and, of course, many more would have traded uninsured. The majority of eighteenth-century breeches-makers were men, though by the 1790s some of them were taking female apprentices. For example, in Poole in 1794 Elizabeth McCannon was apprenticed to George Bedloe,[31] while in the same decade the trustees of the Barnstaple charity apprenticed a series of pauper girls to learn the trade.[32] It would seem that, for much of the century, slop breeches were usually made by slop-tailors rather than by seamstresses, but by 1800 things were changing.

Some older men continued to wear knee breeches into the 1840s, but by the late 1790s many men had adopted the new fashion of trousers. To begin with, these were quite slim-fitting but, as the century wore on, trousers became wider. Quite garish patterns of stripes and checks were popular for leisure wear for both the well-to-do and working men, and trousers were often made of quite lightweight fabrics. Such items were supplied by the slop-sellers, many of whose workers were now seamstresses. A list of items stolen from a Philadelphia slop-seller in 1795 illustrates the range of items such traders sold, and there is no reason to suppose that the stock of their English counterparts was radically different. The list included a pair of cotton trousers striped in purple, yellow and white, three pairs striped in yellow and white, two pairs of red-and-white striped cotton and one in black and white, plus one nankeen pair with a fringe.[33] Such designs continued to be popular into the mid-nineteenth century.

By the time of the 1851 census, many seamstresses described themselves as 'trouser makers' and no doubt some of them were making up these brightly coloured items, though more sober colours – drabs, browns and greys – were probably more usual.

Figure 5.4 Trade card for Foster, breeches-maker, *c.* 1800.

Waistcoats

Early eighteenth-century waistcoats were like coats, knee-length and sleeved, although only the fronts and cuffs – the visible parts – would have been of rich fabric, while the back and sleeves were usually made of linen or a lighter-weight textile. As the century progressed, sleeves were abandoned and waistcoats became shorter until by the 1780s they were waist-length, of similar proportions to those worn today.

Silk waistcoats with elaborate embroidery in silks and metal thread, sometimes decorated with sequins, were worn by eighteenth-century gentlemen for formal wear. The front panels and pocket flaps were separately embroidered on lengths of silk by specialist embroiderers and were then made up by the tailor or workwoman to the client's specification. The fronts were not darted to fit as that would have spoiled the design, shaping was done at the back, as it is today, by means of a strap and a buckle.

Poor men wore waistcoats too and, although these were not usually decorated, they were often of coloured or patterned fabric. The seven waistcoats stolen from the Philadelphia slop-seller in 1795 were as garish as the trousers he sold, patterned in bright red and blue with spots and stripes. Dickens' John Chivery, son of the turnkey at the Marshalsea prison, dresses in his finest clothes when he attempts to court Little Dorrit. His outfit included a silk waistcoat 'bedecked with gold sprigs' but, fancy though it appeared, it was 'mere slop-work – if the truth be known'.[34]

Gentlemen's waistcoats were often made by their tailors, particularly if they were part of a matching suit, but ready-to-wear slop waistcoats were frequently made, and sometimes sold, by seamstresses. By the early 1800s, the six specialist waistcoat-making firms in London which were insured with the Sun Fire Office Insurance Company were all run by women.[35] An advertisement in the London-based *Morning Chronicle* of 18 September 1818 addressed itself specifically to 'women waistcoat makers' and offered 'constant employ' making white waistcoats for a firm in Soho. However, most advertisements of similar date offering work to waistcoat makers did not specify gender. The change seems to have crystallized in the 1840s. Mayhew in his 'Letter XVI' in the *Morning Chronicle* of 11 December 1849 recorded an interview with a waistcoat hand. The man told him 'since the last five years the sweaters have employed females upon cloth, silk and satin waistcoats as well, and before that time the idea of a woman making a cloth waistcoat would have been scouted', – he, not unnaturally, blamed the employment of women for the significant reduction in his wages.

Handkerchiefs

Handkerchiefs were an important part of the eighteenth-century wardrobe for both men and women. They were not only for blowing the nose. Women often described the neck-cloths that they wore as 'handkerchiefs' rather than 'neckerchiefs' and they were usually squares folded in half diagonally. Men might wear a handkerchief – particularly a coloured one – knotted at the neck over a smock or open-necked shirt. Silk or lace-trimmed handkerchiefs were mainly for show, to cascade elegantly out of a pocket or protrude from a sleeve, while plain linen or cotton squares were for use. According to Parson Woodforde's diary, some were designated 'night handkerchiefs'.[36] We also know that there were cheap coloured handkerchiefs that were specifically for people who took snuff.

Wealthy people had large quantities of all sorts of handkerchiefs; when his inventory was taken in 1747, for example, the Honourable William Monson in Lincolnshire had forty-three white handkerchiefs and 149 coloured ones.[37] Fine handkerchiefs were expensive. In Leicestershire in 1790 Sir Willoughby Dixie paid £2 12s. to have six fine cambric handkerchiefs made and 'marked', probably with an embroidered monogram, which works out at around 8s. 6d. each for making alone.[38] Ladies bought and sometimes made the handkerchiefs they wore round their necks. In 1769 Elizabeth Shackleton listed thirteen neck-handkerchiefs and a 'sute of linnen' (neck-handkerchief, sleeve ruffles and an apron) that she had embroidered herself.[39]

Even small drapers sold quantities of plain handkerchiefs. For example, Richard Ducker, a draper in the little Welsh town of Wrexham, had almost 1,500 handkerchiefs, of various qualities and prices ranging between 9d. and 6s. 6d., in stock when his inventory was taken in 1717.[40] The practice of taking snuff, by both men and women, necessitated special handkerchiefs which could be thrown away when they became too stained. In 1717, for example, Lady Grisell Baillie bought four 'snuf' handkerchiefs at 2s. 8d. each; she was a big spender, her expendable snuff handkerchiefs cost more than three times the price of Richard Ducker's cheapest ones. Hemming handkerchiefs for a penny or two a dozen occupied many seamstresses nationwide.

Caps

Caps were an important part of a woman's wardrobe, particularly as she got older. In 1717 Lady Grisell Baillie paid nineteen shillings for 'cambrick and making a sute of head cloaths and Ruf', for example. In 1769, as we have seen, Elizabeth Shackleton listed no fewer than fifty caps in her inventory.[41] While a young unmarried woman in the eighteenth and nineteenth centuries could sometimes go bareheaded, some form of head-covering was *de rigueur* for her mother, grandmother and married sisters. Servants and working-class women wore simple caps that covered the hair and framed the face but were not particularly decorative, and gentlewomen wore something similar for everyday wear in the eighteenth century. (See Figure 10.1.) For paying and receiving calls caps were more elaborate, trimmed with frills, ribbons and laces, and wired or starched, while, for dress wear, caps could be extravagant – and expensive – concoctions (see Figure 1.12 for a particularly extreme example) and were usually made to order by a milliner. The fashionable shape changed from decade to decade, but caps were worn by most women at least until the last decades of the nineteenth century.

Caps of the early 1800s were small and neat and could be replaced by a sort of wreath of ribbons or artificial flowers. By the 1830s day caps could be as elaborate as the bonnets of the time, romantic frames for the face to balance the big sleeves and full skirts of fashionable dresses. By the middle of the century, a lace shape with short lappets, perched on the head and held in place with hairpins, would suffice for a young married woman, while her younger unmarried sisters could eschew caps altogether.

Night caps were worn in bed by both men and women, and these were usually tied under the chin with strings to hold them in place as the wearer slept. They were mainly worn for warmth in unheated bedrooms, but a young bride might have frilly lace-trimmed caps in her trousseau to wear on honeymoon. In 1833 in Shropshire Charlotte Kenyon, for her marriage to a wealthy clergyman with aristocratic connections, had caps made trimmed with Valenciennes and Chantilly lace, for example.[42]

Men, who, in the seventeenth and eighteenth centuries, customarily wore wigs often wore a coloured cap around the house. William Hogarth painted a number of self-portraits of himself wearing coloured caps of cloth or velvet (Figure 5.5). In the 1650s on trips to London, Reverend Giles Moore,[43] from Horsted Keynes in Sussex, bought himself several caps of satin and 'taffety' at between three shillings and six shillings each; in May 1674 he acquired '6 Caps bought at London ready-made. Payd at 9d. ye Cap'.

Servants continued to wear caps long after their mistresses had given the fashion up and, by the 1890s, the cap was a hated symbol of domestic servitude. Babies and small children wore caps for warmth and protection; soldiers, sailors, prisoners and others wore them as part of their uniform; working men wore them

Figure 5.5 Self-portrait by William Hogarth, showing him wearing a cap instead of a wig, 1764.

outdoors instead of a hat. Cap-making, in all its various forms, employed large numbers of women home-workers throughout the eighteenth and nineteenth centuries.

Stays or Corsets

Seventeenth- and eighteenth-century stays were rigid, made of layers of stiffened and starched fabrics and sometimes even of leather. Stitching them was hard manual work and traditionally was the preserve of men. Some tailors made stays; some tradesmen were specialist stay-makers. However, as in many other branches of needlework, by the nineteenth century women had taken over much of the work. This was partly because stays had become somewhat lighter and easier to sew, but largely because women workers were cheaper to employ than men and manufacturers were anxious to keep their costs as low as possible.

Early nineteenth-century stays, worn under soft, flowing Regency dresses which showed off the body's contours, were comparatively short and light, with very little, if any, boning; the emphasis was on pushing up the breasts rather than confining the waist. At least some of them were made by women. In Leicester, in 1823, for example, young Eliza Stone had her stays made by a Mrs Bracey.[44]

By the 1830s the fashion was again for small waists and stays became longer and more rigid, though they were often corded rather than boned. Corsets that gave women the tiny waists fashion demanded were worn throughout the 1830s, 1840s, 1850s and 1860s and as time went on they became more rigid and constricting. By the latter part of the century, dresses fitted closely over the hips and waist and stays got longer, tighter and much more heavily dependent on whalebone and steel. In corsets of the 1880s and 1890s there could be as many as twenty-four 'bones', plus a rigid central 'busk' at the front.

By the 1870s and 1880s, most stays were machine-made. Symington's of Market Harborough, one of the biggest corsetry-making firms in the country, had a series of factories in Leicestershire and Northamptonshire where corsets were cut out, steamed, shaped, trimmed and finished, but the actual stitching was farmed out to an army of home-working seamstresses to whom the firm supplied sewing machines on 'easy terms or hire purchase'. A reporter who wrote an article about Symington's in the *Rugby Times* of 31 December 1881 claimed that: 'By giving out work they enable many who could not come into the factory an opportunity of assisting the breadwinners.'[45] No doubt this was what the proprietors had told him about a practice that was actually designed to cut costs.

It is not clear how much Symington's paid their outworkers but, in general, stay-makers were exceptionally poorly paid. One of Mayhew's informants in 1849 claimed that stay manufacturers sent work out to seamstresses in the country who would work for lower wages than their city counterparts;[46] certainly of the hundreds of seamstresses in Whitechapel in 1851, only twenty-three made corsetry.[47] There was a lot of stitching in a mid-nineteenth-century corset, whether corded or boned, but one woman who came before the courts in Norfolk in 1847, probably one of the countrywomen working on the cheap for a city manufacturer about whom Mayhew's interviewee complained, claimed to be paid just three farthings per corset and that each one took her almost a full day to make.[48]

Figure 5.6 'Pretty Housemaid' corset made by R. and W.H. Symington of Market Harborough. The design was registered in 1886 and it became one of the firm's best-selling items. The stitching was done by outworking seamstresses using sewing machines.

Underwear

Seamstresses had always made undergarments, shifts for women and shirts for men. The nineteenth century saw women weighed down by more and more undergarments, although most men still wore their shirts next to the skin and for them the wearing of drawers remained optional.

The shift was still the basic undergarment for women. By the nineteenth century shifts had short sleeves, were mid-calf or just below-knee-length and were worn next to the skin, under the corset. While the loose shift would be gathered in tightly and the resulting pleats and ridges would have pressed into the wearer's flesh, the idea was that the shift (now often called a 'chemise') could be washed, whereas washing a corset was a major operation, undertaken only once or twice a year, if at all. Drawers were generally worn by the 1820s. They fastened over the top of the shift which was tucked between the legs, and they also went under the corset. With a back-lacing corset holding the waistband of the drawers firmly in place, and worn under a dress with a tight-fitting bodice, single-handedly removing one's drawers would have been impossible, hence the wearing of crotch-less 'divided drawers'.

'Petticoat-bodies', like little short-sleeved blouses, went over the top of the corset, as did waist petticoats or underskirts. Petticoat-bodies changed as the shape of dresses changed; early ones were shaped and fitted to avoid extra bulk under a tight-fitting bodice but, as bodices became looser and pouched in the 1890s, so did the petticoat-bodies, now renamed 'camisoles'. As dresses became fuller and fuller from 1830 onwards, increasing numbers of full petticoats or underskirts were worn to make the skirt stand out. These petticoats were often tucked or corded for extra fullness and were often trimmed with lace at the hem in case a gust of wind or careless movement allowed onlookers a momentary glimpse. Not until the 1850s did the crinoline frame make its appearance and reduce the number of petticoats the fashionable lady needed. It was superseded by various other foundation garments, like the crinolette, or half-crinoline, and various types of bustle, as the fashionable shape changed. Petticoats also changed in shape, becoming narrower as skirts became more fitted, and with ingenious arrangements of cross-over tapes that allowed them to be gathered at the back and remain smooth over the front and hips to enhance the effect of the bustle.

As well as wearing far more undergarments than her eighteenth-century predecessors, after the middle of the century the respectable nineteenth-century lady no longer slept in her shift, or even in a night shift, she wore a purpose-made nightdress with long sleeves, a yoke, a buttoned opening at the neck, a collar and frilled decoration. (Figure 5.7) Her husband would have worn a nightshirt, though by the 1880s younger men were opting for 'sleep suits' or pyjamas. Both men and women wore night caps in bed. Nineteenth-century bedrooms were cold.

Some underwear and nightwear was still made at home but, increasingly, it was bought ready-made or, less often, commissioned from a seamstress. In 1813, sixteen-year-old Eliza Stone in Leicester received her first clothing allowance of £3 17s. a quarter. That first year she spent much of her money on new dresses and shoes, but she also bought four ready-made chemises for a guinea (5s. 3d. each) and a petticoat for 6s. 1½d., plus calico costing 9s. 6d. for two nightdresses which presumably she made up herself.[49]

Figure 5.7 *Le Reveil* by John François Rafaelli, 1890, showing a woman wearing a nightdress typical of those worn in the second half of the nineteenth century.

Respectable ladies had large quantities of underwear, usually provided as part of their trousseaux and expected to last for many years, if not a lifetime. When Charlotte Kenyon married the Reverend John Hill in Shropshire in 1833, for example, she had thirty chemises and twenty-four nightdresses, nine dressing gowns, nine night caps and twelve petticoats. She did not list anything as indelicate as drawers and corsets (other than one pair of French stays that had cost £1 5s. 'from Worton, the Oswestry staymaker'), although she must have had some. There were no petticoat-bodies as they were not yet in fashion. Much of her lingerie – at a cost of £106 18s. 11d. – came from London, from Ware and Co. on Davies Street, off Berkeley Square, Robertshaw's on Oxford Street and Christian and Son on Wigmore Street, all of whom must have employed seamstresses, while some of it may have been made up by Miss Pritchard of Pritchard and Lloyd in Shrewsbury, whom she also patronized extensively. A muslin dressing gown that cost a guinea and a night cap trimmed with Valenciennes lace that cost eighteen shillings came from Hillhouse on Bond Street and were probably intended for the wedding night.[50] Charlotte was marrying well, her husband's uncle was General Rowland Hill, first Viscount Almarez, and her brother-in-law would inherit the title, but, while large and expensive, her trousseau was not so very exceptional for someone of her social background.

An unknown Hampshire lady married in 1846. Beyond this, we know very little about her except that her husband was called 'Robert' and her son, born a year or so after the wedding, was 'Bobbie'; her family must have been fairly wealthy, although nowhere near as well-off as the Kenyons. Like Charlotte Kenyon, however, she kept a notebook entitled 'Wedding trousseau and baby clothes'. The seamstress-made part of her trousseau consisted of twelve day and twelve night shifts, four morning petticoats, four for evening and two 'plain' ones, four flannel petticoats and four flannel waistcoats, thirty pocket handkerchiefs, fifty-six 'squares', eight night caps and five 'chemisettes' (yet another name for petticoat-bodies). She also tells us the day shifts were made of Irish linen at 2s. 8d. a yard and the night ones were of fine long cloth (cotton) at 1s. 2d. a yard, and that the day shifts had frills of cambric that cost 10s. 6d. a yard while the night shifts had much cheaper frills of 'Scotch cambric' at 1s. 10d. a yard, all bought from 'Wilson and Swales'. It seems the day shifts cost 7s. 8d. apiece, though it is not clear whether that included the cost of making up. If it did, the seamstress can only have earned at most a few pence per garment.[51]

Children's Clothes

Seamstresses had always made clothes for babies and toddlers and, as we have seen, by the 1740s if not before, 'baby linen warehouses' had been established in London and elsewhere. There must have been seamstresses who made goods for these establishments as well as for private clients. However, until the end of the eighteenth century, children were dressed as miniature adults when they were little more than toddlers, and their clothes would then have been made by their parents' tailors and mantua-makers.

Jean-Jacques Rousseau in *Émile, ou de l'éducation*, published in 1762, was the first person to publicize the idea that children were not simply miniature adults. He believed that they should be brought up free of the constraints society imposed and should be allowed to develop as 'naturally' as possible. This carried through to the clothing they should wear. He opposed the traditional belief that babies should be swaddled from birth: 'When the child draws its first breath, do not confine it in tight wrappings. No cap, no bandages nor swaddling clothes. Loose and flowing flannel wrappers, which leave its limbs free and are not too heavy to check his movements, not too warm to prevent him feeling the air.'[52] This, he believed, should continue as the child grew: 'The limbs of a growing child should be free to move easily in his clothing; nothing should cramp his growth or movement; there should be nothing tight, nothing fitting closely to the body, no belts of any kind.' He went on to advocate keeping children in frocks for as long as possible and then putting them into 'loose clothing', preferably brightly coloured. However, rich fabrics were to be avoided and, if the child expressed a wish for these, they should be made into garments that were as uncomfortable as possible to make sure he or she did not enjoy wearing them.[53]

Not all parents espoused Rousseau's beliefs, but by the end of the century swaddling had gone out of fashion and children's clothes tended to be lighter and looser, although the fashion for white dresses for little girls and buff-coloured suits for little boys ignored his suggestion that children liked wearing bright colours and also created garments that were grossly impractical.

The unknown Hampshire lady mentioned above listed the items she prepared for 'Bobbie's' arrival in 1846–7 and the prices – although, as all the items were apparently 'made at home', those prices presumably only relate to the cost of fabric.[54] However, the list does give us some idea of the number of items a respectable middle-class family would lay in for a new baby at that date – and no doubt many mothers were less industrious than Bobbie's was and paid a seamstress to make at least some of the items. Baby Bobbie's layette contained: fourteen shirts (£4 15s.), fourteen bedgowns (£4 18s.), fourteen pinafores (£2 15s. 7d.), six blankets (£1 14s. 10½d.) five dozen 'pieces', presumably for nappies (£3 15s.), seven robes (price illegible), eight petticoats (£1 2s. 9d.), six flannel ditto (£1 1s. 4½d.), three pairs of stays and two muslin mantles (£2 9s. 2½d.), two flannel mantles (19s. 2d.), ten lace caps (£2 15s.), six night caps (18s. 7½d.), one flannel ditto and six flannel half squares (6s. 10½d.), two rollers and six pairs of socks. There were also slippers, two flannel aprons (7s. 4d.), six 'diaper binders' (12s. 6d.) and a short dressing gown (£1 7s.), presumably for his mother, along with 'old linen', flannel for bands and four pairs of calico cot sheets and pillowcases, not to mention a basket with covers, a bassinet, a powder puff and box, cold cream, a pin cushion and, for some unexplained reason, a 'needlestand'.

By the nineteenth century it was generally accepted that children should have special clothes. One of the first such outfits was the 'skeleton suit' for little boys, popular in the 1790s and early 1800s, which consisted of a short jacket with buttons and long trousers which were buttoned on to it. Dickens described it as:

> one of those straight blue cloth cases in which small boys used to be confined, before belts and tunics had come in, and old notions had gone out: an ingenious contrivance for displaying the full symmetry of a boy's figure, by fastening him into a very tight jacket, with an ornamental row of buttons over each shoulder, and then buttoning his trousers over it, so as to give his legs the appearance of being hooked on, just under the armpits.[55]

In fact, such suits came in a range of colours, not just blue, although the one illustrated in the image of the Mabie children (Colour plate IV) does actually happen to be blue.

Both genders wore dresses, usually, at least up to the mid-nineteenth century, over cotton trousers or 'pantalettes', and little boys might be as old as seven before they were 'breeched'. Boys' dresses, however, were usually of darker colours than those of their sisters, or of a pattern, like tartan, that was thought to be more 'masculine'. Children's dresses were relatively short, not ankle-length like those of their mothers, and girls wore mid-calf-length dresses into their early teens, but often that was the only concession to children's needs. Dresses were watered-down versions of those worn by the children's mothers, uncomfortably wide necklines and puff sleeves in the 1820s and 1830s, full skirts in the mid-century, dresses cut with 'back interest' to simulate the bustles worn by women in the 1870s and 1880s. (Figure 5.8) Boys continued to wear versions of the skeleton suit once they were breeched but, by the 1830s, they were often dressed in strange full-skirted and full-sleeved jackets or tunics over white or beige trousers. In the second half of the century, knickerbocker suits with belted jackets and plus-fours worn over thick stockings were the usual wear for boys from the age of about seven into their mid-teens. Certain other garments, like girls' pinafores and boys' sailor-suits, came to be particularly associated with childhood in the second half of the nineteenth century and, by the 1890s, knee-length dresses with smocked yokes, often in white, were worn by little girls and their toddler brothers. (Figure 5.9)

Some children's outfits were no doubt made at home or bought from their parents' dressmakers and tailors; but families were often large and buying children's clothes ready-to-wear from a shop made mothers' lives easier. Shop-bought children's wear was, of course, made by seamstresses, so directly or indirectly, the changing fashions in children's clothes created more work for home-based needlewomen.

Figure 5.8 Fashion plate from the *Revue de la Mode* of August 1881. The boys are wearing knickerbocker suits; the girls' dresses are similar to their mother's but shorter; the one worn by the youngest girl is loose-fitting, but her elder sisters' dresses are fitted and they may well be wearing corsets underneath them.

Figure 5.9 A photograph of the Fanning family from Newtown, Waterford City in Ireland, *c*. 1885. The young boys are wearing sailor-suits, their little sister wears a white coat with a big collar over a white dress, while the youngest child wears a dress, but with a 'masculine' braided waistcoat and jacket to show that he is a boy.

Conclusion

Throughout the eighteenth century both seamstresses and tailors made slops and ready-made clothing, though for the most part they stuck to their traditional gender-based roles, with tailors working in wool and heavy fabrics and making men's coats and breeches while seamstresses worked in cotton and lighter fabrics and made shirts and dresses. By 1800, however, many things were changing. The class structure was shifting, the lower middle class and upper working class created a growing demand for cheap, outwardly respectable clothing, even if the overall quality was poor. As a result, the tailoring trade divided into the self-styled 'honourable' sector, making traditional bespoke garments, and the 'dishonourable' sector making cheap ready-to-wear. There was considerable hostility towards the men in the 'dishonourable' category from their more fortunate colleagues who accused them of undercutting wages. Women were also beginning to make garments like waistcoats and breeches and parts of uniforms that had traditionally been made by tailors and they were paid even less than men so they, too, were deeply unpopular. The 'honourable' tailors' fears proved justified: wages fell across the sector as more and more ready-to-wear garments were produced; and, as the article in the *Northern Whig*, quoted at the beginning of this chapter, argued, the government and its cut-price contracts had played a major role in effecting this change, which started in the seventeenth century and reached rock bottom in the mid-nineteenth.

Even in the eighteenth century, almost any item of clothing and underclothing could be bought ready-made. Most drapers' inventories from the 1690s onwards show that their shops carried stocks of ready-to-wear clothing and, though much of this was intended for the cheaper end of the market, account books and letters tell us that from time to time well-to-do women also bought ready-made quilted petticoats, caps, accessories and some dresses, mothers bought clothes for their children and even titled gentleman bought some of their shirts off-the-peg.

As time went on, seamstresses began to make a wide range of other things, as well as the items described above, covers for parasols and umbrellas, cheap shoes and slippers, household textiles like sheets, pillowcases, table linen and towels, things which were sold in most drapers' shops. By the middle of the nineteenth century, if not before, it would seem that women had a monopoly of almost all types of slop-work, though the majority of slop-*sellers* were still men. Interviews with seamstresses in the nineteenth century show that there were women who specialized in the most unlikely of work, making convict's caps out of stout leather, for example, or assembling waterproof capes and coats.[56] The rise of ready-to-wear was unstoppable. Cheapness and convenience mattered to many but good quality, off-the-peg garments were increasingly available too.

Advertisements for drapers' shops and department stores in the last three decades of the nineteenth century show that by then it was possible to be clothed from head to toe in ready-to-wear garments. The term 'slops' might still be applied to shoddy, cheap workwear, but ready-made clothing was now respectable and most middle-class families would have bought at least some items. Many people did still have their clothes made to order by tailors and dressmakers, many women still made their own underwear, their babies' clothes and their husbands' shirts, but many did not. Department stores were key in the popularizing of off-the-peg garments, especially as most had workrooms where these purchases could be customized to fit. The items department stores sold were usually of good quality and their middle-class customers soon ceased to feel there was a stigma attached to buying ready-to-wear.

Nevertheless, as we have already noted, all garments that were available ready-made had been made somewhere by someone, more often than not a seamstress working in her own home for a mere pittance, and they were sold for considerably more than she would have received had she worked directly for the customer, so many seamstresses sank into poverty. Not until the 1840s did their plight come to the attention of the public, as we shall see in the next chapter, but it would be a good deal longer before any steps were taken to improve their lot.

6

'Seam and gusset and band'

Written in 1850, Charles Kingsley's pamphlet, *Cheap Clothes and Nasty*, echoed the *Northern Whig* in describing the role the government had played in debasing the tailoring trade and employing women as slop-workers, and he attributed the decline to the early 1800s. While Kingsley's depiction of the tailoring trade in this pamphlet, and in his novel, *Alton Locke* (1850), which is based on the same source material, has been much criticized,[1] in this passage he makes some relevant points through the testimony of a tailor:

> The government ... had really been the means of reducing prices in the tailoring trade to so low a scale that no human being, whatever his industry, could live and be happy in his lot. The government were really responsible for the first introduction of female labour. He would clearly prove what he had stated. He would refer first to the army clothing. Our soldiers were comfortably clothed, as they had a right to be; but surely the men who made the clothing which was so comfortable, ought to be paid for their labour so as be able to keep themselves comfortable and their families virtuous. But it was in evidence that the persons working upon army clothing could not, upon an average, earn more than 1s. 0d. a day.

He went on to list other government contracts, for police uniforms, postal workers and customs officials, all paid for at around one shilling or 1s. 6d. a day: 'Now, all these sorts of work were performed by time workers, who, as a natural consequence of the wages they received, were the most miserable of human beings. Husband, wife, and family all worked at it.'[2] Other bodies, like local fire departments and the various railway companies, also required quantities of uniform which were produced in the same way and at the same sort of prices. The larger the organization, the greater its bargaining power and the less the uniform makers were likely to be paid.

There were actually considerable profits to be made from the supply of uniforms, if not by the people who made them. For example, tenders survive in Kent Record Office for the supply of police uniforms to 'Worshipful the Mayor and Gentlemen of the Watch Committee' of Gravesend in 1836, just seven years after the establishment of the first modern police force in London by Sir Robert Peel. There were two tenders for supplying hats at fourteen shillings and eighteen shillings; these would, of course, have been top hats, domed police helmets were not introduced until 1865. There was just one quotation, from George Sunmore, for supplying the coat, trousers, greatcoat and cape, complete with buttons.[3] Admittedly the items would have taken upwards of ten yards of hard-wearing woollen cloth, but Mr Sunmore's price of five guineas contrasts uncomfortably with the 1s. 6d. Kingsley's informant claimed that the slop-workers would have been paid. (Figure 6.1)

'Grinders' and 'Sweaters'

Along with the government contractors, middlemen and middlewomen – the 'grinders' and 'sweaters' – were often portrayed as cruel exploiters.

Some seamstresses took work direct from shops; West End tailors and dressmakers 'put out' some work, usually finishing or jobs like skirt-making which could be done without access to the customer, but the majority worked for a middleman or woman who acted as agent for a shop or a wholesaler. These people acquired a reputation for callousness and greed.

The heroine of Reynolds' novel, *The Seamstress: or, The White Slave of England* (1853), Virginia Mordaunt, is supposedly a dressmaker doing outwork for a society milliner, Madame Duplessy. In the story Virginia delivers the dress she has made to a middlewoman, her neighbour, Mrs Jackson. She pays Virginia 3s. 6d. and then makes her take the dress to the next middlewoman in the chain, Mrs Pembroke. Mrs Pembroke gives Virginia seven shillings to pay Mrs Jackson and asks her to take the dress direct to Madame Duplessy, who, in turn, gives her fourteen shillings to pay Mrs Pembroke and asks her to deliver the dress to Madame Duplessy's customer, the Duchess of Belmont, together with the bill. Looking at the bill, Virginia notes in amazement that Madame had charged four guineas 'for making up'.

Reynolds' point is clear: at each step of the chain the profit increased and the person who actually did most of the work was paid the least. But the scenario he paints is highly improbable. First, a high-class evening dress of silk velvet, like the one he describes Virginia making, would not have been entrusted to an outworker; it would have been made in Madame Duplessy's workrooms and the client would have come in for at least one fitting before it was completed. While some cheap shops (those designated by Mayhew as

Figure 6.1 Tom Smith, a well-known London policeman, wearing the police uniform, with top hat, current in 1851. The uniforms Sunmore provided for the Gravesend police in the 1840s would have been very similar.

third- and fourth-class establishments which made garments for working men's wives) did put a good deal of work out, particularly skirts, this was not the usual practice in upper-class firms. Second, even those outworkers would have worked directly to the shop, not through two middlewomen. Third, while middlemen and women did profit from seamstresses' work, the amount of profit Reynolds assigns them is ridiculously high. Fourth, four guineas was an enormous sum for making up a dress, even a very grand one, in 1853, although that was not as extortionate as the £42 9s. the Duchess was charged in total! Reynolds' heart was in the right place but he knew too little about his subject matter to write about it credibly.

Middlemen's profits were often actually relatively modest. On 26 October 1843 the *Morning Chronicle* reported a case brought by a middlewoman:

> The applicant was a sort of contractor or needlewoman to a slop-seller, and got large quantities of goods to make up, giving security in a large amount for the safe return. On receiving them she gave out a portion to different people, for whose honesty she had security, and one of those people had, she had every reason to believe, pawned some shirts. In reply to a question by Mr Henry, she said that her contract for the shirts was three-halfpence each, and she gave them out to be done for five farthings, so that she made a farthing each profit.

The court agreed to send an officer to speak to the light-fingered needlewoman but would not issue a warrant for her arrest for reasons which will become clear later in this chapter.

In May 1858 the *Coventry Journal*[4] reported on a middlewoman receiving – and cheating on – a similarly modest profit margin. She had contracted to provide mantles for three shillings a dozen, out of which she claimed her workers would receive 2½d. a garment. In fact, they claimed she only gave them 1¼d., thus upping her profit from a halfpenny a garment to 1¾d. Even at that rate she would have had to give out many dozens of garments to make much of an income.

Admittedly, some middlemen did treat their workpeople very badly. A report in the *Dublin Evening Mail* in 1856, for example, described the trouble one woman, a widow with five children, had in recovering money that she was owed by a middleman who had recently employed her:

> on her depositing 10s., he allowed her to have four shirts [men's 'regatta shirts', a superior kind] to make at the rate of 6s. per dozen; the plaintiff finding her own needles, thread, candles and a place to work in. The plaintiff, having made the first lot, got four more, having to walk eight miles to fetch them, and being kept six hours waiting, declined doing any more, and demanded payment and the return of her deposit. After walking backwards and forwards, and, altogether performing a journey of 72 miles, she was told that only 2½d. a shirt would be paid to her, defendant and shopman maintaining she had agreed to make them for that sum.[5]

The court ruled in her favour.

Those running workshops, often referred to in the press as 'sweating dens', might make greater profits. In 1884, for example, a 'sweater' running a workshop with ten employees was estimated to earn £3 8s. 11½d. a day,[6] an improbably precise amount. Similarly, in 1889, the *Edinburgh Evening News* described men in tailors' workshops working fifteen-hour days for wages of eight or nine shillings a week, while the sweaters who employed them were making eight, nine or ten *pounds* a week 'for doing nothing'.[7]

However, a middlewoman interviewed in 1886 by the *Pall Mall Gazette*, claimed[8] to make just a halfpenny a pair on the slop trousers she put out.[8] She employed ten women and, if a pair of trousers took a 1½ hours to make, as one trouser-maker interviewed by Adele Meyer and Clementina Black claimed a few years later in 1909, working a six-day week of fifteen-hour days, each of her employees would have made around sixty pairs a week, giving her a weekly profit of £1 5s., very considerably less than the sum attributed to the workshop sweater mentioned in the previous paragraph.

The First Inquiries

Nineteenth-century society was deeply divided and class conscious. Country dwellers, often living in close proximity to their poorer neighbours, knew something about them, but respectable people in the cities were not interested in how the 'lower orders' lived and worked. Consumers knew little, and mostly cared less, about the people who made the clothes they wore, so they were oblivious to the increasingly impoverished state of most needleworkers. Not until the 1840s do we find any serious attempts to investigate the desperate state of the garment-workers and bring it to the attention of the public.

The first event of any significance was a meeting in November 1842 in Stepney of five hundred London shirtmakers. It had been organized by a local clergyman, the Reverend W. Allen, and Mr Cummings, a surgeon, who had recently dealt with a desperate patient who had taken vitriol to escape her life as a maker of sailors' shirts. She was paid just a penny a shirt, out of which she had to find a farthing for thread; working thirteen hours a day she could make just sixpence a day, or 3s. 6d. for a seven-day week. Sailors' shirts were simple, more like smocks than shirts, and did not require the elaborate gathering of the front and back pieces into the yoke and the sleeves into the cuffs and armholes. Thus, one could be made, by hand, in just over two hours. For making better-quality shirts, in other words, traditional ones with yokes, cuffs and full sleeves, women could earn sixpence, but such shirts took at least fourteen hours to complete. The meeting agreed that increasing payment to twopence apiece for the simple shirts would make an enormous difference to the workers' standard of living. A committee was set up to look into the issue, but there the matter seems to have ended.[9]

In 1843 the Children's Employment Commission reported on conditions in the dressmaking trade. Its findings were horrifying. The report contained a litany of complaints about long hours, unreasonable customers and callous mistresses, poor food and accommodation, illness and exhaustion. 'The evidence of all parties establishes the fact that there is no class of young people, living by their labour, whose happiness, health and lives, are so unscrupulously sacrificed as those of the young dressmakers and milliners. They are in a peculiar degree unprotected and helpless', wrote R.D. Grainger, the author of the report.[10] If he and his colleagues had interviewed seamstresses, slop-workers and shirtmakers, many of whom were also young, they would have uncovered even worse sets of circumstances. However, it is notable that Mr Grainger, like so many of the would-be reformers, saw women as being in need of protection. Earlier in the century women had been active members of the Chartist movement, agitating for improvements in pay and working conditions, but by the late 1840s and 1850s, for reasons that are not entirely clear, they were seen as incapable of agency and action, needing others to act on their behalf,[11] so that by the 1840s reformers focused on raising men's wages so that women would be less likely to have to work.

An informative article appeared in the London *Evening Mail* of 18 September 1843 which explained in some detail how, why and when things had deteriorated as they had for seamstresses and slop-workers.[12] A representative of Messrs Silver and Co., shirtmakers in Cornhill, was questioned about the low rates of pay shirtmakers received. Silver's employed 3,000 needlewomen and was the second oldest shirtmaking firm in the capital. The representative explained that in 1794 they had paid needlewomen between 2s. 4d. and 3s. 2d. for 'a full-fronted linen shirt'. Such a shirt probably took at least a day to complete, but even making just three shirts a week at the lower rate a woman would have earned seven shillings, not a king's ransom but a living wage, comparable to the weekly earnings of a male farm labourer.

In 1808 Silver's found demand for ready-made clothing was increasing and cotton shirts were beginning to sell better than linen ones. They then employed 'a Person' – in other words, a middleman – in Deptford who got cotton shirts made up at 1s. 6d. for a plain shirt and 1s. 10d. for a frilled one and who could supply them with between two and four dozen a week. This suggests that the middleman was subcontracting on Silver's behalf to about eight women, so it is possible he was running quite a small operation. Of course, if 1s. 6d. and 1s. 10d. were the middleman's prices, the women he employed would have got less.

However, things soon got much worse. In 1835, a year after the introduction of the new Poor Law, Silver's discovered that shirts were being made up even more cheaply in the workhouses and the company found it had to reduce its own prices accordingly. In 1840 Silver's had actually complained to the Board of Guardians of the City of London Union workhouses about the 'monstrously low' prices pauper women in the workhouses were receiving for making shirts (one penny for every *three* shirts), although, of course, these women were getting free board and lodging – of a sort – and were probably told they were lucky to be able to earn anything at all. Silver's much preferred to employ independent needlewomen but, at those rates, they could not possibly compete. At the time of the interview in 1843 they were paying tenpence a dozen for striped cotton shirts, 2s. 6d. a dozen for full-fronted printed cotton shirts, five shillings for plain white ones and ten shillings a dozen for better-quality ones; again, those would have been the prices paid to middlemen who would have taken their cut before paying their workwomen.

Another shirtmaker, Mr Davis in Stepney, also employed independent women to make shirts and claimed to be paying threepence a shirt where a few years earlier he had paid sixpence but, again, that would have been the middleman's price, not the worker's. The *Evening Mail* journalist also interviewed two shirtmakers: Anne Foreman said that, before she was forced to go into the workhouse herself, she had been getting ninepence for the sort of shirts which would have earned her 1s. 4d. before the introduction of the new Poor Law; while Harriet Rothwell said she was getting eightpence for shirts that in 1833 would have given her 1s. 9d. She added that 'a few months previously' 'a Lady' had offered to have her make a dozen shirts at 1s. 3d. apiece but withdrew the offer when she learned she could get the same shirts made at sixpence each in the workhouse.

The Causes of the Problem

It seems that there were several key factors depressing needlewomen's wages. First, needlework was one of the few trades open to the great army of widows, deserted wives and women without families to protect them. It was done at home and so was open to women who had caring responsibilities. It required very little in the way of equipment, just needles, thread and scissors, and there were no entry requirements, and as a result the trade was grossly oversubscribed.

There was no scope for a woman to negotiate higher rates for her work because there were plenty of others out there able and willing to take her place if she objected to the price she was being offered and, with women working from home for long hours and in isolation, cooperative action was all but impossible.

Second, the country as a whole was becoming increasingly prosperous and more people wanted, and could afford to buy, more clothes than ever before. Respectable outfitters, like Silver's, therefore increased production to keep up with demand. Increased demand could have been good news for seamstresses, meaning there was plenty of work for all, but working men wanted more new garments too and purveyors of cheap, ready-made clothes prospered. However, clothes that were to be sold cheaply also had to be produced cheaply. The sellers of cut-price goods could only afford to pay cut-price wages.

The third, and probably the most serious, factor depressing wages was, as the Silver's representative indicated, the new Poor Law of 1834. The problems began soon after it came into operation. To defray costs and provide the pauper inmates with useful work, workhouse after workhouse contracted to produce shirts and other slops at very low rates which they could do because they had an endless supply of captive labour; indeed, many workhouse inmates had once been independent needlewomen so they required no training. Even if they paid the pauper women a pittance, as the City of London guardians apparently did, most of the money that firms paid for the goods the pauper women made was pure profit for the workhouse. The *Hereford Journal* recognized the problem in 1843: 'As regards the horrible grinding-down of the workwomen by the slop-sellers and the ready-made linen shops, one means, we apprehend, of effecting an amelioration rests with the poor law guardians. They ought at once to prohibit the taking in of slop-work at the workhouses.'[13]

In November 1843[14] *Bell's New Weekly Messenger* listed the quantities of articles that had been made over the summer quarter in various workhouses. The pauper women in Wapping workhouse had produced 2,064 items for slop-sellers; those in St Georges-in-the-East had produced between eight and twelve dozen items a week; those in Bermondsey had made around 200 shirts and 1,100 other garments a week. A month later the same newspaper recorded approvingly that the St Pancras guardians had refused an offer to make shirts for 1s. 6d. a dozen; but most boards of guardians were less scrupulous, which inevitably had a catastrophic effect on the rates that could be offered to independent seamstresses in the community. Thus, we see shirtmakers outside the workhouse being paid as little as three-farthings a shirt.

The Distressed Needlewomen's Society was set up about this time to create a register of capable needlewomen, to train girls, to stand surety for goods placed with women to make up and, most importantly, to try to persuade workhouse masters not to undercut seamstress's wages.[15] A letter in the *Evening Mail* of 16 October 1844 excoriated the union workhouses: 'these establishments set up their capital and their machinery, and used the uncontrolled power which they possess over their inmates, in beating down to the lowest possible rate the wages of the independent workwoman. . . . By dint of this system, many hundreds of industrious women who abhorred the workhouse . . . were driven into it.'

Nevertheless, by the time the letter appeared, the matter was apparently already in hand. A deputation from the Distressed Needlewomen's Society had had a meeting with the Poor Law Commissioners that same month and they 'were pleased to express their anxious wish to afford all proper assistance to meet the wishes of the deputation'.[16] Eventually they did so. By 1850 the Poor Law Commissioners had indeed ordered the cessation of contract needlework in all workhouses other than work for the inmates, but the government had already turned to prisons as another source of cheap labour to make uniforms, with similar results.[17] A spoof letter from 'Sarah Jones' in the *Durham Chronicle* of 1848[18] purported to come from a needlewoman who was anxious to get into either prison or the workhouse so that she could be fed and housed while she sewed. It claimed that at Milbank Penitentiary sailors' jackets and soldiers' greatcoats were being made for a paltry 2½d. and 5d. apiece, respectively.

The Response

Nineteenth-century society was surprisingly ignorant about the various grades of garment-worker but it was not indifferent. People did not seek out information about the poor but, when that information was presented to them, the response was largely sympathetic. The 1843 Children's Employment Commission Report on Dressmakers and Milliners aroused considerable concern amongst the liberal élite and spawned a wave of novels, paintings, cartoons and, most influential of all, Thomas Hood's *Song of the Shirt*. We shall examine these responses in more detail in Chapter 10.

There were also some practical initiatives that tried to alleviate the needlewoman's lot. The best known was the Association for the Aid and Benefit of Dressmakers and Milliners which was founded in March 1843 with the aims of creating a register of employers and employees who met the Association's criteria, persuading proprietors to limit the working day to twelve hours, encouraging them to improve the ventilation in workrooms, urging ladies to place orders in plenty of time to avoid workers having to stay up late to complete them, providing financial support to workers who were temporarily unemployed and securing medical assistance for those who became ill.[19] Lord Shaftesbury chaired the Association and numerous newspapers reported breathlessly that Queen Victoria herself had donated £50 to its funds. However, despite royal patronage, and noble though its aims were, the Association had no legal powers to enforce its recommendations, nor did it ever have the funds to provide support to the many workers who needed it[20] and, in any event, most home-working seamstresses fell outside its remit.

It was a similar story elsewhere. We have already mentioned the Distressed Needlewomen's Society of 1844. While it did some good work and supported a number of women, it was dogged by allegations of misappropriation of monies and the questionable honesty of the Honorary Secretary, a Mr Roper,[21] and it finally folded in 1870. The Milliners' and Dressmakers' Provident and Benevolent Institution was founded in 1849 to offer financial and medical assistance to workers in need, so clearly the Association for the Aid and Benefit of Dressmakers and Milliners was failing to fulfil its objectives in this regard, but it too lacked funds, so many workers still became sick and destitute.

The Needlewomen's Institution was founded in 1860 with the stated aim of tendering for government contracts for army and navy uniforms. It offered women a 'fair rate of pay'; for example, it paid sevenpence a shirt, rather than the 3½d. – or less – that needlewomen got elsewhere, it provided workrooms which were lit and heated, supplied tea for the women working in them, and arranged for local clergymen to hold regular religious services. It also had a charity fund to help its needlewomen when and if they fell on hard times; most of their workers were women in the forty-plus age group. Like most of such charities, it was supported by donations and subscriptions, and for a time the institution was very successful, employing several thousand women at seven depots in different parts of London. Its annual expenditure ranged from £1,785 in its first year to over £13,000; in total, they spent £69,729 0s. 5d. over the nine years of its existence. It closed down in 1869 because the government changed its policy and transferred the making of military uniforms to soldiers' wives. At that point the institution still had cash in the bank which it used to provide accommodation for elderly seamstresses. A letter in the *Daily News* of 5 April 1869 from Ellen Barlee, a former superintendent, claimed that between 1860 and 1869 the Institution had supplied 300,500 shirts, 35,000 coats, 5,361 pairs of trousers, 111 jackets, 2,436 cloth coats, 10,400 seamen's overcoats, 100 blouses, 2,500 women's 'African frocks', 3,250 waistcoats, 650 'duck jumpers', 29,400 bolster cases, 29,000 'palliass' covers, 64,137 towels, 35,800 sheets, 338,072 biscuit bags and 61,000 other items for private employers. No small achievement, and just one indication of the huge market for seamstresses' work.

These societies were London-based but there were regional organizations too. In January 1843, for example, an article appeared in the *Cheltenham Journal and Gloucestershire Fashionable Weekly Gazette* pleading for the reinstatement of the local Provident District Visiting and Clothing Society, and for 'the price paid to needlewomen to be raised to its former standard', which, it claimed, would save at least two hundred Gloucestershire needlewomen from starvation or destitution.[22] A Kentish group to support destitute needlewomen was founded in December 1843;[23] while immediately after Christmas that year the *Dublin Evening Packet and Correspondent* appealed for funds and clothing for a newly-established Association for the Relief of Seamstresses which set out to provide accommodation and work for fifty seamstresses, and occasional work for fifty-three more[24] – but this was still only a fraction of the number of impoverished needlewomen in the city. The Glasgow Milliners' and Dressmakers' Association was established in 1861 but has left virtually nothing in the way of records. One of the longest-lasting of these provincial societies was the Liverpool Society for the Relief of Sick or Distressed Needlewomen which opened in 1858 and did not close down until 1941. However, in 1862 it helped just forty-two needlewomen and had an income from subscriptions and donations of just £120.[25] In January 1875 it claimed that 'a great deal of suffering had been alleviated' but, even then, the Society had given out just £148 6s. 5d., £91 in cash, £24 18s. 6d. in coal and £9 18s. in medicine. No doubt the recipients were grateful, but there cannot have been very many of them.[26]

The difficulty all these organizations faced was that the scale of the problems they were trying to solve was always going to be far greater than the resources they had at their disposal. The result was that conditions for most needleworkers improved little, if at all, and gradually public interest waned, only to be revived by the occasional reporting of tragedies and crimes.

Destitution

On 29 August 1844 readers of the *Devizes and Wiltshire Gazette* were shocked to read of the attempted suicide by drowning of two sisters, two of the four slop-worker daughters of an unemployed labourer on the London docks. They could make eight shirts a day each and earned 1¼d. (less the price of thread, so a penny) for each one. One of the girls was saved by a passer-by; she explained that her sister's desperation had been compounded by the fact that she had recently been fined three shillings, around three quarters of her week's wages, for quarrelling with a neighbour in the street, and that she had also borrowed money for rent and could see no way of repaying it.

Magistrates seem to have been peculiarly blind to the impossibility of destitute women paying the fines they imposed. A particularly egregious example of this was reported in March 1847 in the *Bury and Norwich Post*.[27] Six starving women had been convicted of stealing turnips from a farmer's field; one of them was a seamstress who stitched corsets for which she was paid a mere three farthings a pair. She could earn just sixpence a week – no wonder she was stealing food. Nonetheless, the magistrates fined her two shillings. We do not know the outcome but the likelihood is that she was imprisoned for failure to pay. At least prison food would have saved her from starvation.

Desperate poverty drove even honest individuals to steal. For example, in 1859 Sarah Dyer stole ribbon and braid worth just under a pound from Shoolbred's on Tottenham Court Road: 'She was a widow, and had borne a good character all her life [she was forty] for honesty, industry, and perseverance.' Ladies for whom she had worked owed her considerable sums of money – £10, £11 and £12 – and, despite her having been ill and requested payment, none of them had settled their bills. She had already been on remand for three weeks. The judge let her go without charge and the 'gentleman of the bar' had a whip-round and presented her with £2.[28] Sarah seems to have been a dressmaker rather than a seamstress, but her case does demonstrate the perils faced by the bespoke worker.

Destitute women who did not steal might indeed starve to death. For example, numerous newspapers reported in December 1846 that Louisa Mordaunt, a needlewoman, had died of starvation and her sister told a shocked coroner's court that Louisa and her mother had repeatedly been refused help by the local guardians. The doctor who had carried out her post mortem described her stomach as 'completely shrivelled up from lack of nourishment ... [and] empty, except for a portion of faeces about the size of a pea'.[29] Was it perhaps her case that persuaded Reynolds to give his 'white slave' the surname 'Mordaunt'?

Another seamstress, Mary Ann Stanton, died in March 1865 of an 'effusion of blood into the ventricles of the brain, brought on by want and long privation'. She lived on Bluegate Fields, Ratcliffe Highway, a notorious London slum, and made waterproof capes for a warehouse, sharing rooms with another seamstress

Figure 6.2 A slum street in Bluegate Fields by Gustave Doré, 1874.

who was similarly employed. Between them they earned four shillings a week, of which two shillings went in rent; most days they survived on bread and cups of tea, with a treat of 'bullock's cheek' once a month. Mary Ann slept on a pile of straw on the ground. One day she went to the pawnbroker to pawn her petticoat for which she hoped to get sixpence, but the pawnbroker refused it. She collapsed in the shop and was carried home where she died the next day. The report noted approvingly that, despite her extreme poverty, she had never applied for parish relief.[30] (Figure 6.2)

There were many similar cases and, although the papers usually recorded the women's paltry earnings as the cause of their deaths, this seems to have had little effect on either employers or the public.

Henry Mayhew

In 1849 there were further horrific revelations. Henry Mayhew was a campaigning journalist with a rackety past. He had run away to sea as a boy and served with the East India Company. He spent a period as a trainee lawyer in Wales and lived for almost ten years in Paris to escape creditors at home. He wrote a series of plays and potboiler novels. In 1841 he was one of the co-founders of the satirical magazine, *Punch*. Towards the end of 1849 he embarked on the work for which he is best-known, a survey of working-class life in London. This began as a series of 'Letters' in the *Morning Chronicle* which were eventually recycled as the three-volume, *London Labour and the London Poor*, first published in 1851 as histories of 'Those who work', 'Those who can't work' and 'Those who won't work'. Women were not the main focus of Mayhew's attention; he was more concerned with the plight of male artisans like tailors and shoemakers. Nonetheless, he is a valuable source of information about the plight of the seamstress. His style was racy and populist and he was a master of titillating detail.

Not surprisingly, therefore, one of his explorations of the world of the needlewoman focused on the widely accepted connection between seamstresses and prostitution.[31] To that end, he called a meeting in November 1849 of women who felt they had been forced into immorality. He and a fellow journalist concealed themselves behind a screen, ostensibly to preserve the women's dignity and privacy, and encouraged them to give accounts of how poverty had driven them to immoral behaviour. Twenty-five women attended and fourteen of them gave evidence. Of those, five admitted to prostitution in the twenty-first century sense of the word, but the remaining nine either lived, or had lived, with men who were their common-law husbands, or had been taken advantage of by a man who had left them pregnant. If they had then gone on the streets, they chose not to say so and, for the most part, their stories imply that they had not. In Victorian society, apparently, being an unmarried mother or living 'in sin' constituted immorality as gross as providing sex for money. Moreover, lack of a marriage certificate was sometimes also the result of poverty: one woman claimed that her man would willingly marry her 'the first day that he can afford; but he hasn't the money to pay the fees'.

Henry Mayhew had also written popular plays and novels and he understood his audience. His interviewees' stories were presented as mini-melodramas, complete with villainous workhouse masters, callous employers, cruel parents, faithless lovers, dead and dying children and many lamentations and tears of remorse. That is not to suggest that he fabricated evidence, but he almost certainly edited it; the women all come across as articulate, eloquent and coherent to an extent that is scarcely credible.

'I've been out in the streets three years', ran one such account:

> I work at the boot-binding but can't get a living at it. I went with Mr ... and another gentleman, who took me home to my father, but my father couldn't help me. If I get bread, sir, by my work, I can't get clothes. For the sake of clothes or food I'm obliged to go into the streets, and I'm out regularly now, and I've no other dependence at all but the streets. If I could only get an honest living, I would gladly leave the streets. But I can't earn enough at my work to get a living, and therefore I know it's useless returning to it. I've been out a whole fortnight together and not got a meal but what I got in the streets; and I've been forced several times to go into St George's workhouse.

The stories, harrowing though they were, also provided illustrations of human kindness; there was, for example, the landlady of two elderly seamstresses who 'never troubles them during the winter for the rent – never, indeed, asks for it. She is satisfied that they will pay it directly they can.' Grateful as the women were for the landlady's forbearance, they were constantly in her debt and struggling to pay off their arrears, with the result that their diet consisted almost entirely of oatmeal and water.

After recording the women's testimony in heart-rending detail, Mayhew's report continued:

> After having made these statements, they were asked what were their lowest earnings last week, when it appeared that four had earned under 1s. 0d., four under 1s. 6d., four under 2s., one under 2s. 6d. One woman said 3s. 6d. had been earned between two of them; another said she had earned 3s. 6d.; while a third declared she had not earned anything. Three said they had parted with their work for food. It was the unanimous declaration of the whole present, that if the meeting had been more generally known, several hundreds would have attended, who would conscientiously have made the same declaration they had done – that they were forced into a wrong course of life by the lowness of their wages.

Mayhew also interviewed a much larger group of needlewomen about their earnings and standard of living.[32] First, the married women were asked about their husbands' earnings; most of the men earned under ten shillings a week, some significantly under, while at least six had earned nothing for weeks. They were also asked about their rent. The majority paid between a shilling and 2s. 6d. and none paid as much as 3s. 6d. – but they were not asked how many rooms that covered or what, if any, facilities were provided.

Questions about clothing and food also elicited some telling replies: 'the very idea of having a change of garments appeared to excite a smile. One and all declared they had not, and most asserted that even those they wore were not their own.' They had borrowed from friends and neighbours to come to the meeting decently clad. 'The question, how many had meat every day for dinner seemed to these poor creatures an exquisite joke, and they laughed heartily on its being put.' Only those who had husbands or partners ate meat regularly and most of them only had it on Sundays. At the same time, forty-four women admitted to going without food for days at a time. Questions about pawning goods were also met with laughter. Nearly everyone present had pawned goods at one time or another; and fourteen of them had goods valued at under five shillings in pawn at the time of the meeting. Thirteen interviewees had even pawned their beds, twenty-six had pawned their underclothes and nineteen had risked prosecution by pawning their work.

Pawning work was a strategy that was much used. The needlewoman who appears in the section above on middlemen and women ('Grinders and Sweaters') and whom the court refused to prosecute was one of many. In August 1848, for example, Emma Mounser came before Lambeth magistrates' court accused of pawning seventeen shirts she had been working on for Moses and Son on Aldgate.[33] Her husband, son and daughter were all out of work, and she was earning just fourpence a day to keep them all, the proceeds from making two shirts at 2½d. apiece, less the cost of needles and thread. The Moses' representative blamed the pawnbroker who should have recognized that the woman did not own the shirts she was pledging, but the magistrates knew all too well that pawning completed shirts to survive while they worked on others was common practice among needlewomen. Emma was let off with a caution. The story did not end there, because, after reading about her case in the paper, a benefactor in Brighton sent her a half-sovereign. The Victorians were not all heartless.

It was the tragic stories of extreme hardship that hooked the reader in but, as well as being populist, Mayhew was also a good journalist: he provided statistics and facts and figures.

According to Mayhew there were some 33,629 needlewomen in London in the 1840s working in a range of trades; seamstresses, shirtmakers, slop-workers, stay- and corset-makers, stock- and tie-makers, straw-bonnet-makers, glovers, furriers, embroiderers, cap-makers, bonnet-makers, dressmakers and milliners, around 2,000 of whom ran their own businesses, and of whom roughly 28,500 were under the age of twenty.

Table 6.1 Mayhew's findings on prices paid per garment
(In all cases the worker had to provide thread and/or trimmings out of his or her earnings at a cost of between ¼d. and 2d. depending on the type of garment)

Garment type	Highest price paid per item	Lowest price paid per item
Shirt	5d.	¾d.
Trousers	1s.	1d.
Waistcoat	7d.	2d.
Blouse	5d.	2d.
Jacket	2d.	
Coat	1s.	5d.

Mayhew focused on London, but minimal wages were not confined to the capital. As a comparison, in July 1850[34] *The Advocate, or Irish Industrial Journal* carried an advertisement for Darby and Co., shirt-cutters and outfitters of Waterloo House, Great Britain Street, Dublin, featuring their 4s. 6d. shirts: 'Gentlemen feel surprised … and recollect what they have hitherto paid for similar goods.' To appease their customers' consciences, the company purported 'to keep in view to pay the needlewoman a fair proportionate price for her labour' – but, given that they also sold shirts priced between 1s. 6d. and 3s. 6d., that claim sounds very hollow. It was obviously catering for the lower end of the market.

Mayhew also interviewed a number of workers in their own homes, all of whom spoke of declining prices and changing conditions which affected their wages.[35] A stay-stitcher told him she could earn just three shillings a week (for nine pairs of stays at fivepence a pair, less the cost of thread and candles which she had to supply herself) where once she would have earned at least twelve shillings and had on occasion earned seventeen shillings. According to her, most stay-manufacturers sent work out to the countryside where people were even more desperate and would work for lower wages. She also claimed that stays were made cheaply by Greenwich pensioners who took them in by the bagful, another example of workers already supported by an institution undercutting independent seamstresses.

A cloak-maker claimed she was paid 1s. 3d. for cloaks which would previously have earned her five shillings and for mantles for which she used to earn 3s. 6d. An upholsterer blamed the recent cholera epidemic for keeping people away from London and preventing them from having their city homes refurbished as often as they used to. She claimed to be paid two shillings for a pair of curtains that would formerly have been five shillings, and ten shillings for 'furniture' for a four-poster bed that would previously have been one pound. These workers were probably telling the truth, but few of them indicated at what point in the past they had earned the higher sums they mentioned.

Perhaps the most detailed account of payments past and present came from a young woman who made men's neckwear; her information is shown here in tabular form:

This worker was eighteen and was the sole supporter of her parents: her mother, who could help a little but had problems with her sight and her health, and her father, who used to be a builder's carter but had had an accident and could no longer work:

> I struggle hard to keep him and mother from the workhouse.... [When he had his accident] I was up for three weeks. I never took my clothes off or went to bed for the whole of that time, so that I might support him and pay the doctor's bill ... now I find it very hard work to pay rent, support them, and keep myself respectable without doing as the other girls do. I've been obliged to part with nearly all my clothes to keep them. The doctor said he was to have port wine, and I used to have to give him two gills every day. If I hadn't got rid of my clothes, I couldn't have kept him alive. We have been obliged to pledge one of our beds for £1 as well. But I hope to be able to get on still.

Table 6.2 Prices paid for types of neckwear

Item	Description	Price paid per dozen	Time to make	Former price per dozen
'Albert' ties		6d.	18 in 12 hours	
'Opera' ties		9d. to 1s.	9 a day	2s. to 3s.
'Albert' stocks	Ones with sham pleats and a bow	1s. 9d.	12 in 3 days	3s. 6d. to 4s.
'Burlingtons'	Stocks without ends and with waterproof tops and bottoms to guard against perspiration	2s. 3d. to 2s. 6d.	12 in 3 days	5s.
'Napiers'	With long ends, hemmed both sides and with a knob in the middle	3s. 6d. to 4s.	18 a week	8s. 6d.
'Aeriel' ties	A new fashion	6d.	12 a day	1s. 3d. to 1s. 6d.
'Albert' scarves		9d.		2s.

This young woman was an employer in her own right, with one 'hand' to whom she paid three shillings a week, plus her tea (sixpenny-worth a week), and 'a little girl' who worked for free to learn the trade. In a good week she cleared six to seven shillings. She, too, had her theories about the state of trade. Her employer apparently put notices in his window, 'Hands wanted', to gauge how many unemployed seamstresses there were in the locality which would dictate how low he could set his rates; and most of the price drops she reported had, she claimed, come about in the preceding two months as a result of this policy. She was also adamant that of the fifty or so stock-makers who worked for the same employer, at least thirty were on the game: 'I know by their dresses that they do not get the gowns they appear in out of stock work.'[36] Mayhew praised her as an example of filial piety, but unless her father were to recover her future looked bleak.

Emigration[37]

Mayhew is much quoted, and his findings about pay and the results of extreme poverty are corroborated by numerous newspaper reports, although, like most campaigners then and now, he did focus on the most severe cases of hardship. Various solutions were proposed of which probably the most notable was Sidney Herbert's Fund for Promoting Female Emigration which was launched in December 1849 in the *Morning Chronicle,* in response to Mayhew's articles. On the face of it, it was a neat solution because there were more men than women in the colonies and Britain had an excess of women who could barely support themselves. However, there were many who disapproved of the scheme on the grounds that sending working people from their home country was 'pernicious' and that sending away the 'good, the chaste and the industrious . . . in order that the wages of the less industrious and the less chaste that are left behind may be raised above their present rate' was very unjust.[38] Nonetheless, the scheme went ahead. (Figure 6.3)

The trope of the industrious-but-starving needlewoman who might at any moment succumb to temptation and 'go wrong' was used as an image to raise money to support the scheme, although women who were not needlewomen could and did apply. Between 1840 and 1844 the fund assisted over a thousand women to emigrate to Australia, New Zealand, British North America and the Cape of Good Hope, but the numbers decreased over the next few decades. By 1850, a report in the short-lived London *Standard of Freedom* described a party of

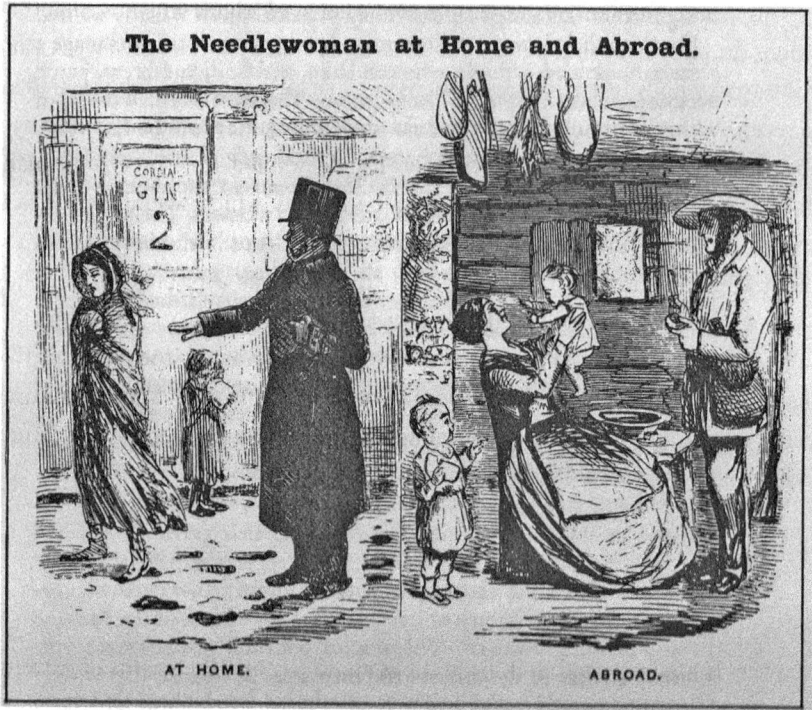

Figure 6.3 Cartoon from *Punch*, 1850. The magazine supported Sidney Herbert's emigration scheme.

sixty-one young women setting sail for Australia but noted that 'the desire to emigrate [is] no means so general as it was a few months ago...and less pressing.'[39]

The fund tried hard to safeguard the women on their journey and to make sure that those who emigrated were of good character. They were interviewed, had to fill in an elaborate form and provide numerous references and a medical certificate. They also had to provide themselves with respectable clothing from a prescribed list – six shifts, two flannel petticoats, six pairs of stockings, two pairs of shoes, two gowns, two pairs of sheets, sixteen towels, 10lbs of soap, a warm cloak or shawl, one bonnet, and a hair-brush and comb (far more items than any of Mayhew's interviewees could have dreamed of possessing) – and the fund gave them money to buy these. It also maintained an Emigrant's Home in Hatton Garden where the women were to stay 'on probation' for several weeks before sailing; and those whose behaviour gave cause for concern were not allowed to emigrate. A matron, surgeon and schoolmaster accompanied them on the voyage and they had to stay in an immigrants' depot on arrival. It all sounds very well organized, but the reality was often rather different. Despite having fulfilled all the criteria, once they were on board ship, the young women were often unruly, drank too much and caroused with the sailors; in other cases, the ship's officers took advantage of vulnerable young girls. Once they landed, the women were all too often prey to unscrupulous would-be employers. Some, undoubtedly benefited, and the fund published letters from women who had settled happily and were prospering to encourage others to apply, but the scandals piled up and eventually the scheme fell into disuse.

Conclusion

Concern about needlewomen was at its height in the 1840s as a result of various reports and inquiries; newspaper readers were given a glimpse of a whole other world, one at once distressing, shocking – and a little titillating. As we shall see in Chapter 10, novels and paintings fuelled interest and sympathy; weeping over the lives of Little Dorrit, Fanny, the 'Little Milliner' or Virginia Mordaunt, the 'White Slave', was cathartic and evidence of the reader's sensibility without the need for him or her to engage with a real poverty-stricken person. Paintings of seamstresses showed them as brave and beautiful, ground down by fate but not crushed by it, inspiring examples of human resilience as much as objects of pity. A donation to one of the numerous charities set up to support seamstresses eased many a conscience, even if the donors were still happy to buy cut-price underwear, shirts and sheets from their local linen draper.

Undoubtedly, the various charities did good work, but many of them were small and can only have helped a limited number of women, and many areas were not covered by any such organizations. Other charities only lasted as long as the enthusiasm of their founders endured, and yet others were ineptly managed. All were dependent on subscriptions or donations and there was never enough money to help all the women who needed it. Sidney Herbert's emigration scheme was widely publicized and, on the face of it, seemed an ideal solution both to the problem of low pay and the fact that Britain had a surplus of single women. However, seamstresses were not really what the colonies needed, they were not robust enough and did not have the skills in agriculture that were needed. No doubt some women settled happily, but the emigration schemes did not live up to their early promise.

The government's own policy of using the workhouses as a source of cheap labour had been a key factor in depressing wages for independent needlewoman and, although they eventually abandoned the policy, the damage was already done. Government needlework was then done in prisons and by soldiers' wives, again taking work away from seamstresses in the community, unbeknownst to most of the population. For the public, there was news of reforms, reports of good work done by charitable organizations and stories of happy emigrants and gradually, interest in the needlewomen began to fade as readers convinced themselves that the problems were being solved. Britain as a whole was thriving and people did not want to think too deeply about the poor and destitute. When a case of a needlewoman committing suicide, stealing food or starving to death came to light, it was now generally viewed as an isolated example or a case for individual charity.

In fact, all was not well. Only government intervention could have addressed the problem, but the government's commitment to the economic doctrine of *laissez-faire* and its reluctance to intervene between employer and worker meant that wages for a large swathe of the working population, not just needlewomen, were, and would remain, unsustainably low. The fact that needlewomen were female, and that women's wages were seen, quite illogically, as less necessary than men's, worsened the problem. While acts were passed to attempt to regulate factories and workshops, the idea of regulating what outworkers were paid for working in their own homes was a step too far for most politicians, and so an army of seamstresses continued to live in poverty.

'Society came and shuddered'

There was another brief flurry of interest in seamstresses in the mid-1860s. In summer 1863 a young woman named Mary Anne Walkley, employed by the élite dressmaking firm, 'Madame Elise' on Regent Street (owned by a Mr and Mrs Isaacson), died in her sleep. It came to the notice of the public because one of Mary Anne's colleagues wrote to *The Times*, and for a short period she was something of a *cause célèbre*.[1] However, the interest was short-lived. The Children's Employment Commission produced a second report on the dressmaking trades in 1864[2] and discovered that conditions in the trade had improved little, if at all, since 1843, but this report did not create anything like the outpouring of literature and art that had followed its predecessor. The public had had its fill of poverty porn.

Meanwhile, a new technological development had come into being that had major effects – both positive and negative – on the lives of seamstresses.

The Sewing Machine

In July 1853 numerous newspapers carried articles heralding the technological invention: 'The patent sewing-machine promises to produce a revolution in the business of the seamstress as great as the power loom effected in that of the weaver.'[3] That October, needlewomen making cloaks and mantles for Messrs Charles Nicholson of St Paul's Churchyard in London went on strike in protest against the introduction of sewing machines by their employer.[4] However, this was something of an anomaly; the machines were still a novelty at that date and were comparatively little used. They were not readily available in the UK until the middle years of the decade and were not bought in any quantity before the mid-1860s. (Figure 7.2)

In Northampton, when sewing machines were introduced into boot and shoe manufacturing in the early 1860s, workers went on strike; a futile protest which

THE HAUNTED LADY, OR "THE GHOST" IN THE LOOKING-GLASS.

MADAME LA MODISTE "WE WOULD NOT HAVE DISAPPOINTED YOUR LADYSHIP, AT ANY SACRIFICE, AND THE ROBE IS FINISHED A MERVEILLE"

Figure 7.1 Cartoon by Tenniel from *Punch*, 4 July 1863, entitled 'The Ghost in the Looking Glass'. It was inspired by the case of Mary Anne Walkley.

resulted in the loss of jobs as many firms relocated to Leicester. Another effect of the increased use of the machine was the establishment of workshops and in 1869–72 seamstresses in Dublin took action in protest. They had preferred working in their own homes, seeing themselves as self-employed; when work moved into workshops, they became 'just employees'. Their protest was not primarily about the use of machines, it was focused more on conditions in the workshops; and they took the highly unusual step of orchestrating a campaign of writing letters to Dublin's *Freeman's Journal*.[5] The campaign was not of itself very effective, but it did demonstrate that women could organize when they wanted to. Overall, however, there was remarkably little hostility to the introduction of machines.

In theory, sewing machines should have speeded up the production of clothing dramatically. It was estimated that a worker could create thirty-five stitches a minute by hand while the machine could make upwards of 1,000, but the early machines were temperamental and not particularly easy to

Figure 7.2 Engraving of a sewing machine demonstration at the Paris *Exposition universelle* held on the Champs-Élysées in 1855. A functional sewing machine had been invented in the United States in the 1840s but the machines were still a novelty in 1855.

manoeuvre when it came to the trickier parts of a garment. The earliest ones were chain-stitch machines, and the seams they created had to be finished by hand because otherwise a tug on the loose end of the thread would cause the whole seam to unravel. They were superseded by the lock-stitch machine in the 1860s: it used two interlocking threads which obviated the unravelling problem; a version of the system is still in use today. However, different makes of machine still had their own peculiarities and, when firms advertised for machinists, they advertised for workers who had experience of the particular brand of machine they used. This meant that factory and workshop machinists were seen as skilled workers and thus received higher wages than hand-sewers – around twelve shillings a week as against the hand workers' six shillings.

Not until the 1870s were machines in general use amongst slop-makers. Most workers bought their machines on hire purchase – Singer had introduced the system in 1856 – and by 1888 the firm employed thirty collectors in the East End alone who visited purchasers to collect their weekly payment instalments of 2s. 6d. Other manufacturers followed suit, some offering rather lower rates. There was, however, no protection for women who fell behind with their payments. If that happened, their machine would be repossessed and there would be no refund of any of the money they had already paid. For a time, the Jewish Board of Guardians purchased machines and ran their own loan scheme to avoid this happening.[6]

The Labour Aid Society, which was founded in 1886, also came up with a scheme to help. Machines could be bought on hire purchase but a deposit of ten shillings was required before the manufacturer would release the machine, and the weekly payments thereafter were expensive for women whose earnings seldom exceeded five shillings. The society appealed for funds so they could negotiate with manufacturers to provide machines without a deposit, to reduce weekly payments to sixpence a week, to take the machine back if the worker fell behind with her payments but to keep it for her until she could resume them and, then, at the end of three years, to allow her to keep the machine.[7] However, it is not clear whether this scheme ever came to fruition; it would have been an enormous boon to seamstresses if it had.

For most seamstresses the machine had become a necessity by the 1880s, but its cost, plus the cost of oil, machine needles and repairs came to be yet another drain on needlewomen's meagre earnings.

'Outcast London'

Needlewomen only became a focus of attention again for most people in the mid-1870s as what was known at the time as the 'Great Depression', the first truly international economic crisis, began to take effect. It had begun in 1873 in Vienna with the collapse of the Austro-Hungarian Stock Exchange and had worldwide repercussions, most noticeably in Europe and North America. By that point, Great Britain's economic and industrial supremacy was starting to be challenged by Germany and the US. The decline was particularly apparent in the iron and steel industry: in 1870 Britain supplied 43 per cent of the world's steel, by 1913 she supplied just ten per cent, but other industries were affected too. The economic situation was exacerbated as a series of poor harvests drove up the price of bread and, as wages in the countryside fell, more and more country people moved to the towns in search of work.[8]

Jewish immigrants fleeing pogroms in Eastern Europe also arrived in large numbers in the 1880s and 1890s. Pogroms had always been a fact of life for Jews in the Russian Pale of Settlement, but they intensified in frequency and ferocity after the assassination of Tsar Alexander II in 1881, which was blamed on a Jewish group. As a result, between 1881 and 1915 an estimated 150,000 Jewish refugees arrived in the UK, settling mainly in London, Leeds and Manchester. Many more passed through on their way to America and elsewhere. By the mid-1880s the established British Jewish community was providing support to the newcomers, setting up a Temporary Shelter in Leman Street for those who arrived without any contacts in the UK, establishing their own Board of Guardians in the East End and developing a wide range of other charitable initiatives.[9]

The poorer parts of cities, and especially London's East End, thus became increasingly overcrowded. Slum clearances had actually worsened the situation by forcing the truly poor into the surviving dilapidated tenements. The 1880s saw a growing awareness – and fear – amongst the middle classes of the existence of a large, impoverished, supposedly degenerate and immoral underclass, living in appalling conditions and increasingly separate from mainstream society. The fact that the two classes seldom crossed each other's paths made the desperately poor all the more frightening.

In 1883 the Reverend Andrew Mearns produced a sensationalist penny pamphlet entitled *The Bitter Cry of Outcast London* that fuelled these fears. Much of it was concerned with the fact – guaranteed to shock respectable middle-class Victorians – that few slum-dwellers ever attended a place of worship, but it also described their insanitary, overcrowded, ramshackle dwellings. He related how whole families lived in a single room sleeping on piles of straw or bare boards, some sharing their accommodation with livestock, their living conditions made even worse by the types of labour taking place in so many homes: foul-smelling glue used in assembling boxes, animal dander from fur-pickers, dust and grime from rag-picking.

The Lancet followed this up with its own inquiry which laid the blame for overcrowding and low wages squarely on Jewish immigrants and caused so much concern that the Board of Trade despatched its own labour correspondent, John Burnett, to the East End to report on conditions. In fact, Burnett only spent one day in the East End, and his report relied very heavily on Kingsley's 1850 pamphlet. He, too, lambasted Jewish employers for paying poverty wages and Jewish employees for accepting them and thus, he argued, lowering the wages for all workpeople, immigrant and native-born alike.[10]

In 1888 *The Lancet* also reported on the spread of illness through garments made in tenement rooms where some of the inhabitants were ill. Mayhew had highlighted the risk of this in 1849, Kingsley presented it as a recognized fact in *Alton Locke* and it was claimed that Sir Robert Peel's daughter died of a fever that was traced back to the family of the tailor who had made her a new riding habit.[11] There is some evidence that scarlet fever might be passed on through infected clothing, and typhus would have been a genuine risk if the item was infested with lice, but other illnesses like typhoid, cholera and smallpox could only be transmitted if the garment was heavily soiled. The likelihood of diseases being transmitted through clothing thus seems to have been rather exaggerated though there were probably rare examples.

At around the same time as these concerns were being raised, Charles Booth was pursuing his enquiries into working-class life in the East End. Booth was a wealthy man, a partner in a Liverpool firm of ship owners. He was also attracted to radical politics and, after he moved to London in 1875, he developed an almost anthropological curiosity about life in the slums. In 1886 this led him to attempt a proper survey of urban poverty and he recruited a group of volunteers to help him. One of these was Beatrice Potter, who later married a fellow volunteer, Sidney Webb. Booth's volunteers had a deeper understanding of conditions in the East End than either Charles Kingsley or John Burnett and they rejected the assertion that the influx of foreign labour was the cause of all the problems in the garment trade. It would, however, be some years before their opinion was generally accepted. Booth's enquiries resulted in the enormous seventeen-volume series, *Life and Labour of People in London*, volume one of which appeared in 1889. Unlike most authors who regarded a pound a week as the bare minimum on which a family could live decently, Booth's findings were less optimistic. He set ten shillings a week as the poverty line; he only counted households earning less than that as truly poor – but he did discover that there were a great many of them.

Initiatives to Help

Seamstresses – or many of them – were amongst the poorest of the poor, many earning considerably less than ten shillings a week, but they worked in a trade that could be seen as 'womanly' and decent, and there were numerous piecemeal attempts to help them. In July 1884, for example, the *Pall Mall Gazette* reported that a Mrs Heckford, who had a shop on Shadwell High Street, had set up a Working Women's Co-operative with £500 collected from like-minded friends.

Her workers worked for a maximum of eight hours a day and she paid them a fair price and sold the goods they made in her shop.[12] Her enterprise was much applauded but it can only have helped a few dozen women.

Two years later, in 1886, the Labour Aid Society was established. It set out to create a register of employers who would pay fair rates and, where that failed, to encourage emigration to the colonies, and it supported both men and women from a whole range of trades. As we have seen, one of its specific objectives for needlewomen was to help them acquire sewing machines. The society also attempted to set up a cooperative of needleworkers, something that already existed in the form of the London Cooperative Clothing Manufacturing Society, and which many saw as the best solution to the problem of poverty wages. However, the biggest obstacle to setting up cooperatives was organization. Needlewomen worked in isolation in their own homes or with one or two family members. They had no leisure to attend meetings; many were barely literate or had no access to printed matter; and the sweaters who employed them were hardly likely to keep them informed about the formation of cooperatives. 'The most potent weapon in the hands of men-workers, combination, does not reach them', wrote W.H. Wilkins in the August 1893 edition of *The Nineteenth Century*: 'This isolated position, the long hours, the under-feeding, the scanty wages crush out any spirit they may possess, and with them, resistance becomes impossible.'[13] He was not entirely correct but well into the twentieth century many working women resisted joining trades unions for similar reasons. Kathleen Woodward in *Jipping Street: Childhood in a London Slum* (1928) wrote:[14]

> the women in the factory were too tired for the revolt urged upon them, too deeply inured to acceptance ... the[y] continued stonily to eye the preachers of revolt ... too palpably unblemished by the experience that was ours. Yet I do not think their insufficiency proved so great an obstacle as the subscription fees to the Trade Union from women to whom even two pennies a week represented a loaf of bread.

For women with hungry families to feed, immediate need always had to trump possible benefit at some point in an uncertain future.

Most support groups were therefore purely philanthropic. The Dublin-based Ladies' Committee for the Relief of Distress in the Western Islands was active in supporting needlewomen and finding them work, and reports of their activities and funds appeared regularly in *Freeman's Journal*. On 5 April 1886, for instance, they reported that they had provided work for 359 needlewomen for a period of weeks and that the women had earned all of five shillings a week apiece; better than the earnings of many of their sisters in London, admittedly, but still barely a living wage. The committee was entirely supported by charitable donations and, although these amounted to thousands of pounds, they were never enough. Dublin also had a Ladies' Association for Employing Seamstresses and one for Clothing the Western Islanders, all of which were subsidiaries of the Mansion House Relief Fund. Nonetheless, most needlewomen in the Irish capital still struggled to make ends meet.

There were various small local initiatives too. For example, the grandly named Society for the Improvement of the Condition of the Lower Classes established a lodging-house with rooms for 123 seamstresses at the subsidized price of one shilling a week in 1850;[15] and on 5 October 1884 *Lloyds Weekly Newsletter* recorded the formation of a Workgirls' Protestant Society. Others set out to address small parts of the problem. In 1888, for example, the *Daily News* reported the creation of a 'Spectacle Mission' in Maida Vale. Applicants had to produce a letter of recommendation from a doctor, clergyman or other respectable member of the community and suitable spectacles would then be provided free of charge; 'This special form of philanthropy is directed chiefly towards printers, seamstresses, tailors, shoemakers, and others whose occupation necessitates clear vision.'[16] It was founded by a doctor whose own career had been impacted by his poor sight. In 1896 726 pairs of spectacles were provided.[17] However, the number of East End needlewomen who had heard of the mission and were able to make their way across town to Maida Vale was probably small.

The Select Committee on the Sweating System

In March 1888 the government finally felt pressured into instituting an inquiry into sweating and set up a committee chaired by Lord Dunraven. The Select Committee on the Sweating System (SCSS)[18] lasted for two years and early in 1890 produced a fifty-page report, with harrowing testimony from workers and details of poverty wages. However, the Committee's methods and findings were deeply flawed. Numerous trades were excluded. Workers were unwilling to come forward because the committee only paid one day's wages to interviewees and, crucially, was unwilling to indemnify them against the risk of being sacked if their employers found out they had given evidence. As a result, the SCSS enlisted Arnold White, a journalist, to find sweated workers for them and his bias was very much anti-immigrant so the witnesses he came up with all blamed immigrant workers and employers for their situation. He was, for example, careful to dismiss the evidence of three women who worked for Moses and Son, slop-tailors, because he claimed Mr Moses – a Jew – lied about the wages he paid. Arnold White was not alone in his hostility to Mr Moses, as we shall see in Chapter 10.

Only twenty-eight female garment workers, out of a total of 291 witnesses, were interviewed and these included a number of women who only worked part-time as seamstresses, as well as one middlewoman and two social investigators, one of whom was Beatrice Potter. She, too, had her biases. She blamed the 1878 Factory and Workshop Act because it excluded home-workers and thought the solution was to extend it to cover them. This, she believed, would make outworking unprofitable and force employers to provide civilized conditions in workshops or factories, even though, despite the best efforts of the factory inspectors, dire conditions still prevailed in many such workplaces. She also argued that the women were their own worst enemies because they would accept work at any price. In a Fabian Society tract of 1896, *Women and the Factory Acts*, she later argued:

> The real enemies of working women are not the men . . . but the 'amateurs' of her own sex. So long as there are women, married or unmarried, eager to take work home, and do it in the intervals . . . of domestic service, we shall never disentangle ourselves from the vicious circle in which low wages lead to bad work, and bad work compels low wages.

Like so many middle-class investigators, she failed to understand that for the individual and her family, the result of refusing poverty wages would be destitution.

The report was debated for several days but was ultimately rejected. In February 1890 the press reported that the committee had blamed the introduction of machinery, the minute division of labour which enabled relatively unskilled individuals to be employed but limited their ability to change jobs, the 'depressing effect' of foreign immigration, the decline of the apprenticeship system and the growing demand for cheap goods. They had recommended the extension of the number and powers of factory and sanitary inspectors and the compulsory registration of all workshops employing more than two people; presumably that would have applied to, for example, a mother and daughter working together at home. It had also recommended the development of technical education in industrial schools.[19] Unfortunately, the recommendation for an increase in government oversight of the relationship between employer and worker was a bridge too far for most Conservative MPs who were heavily wedded to the economic doctrine of leaving the market to find its own level. Lord Thring, another member of the Committee, undertook to produce a watered-down version of the report, but this, too, failed to meet with their lordships' approval.

There were several other attempts to get the findings accepted and in May 1890 the SCSS produced its fifth and final report. This time a good deal of space was devoted to the definition of sweating; some believed that long hours and low wages constituted sweated labour wherever the worker actually worked, others believed it had to be labour sub-contracted through middlemen or women. While this time the report acknowledged that some trades were very much the preserve of Jewish immigrants from Eastern Europe, it recognized that others were not. The report therefore absolved the immigrants from creating the sweating system but did suggest they were 'thrifty and industrious' and willing to work harder and longer, and accept lower wages, than their English counterparts. The fact that Jewish workers who fell on hard times were supported by charitable organizations within their own community, so 'seldom or never come on the rates', was also noted with approval. Overall, however, the report pandered to comforting nineteenth century preconceptions by suggesting the poor were to blame for their own misfortune: they married too young, had too many children and willingly accepted a low standard of living. It also suggested that women working at home were prepared to accept lower wages than men because they were not the sole breadwinners, totally ignoring the numbers of widows, deserted wives and orphan girls who had to support themselves and their families because there was no male breadwinner to do it for them.

In so far as the report suggested any remedies, it fell back on the old chestnut of 'cooperation' but without any suggestion as to how this was to be achieved. It did, however, try to address the issue of government contracts, though with limited success:

> Proposals have been made as follows: First, to insist on the observance of the conditions now commonly annexed to such contracts, which hitherto it has been no-one's duty to enforce – namely, that the work should be done in factories; and secondly, a proposal has been made by Mr Nepean, the Director of Contracts, to bind contractors not to pay less than a specified minimum rate of wages approved by the department,

and it specifically mentioned that this applied to municipal and other public bodies. However, the proposals had little effect.

Overall, no one was satisfied with the enquiry, not Lord Dunraven, not Lord Thring, not their lordships who had authorized the committee, and certainly not the workers whose lot it failed to ameliorate. As a sop to popular opinion, new Factory and Workshop Acts were passed in 1891 and 1895, but they were inadequately enforced and had little impact. Nonetheless, the problem was not going to go away.

More Initiatives and Inquiries

In 1889, even before the SCSS report was submitted, there had been moves to set up an Anti-Sweating League. However, this came to nothing as various people – notably the bishop of London – refused to join until the SCSS reported and, when it did, the fact that the bill was rejected, discouraged the formation of such a league for over a decade. Numerous new local initiatives were being established, however, like the British Needlewomen's Self Help and Training Institute, established in Newcastle in 1887,[20] the Tailoresses' and Needlewomen's Workrooms,[21] the Hampstead Charity Organisation, the Catholic Needlework Guild and the Women's Help Society.[22]

There were other initiatives aimed at addressing the problems of working women in general. The Women's Protective and Provident League was founded in 1874 and was replaced by the Women's Trade Union League (WTUL) in 1889. The WTUL's secretary, Clementina Black, moved the first successful equal pay resolution at the Trades Union Congress in 1888, although the motion was never acted upon, and she also campaigned widely for the extension of protective legislation for women workers. Other all-female organizations, like the Cooperative Women's Guild (1883) and the Women's Industrial Council (WIC), were established. The WIC was founded in 1894 by a group of socialist feminists with the aim of making the public more aware of sweated labour. They also – from 1899 – tried to persuade the government to copy the American system of licensing home-work and agitated for minimum wage legislation. They were followed by the Women's Labour League in 1906 and the Fabian Women's Group in 1908. The impetus for change thus came from groups that were largely middle-class and, though well-meaning, did not always fully understand the problems they were trying to solve. However, most of them, to quote Clementina Black's words at the inaugural meeting of the WIC, were committed to 'special and systematic enquiry into the conditions of working women'.

Some of these 'systematic enquiries' became books which give us an insight into the lives of some individual needlewomen. Mrs Carl (Lady Adele) Meyer and Clementina Black published *The Makers of Our Clothes* in 1909 and Clementina Black published *Married Women's Work* in 1915. A collection of letters from cooperative guildswomen was finally published in 1931, edited by Margaret Llewellyn Davies, as *Life as We Have Known It*, and Maud Pember Reeves' *Round About a Pound a Week* of 1913 looked at working people's budgets and how they managed on low wages. There were investigations into the condition of the working class in provincial centres, too. Seebohm Rowntree's 1901 study of York, *Poverty: A Study of Town Life* is the best known but there were others, like

Eglantyne Jebb's 1906 *Cambridge: A Brief Study in Social Questions*, Lady Bell's 1907 description of the poor in Middlesbrough entitled *At the Works: A Study of a Manufacturing Town*, and the diaries of John Gent Brooks and Joseph Dare, Unitarian 'Domestic Missioners', in Birmingham and Leicester, respectively.[23]

Some newspapers did their own mini-surveys. For example, in 1886[24] the *Pall Mall Gazette* published an article entitled 'How they live in Common Street Commercial Road', a three-page, house-by-house survey of some fifty dwellings on the east side of the street and of their inhabitants, complete with details of the rent they paid, what they did and what they earned. There were 450 inhabitants in the fifty houses, roughly two families per house, and 175 of them were children. Each house entry had a title like 'Never out of work', 'A hard struggle', 'The fault of the foreigner', and, not surprisingly, eleven of the inhabitants were seamstresses and one was a middlewoman employing ten hands. All struggled to get enough work and their earnings ranged between 4s. 6d. and six shillings a week. For those interested in the lives of the poor, there was no shortage of material.

From our point of view, *The Makers of Our Clothes* is by far the most useful source. It was published in 1909 and described research undertaken in the previous year. 'It should be invaluable to politicians and to the large number of persons whose conscience is disturbed by the problems of poverty and underpayment', ran the advertisement for it in the *Westminster Gazette*.[25]

Its published findings were the result of numerous interviews, carried out by a group of volunteers. The interviewees were often selected by church workers or by members of the Women's Co-operative Guild and, probably as a result, most of them seem to have been highly respectable. '[O]f our twelve months' work, the essential virtues of the woman worker – her patience, her industry, her marked sense of fair play – stand out very clearly', Meyer and Black wrote in their introduction. Only one of the women they interviewed admitted to having given up needlework in favour of prostitution; she had earned three shillings a day making underwear – actually a reasonably good rate of pay – but she claimed to have given up sewing on health grounds![26] Several had trained as dressmakers or tailors in the West End and were highly skilled, but had resorted to home-working for health or domestic reasons. Some continued to do outwork for West End firms, but this brought its own set of problems. One worker explained that she would be fined two shillings if anything she had done had to be altered back at the shop, even if it was as minor as repositioning a hook and eye. If she was ever late with her work and the firm had to send someone to her to collect it, she also had to pay the 1s. 6d cab fare.[27]

Carrying work to and from the workshop or middleman who supplied it was time-consuming and ate into the women's working week. (Figure 7.3) One, 'Mrs W', had explained that her husband, who was unable to work himself, collected and delivered her work:

> He is paralysed, but in order to save her time he carries her work to and fro. An hour each way does this poor crippled elderly man spend going with his bundle to the factory and back, and all that he and his wife ask of the world is sufficient work at sufficient pay to enable them to live on in their present way.[28]

Sympathetic though they were, Meyer's and Black's volunteer interviewers were middle-class women with their own sets of prejudices:

> Not a hundred yards from Mr. and Mrs. W., on the outer edge of this depressing district, lives Miss P., also a home worker and also a tailoress. The conditions of her life, however, differ in every way from those of theirs. Her home, which she shares with a brother and sister, is clean and comfortable; her person and dress are neat and immaculate, she speaks carefully and with a good choice of words. . . . The two sisters work together at waistcoat- making, and, when visited, were engaged upon garments of a sort of corrugated stuff that simulated knitting. They put in the front pieces, bind these and the armholes, and make the three pockets. For this they are paid 9s. 0d. per dozen, they providing machine and cotton. Her machine was purchased long ago and has never needed repairing; cotton costs slightly less than fourpence for a dozen waistcoats. Work is fetched and returned twice a week, the sisters undertaking the journey alternately and paying fourpence each time for fares. On the previous day, working together from 9.30 to 7.30 the sisters had earned 7s. 6d., or 3s. 9d. each. . . . Their work is performed in a clean, comfortable and quiet room, the rent of . . . each tenant being thus 3s. 0d. a week. If the two sisters, instead of working at home were obliged to go into their employer's factory, the fares of each would amount to 2s. 0d. a week. Thus to these two worthy women it would be a real injury if homework were to be abolished.[29]

Such stories are telling, but the discursive manner in which the book is written makes it quite difficult to keep track of who earned how much for what, so some of the findings are summarized in tabular form below. The rates of pay varied widely. To an extent, these reflected the skill of the workers, as some of those working for tailors and dressmakers had had three or more years of training, and also related to the type of material being used, but the status of the employer was equally important. Interestingly, some workers claimed that rates of pay had actually fallen over the preceding few years, despite the interest and outrage

Figure 7.3 'The Slaves of the Sweaters', an illustration from *Harper's Weekly*, January 1890, showing women and children carrying piles of garments to the sweaters who employed them. They are in New York City, but British slop-workers would have had to carry equally cumbersome bundles of clothing.

generated by the Sweated Industries Exhibition two years earlier. While, clearly, earnings for many women were still appallingly low, Meyer and Black were even-handed in their reporting and the picture that emerges is not uniformly bleak.

There is some evidence to suggest that by the 1890s manufacturers were finding it less easy to recruit the number of workers they required, partly because the scale of manufacturing was increasing. Up to then, word of mouth had been sufficient but in the 1890s advertisements began to appear in the press. In 1891, for example, a firm in Cork advertised: 'Wanted immediately fifty needlewomen; must be competent to do plain sewing well; good pay; constant employment.'[30]

Table 7.1 Prices from Meyer and Black, *The Makers of Our Clothes*

	Lowest rate per item	Highest rate per item	Rate per dozen	Lowest weekly wage	Highest weekly Wage	Time per item	Where made
BLOUSES							
				5s.	£1		Factory
			4s. (silk)			3 a day	Home
			2s. 6d.–3s. (plain)				Home
	5d. (evening)	2s. 6d.			15s.	2 hours	Home
Blouse finishing			6d.			6 per hour	Factory
BUTTONHOLES							
Buttonholes	1d. large ½d. small						Home
Buttonhole machinist					16s. 6d.		Workshop
			½d.–¾d.	7s.	8s.		Factory
CHILDREN AND BABIES							
Smocking front and sleeves of children's dresses	3d. (cotton)	6d. (silk)					Home
Long robes			2s.				Home
Long petticoats			1s.				Home
Short petticoats			9d.				Home
COATS							
Tweed coats	5½d.	11d.				2 hours	Home
Long alpaca coats		1s.				3 hours	Home
'FROCKS' for officials (government contracts)							
	2s. 1d. (prison contract)	6s. 6d.			18s.		Home
SHIRTS							
					16s. 6d.		Workshop

(Continued)

Table 7.1 (Continued)

	Lowest rate per item	Highest rate per item	Rate per dozen	Lowest weekly wage	Highest weekly Wage	Time per item	Where made
	¾d.–2½d.		9d.–2s. 6d.		10s.–12s.	24 at 9d., 8 at 2s. 6d. in a day	Home
	2½d.–2¾d.		2s. 6d.–2s. 9d.			12 a day	Home
	2d.–4d.		2s.–4s.		8s. 9d.	6 a day	Home
Shirt finisher	7½d.					80 minutes	Factory
SKIRTS							
Skirts – high quality				4s. 6d.	8s.		Workshop
				8s. 6d.	16s.		Home
Skirts – wholesale				5s.	25s.		Home
Shop worker doing skirt alterations				18s.	£2		Workshop
TROUSERS							
Men's drill trousers	4½d.					1½ hours	Home
Men's khaki trousers			1s. 9d.				Home
Trousers	10d.	1s. 9d.		5s.	10s.		Home
Boys' flannel knickerbockers	1¼d.					½ hour	Home
Machine made					2s. 3d.– 3s.		Workshop
UNDERWEAR							
Petticoats	5d. (silk etc.)	7d. (silk etc.)	3s.– 4s. 4d.		15s.–£1		Home
Scalloping petticoat frills by machine			1½d.			1 hour	Workshop
Chemises and drawers			2s.– 3s.			18 a day	Home
Camisoles			2s. 9d.				Home

(Continued)

	Lowest rate per item	Highest rate per item	Rate per dozen	Lowest weekly wage	Highest weekly Wage	Time per item	Where made
Knickerbockers (with insertion)			1s. 9d.				Home
Nightgowns	1½d. (plain flannelette)						Home
WAISTCOATS							
Waistcoats	3d. (machined)	5s.–5s. 6d. (less 1s. 6d. if pockets machined)	9s.				Home
	4½d.				11s. 3d.		Workshop
Dress waistcoats		7s. 6d.					Workshop
Tweed waistcoats		4s. 9d.					Workshop
Waistcoat finisher				6s. 6d.			Factory

S. Flint in Marlow advertised in the *South Buckinghamshire Standard* in February 1893 for '100 good hands, wanted immediately'.[31] In the *Nottingham Journal* of 29 September 1899, C.S. Walker of Marygate in Nottingham advertised for machinists to make ladies' shirts and blouses, 'good wages and bonus paid monthly', while several other local firms also wanted machinists: Copestakes on Houndsgate needed women to make caps, neckwear, aprons and pinafores; Hills on Plantagenet Street advertised for experienced machinists and learners; and Bancroft's on Bath Street wanted machinists to do frilling.[32] A trawl through newspapers of the 1890s will yield many similar examples.

The Sweated Industries Exhibition and Its Aftermath

A major catalyst for change seems to have been the Sweated Industries Exhibition[33] of 1906, financed by the *Daily News* under its Quaker owner, George Cadbury. It came at a propitious time. A Liberal government had come into power that year and contained a number of MPs who were sympathetic to the issue of sweating and anxious to address the social problems that came from old age and poverty, and an Earnings and Hours Commission had recently been established to look into wages.

The exhibition opened in London in May and then toured the provinces. Forty-five home-workers, mostly women, agreed to take part in the exhibition so long as the *Daily News* paid their wages and agreed to support them if they were victimized by their employers. They took their places in the exhibition, doing the work they normally did at home, in front of the visitors and alongside displays of the goods they made and placards detailing their weekly budgets. Few of the workers earned more than a penny an hour in an average week. There were lectures by celebrities of the day like Ramsay Macdonald MP, George Lansbury, Clementina Black, George Bernard Shaw and Will Crooks MP, himself the son of a seamstress mother who had supported the family when his father became disabled, and the sweated workers themselves appeared alongside the speakers and answered questions.

Articles in the exhibition *Handbook* described each of the trades. Shirts were still being made incredibly cheaply (at one shilling a dozen for boys' shirts and 1s. 3d. to 1s. 5d. a dozen for men's) and this included finishing and buttonholes and the women supplying their own thread. (Figure 7.4) There were mini-biographies of workers, often unflattering. Mrs D., for example, was the wife of a labourer and the mother of three small children under the age of six: 'This family occupied two rooms, both filthy in the extreme and almost destitute of furniture. In this case, as in many others, the shirts on which the mother was engaged would, it is absolutely certain, be used as bedding for the family at night.'

The family budget for another shirtmaker and her small daughter was also included. Of the six shillings a week that the mother earned, two shillings went on rent, threepence on coal and just 2s. 4½d. on food – tiny quantities of tea, sugar, flour, oatmeal, margarine, bread, onions and vegetables, with ham worth 2½d. and half-a-dozen 'chipped' eggs supplying the only protein in their diet.

Waistcoat-makers fared slightly better. Cheap waistcoats were paid for at eight to ten shillings a dozen out of which a shilling's-worth of thread and buttonhole silk had to be found by the worker. Nonetheless, given that each waistcoat took two to three hours to complete, the worker's hourly rate was still only 2½d. Workers making 'first-class' waistcoats, however, it was stated, could earn up to £2 10s. – but for a seventy- or eighty-hour week.

The most disturbing discovery for many of the visitors was that it was not only cheap items that were made in sweated conditions. Along with the 'first-class' waistcoats for West End tailors, the trimmings for dresses made in upmarket establishments and the boxes that contained luxury goods, like chocolates and wedding-cakes, were made by workers in their own insanitary homes. Nor were all the workers unskilled. Female visitors would have

Stall XVII.   Worker No. 33.

Description of Work ...	**Chemise Making.**
Rates paid	2d. each.
Worker's outlay for thread, &c. ...	6d. weekly (and sewing machine to be kept in repair).
Time lost in fetching and returning work	Journeys, 1 hour weekly, *but 5 hours weekly lost in waiting.*
Average working day	14 hours.
Average earnings	2/- per day.
Regular or intermittent work ...	Fairly regular, but in slack season can only earn 4d. a day.
Retail price of article	Unknown.
Worker's Rent...	5/3.
No. of Rooms	Two.

Process.—Has to cut out and make entirely.

Remarks.—Worker is married; 2 children. Her husband is out of work.

Stall XVII.   Worker No. 34.

Description of Work	**Making Ladies' Fancy Aprons.**
Rates paid	1/8 and 1/10 per dozen.
Worker's outlay for thread, &c. ...	2d. per dozen.
Time lost in fetching and returning work	Half a day *twice* weekly (also fare).
Average working day...	14 hours.
Average earnings	" Worker must earn 18/- per week, and so works long hours; does not stop for meals and gets help at home."
Regular or intermittent work ...	Intermittent.
Retail price of article	1/6 to 1/11.
Worker's Rent	4/-.
No. of Rooms	One.

Process.—See Stall.

Remarks.—A particularly quick worker, who has done all kinds of machining, both well paid and badly paid.

(138)

Figure 7.4 A page from the *Handbook of the 'Daily News' Sweated Industries Exhibition*, held in October 1906, showing the earnings, expenditure and time spent collecting and delivering the completed goods of two workers who gave demonstrations at the exhibition.

understood the labour involved in garment-making, but they would not necessarily have been aware of the skill involved in making artificial flowers or covering tennis balls, for example; while even carding buttons or making boxes, at speed, required a degree of manual dexterity. Lists of exhibits appeared at the end of the exhibition *Handbook*, together with details of the hourly rates paid to their makers and information about how they managed to live on those wages.

The organizers stressed the risk that goods made in dirty conditions might transmit infectious diseases and also the dangers for the country of allowing what they saw as 'racial degeneration', caused by the fact that families whose members had suffered overwork, poor nutrition and slum living conditions for generations did not produce healthy offspring. This had already been recognized in the low standard of physical fitness of recruits to the Boer War and would resurface a few years later when the First World War broke out.

The impact of the exhibition nationwide was profound. Eyes were opened. A National Anti-Sweating League was established, dedicated to securing a legal minimum wage, and in 1907 a Select Committee on Home Working was set up. This tackled the issue of low wages across the board, in factories and other workplaces as well as for outworkers, although it is clear that there were still many problems to solve. On 1 May 1908, for example, the *Morning Chronicle* reported an interview the Committee had had with a Miss Holden. She worked at home, machining women's costumes, and could make three a day by working long hours. The one she showed the committee members had earned her 1s. 1d. but her wages' book showed she had been paid 1s. 3d. for nine similar ones and 1s. 4d. for six others. She earned thirteen to fourteen shillings a week but this was not all profit: she had to provide her own cotton, her machine needed oiling, repairing and new needles and she paid another woman twopence a costume for putting in linings and sewing on hooks and eyes. She was asked why she worked for a middlewoman rather than going direct to the factory; she replied that factories would not give out work in manageable quantities. To a question about setting up a cooperative with other workers, she said simply, 'I do not know any colleagues whom I could ask.' Like so many women, she worked in isolation.

Finally, in 1909 the first trade boards were created.[34] Their aim was to set a minimum wage, though this was not to be a national standard but the lowest amount needed for subsistence, based on what it was thought a particular trade could stand, and related to the age and gender of the worker. The first trade boards were experimental and only covered four trades, chain-making, box-making, tailoring (bespoke and ready-made) and lace finishing. Boards for shirtmaking, tin-box-making, sugar confectionery and food processing were added in 1913. The criterion for establishing boards was that the industries they represented should be ones where wages were 'exceptionally low compared with those in other employments'. Nonetheless, the effect on women's wages was limited as the boards preserved the traditional differential between men's and women's wages and, although women were represented on those boards for trades with a large female workforce, it was seldom the workers who sat on the board, the places were taken by confident, educated middle-class women who tried to represent them.

The boards' importance lay not so much in what they achieved, which was extremely limited, but in the change in attitude they represented. *Laissez-faire* was no longer the government's guiding economic principle, intervention to regulate wages was at last deemed possible. They also showed what organizing workers could achieve and were a stage in the long, slow process of encouraging women to unionize.

Conclusion

Conditions for seamstresses improved little in the second half of the nineteenth century. Society lost interest in them for a while and, when the focus returned, it was found that conditions were as bad – or worse – than ever. The arrival of the sewing machine had wrought significant change; it brought benefits to some, but extra expense to others, and, overall, conditions for seamstresses in all parts of the trade continued to deteriorate through to the early years of the twentieth century. Various bodies and individuals expressed concern, but there was little agreement about the causes of the problem or how it should be addressed. It is also important to understand that attempts to improve matters for the working poor in general were driven as much by fear of a largely unseen and little-understood underclass – and the 'racial degeneration' their existence was thought to threaten – as by charity.

The government was eventually persuaded of the need to look into the problems of low wages and sweated labour and the Select Committee on the Sweating System was set up in 1888. It was dogged by controversy about what sweated labour actually was and its methods of inquiry were deeply flawed and relied on interviewers who were strongly biased. Despite two years of inquiries, its findings were never fully accepted and it proposed no useful solutions to the problems it had investigated.

Instead, a new selection of charitable organizations and initiatives was established in the last quarter of the century, alongside a range of bodies that sought to improve conditions for women in general, and working women, in particular, not just for needlewomen. These groups were largely the preserve of philanthropic middle-class women – and some men – who were well meaning, but did not always fully understand the problems they were trying to solve or the people they were trying to help. However, through their numerous investigations and reports, many of which were eventually published in book form, it became clear that a large swathe of the working population was, through no fault of its own, unable to earn a living wage.

The Sweated Industries Exhibition of 1906 played a major part in bringing this to the attention of the public, in publicizing long hours, dire poverty and hunger and in highlighting the shocking and insanitary conditions in which so many lived and worked and the risks these posed to people who bought the goods they made. The workers emerged as real people, albeit ones battling against insuperable odds, and gradually public opinion began to swing in their favour.

The newly-elected Liberal government of 1906 recognized that action was necessary and, inadequate though they were, some efforts were made to improve wages through the wages boards and a programme of reforms and innovations – like old age pensions – began to improve the lives of the most disadvantaged. A global conflict in the form of World War I changed the dynamics between worker and employer, and between women and work, at least in the short term. Gradually, an understanding grew that society as a whole had to accept some responsibility for the poor. Change came slowly and wages in the garment trades remained – and remain – low, but the days of workers receiving a penny an hour or three-farthingss a shirt were coming to an end.

8

Bespoke needlework

On 9 February 1850 the *Illustrated London News* carried an article entitled 'The Needlewoman'. 'Shirts by the thirty thousand are made at twopence-halfpenny each'; it ran:

and, in the meanwhile, no needlewoman, distressed or other, can be procured in London by any housewife to give, for fair wages, fair help in sewing.... In high houses and in low, there is the same answer. No *real* needlewoman 'distressed' or other has been found attainable.... Imaginary needlewomen, who demand considerable wages, and have a deepish appetite for beer and viands, I hear of everywhere; but their sewing proves too often a distracted puckering and botching.... Good sempstresses are to be hired in every village; and in London, with its famishing thirty thousand, not at all, or hardly.

If the number of advertisements in the nineteenth-century press for ladies' maids and companions, housemaids, parlourmaids, nursemaids and even barmaids, all of whom were explicitly required to be 'a good needlewoman', is any guide, needlewomen were in short supply in most provincial towns and cities as well as in London.

So why was this the case when so many needleworkers were starving and destitute? It is unlikely that the underpaid shirtmakers and slop-workers really 'botched and puckered' their sewing; middlemen were ever anxious to find reasons not to pay their workwomen what they were owed and they would not have accepted poor work. The simple fact was that needlewomen who lived, and in many cases had grown up, in slum conditions, did not have any of the other attributes that would have made them employable as servants. They did not know how to set tables, make beds, black grates or do any of the myriad other tasks required of a house-servant because they had never done them or seen them done; their own homes lacked tables and table linen, their beds lacked sheets, many rented rooms in the slums lacked grates. Most of the women did not even have respectable clothes in which they could attend interviews and few of them would have seen, or been able to read, advertisements in the newspapers.

The gulf between them and the women who might have been willing to pay for their sewing skills was all but unbridgeable.

That is not to say that there were no needlewomen working in the bespoke trade. As in the previous century, there were women who worked directly for individual clients, others who did bespoke work for shops and yet others who did needlework as part of their duties as servants, but, while these women might have become slop-workers if they fell on hard times, the trade saw little mobility in the opposite direction.

Unfortunately, the low wages paid in other branches of the needlework trades and the increasing availability of cheap ready-made goods, combined to depress wages for the bespoke seamstress. Various articles and letters in the press urged housewives not to economize on the money they paid for needlework; in the *Newry Telegraph* of 17 September 1840, for example, under the heading 'Advice to Wives' came the plea, 'I beseech you not to extend your economising to the wages you pay to seamstresses or washerwomen.' Similarly, in March 1842, the *Reading Mercury*[1] printed a letter from 'P.P.' excoriating ladies who underpaid their seamstresses. 'I fear', it ran, 'ladies seem only to calculate how much can be done for them, and at the least possible expense to themselves – so that the poor seamstress has only a choice of evils, either to accept the pitiful sum offered her, or lose all chance of employment.' Some readers may have heeded these strictures but, overall, rates of pay for bespoke needlework continued to decline.

Lady FitzHerbert

Lady FitzHerbert provides a case in point. She lived at Tissington Hall (Figure 8.1) in Derbyshire and in the 1830s and 1840s she employed Ann and Sarah Alsop as needlewomen, though whether she offered a 'fair rate of pay' is open to question. Anne Alleyne had married Sir William FitzHerbert in 1836 and they had ten children. Table 8.1 shows a range of the items the Alsops made for the family and the payments they received.[2]

'Turning', often known as 'turning sides-to-middle', meant cutting the item in half, seaming what had been the outer edges together and hemming the raw edges. It gave the item a new lease of life by moving the central, thin, worn part of the sheet or cloth to the edges and putting the less worn part in the centre, albeit with a central seam which on a sheet was uncomfortable and on a tablecloth rather unsightly.

Figure 8.1 Tissington Hall in Derbyshire, home of the FitzHerbert family, 2009.

'Marking' meant embroidering a motif and/or initials. *The Workwoman's Guide* of 1838 devoted a whole section to explaining what marking should look like and it was not as easy as one might suppose:

> In marking, two threads are generally taken each way. There are three ways in which the needle is passed before the stitch is perfect. One is aslant from you towards the right hand; the second is straight downwards towards you; the third is across from you or aslant towards the left hand, taking care to bring out the needle at that corner of the stitch nearest the one you are going to make. The generality of markers make the first stitch aslant twice over to make it clearer before proceeding onwards.[3]

Each letter had to be embroidered separately and the thread should not be carried over between letters. Various stitches could be used and there was a sampler showing how they were to be worked. The mark had to include the owners' initials, ideally it should also have initials to describe the item, e.g. 'G C' for 'glass cloth', and a number from one to however many similar items the family owned. Markers certainly earned their penny (or less) an item, although it has to be said that most surviving items are not as fully marked as *The Workwoman's Guide* decreed they should be.

At tenpence each the Tissington Hall baby's bed gowns of 1837 were probably the most expensive items in the list below and may well have been tucked and embroidered as befitted clothing for the family's firstborn, and many of the other

Table 8.1 FitzHerbert commissions

Date	Item	Price
1837	6 baby's bed gowns	5s. 0d.
	2 baby's nightgowns	1s. 0d.
	10 'slops'	2s. 0d.
	4 tablecloths	1s. 6d.
Unknown	Repairing 3 shirts and altering 2 petticoats	1s. 6d.
Unknown	Turning and hemming 12 pairs of fine sheets	6s. 0d.
	Ditto 11 pairs of coarse sheets	4s. 7d.
	Turning and darning 8 tablecloths	1s. 6d.
	Making 6 new cloths	2s. 6d.
	Making 2 tray cloths	4d.
	Making 5 flannel petticoats	1s. 0d.
Unknown	Making 1 pair of sheets	1s. 0d.
	Making 9 flannel petticoats	3s. 0d.
1841	Making 1 dozen 'chamber towels'	2s. 0d.
	6 napkins	9d.
	6 kitchen cloths	1s. 0d.
	6 'jack' towels	6d.
	9 knife cloths	9d.
	5 tablecloths	2s. 6d.
1841	10 shifts	17s. 6d.
1842	Frilling a night shift, adding 2 gussets, making 24 napkins, making and marking 24 cloths, repairing 2 shirts, making 2 shifts, making 6 pillow slips out of 4 large ones, marking 7 pairs of sheets, making 7 pairs of drawers, making 3 pairs of crib sheets and marking 6 pairs	Plus -
1842	Turning and repairing 8 tablecloths (18d.), making 9 flannel petticoats, making 7 towels, turning 2 pairs of fine sheets, repairing 1 shirt, making 2 night shifts and 2 flannel petticoats, turning and repairing 2 tablecloths (6d.) and 1 coarse sheet (3d.)	Total 16s. 10d.
1842	Making 3 sheets	1s. 3d.
	Making 3 pairs of crib sheets	10d.
	Making 1 flannel dressing gown	8d.
	Making 6 flannel petticoats	2s. 0d.
	So presumably she got a 3d bonus on this order!	Total 5s. 0d.

shifts and petticoats listed were probably child-sized, but, nonetheless, Lady FitzHerbert was paying derisory wages, less even than the parsimonious Earl of Gainsborough in Rutland paid his seamstresses back in the mid-1760s.[4] Indeed, the overseers of the poor in some villages were more generous than she was. At Sandhurst in Kent, for example, they paid four shillings for a pair of flannel drawers in 1802, 1s. 2d. apiece for shifts in 1824 and 3s. 6d. for a 'round frock' in 1830.[5]

However, while the few pence that the Alsops earned per item made or repaired is similar to the sums earned by city shirtmakers and slop-makers, their circumstances were entirely different. Both women lived in Tissington village, both were in their fifties and both were married to farm labourers; their husbands were probably related. The 1841 census does not record Ann as having any occupation so Lady FitzHerbert must have learnt by word of mouth that she could sew, probably from one of the Tissington Hall servants. Sarah, on the other hand, worked as a washerwoman and the trades of seamstress and washerwoman often went hand in hand. For women like Ann and Sarah, doing occasional work for Lady FitzHerbert eked out their husbands' wages and allowed their families to live a little bit more comfortably; no doubt there were many countrywomen like them. Their position was nowhere near the same as that of unmarried or widowed seamstresses in the cities struggling to pay rent and survive on poverty wages.

Henry Mayhew – Again

In 1849 Mayhew interviewed women who earned their living in the city as bespoke needlewomen, working both for shops and for private customers, and he submitted his findings to the *Morning Chronicle* in a series of letters. In 'Letter IX' to the *Chronicle*, 16 November 1849, he wrote of one lady that he could: 'tell by the regularity of her features that her family for generations past had been unused to labour for their living, and there was that neatness and cleanliness about her costume and appearance which invariably distinguish the lady from the labouring woman'. Interviewing gentlewomen was something of a novelty for Mayhew but he knew his readership; he was writing for respectable, class-conscious readers and he probably shared their prejudices despite his undoubted sympathy for his working-class subjects. The 'lady' needlewoman told him:

> Since Wednesday myself and my daughter have made one flannel Jacket and just upon four night caps; that's all, and they will come altogether to 2s. . . . Latterly I've had no work at all, only that which I got from an institution for distressed

needlewomen. They were children's chemises. I think I made seven. . . . I did the seven chemises in a fortnight, and got 7s. for them. I have also within this time made one dozen white cravats for a shop; they are the wide corded muslin cut across, and the very largest. I have 6d. a dozen for hemming them and had to find the cotton, of course. I have often said I would never do any more of them, I thought they would never have been done, there was so much work in them. Myself and daughter hemmed the dozen in a day. It was a day's very hard work. It was really such very hard work I cried over it, I was so ill and we were wanting food so badly. That is all that myself and daughter have done this last month. During that time the two of us (my daughter is eighteen) have earned 6d., and 7s., and 2s., making in all 9s. 6d. for four weeks. . . . I have not been constantly employed all month. . . . But there is a great difficulty in getting work – oh yes, very great. The schools injure the trade very greatly. Ladies give their work to the National Schools, and thus needlewomen who have families to support are left without employment. That, I think, is the principle cause of the deficiency of work . . . also the cause of the price being so low.[6]

This lady claimed to be the daughter and granddaughter of army officers and the sister of a clergyman. Her husband had also been in the army but had died some years before, leaving her with three children, two daughters who lived and worked with her, and a seventeen-year-old son who was in the West Indies and 'doing well'. She hoped to receive some support from him in the near future. Her husband had been of Spanish extraction and she and the daughters spoke Spanish and French – she urged Mayhew not to put that in his article as it would identify her and: 'I would rather starve than have it be known who I am.' He seems to have forgotten or ignored her request.

He described her room. It was bare, save for two chairs and some trunks which served as tables, but 'was at least untainted by the *atmosphere* of poverty'. He was 'no longer sickened with that overpowering smell that always hangs about the dwellings of the very poor' and recorded diligently how many items she had pawned (including her bed, bedding and underclothes) and how much she had received for them. A bible and prayer book were prominently displayed on the mantelpiece – a detail calculated to win the readers' approval – while a 'lady of high rank' was paying their rent. Nonetheless, the family were starving and the needlewoman said she had chewed camphor and drunk warm water to stay her hunger and as a result suffered severely from flatulence. No detail was ever too intimate for Mayhew to omit.

Another gentlewoman he interviewed was unmarried and 'had been reduced from a position of great affluence and comfort to one of absolute want', but 'you would hardly have believed, from the neatness of the room in which she lived, and the dress of the lady herself, that you were in the presence of one absolutely in want of bread'. She was Eurasian and her family had lost an enormous £140,000 when Ferguson's bank in India failed, just a matter of days after her father's death, leaving the family penniless. Her mother and artist brother lived abroad and she had to support herself.

'I do any plain work I can get', she said:

I make chemises, children's drawers, nightcaps, shirts, petticoat-bodies, etc. . . . I am a good needlewoman and nothing comes amiss to me. I get for chemises 1s. 3d. if they're plain; and if there's much stitching, 1s. 6d. For children's drawers I have about 6d. or 8d. per pair; nightcaps fulltrimmed [*sic*] about 10d.; petticoat bodies about 1s. 0d. There's a great deal of work in a petticoat body. If they're trimmed I get 1s. 6d. for them. For hemming pocket handkerchiefs I get ½d. a side and 1d. a side for towels. I work usually for private hands, and they, knowing my case, give me a better price than the shops would. Oh dear yes, decidedly better. Last week I had two petticoat bodies; those I made from Friday to Wednesday, and earned 3s. in three days. Everything was found for me – cotton, tapes and all; but generally speaking I have to find those myself.

She also made money by sending items to 'the bazaar' – doilies, antimacassars, a dressed doll – but claimed that in the five or six years she had been a needlewoman she had never made more than five shillings a week and usually made about 2s. 6d., mainly because there was so little work to be had. She, too, blamed the schools.

These two ladies fitted the stereotype of the gentlewoman-fallen-on-hard-times, familiar to Mayhew's readers from numerous novels and paintings, but, in fact, she was a comparative rarity. Most needlewomen came from much humbler backgrounds.

Other Case Studies

By the nineteenth century, seamstresses were the poor relations of the clothing trade. They appear in account books, but less frequently, and usually with less detail of their work than was accorded dressmakers, milliners and tailors. The goods they made – underwear, shirts and baby linen – were quite often made at home or bought ready-made; only the old and infirm, the hard-pressed mistresses of large households, the philanthropic and the really wealthy who saw utilitarian needlework as being beneath them put much work out to seamstresses. Some seamstresses also made handkerchiefs, caps and aprons, but the fancier

Figure 8.2 Two seamstresses at work in a tenement attic in Elizabeth Street, Manhattan, *c.* 1890. British seamstresses lived and worked under similar conditions. Photograph by Jacob Riis from his book, *How the Other Half Lives: Studies among the Tenements of New York* (1890).

versions of these were quite often entrusted to milliners who were felt to have more 'taste', so references to such items in account books have to be treated with caution. As in previous chapters, this section will examine a handful of case studies.

(i)   In the early years of the nineteenth century, the Grey family of Dunham Massey in Trafford, in what is now Greater Manchester, patronized Mary Dean, a seamstress.[7] We do not know whether she was local, or someone they employed on their numerous visits to London. The Greys were wealthy and they spent heavily on clothes; in 1814, for example, Lady Amelia Grey spent an enormous sixteen guineas with the court dressmaker, Madame Sarel in London, on a dress trimmed with flowers and ribbons. Mary Dean seems to have run a shop as well as making up linen; in the early 1800s she charged the Greys £9 1s. 1d. for flannel, linen, tape and making twelve petticoats (for £1 4s. or two shillings each), eight caps (ten shillings), eighteen pairs of stockings (six shillings) and six pairs of pockets (nine shillings). She sold a range of fabrics, not just cottons and linens, but woollens like 'blue shag' and cashmere. A couple of years later she charged £5 2s. for handkerchiefs, stocks and shirts; eighteen shirts cost £3 18s. (4s. 4d. each), twenty-four stocks came to £1. 4s. (one shilling each) and eighteen handkerchiefs were 10s. 6d. (sevenpence each). As these prices do not seem to have included the cost of the fabric, Mary's charges were actually quite high.

(ii) Lady Langham's clothing account book for 1845 to 1855 is in the Northamptonshire Record Office.[8] She was the sister of the politician, Sir Francis Burdett, and the wife of Sir James Langham, 10th Baronet of Cottesbrooke in Northamptonshire and Langham House in Middlesex. She had married in 1800 at the age of twenty-two, and by the time her account book begins she was sixty-seven and a grandmother. She had given birth to eleven children and by 1845 had buried six of them. Lady Elizabeth Langham died in 1855 – her account book ends half-way through that year – so it gives us a picture of her expenditure in the last decade of her life, but even then she was spending a lot of money on clothes. It would be interesting to know how much she had spent when she was in her prime.

We do not know who Lady Langham's seamstress was, the account book sometimes lists the garments made and the price paid and sometimes simply records a lump sum to 'Sempstress'. She spent a considerable amount with linen drapers, presumably on fabric for the seamstress, and maybe her servants, to make up. We do not know where she shopped, but the fact that she made regular purchases from a 'Linen draper' every August (see Table 8.2) might suggest she made an annual trip to London.

The accounts are quite frustrating. They are neatly kept and very legible, but Elizabeth seldom tells us how much fabric she bought or how many items her entries refer to.

Like most old ladies, caps were an important part of her attire and some of them were probably made up by her seamstress. A cap cost her ten shillings in April 1846, for example, and a net one cost 10s. 6d. two months later. A dress cap set her back 18s. 6d. in May 1848, though that one almost certainly came from a milliner, and some more caps came, probably ready-made, from 'Seatons' for 11s. 10d. in September 1848. However, the 'undercaps' she bought for £1 4s. 5d. in July 1848, the night caps she had made for twelve shillings in May 1851 and the fancy muslin night cap

Table 8.2 Lady Langham's purchases of fabric

Date	Fabric	Price
August 1845		£2 2s. 3d.
August 1846		£3 9s.
December 1846		£1 11s.
August 1848		£4 1s. 9d.
August 1850	10 yds flannel	£1 7s. 6d.
November 1850	Flannel	17s. 6d.
April 1852	Irish linen	£2 1s. 8d.
October 1852		£1 3s.
August 1853		£2 6s. 4½d.
May 1854	Cambric	£1 7s. 4d.
August 1854	'Linnen Bill'	£3 14s.
September 1855	Flannel	12s.

she had made in September 1855 at a cost of 6s. 6d. (from eighteen shillings'-worth of muslin) were very probably seamstress-made.

Lady Langham bought a considerable number of new dresses in the decade covered by the account books; she lists twenty-three, but additional lump-sum payments to the mantua-maker suggest there were probably more. She had spare cuffs and sleeves made, probably by her seamstress, to smarten up the outfits she already owned; the fashion was for white cuffs and collars and, if they were pristine, the fact that the dress itself might be shabby or even grubby was less obvious. In April 1845, for example, Elizabeth spent three shillings on muslin sleeves and in May 1847 'Cuffs etc.' cost her 14s. 8d., while another set in April 1846 came to 7s. 6d.

Elizabeth Langham also spent a lot on handkerchiefs. Throughout the accounts, cambric handkerchiefs feature largely and they were expensive. In July 1847, for example, she spent £1 13s. 6d. and in April 1848 she bought some more for £1 16s.; they are listed as 'handkerchs' (plural) but we do not know how many there were. Neither do we know whether or not they were made by her seamstress or bought ready-made, the work of some unknown needlewoman employed by a shop.

However, two entries in the account book simply list payments to 'Sempstress' – £1 5s. 9½d. in August 1848 and five shillings in May 1849. We do not know what this woman did for the money, though we may deduce that in 1848 she was making up some of the fabric bought from the linen draper earlier that month. We know she also made a 'night shift' for a pound in October 1846. By the 1840s women's nightwear was quite elaborate with set-in sleeves, a yoke and collar, tucked decoration and lace trimming, much more complicated to make than the term 'shift' implies, although perhaps Lady Langham preferred the simpler night shifts of her youth. Nonetheless, a pound was a substantial sum of money, perhaps it was balanced out by the 5s. 3d. that she was paid for making petticoats the following January. By the mid-1840s women's skirts were becoming fuller and fuller. The crinoline would not make its appearance for another few years, meanwhile fashionable ladies wore layers of full petticoats, stiffened with tucks and sometimes corded, to make their skirts stand out; making such petticoats would have been very labour-intensive and it is to be hoped that the 'Sempstress' didn't have to make too many of them to earn her 5s. 3d.

(iii) Needlewomen quite often still did more than sewing. In a letter to her husband in December 1853, Margaret Peek wrote about the linen belonging to a single friend: 'Did you tell Mr Winch about the sempstress coming on Monday to mend the clothes of those who wish – if he will excuse my suggesting it I think as he has such an immense stock of things it would be well for Mrs Hollingworth to look them over and leave out a sufficient number of everything for use and the remainder be rough-dried and locked up. As they are <u>now</u> they may be lost or stolen without his being any the wiser.'[9]

(iv) In Cambridge in the late 1890s, Eliza Johnson[10] applied to the Cambridge Charity Organization Society for financial assistance. Eliza was fifty-eight and had been a needlewoman most of her life. She had worked for a local shop but claimed that she was then being paid 2s. 8d. a day for work which would previously have earned her 5s. 6d. There is no reason to doubt her claim, but the Society, ever willing to find reasons to refuse aid, dismissed her application, describing her as 'a great beggar'.

Schools and Institutions

While bespoke needlewomen existed, they do seem to have been a dying breed. Ladies who wanted garments made up were as likely to take items to their nearest school or institution as to find a needlewoman, as Mayhew's two gentlewomen seamstresses suggested. The practice dated back at least to the late eighteenth century. An account book (1794–1853) survives for a 'Female School of Industry' in Northumbria[11] and records donations of linen and items ready-cut-out for the girls to make up. For example, in 1795 Eleanor Martin supplied two shifts for making up and a Miss Wake gave seven yards of check for aprons. In 1796 Edward Makins had eight neckcloths made and Cuthbert Brown donated three yards of 'common linen' to be made into a shirt; while Isabella Readhead had three shifts made, Mrs Thorp had a whole lot of 'necks' and 'wrist bands' and Miss Spours gave enough linen for nine fine shirts. The girls also undertook spinning and knitting.

In March 1820 in Leicestershire and Rutland a competition was held for village schoolgirls to judge who could make the best shirt, unaided, in a set amount of time. It was sponsored by clergymen, local overseers of the poor, the Earl of Gainsborough and a group of trustees selected from among the great and good of the district.[12] Some of these shirts were sold when the competition was over.

A receipt book, dating from the 1840s, for the London Foundling Hospital claimed: 'All kinds of Plain Needle-Work are taken in and executed by the Children at the following Rates ...'. Those rates varied from three shillings for a fine, trimmed shirt or a gentleman's neck handkerchief to fourpence for a pillowcase or a penny for hemming a breadth of cambric.[13] Part of the hospital's expenses were funded by the girls' work.

Being able to do plain needlework continued to be seen as important for working-class girls throughout the nineteenth century. Maria Hull went to a board school in Derbyshire between 1884 and 1893. She remembered that at the age of nine 'we girls made calico underwear and did much knitting as well' and a year later:

> In 'scientific' needlework lessons, we cut out paper patterns of undergarments – drawers, chemise and nightgowns – to our individual measurements. I kept the patterns for a long time and found them useful. We were taught how to patch on both calico and flannel, how to gather and make buttonholes and a gusset. I made a maroon-coloured flannel petticoat, feather-stitched in golden silk on the hem.[14]

In 1904 the headmistress of Stapleford School in Nottinghamshire recorded details of what girls in each of the seven standards was expected to learn and produce, from hems and simple seams for the eight year-olds in Standard One, who were then expected to make a duster, to 'tuck running', fancy buttonholes, mending calico and making a girl's dress or blouse, following the 'Rodmure' dressmaking system, at age fourteen in Standard Seven.[15]

Many schools, encouraged by their local governors, sought to defray expenses by selling items the children had made or by taking in needlework for the girls to do, aided and overseen by their schoolmistresses. In 1865 the *Louth and North Lincolnshire Advertiser* described an exhibition of work from nine schools and described in some detail, class by class, how schools could defray expenses by exhibiting:

> For ordinary first class work – 4 yards of shirting at 10d. per yard, would make a working man's Sunday shirt, and 2d. for cotton and buttons would cause an outlay of 3s. 6d., sufficient to provide exhibition work for 8 or 10 girls, at a trifle under 5d. per head, which shirt would be well worth 4s. 0d. when made. Of course it is in the nature of a speculation but we think it is one that would return as good interest as many of those now entered into.[16]

It would seem that each article was the work of a number of girls, even handkerchiefs. For 'fourth class' work, the article recommended 'a cheap pocket handkerchief which can be got for 3d. would suffice to exhibit the work of 4 fourth class workers, and which, when done, could be sold for 3½d., thus covering the expense of needles and cotton'. Presumably each girl hemmed one side.

Even if ladies did not actually order garments from schools, many schools held displays and sales of the girls' work. On 2 June 1887, for example, Wootton Bassett National School in Wiltshire held a sale of needlework in the vicarage garden, along with tea, entertainments and a lecture on education by someone from the London Education Board.[17] The women who patronized such sales could congratulate themselves on contributing to the children's education while at the same time buying useful items cheaply.

At All Saints' School in West Sussex in 1880 it was even suggested that the girls should do sewing for the workhouse to help cover costs.[18] Part of the needlework curriculum also consisted of mending and ladies were encouraged to supply items for schoolgirls to repair. A letter from a former headmistress in the *St Neots Chronicle and Advertiser* on 1 May 1880, for example, complained about the amount of needlework girls were expected to produce to satisfy the inspectors, but also added a plea, 'The expense of materials is great, and it is difficult to find old garments to mend. Benevolent ladies would confer a favour by sending old garments to schools to be mended.' It is unlikely that many of the women trying to make a living as seamstresses would have agreed.

Another unexpected problem needlewomen faced was the input of the charity bazaar. Bazaars to raise money for local churches, schools, charities or other organizations were very much a feature of nineteenth-century life, and making goods to sell at them occupied the leisure time of many middle-class ladies and their daughters; women's magazines were full of designs for decorative items that were supposedly suitable for sale and there was a good deal of genteel competition about whose work made the most money for the cause in question and about who bought it. However, not all ladies were good at sewing, and some apparently went so far as to commission seamstresses to make articles for them which they then passed off as their own work. The purpose of the bazaar was to make money, so the goods for which the seamstress had been paid a pittance were sold on at bazaars at many times the price paid to the original maker, much to the annoyance of one Herefordshire seamstress who wrote to the press to complain.[19]

Shops

Mayhew's two 'superior' needlewomen did work for both private individuals and shops. While, as the nineteenth century progressed, more and more garments were available ready-made, particularly those items like shirts and underwear that had traditionally been the preserve of needlewomen, many shops did continue to offer a bespoke service.

Some of these were small local drapers anxious to 'oblige' customers. Dodds of Alnwick in Northumberland was one such and they are unusual in that they kept meticulous records. Their daybook for 1845–6 records a handful of seamstress jobs. Their prices for shirtmaking varied widely and it is difficult to see why. For example, J.W. Craster Esq. bought nine yards of Hoyle's shirting at 7s. 6d. a yard and two dozen buttons and then paid 4s. 6d. for having three shirts made up. That July he paid 1s. 6d. for four more shirts. Why did one lot of shirts cost 1s. 6d. each and another batch just 4½d.? Why did other customers pay two shillings as W. Forster Esq. of Belvedere did in April 1846? Others paid even more. In June 1845 Edward Mole of Newton Barnes paid fifteen shillings for having shirts made, while Rowland Bell 'of Jamaica' paid £1 7s. for twelve shirts at 2s. 3d. each and four shillings for their carriage to London.[20]

Some city shops offered a much more expensive and exclusive service. There are numerous advertisements for high quality shirtmakers in towns and cities across the UK, and they must have employed well-trained seamstresses, but little or no detail survives of the wages they paid. There is some evidence, too, to suggest that in some firms, shirtmaking was actually done by male tailors rather than by seamstresses; this may well have been the case at David Lord's.

David Lord, 'shirtmaker, hosier, glover and outfitter' had a prestigious address on Burlington Arcade, just off Piccadilly. Between 1888 and 1905 Sir William St Andrew Rouse Boughton of Downton Hall, near Ludlow in Shropshire, patronized the firm extensively. He was thirty-five in 1888, a wealthy and fashionable young man. Over the next seventeen years Lord's sold him forty-one shirts, 178 collars, fifty-three bands for fronts, collars and wrists, nine 'sleep suits' (pyjamas) and one night-shirt that cost him 8s. 6d. His day shirts usually cost between 8s. 6d. and 9s. 6d., but flannel ones were 14s. 6d. The collars and bands cost between one shilling and 2s. 6d. apiece and the dozen white ties he bought in 1888 cost one shilling each. His pyjamas were made of flannel and cost between twenty-five and thirty shillings a pair. These items would nearly all have been made in-house by the firm's own seamstresses or tailors, and the shirts at least were almost certainly made to measure and some of them were sent to Sir William in Shropshire by post. Lord's also did some washing for him and 'marked' his items with the monogram 'WRB'.[21] Sir William also purchased numerous other garments from David Lord but it is the type of goods seamstresses would have made that concern us here. This was a fashionable firm, charging high, though not top-of-the-range, prices. (Figure 8.3)

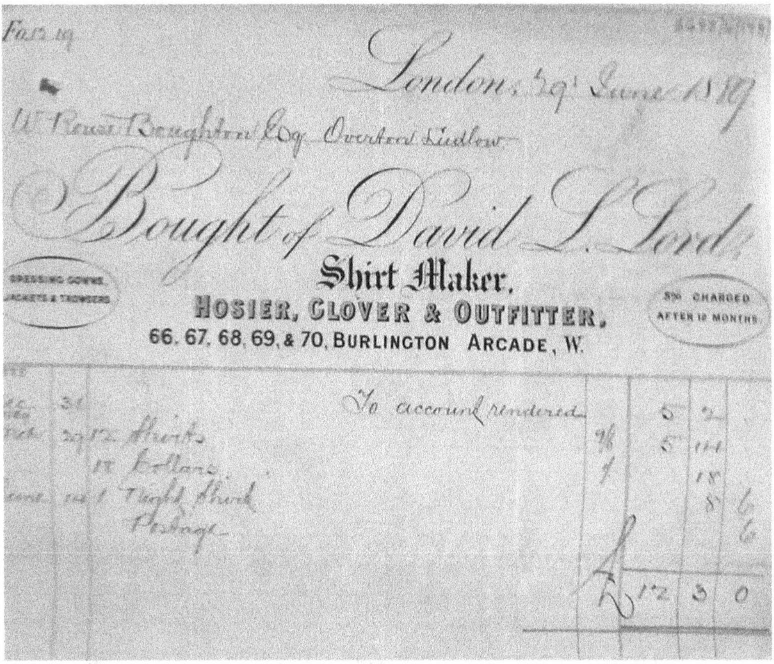

Figure 8.3 Bill from David Lord to W. Rouse Boughton in Ludlow, June 1889.

At much the same period Edward Jackson's in Reading (Berkshire) sold a range of ready-made goods but also described themselves as 'shirtmakers' who would make bespoke goods. Their prices were actually higher than David Lord's. One of their bills survives, showing that in 1887 they were selling shirts at an enormous 26s. 6d. each.[22] (Figure 8.4)

By the second half of the nineteenth century a bespoke service was available in all towns of any size, not just in London, and advertisements appeared in most local papers. To give just a handful of examples: in Preston (Lancashire), Shorrock and Wood advertised Oxford and long cloth shirts 'made to measure'; in Wigan (now in Greater Manchester) J.S. Read on King Street described itself as 'the noted hosier, glover and shirtmaker' and supplied clothes for both men and women; in Leicester Lingards at 11 Gallowtree-gate advertised 'Every description of SHIRTS made to measure'. In Liverpool David Anderson offered all-linen shirts made to measure at 12s. 6d. and 14s. 6d.; in Ipswich

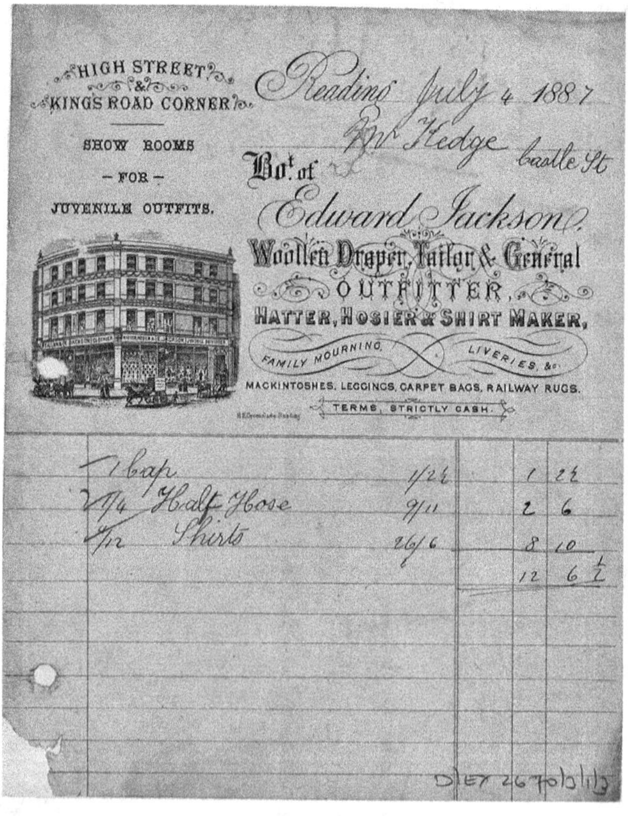

Figure 8.4 Bill from Edward Jackson in Reading, a high-class and expensive shirtmaker, July 1887.

(Suffolk), W. Carter on Tavern Street made shirts on the premises 'on the shortest notice'; while in September 1880 Messrs J. and G. Ross on Exeter High Street (Devon), makers of 'the celebrated ZUGON shirt', had a new set of autumn patterns and would make warm shirts out of 'unshrinkable flannel'. North of the border, Dow and Fender in Edinburgh offered 'Gentlemen's shirts of unsurpassed fit and workmanship made to measure', while, on the other side of the Irish Sea, Taaffe and Coldwell in Dublin offered the 'Best Value in Ireland', making 'perfect fitting' shirts at between 3s. 6d. and 7s. 6d.[23] There were hundreds of similar advertisements.

The second half of the nineteenth century saw a major development in the retail trade, namely the birth of the department store. These had usually started out as drapers and, even in their expanded form, they mostly sold fabrics, clothing and household textiles. Two of the best-known, Kendal Milne in Manchester and Bainbridges in Newcastle, actually opened in the 1830s, but most department stores date from the 1850s, 1860s and 1870s. They helped to popularize ready-made clothing to respectable customers, and most sold clothing for men, women and children. In March 1850, for example, William Walters in Worthing (Sussex) put out a flier saying he was closing his grocery store and re-opening as a drapery business at 11 Montague Street. His new stock would contain 'every description of Ready-Made Clothes for Boys and Youths . . . both home-made and London' so it would appear that some garments were to be made in-house by seamstresses. He prospered. By 1898 he had four shops in Worthing and one at Tarring Crossing and was offering a range of services, including dressmaking.[24] Like Walters, many stores had workrooms where garments could be made, or where ready-made goods could be altered to the customer's specifications. Bainbridge's in Newcastle sold ready-to-wear but by 1860 it also had a department devoted to the making of pit flannels, and by 1869 it was advertising shirtmaking.[25] By 1900 the store had a factory in Leeds that did nothing else. Shepherd and Manning in Northampton opened a dressmaking department in 1872, but ten years earlier they it was advertising 'new, made-up ladies' wrappers for seaside wear' at 10s. 6d. apiece, which presumably were made by workwomen they employed.[26]

Lucks of Darlington (County Durham) sold ready-made goods and does not seem to have had a making-up service, but a brochure for their sale in 1912 offered 'All Household Linen Goods in this Catalogue Hemmed Free of Charge during Sale', which suggests that this was a standard service for which they usually charged.[27] There were also firms of clothiers that do not merit the description of department store, but which sold ready-made goods alongside

£2 . 12 . 6.

JOHN WRENN AND COMPANY

10 AND 11, ST. GEORGE'S-CRESCENT,

(TOP OF LORD-STREET,)

Have received an Immense Stock of SCOTCH ANGOLAS and CHEVIOTS, all Wool and thoroughly shrunk (of such value that has never before been offered (from which they can make their CELEBRATED SUITS, at the price quoted above.

Separate Garments can be had, viz. :—

TROUSERS, 15/; VESTS, 8/6; COATS, 30/.

N.B.—No Machines used, all Garments being Made by Hand. Superior SUITS at £3 13s. 6d. and £4 14s. 6d.

Also, a large assortment of the very finest Goods from the CONTINENT and WEST OF ENGLAND, at proportionately low prices.

READY-MADE OVERCOATS
From 18s. 6d.

A LARGE STOCK OF READY-MADE CLOTHING,
For Home, Foreign, and Sea use.

GENTLEMEN'S HOSIERY AND OUTFITTING,

Consisting of shirts, Hosiery, Gloves, Ties, Collars, Braces, Rugs, Portmanteaus, Hat Boxes, Umbrellas, Hats, and every article required for use at home, voyage by sea, or residence abroad.

BEDDING AND LINEN FOR SHIPS' USE. APPRENTICES' complete OUTFITS on the shortest notice.

SHIRTS MADE TO MEASURE;
A PERFECT FIT GUARANTEED.

Figure 8.5 Advertisement for Wrenn's clothing shop in Liverpool from the *Liverpool Mail*, 26 February 1870.

offering a bespoke service, like John Wrenn and Co. in Liverpool whose advertisement appears in Figure 8.5. All this implies that these big stores must have employed seamstresses, but while we have a good deal of information about the employment in-house of dressmakers, tailors and milliners, there is little evidence of seamstresses. It therefore seems likely that they were usually outworkers.

Servants and Others

When Margaret Langley was a teenager in Hove (Sussex) in the early twentieth century and considering going into service, she discussed the matter with her mother, herself a former servant, and was told: 'Well, as you hate needlework, . . .

there's only one place you can go and that is into the kitchen. If you're a parlourmaid you've got to mend all the table linen, and if you're a housemaid you've got to mend all the house linen, and if you're in the nursery you've got to mend, and even make, the children's clothes.' Margaret became a kitchenmaid.[28]

Advertisements would suggest that this was indeed the pattern. Mrs Beeton, writing for middle-class housewives in 1859–61, agreed. 'On leisure days', she wrote, 'the housemaid should be able to do some needlework for her mistress – such as turning and mending sheets and darning the house linen ... for this reason it is almost essential that a housemaid, in a small family, should be an expert needlewoman.'[29] Twenty years earlier, the inventory of the contents of Burford House in West Oxfordshire contained a list of draconian 'Rules for servants', which includes instructions such as 'The under servants to have new milk but no cream in their tea'! It also included rules about needlework: 'The laundrymaid to mend the linen the week she is not washing'; 'The housekeeper to get as much needlework done as possible'; and 'The maids can only work for themselves after 8pm.'[30]

Some big households employed designated needlewomen. Petworth House in Sussex, for example, listed numerous seamstresses in their wage accounts between the mid-1840s and the 1880s. The earlier accounts do not always give the amounts paid, though where they do, the going rate seems to have been two shillings a day, or twelve shillings for a six-day week, a fortune compared to the wages of independent needlewomen in the cities. By the 1870s and 1880s prices had risen and the Petworth seamstresses were usually paid thirteen shillings a week, or a daily rate of 2s. 2d. One or two women got six shillings a week, probably as assistant needlewomen, although this isn't specified in the wage accounts, and there were a few exceptions. Mrs Chandler, for example, got a shilling a day for an unspecified period in the 1870s for 'altering furniture', in other words working on upholstery and bed-curtains. Most of the women did not stay long, usually a matter of months, but Mrs Botting was unusual in that she remained in post for nine years – December 1873 to January 1883 – at the high rate of fifteen shillings a week.[31]

Skill in needlework was, of course, also required of schoolmistresses who were going to have to train the next generation of servants. As we have seen, schoolgirls were required to reach a satisfactory standard in needlework as well as in English and arithmetic and their work was examined by the school inspectors. There were also full-time posts for needlewomen in various institutions like workhouses, prisons and asylums where the role would involve overseeing the inmates making and mending garments, and in hospitals where much of the work would have been repairing bed linen. Such posts were comparatively well paid and the women would have had their board and lodging as well as their salary. In the 1850s, for example, the Llanfyllin (Powys, Wales) Poor Law guardians paid their workhouse seamstress sixteen pounds a year, all found, while their colleagues in Newport Pagnell (Buckinghamshire) paid fifteen pounds. In Bromsgrove (Worcestershire), the guardians only paid ten pounds, while in Southampton (Hampshire) their seamstress, grandly styled an 'industrial trainer' because she taught the inmates needlework, earned twenty-five pounds.[32]

Such institutions generated a huge amount of needlework. For example, at Colney Hatch asylum in Middlesex in just one year (1858) the sewing department made up, among other things, 3,946 gowns and 2,304 shirts for inmates and staff uniforms, and 4,664 sheets and 3,408 pillowcases from 1,593½ yards of sheeting and 1,148½ yards of calico bought at the bulk purchase prices of 1s. 2d. a yard and fivepence a yard, respectively.[33] Just as in the case of house-servants, needlewomen from the slums, however skilled they might have been at sewing, would not have been considered for jobs in institutions. Workhouse staff and asylum staff were expected to set a good example; these jobs were for 'respectable' applicants only and they were better paid than most servants.

Charity

The needlewomen's complaints did not go unheard and many charitably inclined individuals tried to help them. The easiest way to do this, for those who could afford it, was to donate money to one of the various organizations and institutions set up to support the poor and needy. However, charities were not always what they seemed.

In January 1855 the London *Morning Post*[34] carried an appeal for donations to the Distressed Needlewomen's Home, at 15 Carburton Street, just off Fitzroy Square. It had been:

Established February, 1852, under the distinguished Patronage of several Clergymen and Ladies of Title and Distinction.... The purpose of this Institution is to afford a Home or Asylum to Aged or Distressed Females, who, from reverses of fortune, have nothing to depend upon but working at the needle: to secure to the inmates and others regular employment at reasonable remuneration; and to afford them relief in sickness, infirmity, or age.

It claimed to have supported over a hundred women, many of whom were 'officers', solicitors' and clergymen's widows' – the suggestion that recipients of charity were members of the middle class who were down on their luck was always effective – and many of the needlewomen were also 'over seventy'. Numerous other advertisements appeared in the press, encouraging ladies to order work for themselves or 'for the making up of Clothing for the Poor from ladies in the habit of distributing such',[35] and a short article about the home, complete with a price-list for the work the inmates performed, appeared in the one and only edition of *The Sempstress*, published in October 1855, price one penny. The home sounded like a worthy initiative, and many no doubt assumed it was an offshoot of the Distressed Needlewomen's Society; money poured in. Unfortunately, however, the secretary, the self-styled 'Reverend' Charles Geary, was a conman, with a history of offending, and in May 1857 he was imprisoned for obtaining money under false pretences.

The home did actually exist, and Mrs Meller, the superintendent, was interviewed in court:

> Her duties were to superintend the work done, to receive ladies who called, and to hand over, or account for, to Geary, any subscriptions she might receive. The Home was intended for persons who had been in good circumstances but who were not sufficiently skilled to be able to maintain themselves by that means. There were at present six persons resident in the Home, the largest number being resident at any one time was nine.

So far short of the twenty-five claimed in *The Sempstress*:

> Many of those persons were very aged. Others were employed at the Home in making up work which was brought for that purpose by ladies. These workers received 1s., 1s. 3d. or 1s. 6d. a day, and the residents in the Home had coals and candles in addition. At one time there had been 70 workers at the Home. The prices paid by ladies for the work done were the usual prices, but the workers were not so quick as the more practised needlewomen, and the institution frequently paid more for the work done than it received from the ladies who gave it.

It sounds as though Mrs Meller was unaware that Geary was siphoning off money for his personal use, or perhaps her salary of eighteen shillings a week encouraged her to turn a blind eye.[36]

That anyone should have sought to profit in such a callous way from the charitable inclinations of the well-to-do towards the desperate and vulnerable is sickening but Geary learnt nothing from his all-too-brief spell in Whitecross Street Prison. In March 1859 he was again convicted for soliciting donations, this time for the 'Indigent Sempstresses' Home', also 'founded in 1852', a scruffy little house in Bolsover Street, Marylebone, an area notorious for prostitution. His sentence of three months' hard labour seems surprisingly light, though he clearly didn't think so: he fainted when it was pronounced.[37] What is significant about this sordid little episode, however, is that there was such a willingness to subscribe money to support the seamstresses that a practised conman like Geary saw an opportunity for a lucrative scam.

Fortunately, there were other, genuine, charitable initiatives. The West London Institution for the Employment of Needlewomen was founded in or around 1860. It provided rooms at 5 Hereford Terrace, just off Leinster Square, in which needlewomen could work; the rooms were open from 9.00 am to 8.00 pm and were well-lit and heated by open fires, and tea was served to the workwomen. A matron cut out and allocated the work ordered, and there was a lady superintendent in charge of the operation. The institution kept books which were open for inspection and detailed how much the women were paid and how much the customers were charged, but with only two rooms it can only have helped a small number of women.[38]

A similar institution was founded in Liverpool in 1853 by Archdeacon Brooks at 30 Great Orford Street, under the superintendence of a Miss Skeaping. Advertisements in the Liverpool press claimed 'Orders executed in every Branch of Needlework'; some of the workwomen produced fine bespoke work, while those who were less skilled made garments for clothing clubs and charities. In 1857 there were 323 needlewomen on the books but the institution could only find work for seventy of them, so this organization, too, operated on quite a small scale.[39] In 1870, for example, just 516 items were made.[40]

Similarly, the 'Thimble League' was established in the winter of 1885–6 by a group of philanthropic ladies in London. They cut out work which was then handed out to seamstresses to be made up and was paid for at a 'fair' rate: 'By this means help is given to the needy without pauperising them, while the rich and the poor are brought into contact, very much to the advantage of both.'[41] The league was supported by donations and the proceeds of fêtes and theatrical performances. There were various local branches and advertisements in the press urged ladies to buy the work it subsidized. It too could only support a few seamstresses. Nevertheless, it was still in existence as the 'Silver Thimble League', with a rather wider charitable remit, in the 1940s.

There were numerous other small local initiatives. Most of these charities supplied work ready-cut-out to the needlewomen. This was understandable when needlewomen were working for a shop or a warehouse, but less so when they were dealing with private customers. The fear was always that, if workwomen were to cut out work themselves, they would cheat by over-estimating the amount of fabric required, keeping the extra for their own use and charging the client more than they needed to pay. It was a criticism that was also levelled at tailors and dressmakers – humiliating because it implied they were untrustworthy and unkind because it deprived them of any tiny perks the job might have offered.

Conclusion

Needlework remained an important part of girls' education and from 1880 that education was compulsory. A girl's ability to sew was examined by Her Majesty's Inspectors alongside her proficiency in reading, writing and arithmetic, though it was seen as something that would help her to be a good wife and mother rather than as a qualification for employment.

Indeed, by the 1880s there were comparatively few openings for needlewomen other than as slop-workers. The bespoke trade seems to have declined after 1840, though it did not disappear altogether. There were still women working as independent needlewomen because that was what they had always done or because it was the only avenue of work open to them, but they struggled to make a living as more and more garments were available ready-made and fewer and fewer households needed their services. Women like Ann and Sarah Alsop in Tissington may have been happy to earn a little pin money by doing jobs for Lady FitzHerbert but for Mayhew's two gentlewomen seamstresses it was a completely different story. They were clearly highly skilled at what they did but nonetheless could barely keep body and soul together.

There were still jobs for skilled bespoke needlewomen in shops and department stores, although, as the wholesale trade depressed prices, their earnings shrank and they were usually outworkers, employed as and when they were needed, not salaried staff like the tailors, dressmakers and milliners the stores also employed. There were jobs for competent needlewomen in schools and other institutions and these were taken by the fortunate few but, increasingly, domestic needlework became the preserve of servants. Writers like Mrs Beeton make it clear that by the mid-century it was seen as the laundrymaid's job to check the linen after she had washed it; she, the housemaid, the parlourmaid and the nursery staff would then be responsible for doing any running repairs, probably overseen by the mistress of the house. The jobbing seamstress, visiting every few months to make and mend, was no longer needed in most households.

There were, of course, still jobs in the slop trade, but these continued to be abysmally badly paid. Charitable institutions tried to redress the balance but the level of need was always greater than the help available and, though few charity organizers behaved as egregiously as 'Reverend' Charles Geary, charities were not always effectively run or they were too hamstrung by Victorian notions of propriety to be genuinely helpful to their many applicants, as we shall see in the next chapter.

Clearly, being a seamstress was not a comfortable life at any stage in the nineteenth century – but was it really as dire as the various social reformers suggested? The next chapter will try to answer that question.

Real lives

Much has been written about the downtrodden nineteenth-century seamstress –
as we have seen in previous chapters. She was vilified for being little better than a
prostitute, sermons were preached about her, articles were written about her,
societies were formed for her protection and she was immortalized in numerous
novels and paintings. Some forty years ago Sally Alexander[1] was one of the first to
question the received wisdom about the seamstress's plight. Was the evidence
gathered by the reformers skewed so that it concentrated on the lives of the most
unfortunate? Was it possible, she wondered, that not all seamstresses lived lives of
unrelieved misery? Might some of them have actually had a relatively happy, if
not prosperous, existence? The aim of this chapter is to take an objective look
at some hitherto unexplored sources of information about the lives of real
seamstresses to see whether they cast any light on the issue.

Seamstresses in Whitechapel in 1851

The data in this section is based on census returns and census data must be treated
with caution. People did not always tell the enumerators the truth and sometimes
the enumerators did not record what they were told correctly. In addition, in the
nineteenth century many people did not know exactly how old they were; when
there were no forms to fill in and birthdays were little celebrated, it was easy to
lose track. Illegitimate grandchildren were passed off as children; not all 'married'
women had gone through a legal ceremony; if a woman remarried, her children
from her first marriage might take on their stepfather's name. The pitfalls are
endless and the data may throw up as many questions as it answers. Similarly,
people who were illiterate could not spell their names and the phonetic
interpretation written down by one enumerator might differ radically from that
of another enumerator a decade later. Nonetheless, for all its faults, the census is
one of the best sources we have to examine the minutiae of individual lives,

Figure 9.1 Whitechapel High Street in the 1830s.

particularly in a trade which is under-recorded, though, of course, what it cannot tell us is what people earned and how they spent their money.

In 1851 Whitechapel in London's East End had a population of 37,848, of which roughly a third was made up of women of working age. And most of those women did work. Whitechapel was a poor area and working-class families could seldom manage without the earnings of wives and daughters. Women in Whitechapel worked as servants and charwomen, washerwomen and wet nurses, shop girls, feather-dressers, rag-pickers, cigar-makers and in many other trades, and there were a surprising number who openly identified as 'prostitutes'. A great many Whitechapel women also worked in the clothing trades and many of them fit our definition of seamstresses, though they used a range of terms as well as 'seamstress' to describe what they did – 'needlewoman', 'shirtmaker', 'waistcoat-maker', 'slop-worker' and so on. It is the women who pursued these trades who form the basis of this analysis.

There were other women who probably fitted the profile of seamstress, like stay-makers (surprisingly few, just twenty-three of them), slipper makers and shoe-binders, some of whom worked from home stitching uppers, and umbrella makers, some of whom no doubt sewed covers for umbrellas and parasols in their own homes, but they have been excluded because of the uncertainty about how and where they actually worked. Similarly, hundreds of Whitechapel women described themselves as tailoresses (367) and dressmakers (353); some would have worked in the bespoke trade but it is certain that some were seamstresses to whom tailoring or dressmaking firms 'put out' certain types of work. Again, it is impossible to distinguish which part of the trades they belonged to, and so they too have been excluded from the calculations.

This leaves some 612 women who we can be reasonably sure worked as seamstresses. They ranged in age from a girl of eight – Sarah Keeping on Spectacle Alley, working alongside her widowed mother and seventeen-year-old sister – to women in their seventies. As outlined above, we have to allow for a certain amount of inadvertent or deliberate misinformation when it comes to ages in the census but, taking the data at face value, it seems the majority of seamstresses (fifty-five per cent) were in their late teens, twenties and early thirties, as would be expected given the relatively low life expectancy in the area. Just eight per cent were fifteen or younger. A significant number were in their late thirties, forties and fifties (thirty-one per cent) and a handful (six per cent) were over sixty. In the optimistically named Providence Court, for example, seventy-year-old Susannah Raymond and her 45-year-old daughter worked at 'slop-work', along with their 72-year-old 'visitor', Mary Winter, while at 33 Fieldgate Street Rose Jenkins was still working as a needlewoman at the age of seventy-five.

The majority of seamstresses – 43.3 per cent – lived with family, usually their parents but sometimes with their grandparents, aunts and uncles or siblings. At 20 Oxford Street, for example, 66-year-old Abigail Childs had rooms with her fifteen-year-old granddaughter, Jane, and both were needlewomen. On Bakers Row, sisters Sarah and Louisa Tarry, both in their early twenties, supported themselves by needlework. Even quite prosperous families set their daughters to needlework. For example, on Thames Street, John Warner was a carpenter; his wife didn't work and had four young children to look after, but their sixteen-year-old worked as a seamstress. Phineas Fonseca had a business as a 'general dealer', his wife did not work and they had a servant, but, nonetheless, his nineteen-year-old daughter made waistcoats and his older daughter was a furrier.

Just 16.3 per cent of the total were married women living with their husbands and, in those cases, the husbands were usually in precarious or poorly paid jobs like tailors and shoemakers, who could be put out of work at a moment's notice if someone better or cheaper came along, or labourers, particularly on the docks, who were hired by the day as and when needed and probably seldom worked a full week. For instance, Peter and Eliza Sheen, aged twenty-six and twenty-four, respectively, had rooms at 52 Rosemary Lane: Peter was a 'dock labourer'; Eliza was a seamstress. An older couple in the same building were Christopher and Diana Hyde: at forty-seven Christopher had the unenviable dockland job of 'ballast heaver'; she, a decade his junior, was a seamstress. In Bear's Head Yard, Peter Briscomb was a 'coal whipper', an arduous job that involved getting loads of coal out of the hold of a ship by means of a rope and pulley, while his wife and teenage daughter were slop-workers. In Wagener Buildings lived Charles Roper, a labourer in his fifties who also worked on the docks; his wife and two daughters made waistcoats and blouses to eke out his wages.

There were husbands whose jobs sound a little more secure, shopkeepers, hairdressers or skilled men, like the 24-year-old German immigrant, George Werner, who was a pianoforte maker on Charlotte Street, and whose young wife, Elizabeth, a local girl from Tottenham, worked as a seamstress. Perhaps she planned to give up work when his business was better established and children started to arrive. In Tower Hamlets, Edward Winslow identified as 'clerk to a solicitor general' but his fifty-year-old wife, Frances, was 'employed at home in needlework'. Joseph Martin was a gun-maker, a skilled trade, he was fifty-nine and so, presumably, an experienced worker, and his 25-year-old son worked with him. Nonetheless, Joseph's wife and their four unmarried daughters, the youngest of whom was just fifteen, were all slop-workers. Of course, we have no way of knowing how successful any of these men really were, and some of them may have been drinkers or gamblers, leaving their wives or daughters to earn the money that put food on the table.

The remainder of the cohort – some 40.4 per cent – many of them widows, headed their own households, lived alone or boarded with families who relied on their rent. Some describe themselves as 'visitors' but that usually simply seems to have meant being in temporary lodgings. Many of the household heads supported families by their needlework, sometimes assisted by their older children, but there were many lone mothers struggling to work while looking after small children. At 11 Dowson Place, for example, Harriet Meade was already a widow at twenty-five and was trying to support herself and two little boys aged three and five by needlework; while, sharing a house at 28 Wellington Street, Charlotte Jolly was single-handedly providing for three children under ten. On Well Close Square, 32-year-old Sarah Alster lived with her twelve-year-old daughter and a three-year-old. She worked as a seamstress and let space to a corn merchant and a shoe-binder, both described as 'visitors'. Their rent seems to have made a difference; unlike many girls her age, young Amelia Alster was in school. Just round the corner in Charles Court, Ann Whittington, working as a seamstress, was also able to keep her eleven-year-old son in school, although her two teenage daughters worked with her as seamstresses and her fourteen-year-old was an errand boy. In Well Yard, twelve-year-old Mary Ann Maunder, the eldest girl of the nine children of a chairmaker father, was already working as a seamstress alongside her mother. On Conants Place, widowed Elizabeth Peasgood's thirteen-year-old daughter worked with her as a seamstress and, between them, they had to support five younger children, one just a baby. On Colchester Street, Sarah Bridges and her twenty-year-old daughter were supporting four younger children, although fifteen-year-old Frederick and twelve-year-old Francis were bringing in a few pence a week as errand boys and the family had a seamstress lodger.

We do not know for whom they all worked, but there were many clothes-dealers in the area, ranging from slop-sellers to respectable linen drapers employing numerous hands. On Castle Street, Mary Polack described herself as 'head of the household' and a needlewoman and, though she was unmarried, she had four tiny children; Edward Anderton, their 28-year-old 'visitor' who was a baker from Gloucester, may have fathered some of them. Mary's mother, Frances, lived with the family and described herself as a clothes-dealer, so Mary may well have worked for her. The census also records a few men who described themselves as 'cutters out of clothes': for example, Robert Skinner who lodged with a widowed laundress on Little Prescot Street; Joseph Johnson, a married man in his twenties living on Everard Place with his wife and two toddlers; 48-year-old John Varley 'cutter to clothiers' living at 31 Colchester Street with his family; and James Hoyland who lived in Black Lion Yard and was a 'cutter at outfitters'. His wife was a tailoress – did she perhaps work for the same outfitter? There must have been many more cutters-out to keep so many seamstresses in employment, but they are probably listed as 'assistants' to the clothiers, drapers and tailors who employed them.

Bearing in mind that most seamstresses earned no more than four or five shillings a week, none of the women listed above lived particularly comfortable lives, but those who had husbands or adult children in employment probably managed best. The outlook for single mothers like Harriet Meade and Charlotte Jolly and their young families was indeed bleak. Just occasionally we catch a glimpse of those who were slipping through the net. For example, at 16 Charlotte Court, Sarah Jason, a widow in her fifties, living alone, described herself as 'sempstress receiving p[ar]ish aid' – but at least she was still living in a home of sorts. The records of the Whitechapel workhouse point to the fate that awaited many seamstresses; in 1851, out of 439 female inmates, 115, more than a quarter, had been needlewomen of one sort or another.

So how did the seamstresses we have encountered in this section fare? It was possible to trace quite a number of them in the records of marriages and deaths and in the 1861 census. Little Sarah Keeping, the youngest of them, was eighteen and married by 1861. Her husband was James Charles Blore (or Tukenbloore according to the marriage index) but on census night she was staying with her mother. They were both still earning a living by needlework but old Mrs Keeping now described herself as a 'tailoress' and Sarah was a specialist, making fringes, though she was probably paid no better than she had been as an ordinary seamstress. Her elder sister, Martha, was married to Charles Welch, a platemaker, they had a baby boy and she no longer worked.

Not surprisingly, the three needlewomen in their seventies who were still working in 1851 had all died by 1861; in fact, Mary Winter died within months of speaking to the enumerator, and Susannah Raymond's daughter, Deborah, could not be traced. Abigail Childs died at the age of seventy and her granddaughter, Jane, moved in with her stonemason uncle and his family and was still a seamstress in 1861. Louisa Tarry was working as a housemaid in Marylebone and it would be nice to think that her sister had become the nursemaid employed by the McPhersons in St Pancras to care for their five children. Mr McPherson was a ship-owner and the family were well-to-do. However, there was another Middlesex-born Sarah Tarry of the same age in the Essex workhouse and we cannot be sure which one was Louisa's sister. Elizabeth Warner, the carpenter's daughter, died in 1856 aged twenty-one. By 1861 Eliza Sheen was a widow with a six-year-old daughter and her occupation was recorded as 'NK' – not known. We can only speculate how she earned her living. Charles Roper, the former dock labourer, had found slightly less arduous work as a brass-finisher and his wife no longer worked as a seamstress; their daughters had left home and cannot be traced with any degree of certainty, though an Elizabeth Roper died in 1856 in the right area. Sarah Martin, the gunmaker's wife, was sixty-four and had also retired from sewing, but two of her daughters, Emma, who was twenty-three and unmarried, and Mary Ann, now Mary Ann Lindsey aged twenty-nine, who was back home with her two toddlers, were still slop-trouser-makers.

Phineas Fonseca's daughter could not be traced, nor could the Hydes or the Briscombs, Frances Winslow, Mary Ann Maunder or Sarah and Amelia Alster. The German pianoforte maker and his seamstress wife had also disappeared by 1861 but there is no record of either of their deaths; it is to be hoped that they returned to Germany and set up a successful business. Of Harriet Meade and her children there is no trace. However, Charlotte Jolly remarried and moved to Hornchurch. Her new husband was George Willers, an agricultural labourer, and in 1861 Charlotte's son, Samuel, who was a baby in 1851, was ten and had taken his stepfather's name, and she also had a one-year-old called Robert. Of Charlotte's older son there is no trace, but her daughter, Hannah, died in 1857 aged fourteen. An agricultural labourer's pay was unlikely to be more than about eight shillings a week but, nonetheless, Charlotte was no longer doing paid work.

In 1861 Ann Whittington was still working as a seamstress, as was her daughter, Caroline, then aged twenty-five. Thomas, a schoolboy in 1851, was a lighterman, and the family were also looking after three small boys, surnamed Whittington, presumably the children of Ann's other son, George. Of Elizabeth Peasgood and her brood, only Thomas was still in Whitechapel in 1861. He was married with a child and made packing-cases for a living. Sarah Bridges and her daughter – by then Sarah Watts – were working as 'tailoresses' in 1861. As were Mary Polack and three of her daughters. Her two sons were no longer at home, but despite having no husband in evidence, Mary had had three more children. She now described herself as 'married' – though her surname had not changed and back in 1851 she had said she was single.

Unfortunately, the findings about the women's lives a decade down the line do not do much to contradict the depressing histories that appeared in the press and in the reports of the Children's Employment Commission. Of the twenty-three women working as seamstresses in 1851 whose careers can be traced, six had died by 1861. Most had lost at least one family member. Five young women had married but only two had been able to give up work and appeared to be living with their husbands. Of course, the other three were not necessarily deserted wives, their husbands may have been seamen, working away from home in some other capacity, or simply doing a night-shift on census day. One girl, or possibly two, had gone into service. Just two older women had given up seamstry. Nine of the cohort were still needle workers and four girls who had been children in 1851 had joined their mothers in the trade. Two – Eliza Sheen and Mary Polack – may well have found less respectable ways of making or augmenting their livings. Needless to say, we do not know for certain that the women who were seamstresses in 1851 and were still seamstresses in 1861 had plied their trade consistently for the intervening decade, though the likelihood is that they had.

Concern about seamstresses was at its height in the 1840s and 1850s, but the various attempts at reform had minimal impact on their plight and, while there was still some agitation for reform, popular interest in the needlewomen's case had diminished by the 1860s. As we have seen, it only resurfaced in the 1870s and 1880s as poverty, the supposedly debased condition of the working class, and the cost of alleviating the problems this caused, once again became causes of concern. Middle-class reformers approached the issues with varying degrees of understanding. Few were as insightful as Lady Bell in Middlesbrough, the wife of an industrialist, who wrote *At the Works*, published in 1907. In two chapters about the wives and daughters of working men she writes with genuine admiration and respect about working women who kept clean, comfortable homes while bearing, raising – and burying – numerous children, and managing on tiny, uncertain incomes. She also writes with empathy and understanding about wives who managed less well and is keen to point out to her middle-class readers just how hard life was for women who had no servants and too little money. Much more common were do-gooders who subscribed to the very Victorian notion of the 'deserving' and 'undeserving' poor. The following two sections depict examples of charities where those beliefs held sway, but both are valuable for the detail they give about individual lives.

The Cambridge Charity Organization Society

The charity organization societies were founded in England in 1869, following the twenty-second report of the Poor Law Board (Appendix A, No. 4) which sought to cut the amount of outdoor relief distributed by the boards of guardians. Amazingly to modern readers, the societies saw this as a *good* thing and embraced 'scientific philanthropy' as a way of alleviating the effects of poverty, rooting out 'scroungers' and only supporting people deemed worthy of support, while encouraging self-help and championing limited government intervention. Various branches were soon established throughout the country.

The Cambridge Charity Organization Society was formed in 1880. Its stated aim was 'the improvement of the condition of the poor' and it worked in cooperation with the Poor Law guardians, churches and other charities to find work for applicants, to provide regular payments over short periods of crisis and to give donations – or more usually loans – to purchase items like sewing machines or laundry equipment to enable families to be self-reliant. It also tried to put people in touch with other sources of aid where appropriate, as, for example, in October 1891 when they referred Susan Wilson,[2] a former shirtmaker, to the Trust for the Blind in London. The society also interested itself in a range of other undertakings and reforms to improve conditions for the poor, but dealing with individual cases of hardship took up the greater part of its time.

The moving spirits behind the establishment of the Cambridge society were Henry Sidgwick, the philosopher and economist, and his wife, Eleanor, who became the second principal of Newnham College and was the sister of Arthur Balfour, MP, prime minister between 1902 and 1905. There was strong membership from the town, local churches, and from the Cambridge colleges; the first chairman of the society was the Master of Pembroke. Margaret Keynes, mother of the economist, John Maynard Keynes, was a member, as was her friend, the social reformer, Eglantyne Jebb, who wrote about the Society very approvingly in her book, *Cambridge: A Brief Study in Social Questions*. The Cambridge society had premises at 82 Regent Street which were open every afternoon and people were referred by well-wishers, churches, the Poor Law guardians and charities. It was funded by donations, never sufficient for its needs, and individuals willing to support particular people or families could do so through the charity, secure in the knowledge that the recipients had been well-vetted and the spending of their money would be monitored.

A sub-committee met weekly to review applications and a salaried agent was employed for home visits. Casework formed a major part of the society's work, but visiting the homes of the poor was not something the respectable middle-class members were comfortable doing. Applications for aid were carefully scrutinized, details of family members of applicants were recorded, as was the number of rooms in which the family lived and how much rent they paid, whether or not they were in arrears and whether there were any other debts. Referees were contacted, neighbours, former employers, teachers and employers of family members were questioned. Details were sought of relatives who might contribute to the applicant's support and pressure was put on them to do so.

It was important to have a clean, tidy home when the agent visited. Mary Jane Melton[3] applied for money to buy a sewing machine in May 1881. She was a widow with two small children and the family all lived, ate, cooked, washed and slept in one room for which she paid two shillings a week. The agent called shortly after she had got the children off to school one morning and reported, rather sniffily, that the room, though clean, was 'not very tidy'! Mary Jane did, however, get her machine. Nonetheless, despite their stated intention of helping people to help themselves, many such requests were refused. Caroline Burgess wanted a mangle but was refused; Phoebe Ann Camps wanted help to hire a sewing machine but was refused; so was Sarah Ann Miller because one referee accused her of having 'intemperate habits'. Another referee even accused Elizabeth Ann Pettit of 'cheek' for applying for money to buy a sewing machine a matter of weeks after her husband died.[4]

Disparaging remarks from neighbours could put paid to the most reasonable of claims. A month after Mary Jane Melton got her sewing machine, another widow, Martha Norman,[5] applied for a hospital ticket. Hospitals, convalescent homes and similar institutions issued 'tickets' to their subscribers and supporters to be doled out by them to sick individuals they deemed worthy of treatment; even medical treatment for the poor was dependent on their being 'deserving'. To gain admission, a would-be patient had to persuade someone to give them a ticket. Martha had consumption and the doctor had advised that she needed to go to a convalescent home. However, the trustees failed to find anyone who would supply her with the necessary ticket, despite the fact that most of their supporters would have been ticket-holders. It seems likely that it was her neighbours' comments that sealed her fate; they alleged that Martha's sister-in-law was a prostitute and that Martha's own behaviour before her marriage had been questionable. There is no way of knowing whether a spell of convalescence would actually have helped, but Martha died of consumption six years later, aged just thirty-three.

Neighbours accused Harriet Shallow, who described herself as a 'needlewoman and lodging-house keeper' of being a 'professional beggar', certainly not someone who lived up to the society's high standards of behaviour. Her application for assistance was dismissed out of hand. Allegations of drunkenness were equally damaging. Harriet Holden was fifty, a deserted wife with two adult children who between them earned less than a pound a week. She applied for money to buy coal so she could make hot food. Her case was dismissed as 'undeserving' because the neighbours said she drank. Hannah Smith had been a needlewoman and had worked for Mr Bradwell 'opposite the station' but she had been out of work for a year because trade was slack. He acknowledged that she was a good worker but that carried no weight when her children and neighbours accused her of being a drunk. Mrs Johnson was refused help because she had had an illegitimate child after her husband died; Ellen Fletcher was dismissed as 'a bad lot'; Eliza Newman, severely disabled after a pile of sacks fell on her, was nonetheless refused help because she was said to be a 'a drunken good-for-nothing'.[6]

Cambridge was not a city noted for clothing manufacture and, although it had its fair share of seamstresses and shirtmakers working for drapers who provided bespoke items, and others who did making and mending for private individuals, the 1881 census listed just ninety-two women who earned their living that way, serving a population of 35,653. Nonetheless, seamstresses, needlewomen and shirtmakers applied to the Cambridge Charity Organisation Society in considerable numbers. In the first two years of the society's existence, twenty-two women in these categories applied for assistance, almost a quarter of the number listed in the census as needleworkers, and by 1890 another thirty-six had sought help. Just twenty came forward in the 1890s and, though the society remained in touch with some of the women it had assisted into the twentieth century, no new applications from needlewomen were recorded after 1900.

Many of the women who sought help were quite young: Miriam Hayden, Emily Brown, Mary Stretch and Elizabeth Chapman[7] were all in their twenties but unable to find work. Miriam did find work helping out at the Mission House but was refused further help because she was said to be unreliable and 'not very clean'. Emily Brown's case was dismissed as ineligible for no discernible reason. Mary Stretch's husband was suffering from lead-poisoning and had been prescribed milk and soda water which were expensive; she was refused a regular payment but did receive fairly frequent payments of three shillings. Elizabeth Chapman's case was regularly deferred but she eventually found herself work at Pembroke College. She came back to the society in 1928 to ask for help to find a place in an almshouse but, as she was in receipt of a college pension of fifteen shillings and an old age pension of ten shillings she was deemed to have too high an income to qualify.

Only a handful of applicants (nine out of seventy-eight) were over sixty: women like 73-year-old Lydia Chapman,[8] who needed money to buy herself a pair of glasses so she could continue to do plain needlework; or 69-year-old Sophia Lucretia Lansdowne,[9] who could no longer sew and needed food and clothing. Lydia was described as 'unsatisfactory' and a 'bad character' and the best the society would offer was the recommendation that she go to the workhouse. Sophia did rather better. She was a spinster and had lived at home with her parents until she was fifty, she then worked as a teacher and as a needlewoman but was said not to be very good at either job! Nonetheless, seven people contributed to her upkeep giving her 3s. 6d. a week, on top of the 3s. 6d. a week she received from the parish, along with a weekly parish gift of two pounds of meat, soup from St John's College and charitable gifts at Christmas. Somehow, Sophia had established a very supportive network of friends and contacts. However, it did not last. In April 1881 Sophia Lucretia Lansdowne was admitted to the Cambridge Lunatic Asylum and a month later she was diagnosed as 'permanently insane'. She died there in 1887.

The majority of applications came from women with families, widows or wives whose husbands were too ill to work. Most of the requests (twenty-seven out of seventy-eight) were for financial support: money to pay off debts, money to support families while one of the breadwinners was ill, money for food, money for fuel, money for rent. In 1880 Elizabeth Murcutt asked for five pounds to pay off her debts and the society gave her a loan. Louisa Ayres had obviously taken advantage of one of the numerous emigration schemes touted as a solution to the needlewoman problem but needed help to pay off her debts before embarking for Brisbane. They added up to ten pounds but it is not clear whether or not the society helped her; the records are sometimes unclear or the 'Decisions' sheet is missing. Twenty-nine-year-old Annie Dickinson requested a loan of just one pound to pay off some small debts and buy some decent clothes so she could go out to look for work. However, Annie had been in prison for theft and, as one of the people contacted by the society put it, 'If she has reformed, it is within the last week.' Annie did not get any help. Joanna Green's husband was in the army and she needed help to travel to be with him in Aldershot but was refused.[10]

Many of the requests show just how precarious family budgets were. In September 1882, for example, Caroline Munson[11] applied for financial assistance. Her husband had been a painter and decorator but he had been ill for five years, had earned nothing for the previous two months and was currently in the Brompton Hospital, and she had been warned his prognosis was not good. Caroline had five children aged between two and twelve and Edith, her six year-old, was 'delicate'. She paid five shillings a week for four rooms and let part of one of them to a lodger for 1s. 6d. a week. She was already thirty shillings in debt and was expected to pay the hospital 1s. 3d. a week to do her husband's washing, this left her with just 6s. 9d. a week to support the six of them – though she was hoping to pick up some sewing work by which she expected to earn another three shillings. Her references were excellent: her husband had been 'steady and hardworking'; her home was clean and the four school-age children attended school regularly (which would have cost her fourpence a week which she could ill afford). The society awarded her a 'pension' of 2s. 6d. for a few weeks but, as it was short of money, the payments kept being deferred so it is not clear how much, if anything, she actually received.

Some thirty-five years later Caroline was forced to apply to the Society again. She was then sixty-six and 'used to do shirt work' so obviously she had eventually found a job. She was a widow and only two of her children were still alive: a daughter, who was also a needlewoman but was suffering from pneumonia and unable to work, and a son, who was in the army. Another son had been killed in the war. The family's only income was the 11s. 6d. the soldier son earned. Nonetheless, the society was again unable to help and referred her to the board of guardians.

The next largest category of requests were for help to find work, something the society claimed to do but at which it seems to have been remarkably unsuccessful; the majority of claimants who eventually found jobs did so for themselves. Others requested tickets for admission to hospital for themselves or for family members, like consumptive Martha Norman in 1881 or Maria Stokes[12] in 1888, who needed, and received, a letter of recommendation to the convalescent home by the sea at Hunstanton. In 1884 Elizabeth Edwards[13] was pregnant and asked for money to pay a doctor when she gave birth as her husband had been ill and unable to work full-time for two years. It is not clear whether she got it. Her referees spoke highly of her, but the society's representative described her room as 'not very clean' and said that she lodged with 'a person given to drink'. Not only did applicants have to be squeaky-clean, so, it appears, did all their associates.

Of course, some people were helped. Elizabeth Peddle applied for help in 1885 and received a shilling a week through the Society until 1894.[14] She finally went into an almshouse and sent a letter expressing her gratitude for the support she had received. Mary Ann Coulson got a semi-regular pension of three shillings a week for several months because she was too ill to work, as did Jane Freestone and Mary Dennison.[15] However, these successful applicants were few and far between and a large number were dismissed out of hand with no apparent reason given, or described simply as 'a case for the poor law'. Overall, it seems the society promised a great deal more than it delivered but, as many of the records are incomplete or inconclusive, it is impossible to estimate the percentage of seamstresses they actually helped.

The charity organization societies believed in self-reliance and in helping families to help themselves and so the applicants most likely to be successful were those requesting money to set up in a small way of business. In 1893 Georgina Sophia Conway[16] got a loan of ten pounds to buy stock for a little shop she had established alongside her dressmaking business. Her referees said she was 'industrious, trustworthy and straightforward' and 'very clean and respectable'. It is to be hoped the business was successful as the trustees expected their loan to be paid back at the rate of ten shillings a week over twenty weeks, quite a tall order for a fledgling business in the 1890s.

Other women requested mangles and laundry equipment. Cambridge in term time had a large population of young men living away from home, most of whom would not have had the first idea about washing their own clothes. Competent washerwomen could make a good living. Unfortunately, Martha Ayres,[17] who applied to the society in July 1882 for help in setting up a laundry business, could not be described as competent. Her husband had been a jeweller's assistant but was in poor health and the doctor warned the couple he would never be strong. They had three children and lived in four rooms for which they paid the standard local rent of five shillings. From the file it sounds very much as though the family had come down in the world, but the Ayres do seem to have been unusually adept at getting people to support them. The children's schooling was paid for by Mr Orpen of All Saints' Church, they had help from 'the Assurance Company' to pay the rent and at one point the church made a collection of £50 for the family.

Martha decided she wanted to set up a laundry business as needlework was 'small insufficient work'. The society paid sevenpence to have a pair of washtubs repaired, fourpence for a screw for one of them, 7s. 6d. for a 'wringing machine', 10s. 6d. for flat-irons and £1 16s. for an 'ironing table'. There was correspondence from one of her husband's friends about an 'ironing stone' that didn't fit over the family fireplace and a request for water to be piped to the residence from a neighbouring wash-house and a suggestion that the church would help with the costs and reimburse the society. The request for the pipeline was a bridge too far and the society refused; Mrs Ayres would have to get her water from somewhere else. Martha then went on to request a combined mangle/wringing machine. It is not entirely clear what she wanted but 'patent chain nets for wringing' were available which squeezed water out of the washing more gently than did a mangle and were preferred for fine items.[18] One can sense the Society becoming more and more concerned as her requests escalated and complaints poured in about the shirts she had scorched and how badly she had laundered a Miss Miller's linen. The trustees must have heaved a collective sigh of relief when Mr Ayres notified them in summer 1883 that he had been offered a job in Exeter at twenty-five shillings a week and would shortly be moving his family down there.

The charity organization societies were reluctant to simply bail applicants out with gifts of money, however 'deserving' they were, but additional money was what most people really needed. Eglantyne Jebb wrote: 'Modern thought has emphasised the far greater importance of personal services than of money in the relief of the poor'; she was on message as far as the societies were concerned but she – and they – were wrong. She admitted that: 'Ultimately prevention is far cheaper than cure, but at present we are sinking large sums of money in establishing and supporting institutions which have to cope with a legacy of difficulties, and whose work has not yet had time to bear fruit in the diminution of sickness, poverty and crime.' However, that, too, was optimistic.[19] Poverty wages, insecure employment and the lack of any form of health-insurance were the root of most people's problems and, until those issues were addressed, working-class families were doomed to live with the ever-present threat of destitution.

Moreover, for those seamstresses who reached old age, particularly those without families able to support them, destitution was a near certainty. Only the lucky few, whose lives of hard work and sobriety earned them a place in some charitable institution other than the workhouse, could hope to escape that fate. Lady Haberfield's Almshouses in Bristol was just such an institution.

Lady Haberfield's Almshouses

Sarah, Lady Haberfield, died on 5 December 1874, at the age of seventy-six. She left instructions that most of her estate should be sold and had appointed trustees who were to use the proceeds to build and endow almshouses in memory of her late husband. He was Sir John Kerle Haberfield (1785–1857), a solicitor and attorney, a magistrate, patron and member of various local organizations, a philanthropist and a bon viveur who had been Mayor of Bristol six times. The couple had lived in some style at 41 Royal York Crescent in Bristol, and Sir John was well-known for driving round the city in an old-fashioned coach, complete with postilion.[20]

Figure 9.2 Lady Haberfield's Almshouses, Hotwells, Bristol, 2022. The almshouses lie on a particularly steep stretch of road which must have made life difficult for their ageing tenants.

Lady Sarah's almshouses were built on Joy Hill in Hotwells, a district south of Clifton, and were to provide accommodation for 'Twenty-four Almspeople as Inmates – one half of whom shall be parishioners of the old Parish of Clifton and the remaining half shall be parishioners of the Parish of St Mary Redcliffe.' The almshouses were open to both men and women but only 'such as are poor and impotent, and of good character, and members of, and, so far as they may be able, regular attendants on the services of the Church of England'. They also had to be over fifty-five and never to have been in receipt of parish relief.[21] Through the endowment fund, the trustees were also able to provide out-pensions for those needing some financial help but not accommodation. With its stress on adherence to the Anglican religion, good character and an industrious past in which the applicants had supported themselves without recourse to poor relief, it was a typically Victorian venture to which only the most deserving of the deserving poor would have access.

Applicants had to fill in a printed form and provide the names of referees, one of whom had to be their parish priest, and the early applicants often also supplied letters of recommendation. Some of the questions on the form were quite intrusive: as well as their name and address, the applicants had to say where they were born; how long they had lived at their current address; what they had done for a living; whether they had ever been in business on their own account; whether they had ever saved any money and, if so, what had happened to it; how they were supporting themselves at the time of the application (asked three times in different words); whether they had any pensions or annuities; and whether they had ever been in receipt of parish relief (even though the introductory notes on the form would have told them that never having received such relief was a necessary qualification for entry). Similarly, applicants had to confirm they were members of the Church of England and had to answer numerous questions about their family – whether they had ever been married, whether their spouse was still alive, how many children they had and what those children did for a living. Most pertinently of all, as far as the trustees were concerned, applicants had to give details of who would support them financially if they needed medical attention or incurred any other 'extra expenses'.

The first residents were chosen in April 1891. Amongst them, almost inevitably, were seamstresses. Bristol, like Cambridge, was not noted for its clothing manufacture but, like all cities, it had its fair share of needlewomen employed by manufacturing drapers and tailors and women who did sewing for private clients as and when they could.

Jane Fowles from Alma Vale in Clifton was one of the first inmates, admitted at the end of April 1891. She had been a needlewoman but by 1891 'could hardly earn enough to live on' and her failing sight 'prevented her from doing much'. Jane was only sixty-six but, along with her poor eyesight, she also suffered from bronchitis and rheumatism. Her referees offered the staple nineteenth-century recommendations: she was 'steady', 'honest', 'industrious' and 'doing her utmost to obtain a living'. Admission to the almshouses was her salvation; she was there for twelve years before her health gave out. A letter from her brother in 1903 informed the trustees that he and his wife had agreed Jane could move in with them as she could no longer look after herself; the tone of the letter suggests that pressure had been put on them to take her in, but they only agreed on condition she continued to receive a pension from the Haberfield trust fund.[22] We do not know how long she lived with them, but a Jane Fowles of the right age died in Whitby in 1904 – though we cannot be certain it was Jane from Bristol.

Another needlewoman, Eliza Davies, was admitted at the same time. She too came from Clifton parish and, for the previous decade, had lived on Argyle Place, though she was a Shropshire woman by birth. She was seventy-five years old and three years a widow. Her husband had been a carpenter and they had married in Ludlow in 1835; he had died of prostate cancer in 1888. At some point the family had been quite prosperous and had had £300 in savings, but most of it was lost when the small business she had established failed. It seems she was well thought of in the district because, under the question about how she was surviving, she put 'help from ladies in Clifton' –perhaps they were former customers. She had had nine children, of whom only three were still living. All those three were married with families of their own: her son was a draper's assistant with a 'delicate wife'; her younger daughter was married to a lawyer's clerk and they were 'in poor circumstances'; her elder daughter, Mrs Langdon, was a needlewoman like her mother and worked for 'Mr Chapman, The Triangle' (a tailor) to support herself and her three children because Mr Langdon had spent the last fourteen years in a lunatic asylum. The tragedy and heartache that must have lain behind those bald statements of fact does not bear thinking about. Eliza now had chronic rheumatism and couldn't sew. Her referees described her as 'very respectable', 'industrious' and 'thoroughly well-conducted', altogether a desirable almshouse inmate.[23] Comfortable living arrangements and a regular income worked wonders and Eliza spent ten years in the almshouses up to her death in 1901.

The third needlewoman admitted to Lady Haberfield's Almshouses in April 1891 was Jane Hallett and she made a particularly strong claim for a place, in that she 'was well-known to the late Lady Haberfield and worked in her house and was there at the time of her death and performed the last sewing for her'. From her references it would seem she moved from big house to big house doing sewing work and had done so for many years; she solicited support from Lady Jane Phillips of Edgecumbe Villas, who claimed she had known her over a fifty-year period (probably something of an exaggeration as Jane had only been in the area for twenty-three years and fifty years earlier would have been a child of fourteen) and, rather less successfully, from Mehitabel Allen at Kensington House in Clifton, who claimed not to know her at all! It very much looks as if it was the connection with Lady Haberfield that secured her admission. Jane came from Somerset, had been widowed twenty-one years earlier, had no children and was sixty-four years old. She died at the beginning of 1914.[24]

All three of the needlewomen admitted to the almshouses in 1891 seem to have thrived there, but places for other seamstresses did become available when inmates died. Another needlewoman, 67-year-old Elizabeth Back, was admitted at the beginning of 1897 on account of her poor general health and worsening eyesight. Like Eliza Davies, it would seem she had known better days. Her husband, when he was alive, had earned twenty shillings a week working in a vinegar factory, for a time she had been in business on her own account, and the couple had had only one child to support, a son who now worked as a commercial traveller and was willing to support his mother financially if she needed it.[25]

No more seamstresses were admitted to the almshouses in the nineteenth century, but Emily Bowring and Kate Drewett arrived in 1908, Elizabeth Anderton in 1909 and Annie Parker in 1912, though none seem to have been quite so destitute as the early applicants. Emily Bowring was described by her vicar as the 'most deserving' of three good candidates, but at fifty-nine she was still relatively young and had an annuity of thirteen guineas a year or roughly five shillings a week.[26] Kate Drewett still had twenty pounds which she had inherited from her aunt; she had been a housekeeper but had taken up needlework because: 'For some time past it has not been possible for her to do Cooking etc. to which she had been accustomed.' However, her sight was failing and even at needlework she could 'scarcely make a living'. She had never married and under the question about her marital status she wrote 'No. And not given to drink.' No doubt she hoped her assertion of determined sobriety would impress the trustees![27]

Elizabeth Anderton and her husband had had savings, most of which had been spent when he was ill, but she still had fifteen pounds left. She too suffered from failing eyesight: 'I am sorry to say the sight of my right eye is nearly gone with so much sewing.'[28] Annie Parker had a 'pension' of five shillings a week from her church and 2s. 6d. a month from her daughter and was still able to earn about two shillings a week from 'a little private sewing', but wrote: 'My health and eyesight have been very imperfect lately and I could not do much needlework even if I could obtain it.'[29] Opticians were less skilled at correcting defective vision than they are today; there were only two of them in Bristol in the early twentieth century and spectacles were expensive. It is quite possible that, with a good pair of reading glasses apiece, Kate, Elizabeth and Annie, and Jane Fowles and Elizabeth Back before them, might have continued to earn a living of sorts by needlework.

For all of the almswomen, a comfortable home, a regular allowance, company and freedom from worry about the future ensured as good an old age as they could reasonably have hoped for, but they were the lucky few. At the same time as Jane Fowles, Jane Hallett and Eliza Davies were being given places in the almshouses, nineteen of their fellow seamstresses, along with eleven tailoresses, seven dressmakers, two cap-makers, a stay-maker and a milliner, were amongst the 456 female inmates in Bristol City workhouse. Thirteen of the seamstresses were over sixty and one of them, Mary Lewis, was eighty-five, while Emily Hughes, a spinster, who no longer knew how old she was or where she came from, was labelled an 'imbecile'.[30] No doubt many of them also suffered from failing eyesight and hands crippled with rheumatism, but they would end their days in much less comfortable surroundings than the almshouses, with the additional stigma of being inmates of the workhouse.

Out in the community, other old women tried to get by on a combination of meagre earnings from needlework and charity from family and friends, women like Eliza Davies' former next-door neighbour on Argyle Place, 69-year-old Sarah Smith, or Mary Ann McGoldrick, lodging with the Smith family at 17 Ambrose Road, Clifton, a 79-year-old widow still struggling to earn her own living by sewing.[31] The sober, industrious, Christian lives the almswomen had led may not have been much fun, but they paid dividends in the end.

Conclusion

This examination of evidence of the lives of a small number of flesh-and-blood seamstresses does not do a great deal to overturn the grim picture painted by the reformers. The census evidence shows that some women remained seamstresses for many years, which does suggest that for women with reasonable health and stamina, taking in sewing was not necessarily as speedy a shortcut to starvation and death as some contemporary pundits would have had us believe, but nor was it a route to a comfortable, secure life.

Few of the Whitechapel women we discussed were able to give up work or find better paid jobs in the course of a decade, many did not survive, nearly all had suffered one or more bereavements. Women who had husbands, fathers or sons in employment, and family groups of women working together as seamstresses, probably fared best and lived less miserable lives than some of their contemporaries. The Whitechapel women only represent a small fraction of the women working as seamstresses in the capital, however. The sheer number of needlewomen who came forward to speak to reformers and journalists about the hardships they endured suggests that those hardships were widespread, if not universal, and the number of lone women in the Whitechapel cohort, living in rooms in other people's homes or supporting young families, make those accounts credible.

There were many factors that could overturn the lives of the just-about-managing as the applications to the Cambridge Charity Organization Society show. Illness, the death of one of the breadwinners, being laid off work when trade was bad by an employer who had no obligation to protect his workers, a rent rise, even something as simple as the need for a pair of boots for a son starting work, all could derail a precariously balanced budget. Small wonder that so many families got into debt. The women who applied to the Cambridge Society, even the ones whose applications were refused, were nearly all better at managing their money than the society ladies setting out to advise them could ever have been. They had always had to be; the advice they received from their 'betters', however well-intentioned, must often have grated.

Once she became a seamstress, a woman – and often her daughters – was likely to remain a seamstress for the rest of her life and face a grim old age as her eyesight failed, rheumatism crippled her fingers and sewing became more and more difficult. Very few were lucky enough to end up in places like Lady Haberfield's Almshouses but, for those who did, their life expectancy increased dramatically, showing just what a difference decent living conditions and an adequate pension could make.

The lives of needlewomen everywhere in the country were precarious and for the most part impoverished, but they were not unique. Workers nationwide in many sectors, both male and female, struggled to make ends meet. Reform was urgently needed, but it had to take the form of improved wages, security of employment and insurance against illness and old age; and no amount of do-gooding could replace those.

10

The seamstress in art and literature

A woman doing needlework was, for many men, the very epitome of industrious femininity. Eighteenth-century artists often chose to depict women, both wealthy and poor, at their needles, and both made attractive pictures. (Figure 10.1) These images did not suggest any form of exploitation; they were simply nice pictures showing women doing something womanly, in the same way as a scholarly man might be depicted with a book, a country squire with his dogs and his gun or farm labourers might be shown getting in the harvest. However, the way needlewomen were portrayed in print, particularly in eighteenth-century novels and plays, was often much less benign.

Probably the first play about a seamstress was *The Fayre Maid of the Exchange* of 1607.[1] The 'fayre maid' was Phillis Flower and we know she is a seamstress because in her opening scene she enters speaking to Ursula, her apprentice or journeywoman; 'Stay Ursula: have you those suits of ruffs, those stomachers and that fine piece of lawn mark'd with the letters double C and S?'[2] So we learn that Phillis has a shop in the Exchange selling wares she and Ursula have worked on. However, for half the play that is the only hint we have of what she does. Phillis is the object of the attentions of three brothers, Ferdinand, Anthony and Frank Golding, though she herself is in love with a character called 'The Cripple' – political correctness was an unknown concept in seventeenth-century England! He is described as a 'Drawer', drawing patterns for embroidery on fine fabric, hence his contact with Phillis. In Act 3, Scene 1 she is allowed to puff her wares as a way of deliberately misunderstanding the attentions of Richard Gardner, another gentleman who pursues her and who claims he wants to see more of her:

My shop you mean, sir; there you may have choice of lawns, cambrics, ruffs well-wrought, shirts, fine falling-bands of the Italian cut-work, ruffs for your hands, waistcoats wrought with silk, nightcaps of gold or such-like wearing linen fit for the chapman of what'ere degree . . .

Figure 10.1 *The Seamstress*, engraving by Richard Purcell after Phillippe Mercier, 1754.

In truth, Phillis's profession is entirely incidental to the plot, she could equally well be a seller of books or confectionary. However, unlike similar plays a century later, Phillis's admirers do at least want to marry her rather than seduce her.

Unlikely as the *Fayre Maid* scenario seems today, the ever-lascivious Samuel Pepys was reputed to have had an affair with both Mrs Lane (née Betty Martin) who ran a draper's stall and her sister. On 25 August 1660 he bought a 'half-shirt' from her. On 4 April 1665, having seen another woman he fancied, he wrote:

and then went up to the 'Change to buy a pair of cotton stockings, which I did at the husband's shop of the most pretty woman there, who did also invite me to buy some linnen of her, and I was glad of the occasion, and bespoke some bands of her, intending to make her my seamstress, she being one of the prettiest and most modest looked woman that ever I did see.

No doubt it was her prettiness rather than her modesty that appealed to Samuel!

Much eighteenth-century literature denigrated needlewomen. Milliners, mantua-makers and seamstresses were frequently depicted as immoral and predatory, or at best as easy prey for randy young men. Alternatively, they were a literary device to cross the social divide, like ladies' maids, used as a means for young men to contact young women they fancied they loved without the women's families knowing. Where they were given any sort of personality, needlewomen were brash, vulgar and over-dressed, schemers and inveterate matchmakers, or naïve innocent young things ripe for seduction. However, like the *Fayre Maid*, their profession was largely irrelevant to the various narratives. There were numerous plays of this type: *The Intriguing Milliners and Attornies' Clerks* (1738), Robert Drury's *Rival Milliners* (1753), Douglas Jerrold's *The White Milliner* (1825) or John Madison Morton's *The Milliner's Holiday*, also published in 1825, for example. Novels followed a similar path; their subjects were often cheerfully debauched, like Serena Tricksy in Eliza Haywood's *The Anti-Pamela: or, Feign'd Innocence Detected* (1741), or John Cleland's eponymous heroine in *Fanny Hill: Memoirs of a Woman of Pleasure* (1749), working in a brothel concealed behind the 'outward decency' of a milliner's shop.

The belief that needlewomen were immoral died hard but seems to have had little basis in reality, though it was repeated as fact by Robert Campbell in *The London Tradesman* (1747), ostensibly a book designed to help parents choose an appropriate trade to which to apprentice their children: 'The vast Resort of young Beaus and Rakes to Milliners' Shops, exposes young Creatures to many Temptations. ... [N]ine out of ten of the young Creatures that are obliged to serve in these shops are ruined and undone.' Moreover, 'the Title of Milliner [is] a more polite Name for a Bawd, a Procuress, a Wretch who lives on the Spoils of Virtue.' Mantua-makers' shops were no better because in going there, 'Men pride themselves in debauching such as betray any Marks of modest Virtue.' Did Campbell influence the likes of Drury and Cleland or vice versa? Either way, the suspicion about needleworkers' morals lingered on well into the next century. However, the 1840s saw other concerns being raised.

'The Song of the Shirt'

[1] With fingers weary and worn,
    With eyelids heavy and red,
A woman sat in unwomanly rags,
    Plying her needle and thread –
        Stitch! stitch! stitch!
In poverty, hunger, and dirt,
    And still with a voice of dolorous pitch
She sang the 'Song of the Shirt'.

[2] Work! work! work!
While the cock is crowing aloof!
    And work – work – work,
Till the stars shine through the roof!
It's O! to be a slave
    Along with the barbarous Turk,
Where woman has never a soul to save,
    If this is Christian work!

[3] Work – work – work,
Till the brain begins to swim;
    Work – work – work,
Till the eyes are heavy and dim!
Seam, and gusset, and band,
    Band, and gusset, and seam,
Till over the buttons I fall asleep,
    And sew them on in a dream!

[4] O, men, with sisters dear!
    O, men, with mothers and wives!
It is not linen you're wearing out,
    But human creatures' lives!
        Stitch – stitch – stitch,
    In poverty, hunger and dirt,
Sewing at once, with a double thread,
    A Shroud as well as a Shirt.

[5] But why do I talk of death?
    That phantom of grisly bone,

I hardly fear his terrible shape,
   It seems so like my own –
It seems so like my own,
   Because of the fasts I keep;
Oh, God! that bread should be so dear.
   And flesh and blood so cheap!

[6] Work – work – work!
   My labour never flags;
And what are its wages? A bed of straw,
   A crust of bread – and rags.
That shattered roof – this naked floor –
   A table – a broken chair –
And a wall so blank, my shadow I thank
   For sometimes falling there!

[7] Work – work – work!
   From weary chime to chime,
Work – work – work,
   As prisoners work for crime!
Band, and gusset, and seam,
   Seam, and gusset, and band,
Till the heart is sick, and the brain benumbed,
   As well as the weary hand.

[8] Work – work – work,
In the dull December light,
   And work – work – work,
When the weather is warm and bright –
While underneath the eaves
   The brooding swallows cling
As if to show me their sunny backs
   And twit me with the spring.

[9] O! but to breathe the breath
Of the cowslip and primrose sweet –
   With the sky above my head,
And the grass beneath my feet;
For only one short hour
   To feel as I used to feel,

Before I knew the woes of want
  And the walk that costs a meal!

[10] O! but for one short hour
  A respite however brief!
No blessed leisure for Love or hope,
  But only time for grief!
A little weeping would ease my heart,
  But in their briny bed
My tears must stop, for every drop
  Hinders needle and thread!"

[11] With fingers weary and worn,
  With eyelids heavy and red,
A woman sat in unwomanly rags,
  Plying her needle and thread –
    Stitch! stitch! stitch!
  In poverty, hunger, and dirt,
And still with a voice of dolorous pitch, –
Would that its tone could reach the Rich! –
  She sang this 'Song of the Shirt!'

Thomas Hood's poem appeared in the December 1843 edition of the satirical magazine, *Punch*. It was, wrote his son, 'undoubtedly the first thing that drew attention to Hood as a serious poet of great power.'[3] To the modern reader it is a rather mawkish piece of social commentary, but in 1843 the poem did indeed have power.

It was, Hood claimed, based on a real incident, when a widowed seamstress named Biddell, the mother of two small children, was prosecuted for pawning her work by her employers, the slop tailors, Moses and Son. The report of the case appeared in the *Evening Mail* in October 1843:

According to our Police Report of yesterday, a wretched-looking woman named BIDDELL with a squalid, half-starved infant at her breast, was placed at the bar of the Lambeth-street-office on Wednesday, and charged before Mr HENRY with having unlawfully pawned several articles of wearing apparel which she had been employed to make up for Mr MOSES, a slop-seller on Tower-hill. It appeared that MOSES had 'taken security' – for he, like SHYLOCK, 'will have his bond,' – to the amount of 2L for the safe return of the articles intrusted to the workwoman, and having heard that some of them had been pawned, gave the poor wretch into custody for the offence. Her tale, on the correctness of which no suspicion whatever was attempted to be cast, was sad enough, and, as the worthy magistrate stated 'the affair was one of *very common* occurrence in that part of the metropolis.' By the violent death of her husband from an accident, last January, she had been left a widow with one child two years old, and pregnant with the infant she then held in her arms. After the death of her husband, she had attempted to support herself and the two children by her needlework, principally in making trousers, for which she was paid SEVEN PENCE a pair, out of which she was obliged to buy the thread to make them; and, in order to provide *dry bread* for herself and her infants, she had been compelled to pawn a portion of the work which she had finished while she proceeded with the remainder. The slop-seller's foreman, probably well experienced as to what was sufficient to keep life in the miserable drudges who slaved for his master, asserted that if she was honest and industrious, she might make a 'good' living at her trade, and, on being questioned by the magistrate as to what he considered a 'good living for a woman who has herself and two infant children to support' he explained it TO BE SEVEN SHILLINGS A WEEK.

This was thought by the court, and by Thomas Hood, to be outrageous, but as many women, including the ones Mayhew would interview six years later, earned five shillings a week or less, and all firms required a security payment before handing work out, the foreman's assertion was not wholly unreasonable. Indeed, as late as 1908 there were still women earning just 4½d. a pair for making drill trousers (see p.180). Messrs Moses were actually paying *above* the minimum rate, but they were both highly successful and Jewish which made them doubly unpopular, hence the criticism and the unnecessary reference to Shylock.

There had been other similar cases in the press, and most magistrates understood that pawning completed work to raise enough money to survive till payday was a recognized strategy amongst needlewomen, and did not punish them. Messrs Moses were within their rights to prosecute, but many employers did not; the worst interpretation of the Biddell affair is that the firm was being unnecessarily officious.

Hood may have been inspired by the incident, but his protagonist in 'The Song of the Shirt' was actually a shirtmaker, working alone in her garret, not a trouser-hand like Mrs Biddell. It was not Hood's first foray into verse about needlewomen and their exploiters. In 1840 he had penned 'Miss Kilmansegg and Her Precious Leg', which, despite its rather comical title, was about a spoilt young heiress who wore rich clothes and was not born:

to sit all day and hem and sew
As females do, and not a few
To fill their insides with stitches.

In January 1843 he had written a story called *The Defaulter* which urged young ladies to consider the plight of respectable young seamstresses being paid a pittance for making shirts and shifts. Nor was it to be his last. In February 1844 he wrote 'The Lady's Dream' about people ignored by society, including those needlewomen who:

For the pomp of pleasure of Pride
We toil like Afric slaves,
And only to earn a home at last
Where yonder cypress waves.

In April that same year he wrote 'The Workhouse Clock', listing all sorts of hopeless, starving workers, among them:

The sempstress, lean and weary and wan,
With only the ghosts of garments on . . .

Hood wrote many poems but it was 'The Song of the Shirt' that everyone remembered. It was quoted in the press and in parliament, schoolchildren memorized it and references to it were understood decades after it was published. It was even translated into German and French; English seamstresses were not the only ones who were overworked and lived in poverty. Hood was proud of it and actually had 'He sang the Song of the Shirt' inscribed on his gravestone when he died in 1845.[4]

Images of Needlewomen

Lines from Hood's poem formed the titles of numerous paintings. In 1849 John Thomas Peele painted a seamstress in a bare room with an unpainted wall on which her straw bonnet hangs on a nail. The table at which she sits is covered by a drab-coloured cloth on which lie her workbox and the shirt she is working on. She wears a rust-coloured dress and a cream shawl – we are to deduce that the room is cold – and she is resting her chin on her hand and gazing pensively into the distance. Peele called it *The Song of the Shirt*.[5] (Colour plate V) George Frederick Watts painted a picture with the same title at about the same period.[6] His shirtmaker also wears a drab rust-coloured dress, un-enlivened by collar or cuffs. She sits on a wooden chair at a plain wooden table, her face resting on her left hand, the shirt she has been stitching draped across her lap. There is a guttering candle on the table, so we know it is late, the rest of the room is in darkness and the only thing we can discern is a small, high window-frame, suggesting an attic room, and a pale patch at her feet which may be more shirts. In 1875 William Daniels used the title again for a picture of a woman (modelled by his eldest daughter) in a shapeless grey cloak seated at a table in a darkened room, head resting on her hands, shirt on her lap and scissors, thread and an almost-burnt-out candle on the table before her.[7]

Anna Blunden also painted a shirtmaker in 1854.[8] Her needlewoman is wearing a green dress and is shown in profile, seated at a table, gazing upwards with hands clasped as though in prayer. A shirt, a reel of cotton and a workbox lie on the table. Beyond her is a window, quite a large one, to enable Blunden to show the scene beyond. She is at rooftop height, so this is an attic. Blunden chose the title for her work, *For Only One Short Hour*, from a line in 'The Song of the Shirt', invoking memories of the seamstress's country childhood amongst 'cowslip and primrose sweet – with the sky above [her] head, and the grass beneath [her] feet'. (Colour plate VI)

John Everett Millais painted *Stitch! Stitch! Stitch!*, again a line from 'The Song of the Shirt', in 1876.[9] It shows a three-quarters-back view of an attractive young woman, her hair neatly dressed in a bun, wearing a grey dress with a smart white frill at the neck. She is sitting on a mahogany chair, a finer piece of furniture than Peele, Watts, Daniels and Blunden gave their seamstresses, but the rest of the room is drab and in shadow. She is holding a white piece of fabric, probably a shirt, but is looking away from her work at something which is out of the picture. She appears sad or worried, but looks healthy and well-nourished.

References to Hood's poem continued to be used long after his death. In 1891 Claude Andrew Calthrop produced a painting called *It Is Not Linen You're Wearing Out, But Human Creatures' Lives*, which shows a group of five women in dark dresses with white aprons.[10] Two are stitching busily, one is clearly exhausted and is resting her head on the table and one is looking towards the door where a fifth young woman is standing with another bundle of what appear to be more shirts to be stitched. In the early twentieth century (1907–17), Beatrice Offor used the same title for a portrait.[11] It shows a middle-aged lady, smartly dressed in a black dress with a collar and wearing a string of coral-coloured beads, sewing what looks like a shirt. The background is in darkness, and she is looking sorrowfully straight ahead at something behind the viewer. Her expression fits the title, but she is well-dressed and again, apparently healthy; her life seems some way off from being 'worn out'.

Numerous other artists painted distressed needlewomen. Richard Redgrave prided himself on his contribution; he claimed, 'It is one of my most gratifying feelings, that many of my best efforts in art have aimed at calling attention to the trials and struggles of the poor and oppressed.' He painted a number of versions of *The Seamstress*, (1844–6),[12] depicting a young woman in a bare, dark room, gazing upwards, a shirt on her lap and a candle lighting the table where she sits. He also painted *Fashion's Slaves* (1847)[13] showing an indolent young woman lolling on a settee with a poorly dressed young dressmaker or milliner at her side with a bandbox, and images of other young working women like *The Poor Teacher* (1843)[14] and *Going into Service* (1843), which shows a young girl bidding a sorrowful farewell to her family.[15]

Philip Hermogenes Calderon's *Lord, Thy Will Be Done* shows a young woman nursing a baby. She is a seamstress and her work lies on the table alongside her. The room is poor but the family are not destitute, there is a loaf of bread on the table, ornaments on the mantelpiece and coal in a hod. However, the painting is dated 1855, the period of the Crimean War; a letter discarded on the floor and a dishevelled pile of pages of newsprint suggest that the young woman has just received bad news, and the small portrait of a man in soldier's uniform to the left of the fireplace hints at what that bad news has been. Henceforth the discarded needlework on the table is going to be her sole source of income.[16] (Colour plate VII) George Elgar Hicks' *Snowdrops* dates from 1858[17] and shows a young needlewoman in a striped dress admiring a pot of snowdrops while sitting at a table in what we know must be an attic because of the sloping ceiling, by a small window, with a shirt on her lap and a cup of tea on the table.

Frank Holl's *The Slaves of the Needle* dates from the 1860s[18] and shows three young needlewomen in black dresses sewing in a pleasant room with a fireplace and a picture over it, suggesting that at one point they lived in some comfort. One of them has fallen asleep over her work. Edward Radford's *Weary* (1887)[19] shows another exhausted seamstress almost asleep in her chair in her attic room. Her bed is just behind her, covered with a patchwork quilt, a lit candle and cup of tea stand on the table beside her, a shirt is on her lap and another is on a chair under the window, while a child's toy lies on the floor telling us she is a mother working to support a young child.

These pictures were painted to draw attention to the plight of the wretched, overworked 'distressed seamstress'. It was fertile subject matter, however none of the women in the paintings look particularly distressed. Their surroundings are poor, but apparently clean, they are decently dressed and there are hints of better circumstances – a pot of snowdrops, a child's toy, a china cup and saucer. Unlike

Mayhew's interviewees, these women have not been reduced to pawning their clothes and bedding and, although some of them look sad, or at least pensive, and some have fallen asleep from exhaustion, none of them appear to be starved or ill. They invite the viewer's sympathy but also respect for their courage and industry. They are not (yet) ground down by fate. It would, of course, have been difficult for painters to find models who were as emaciated and exhausted as real seamstresses often were and, besides, though they may have hoped the scenes they depicted made a point, at the end of the day artists wanted to sell their work and, if they made their models too unattractive, no one would buy their paintings. There were practical limitations to the power of the painted image to reform society.

Cartoons and Magazines

Cartoons and book illustrations present less sanitized pictures. *Punch* was founded in 1841 by Henry Mayhew and Ebenezer Landells and became a leading protagonist for social change, particularly in the middle years of the century. The historian Richard Altick wrote that: '*Punch* had become a household word within a year or two of its founding, beginning in the middle class and soon reaching the pinnacle of society, royalty itself.'[20] It was, of course, *Punch* that first published 'The Song of the Shirt'. In August 1848 they published a cartoon depicting the final line of the fourth verse, 'A shroud as well as a shirt', showing an image of a shirt printed with skulls and the figures 2½ for the 2½d seamstresses were paid per shirt. The brief article above it referenced the case of Emma Mounser (see Chapter 6, section 'Henry Mayhew') and took the opportunity to denigrate Moses and Son, her employers: 'By the kindness of the pawnbroker we are enabled to furnish a pattern of the "Twopenny-ha'penny Shirt" which can be had ONLY (it is to be hoped) of MESSRS. HENRY EDWARD AND MORRIS MOSES of the Minories.' (Figure 10.2) Twopence-halfpenny was indeed a pathetic wage but, as we have seen, there were at the same date women working for a penny or a penny-halfpenny a shirt, less the cost of thread.

The magazine had it in for Messrs Moses. There were cartoons of Mr Moses and his son 'Attiring young England' in 1844 and 'Mr Smith and Mr Moses' in 1848, both showing caricatures of hook-nosed Jews attending to their supposedly hapless customers. (Figure 10.3) In 1844 there was a spoof piece based on the idea that Moses and Son would supply anything their customers required: 'State of the matrimonial trade. LOVERS – A large cargo of fine lively Lovers just landed in prime condition. Dressed every day by Moses and Son in the highest

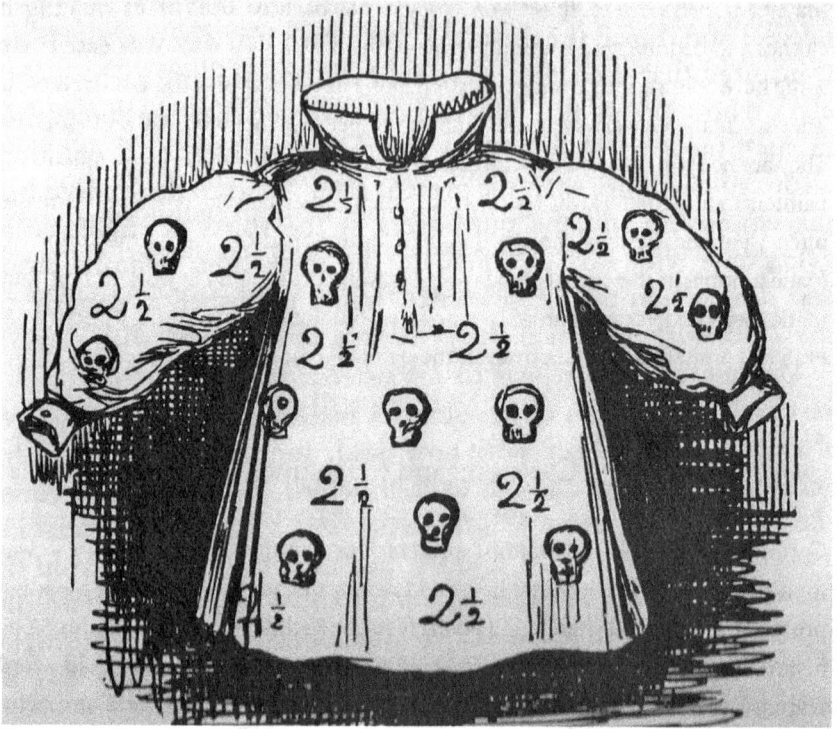

Figure 10.2 Cartoon from *Punch*, 'A shroud as well as a shirt', referring to the Mounser case of 1848.

perfection and sent to any part of Town or Country. Allowances to Widows or to Families having two or three daughters according to the quantity taken.'

The same year there was also a mock book review of *The Commercial Phenomenon: Moses and Son*, complete with a suggested design for a memorial to them, the base supported by an impoverished tailor and a seamstress clad in rags.

In fact, at this period Moses and Son were one of the pre-eminent men's tailoring firms in London. They had recognized the growth of a new and expanding market for affordable fashion and catered for it by aggressive and innovative marketing. Their shop on Aldgate was grand, almost palatial, as was its successor in Tottenham Court Road. In the fifty-five years they were in business (1829–84) they played a major role in laying the foundations for modern mass-market retailing in men's fashion by a strategy of carrying extensive stock, aiming for a high turnover, and keeping profit margins as low as possible, obviously at some cost to their workpeople.[21] Nonetheless, they were probably no more exploitative of their workers and customers than many other

MR. SMITH AND MOSES.

Figure 10.3 Cartoon from *Punch*, 1848, lampooning the business practices of Moses and Son and emphasising their Jewishness.

clothes dealers, but they were Jewish, and much of nineteenth-century England was deeply anti-semitic. *Punch* knew its readers and gave the firm a bad press.

Punch magazine addressed other aspects of the needlewoman question too. In December 1849, for example, it published a cartoon entitled 'Pin money/ Needle money', depicting a well-to-do young woman sitting at her dressing table attended by a servant, trying on items she has bought with her 'pin' (or pocket) money, contrasted with an emaciated black-garbed needlewoman sitting stitching for 'needle money'; it was probably a reflection of Mayhew's recent 'letters' in the *Morning Post*. (Figure 10.4) In 1850 when needlewomen were being urged to emigrate, *Punch* joined the debate with *The needlewoman at*

Figure 10.4 Cartoon from Punch, 'Pin money/Needle money', 1843, highlighting the difference between the rich young lady and the poor seamstress.

home and abroad, showing an impoverished girl huddled in a shawl in the street in front of an advertisement for cheap gin, contrasted with a young woman happily playing with a baby in a log cabin watched by her husband and toddler. *Punch's* position was clear; emigration was a good thing. (See Figure 6.3.) In July 1863 at the height of the Mary Anne Walkley scandal, they published *The Ghost in the Looking Glass* by Tenniel, which showed a fashionable young woman looking in the mirror and seeing the starving, exhausted needlewoman who has made her new dress. (See Figure 7.1.)

Book illustrations sometimes used similar types of contrasts. The frontispiece of Reynolds' *The Seamstress,* for example, was divided in two by a giant pair of scissors, a thimble and various reels and hanks of thread: one side showed the industrious needlewoman bent over her work late at night, the other the gay young things going to a ball in garments she had made. (See Figure 0.1.) Short stories and serials in magazines continued the theme of the overworked, exhausted needlewoman struggling to make a living in miserable surroundings.

Millais painted a picture called *The Seamstress* in 1860,[22] which was intended as an illustration to a story called 'The Iceberg' by J. Stewart Harrison, which was published in the periodical *Once A Week*.[23] The story tells of Ben, a sailor, who is engaged to Esther, but, when he returns from a voyage, he discovers she has borne a son by another man. He abandons her and she is reduced to earning her living as a seamstress to support herself and her baby boy. Millais' illustration shows Esther in a smart, blue-and-white striped dress and matching snood, sitting sewing a shirt in a large, empty, but quite grand room (there is a large fireplace with a small fire in the grate and a gilt-framed mirror), next to a baby in a cradle. The bareness of the room suggests Esther has already sold many of her possessions. (Colour plate VIII)

Figure 10.5 is a typical example of another common theme: it shows a young woman taking a break from her pile of sewing and talking to her pet canary. Potted plants, suggesting the subject's love of nature from which her work

Figure 10.5 Magazine illustration by Kate Edwards, London, 1868, showing a seamstress and her caged bird. Birds in cages were often used in illustrations of seamstresses.

separates her, and birds in cages, trapped like she is, are often associated with images of needlewomen. The symbolism is glaringly obvious. The writer of the spoof letter of 1848 in the *Durham Chronicle* (see Chapter 6, section 'The Causes of the Problem) referenced this trope, when she claimed to have both a linnet and a geranium which she was willing to give to whoever procured her a place in prison or the workhouse where she would be able to do her needlework without having to pay rent or buy her own food.

Novels

While artists were inspired by Hood's poem, it was by no means the only source of information about the plight of needleworkers. The report of the Children's Employment Commission on the dressmaking trade also came out in 1843 and highlighted long hours, meagre pay, unsympathetic employers and dreadful working conditions. That report as a whole caught the public imagination in a way subsequent reports on other, equally exploitative industries, failed to do.

Novelists of the second half of the nineteenth century wrote about needlewomen – with varying degrees of credibility – and several of them were directly influenced by the report. Elizabeth Stone's *The Young Milliner* appeared in 1843 within months of the report's publication and she credited it as her source in the introduction and in footnotes. Her heroine, Ellen Cardan, worked for 'Mme Sarina Mineau' (Sally Minnow) and witnessed all the abuses the report had highlighted, long hours, abusive mistresses in the shape of a Mrs Modish, who called in on the girls toiling in her workroom on her way to bed, glass of gin in hand, and through Bessy, a fellow worker, who became a prostitute, the temptation to which so many girls were believed to succumb. (Prostitution, in fact, was scarcely mentioned in the report but, nonetheless, the link between it and needleworkers was still widely believed.) Ellen – or Mrs Stone – had no doubt that the reason for the dressmakers' hard lives lay with selfish customers who expected gowns to be made in double-quick time.

Ellen also had some friends, the Lamberts, who were shirtmakers struggling to make a living against impossible odds. 'It can hardly be called living,' Mrs Lambert tells Ellen:

> Formerly we had 4½d. for a fine shirt and 2½d. for a coarse one; and then I did contrive, somehow, to hold that little decent room upstairs. But I hardly know how it is, hands seem to become more plentiful every week; and then, of course,

when there is so much competition, the prices are lowered; and of late we have not only been without work sometimes, but when we have got it, it was only on the condition that we would make shirts at 1½d., apiece.[24]

Not surprisingly, Mrs Lambert ended up in the workhouse.

Charlotte Elizabeth Tonna wrote *The Wrongs of Women* between 1843 and 1844. It was in four volumes and dealt with different abuses in different trades, and two of them dealt with needleworkers, though not specifically with seamstresses. The first chapter of each volume described the reality of the situation Tonna was about to fictionalize and referenced the Children's Employment Commission reports. Volume one was about dressmakers and milliners, and the fictional protagonists were Ann and Frances King, daughters of a poor, widowed farmer. Ann is apprenticed to a dressmaker and works long, long hours with thirty others in a large workroom which becomes stuffy and smelly as the day wears on, with the fumes from the gas lights that come on in the evening adding to the unhealthy atmosphere. The girls are allowed brief breaks for meals, but the food is poor and unappetising and Ann becomes ill with consumption and has to return home. Frances has a more prestigious post with a milliner but spends most of her time running errands. Though her indenture says meals are to be provided, she is turned out to fend for herself on Sundays when she attracts the attention of young men and becomes a prostitute.

The heroine of volume four is Kate Clark, who went to Nottinghamshire to become a lace runner – in other words, someone who embroidered designs on machine-made net. Kate is, in effect, a specialist seamstress. She lives with her employer, sleeping on a shared palliasse on the floor. Her employers' and neighbours' children work at the same trade, the youngest being a little girl of four, all sitting together at the same table. Kate is horrified to learn that her mistress's baby is kept sedated with laudanum to keep it quiet while they work. Again, the hours of work are long, there is little opportunity to go outside in the fresh air, and Kate becomes ill.

The Unprotected: or, Facts in Dressmaking Life, by an anonymous author, 'A Dressmaker', was published in 1857 and also relied on the report, although it misreferenced it as 'evidence put before the House of Commons in 1855', despite an introduction composed of quotations from the report of 1843. The heroine was Clara, an apprentice to a heartless mistress called Mrs Morterton, who overworked and neglected her staff and lied to her customers and the Employment Commissioners. Many of her staff were respectable and well-educated. However, one of them went missing and was eventually discovered, pregnant and living with a man who was not her husband. Even authors who were familiar with the Commissioners' findings could not divest themselves of a belief in the link between needlework and immorality. Mrs Morterton refused to allow her own daughter, Minnie, to sit with the girls in the workroom because it was so unhealthy: 'If any of them are ill and die, which they sometimes do, I can replace them; but if you were to die, what on earth should I do? No-one can replace you.'[25] Minnie eventually came up with a plan to improve the girls' lot by reducing hours and raising wages, but her mother was totally unimpressed.

Charles Rowcroft's *Fanny, the Little Milliner* (1846), *Lettice Arnold* by Mrs Anne Marsh-Caldwell (1850), Reynolds' *The Seamstress: or, The White Slave of England* (1853), *May Coverley, the Young Dressmaker*, published by the Religious Tract Society in 1860, and *Nellie Graham, the Young Dressmaker* by C.R. Doggett (1874) are all variations on the same theme, involving heroines working long hours in dismal conditions and (usually) hanging on to their virtue against numerous temptations.

A play first performed in October 1852, *Wanted: 1000 Spirited Young Milliners, for the Gold Diggings* harked back to the scurrilous plays of the eighteenth century. Two young solicitors place the advertisement in the hope of acquiring young women to seduce, but the women who respond are feisty older women who attack the young men with their needles when they discover the plot. The women in *The Milliners' Holiday* of 1825 are equally fearsome, terrifying the young men whom they meet on their travels.

Other novels took different approaches. In some, like Margaret Oliphant's *Kirsteen* (1891), needlework is a means, albeit a hard one, to independence and eventual financial security; in *The Sorrows of Gentility* (1856), Geraldine Jewsbury's heroine, Gertrude Donnelly, spends a profitable and comparatively happy period working as an embroideress and embroidery designer for Lady Southend and her contacts to support herself and her child while her useless, spendthrift husband is abroad; in *Girl Neighbours* (1911) by Sarah Tytler, needlework and dressmaking, learnt at a residential college, are presented as a route to independence for modern girls. However, in Ernest Jones' melodramatic short story, *The Young Milliner* (1851–2), the needlewoman, Anna, is seduced and impregnated, then abandoned by her lover, and both she and her child die miserable deaths. *My Milliner's Bill*, a play of 1884 by G.W. Godfrey, centres around the (mistaken) idea that dressmakers routinely overcharged their customers and describes how a man decided to teach his actress wife a lesson when she ran up a bill of £600 for clothes. There were many ways of approaching the needle trades. Better known authors also tackled the seamstress question.

Charles Dickens' *Little Dorrit* was a seamstress who had learnt to sew from a fellow prison inmate. She was a shadowy, elusive figure, working twelve hours a day to support the hapless father and brother with whom she lived in Marshalsea debtors' prison: 'Little Dorrit let herself out to do needlework. At so much a day – or at so little – from eight to eight, Little Dorrit was to be hired. Punctual to the moment, Little Dorrit appeared: punctual to the moment, Little Dorrit vanished. What became of Little Dorrit between the two eights was a mystery.'[26]

What became of Little Dorrit while she worked was actually just as much of a mystery. We learn nothing of her working life, what she sewed, how much she was paid or, indeed, how she was able to cease work so promptly every day when most needlewomen were expected to stay at work until the task was finished, or how she had so much free time. 'Oh! She? *She's* nothing; she's a whim – of hers [Mrs Clennam's]'[27] the old servant tells Mrs Clennam's son when he returns after a long period abroad. Little Dorrit was also Dickens' 'whim', a quiet, modest presence, struggling in a patriarchal environment, but a positive moral influence on all around her; an 'angel in the home', an archetype of his ideal woman rather than a representative of an oppressed workforce. However, at least Dickens did not subscribe to the myth of the needlewoman whore.

In *Nicholas Nickleby* (1839) Kate Nickleby works for a time for Mme Mantalini, in 'drudgery and hard service', twelve hours a day for between five and seven shillings a week. Eventually she is sacked and finds a new job as a companion. Dickens deals with the needlework question more fully in a novella, *The Chimes*, of 1844. 'Trotty' Veck, an elderly working man, is depressed and despairing. On New Year's Eve he dreams he is summoned by bells to the church, where he climbs the tower and meets the goblins who are the bells' attendants. They offer him a series of visions of what the future may hold and this includes the death of his about-to-be son-in-law, Richard, who dies leaving Trotty's daughter, Meg, with a baby. Meg and her friend Lilian are forced to become needlewomen, 'for so many long, long nights of hopeless, cheerless, never-ending work' and live in desperate poverty: 'Meg strained her eyes upon her work until it was too dark to see the threads, and when night closed in, she lighted her feeble candle and worked on.'[28] Lilian becomes a prostitute and eventually dies in Meg's arms. Meg is about to drown herself and the baby when Trotty finally wakes from his dream and finds all is well. Meg blames his dream on indigestion: 'And whatever you do, Father, don't eat tripe again . . .!' The story ends with Trotty dancing happily at Meg's wedding: 'Had Trotty dreamed? Or are his joys and sorrows, and the actors in them, but a dream; himself a dream: the teller of this tale a dreamer, waking now?'[29]

An anonymously written novella, *Christmas Shadows* (1850) recycles *The Chimes* and *A Christmas Carol* as a polemic against the exploitation of needlewomen. Dickens' Scrooge becomes Cranch, an outfitter-employer, employing 'glengarries', who are cutters-out, and needlewomen. One girl, Emmeline, asks for an advance to help her care for her sick brother. Cranch refuses and sacks Emmeline. In the night he, too, dreams. His dream is about the fate of Rose and Kate, his beloved daughters, who have somehow been reduced to living in a common lodging-house and taking in slop-work from their father's old firm. Rose dies and Kate tries to poison herself because she has (like Emmeline) been refused work – and Cranch wakes up a reformed character and model employer. The message is crystal clear.

Mrs Gaskell was also sympathetic and understanding of working-class problems, and she, too, wrote about needlewomen heroines. *Mary Barton* (1848) is based on a relationship that ends in murder. Mary becomes a dressmaker's apprentice as her father has refused to let her work in a factory, partly because of the example set by her Aunt Esther who has become a street-walker: 'That's the worst of factory work, for girls. They can earn so much when work is plenty, that they can maintain themselves any how', John Barton claims.[30]

Mary has two suitors, rich Harry Carson, son of her father's employer, and working-class Jem Wilson. Harry is murdered, Jem is accused but the culprit is actually Mary's father, maddened by the Carsons' treatment of himself and his fellow workers. However, it is the, very brief, description of Mary's work that concerns us here. Her father could not afford the premiums demanded by high-class dressmakers in Manchester, but she was finally taken on by:

> Miss Simmonds, milliner and dressmaker, in a respectable little street leading off Ardwick Green, where her business was duly announced in gold letters on a black ground, enclosed in a bird's-eye maple frame, and stuck in the front parlour window; where the workwomen were called 'her young ladies;' and where Mary was to work for two years without any remuneration, on consideration of being taught the business; and where afterwards she was to dine and have tea, with a small quarterly salary (paid quarterly, because so much more genteel than by the week), a *very* small one, divisible into a minute weekly pittance. In summer she was to be there by six, bringing her day's meals during the first two years; in winter she was not to come till after breakfast. Her time for returning home at night must always depend upon the quantity of work Miss Simmonds had to do.[31]

Mary was a dressmaker, but the anti-social conditions of her working life were not dissimilar to those of young seamstresses working for a shop, and Mrs Gaskell was clearly aware of the meanness and unfairness of those conditions and also of the difficulties seamstresses faced. She describes Mary's friend, Margaret, who was a seamstress: 'a sallow, unhealthy, sweet-looking young woman, with a careworn look; her dress was humble and very simple, consisting of some kind of dark stuff gown, her neck being covered by a drab shawl or large handkerchief, pinned down behind and at the sides in front.'[32] One evening Mary helps her with an order for mourning for a funeral the next day. It seems Margaret worked for a shop but took work home at the end of the day. She explains how much she has to do:

> I only got the order yesterday at noon; and there's three girls beside the mother; and what with trying on and matching the stuff (for there was not enough in the piece they chose first), I'm above a bit behindhand. I've the skirts all to make. I kept that work till candlelight; and the sleeves, to say nothing of little bits to the bodies; for the missis is very particular, and I could scarce keep from smiling while they were crying so, really taking on sadly I'm sure, to hear first one and then t'other clear up to notice the sit of her gown. They weren't to be misfits I promise you, though they were in such trouble.[33]

That evening, Mary also learns that Margaret is going blind, and how and why. She has lost sight in one eye, and though she can see with the other:

> Th' only difference is, that if I sew a long time together, a bright spot like th' sun comes right where I'm looking; all the rest is quite clear but just where I want to see. I've been to both doctors again, and now they're both o' the same story; and I suppose I'm going dark as fast as may be. Plain work pays so bad, and mourning has been so plentiful this winter, I were tempted to take in any black work I could; and now I'm suffering from it.[34]

Another of Mrs Gaskell's novels, *Ruth* (1853), deals with the issue of the supposedly immoral needlewoman and the cruelty of her treatment. Ruth is chosen by her employer to go to a ball to do running repairs on ladies' dresses; long skirts and trains tended to get trodden on and torn. Ruth is an orphan, alone in the world, and very beautiful. At the ball she meets a young man who seduces her, she becomes pregnant and he abandons her. Eventually she is befriended by a Baptist minister and his wife who present her to their community as a young widow with a child. The deception is discovered and she and they are ostracized. Ruth only redeems herself by selfless nursing during an epidemic and by her subsequent death. The clergyman who performed her funeral, and whose unforgiving attitude had informed the behaviour of his congregation, read from the Bible:

> 'And he said to me, these are they which came out of great tribulation, and have washed their robes, and made them white in the blood of the Lamb. Therefore are they before the throne of God, and serve him day and night in his temple; and he that sitteth on the throne shall dwell among them . . .'
>
> Before it was finished, most of his hearers were in tears. It came home to them as more appropriate than any sermon could have been.[35]

However, it was all far too late for Ruth, and Mrs Gaskell wanted her readers to recognize the congregation's – and their own – hypocrisy.

Conclusion

There are two reasons why it is worthwhile to look at artistic and literary depictions of needlewomen. First, amid a good deal of conjecture and guesswork and dramatic effect there are some nuggets of genuine information; for example, the *Fayre Maid* lists shirts amongst the items she sells (sells rather than makes), an indication of just how early ready-made shirts were available to buy. Second, while the paintings and cartoons, novels and plays may present an inaccurate or distorted picture – implying, for instance, that eighteenth-century seamstresses were nearly all immoral and ripe for seduction, and that a disproportionate number of mid-nineteenth-century needlewomen were gentlewomen-fallen-on-hard-times – these depictions show us how contemporaries were led to perceive seamstresses, which in turn explains how attitudes were formed.

Before the 1840s the needlewoman was not seen as a problem; she did her job and earned her money providing useful articles that people wanted. She appeared in plays and novels as a figure of fun or scandal, but for the most part people knew that fiction really was fiction. However, after 1840 the distressed needlewoman became a familiar figure, at least to the Victorian middle-classes, through novels and magazines, through paintings and cartoons, and through reports in the press of tragedies and charities, miscarriages of justice and government interventions. Why then was so little done to help her?

Part of the problem lay with the very works that tried to raise awareness of her suffering. Paintings showed the needlewoman as brave in the face of adversity and, perhaps more importantly, as fit and healthy. Novels often provided happy endings for the good and virtuous as well as reinforcing troubling notions of seamstresses' immorality. Cartoons were, well, cartoons, showing caricatures of reality that were in turn amusing and shocking, but exaggerated and not necessarily credible. Numerous reports in the press of charitable initiatives and government interventions suggested that the problems were being solved, and the occasional reports of suicides, court cases and starvation were just that, occasional regrettable episodes. Contact with real needlewomen at home or in shops allayed many fears, while the truly distressed and destitute stayed out of sight in the parts of towns respectable people did not visit.

Despite the best intentions of people like Richard Redgrave, Mrs Stone, Elizabeth Gaskell and so many others, art and fiction were not necessarily the best ways to publicize real abuses. Moreover, as we have noted before, the problems were actually so great that there were no quick fixes. Only government intervention could improve the seamstress's lot, and it was a long time coming.

Conclusion

Seamstresses were always at the least glamorous end of the spectrum of clothing workers. Because most of the items they created were either made from geometrically-shaped pieces put together according to well-established formulae, or later, from pieces cut out and ready to assemble, their work was seen to require less skill than that of tailors and dressmakers whose creations had to fit, and ideally flatter, their customers. Nonetheless, the garments and household textiles seamstresses produced were of considerable value, both practically and commercially, and almost everyone used at least some of the items they made. Even the poorest man had his shirt or smock, and the poorest woman had her shift, while their richer neighbours also wore shirts and shifts albeit made of finer fabrics, along with aprons, collars and cuffs, cravats and neck-handkerchiefs, and owned cupboards and chests full of household linen. When stolen, some of those same items were highly valued, witness, for example, the fifteen-shilling, fine linen shirt stolen from William Threele in 1607.

The cut of seamstress-made garments may have been simple, but they, and the household textiles seamstresses also produced, had to be considerably better stitched than suits and dresses because they had to withstand soaking in lye, boiling and rigorous scrubbing by laundresses, in a way that fancier garments did not. The number of stitches-per-inch was related to the thread-count, as we saw in Chapter 1, with the result that fine Holland could require twenty-five tiny stitches to the inch, each barely a millimetre long, which must have made sewing high-quality linen very slow work, and far, far finer than the stitching seen on surviving eighteenth-century dresses and suits. In the seventeenth century the women who made these items were recognized as expert craftswomen. They sewed, but they also washed and starched and 'got up', fine wearing linen, and they were familiar with the fabrics on which they worked because many also sold them, along with laces and trimmings, haberdashery and bought-in goods like stockings.

Seamstress-made garments may not have excited the same level of admiration as a fine new suit, a lavishly embroidered waistcoat or a dress of rich brocade, but a pristine white shirt, or a clean shift showing at neck and wrists, trimmed, perhaps, with fine frills, provided a foil for the showier clothes and was evidence of the wearer's gentility and cleanliness, or at the very least of their efforts to appear respectable. Similarly, fine sheets and table linen were a form of conspicuous consumption, intended to impress overnight visitors and dinner guests alike by providing a comfortable night and showing off an embroidered bedspread, or displaying silver cutlery and a dinner-service of fine china to their best advantage.

Nonetheless, like other garment-workers, seamstresses were poorly remunerated, even in the seventeenth and eighteenth centuries. For example, in the eighteenth century a workman's shirt or a pauper's shift made of dowlas or osnaburg or hempen cloth used two, or at most three, yards of material costing between sixpence and 1s. 2d. a yard, but the parish seamstress making it up was usually paid somewhere between fourpence and a shilling per garment, according to the wealth or generosity of the local overseers. At the other end of the scale, fine Holland could cost upwards of eight shillings a yard and an average price for making a good quality shirt was around 4s. 6d. In both cases, seamstresses, like tailors and dressmakers, were paid less for making a garment than the value of the fabric on which they were working. They had to be skilful; they could not afford to make mistakes.

By the mid-eighteenth century, things were getting worse. Fewer needlewomen kept shops and did laundry, and more and more seamstresses were outworkers, contracted to a shop or a supplier. There were still needlewomen keeping small shops and carrying a handful of made items, but city shops were getting larger and keeping stocks of dozens or hundreds of examples of different types of garments. Thomas Walker in London, for example, had 458 petticoats in stock, along with 434 mantuas, 120 gowns and numerous suits and waistcoats as early as 1693.[1] Some of these large shops also employed washerwomen. For example, C. Churchill in London did washing for the Hill family in the 1730s, and M. and E. Nicholas in Oxford in the 1760s and 1770s dressed various caps for Mrs Ives, the alderman's widow. However, these new large shops meant that many needlewomen were no longer autonomous workers making the goods they sold, aided, perhaps, by an apprentice or journeywoman; they were employees, employed only as and when they were needed. While in the mid-eighteenth century Elizabeth Mepham in East Hoathley could make as many 'frocks' as Thomas Turner needed for stock, at the same sort of date a big firm like Webbe and Batten at the Hen and Chickens in London's Covent Garden would have had numerous outworking seamstresses on their books. (Figure 11.1) As their trade

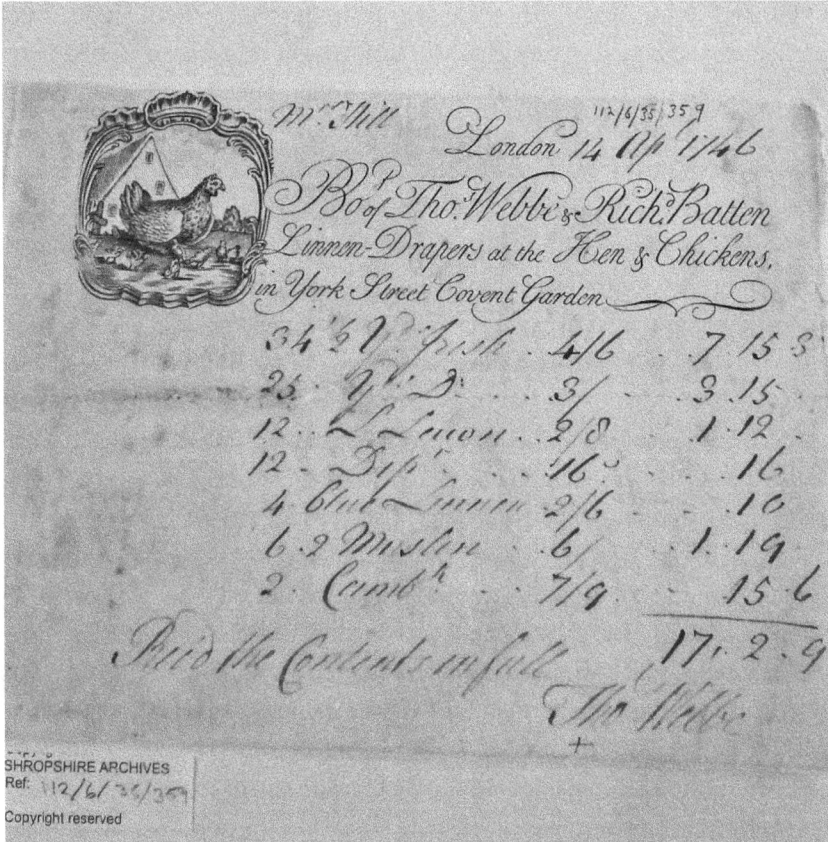

Figure 11.1 Bill from Thomas Webb and Richard Batten at the 'Hen and Chickens', linen drapers, April 1746.

expanded, shopkeepers found it more and more time-consuming to manage all the sub-contracting to needlewomen that their businesses required. Thus, they employed middlemen, like the 'Person in Deptford', contracted by Silver and Co. in the early 1800s. As time went by, even that level of sub-contracting became burdensome, and large firms bought from warehouses or wholesalers. The gap between the seamstress and her customer was growing ever wider and with it, recognition of her skill declined and her wages shrank and shrank.

In fact, however, even those seamstresses employed in the relatively lowly trade of making 'slops', particularly after 1800, were producing useful items that allowed the rank-and-file soldiers and sailors to be adequately, decently and uniformly clad, that helped to provide clothing for the growing number of uniformed civilians, and that made affordable, moderately fashionable, if not particularly high-quality, garments available to ordinary working people. From the eighteenth century onwards, visitors to Britain often commented on how finely many working people were dressed and on the difficulty of distinguishing servants from their masters and mistresses. Servants might actually be wearing their employers' cast-offs, but many other working people were able to dress respectably, at least on high days and holidays, because of the clothes they could buy in the slop-shops. Society may not have recognized it, but the army of seamstresses toiling away in their garrets were providing a valuable service, although it was one from which they, and the rest of the truly poor, were seldom able to benefit.

As they became less and less visible, respect for seamstresses declined. When Lady Anne Clifford in Cumbria in 1676 'kist' the seamstress who had arrived to make new sheets for the household, or when a century later Dr Davenport and his wife in Worcestershire gave Mary Berrington, their needlewoman, five shillings for Christmas in 1776, they were recognizing the value of people who did a job they needed and appreciated. Mr Burden in Ludlow in 1822, campaigning to have parish relief reinstated for his disabled seamstress, Mrs Bullock, was making it clear that she had been a valued employee, not someone who could readily be replaced. Even as late as the 1890s some bespoke seamstresses in Clifton could find satisfied former clients to recommend them for places in Lady Haberfield's Almshouses, but they were unusual; by that date fewer and fewer women worked in the bespoke trade and they tended mostly to be tarred with the same brush as the thousands of slop-workers toiling for middlemen and warehouses.

Indeed, by the 1840s, society had come to see seamstresses as 'a problem'. They were not alone. Working women generally were seen as problematic; a woman's place, respectable Victorians believed, was in the home. Even the Chartists, who in the early years of the century had embraced women as fellow workers in the struggle against exploitative employers, had changed tack and now agitated for higher wages for *men* so their wives could do the womanly thing and be housewives and mothers, not wage-earners.[2] Those women who had no man to support them played no part in anyone's calculations, although in fact they formed a very large part of the cohort of seamstresses. In 1851 there were somewhere between 500,000 and a million more women than men in Britain: many were widows, some were orphans, some had never married and the majority had no inherited wealth. Inevitably, therefore, there were many women who had no option but to earn their own living, and many of them became seamstresses because there were so few other jobs open to them. The employment opportunities available for women had always been somewhat limited, but as society increasingly subscribed to the myth of the 'little woman in need of protection', these opportunities declined yet further.

Another factor was that the Victorians saw poverty as a sin, something to be concealed at all costs. 'Poverty should never have the appearance of poverty', wrote 'Sylvia' in *How to Dress Well on a Shilling a Day*,[3] a manual of fashion advice for middle-class women with limited incomes. 'Sylvia's' readers were not truly poor but they were trying to appear more affluent than they were because affluence signalled respectability. By extension, people were led to believe poverty was something the poor had somehow brought upon themselves: they married too young, made no attempt to save and had too many children. It was their own fault for accepting inadequate wages, not the fault of employers for paying them. As a result, by the mid-century attitudes to giving poor relief had hardened. After the Poor Law Amendment Act of 1834 which created the Union workhouses, society increasingly believed that the workhouse was the only suitable place for the indigent poor and that 'out-relief' should be withheld as often as possible; witness the case of Louisa Mordaunt who was allowed to starve to death by the local guardians because she and her mother wanted to stay in their own home. As we saw in Chapter 9, even the well-meaning members of the charity organization societies believed the Poor Law Board's decision to cut outdoor relief in 1869 was actually a desirable move, despite their closer-than-average involvement with the lives of the poor.

These attitudes created a situation that gave exploitative employers free rein, and many of those employers employed seamstresses. Of course, men were exploited too, men like the slop-tailors catering for the armed forces or making cheap coats for slop-sellers, but women were doubly disadvantaged because of their sex. As women, there were fewer alternative jobs open to them; as women they would always be paid less than men; as working women they were despised because they were in the wrong 'sphere', the marketplace rather than the home; and as single women they were vulnerable to both sexual and workplace exploitation because they had no man in their lives. It was a gross oversimplification and was belied by feisty women like the widow recorded in the *Dublin Evening Mail* in 1856, who took her cheating employer to court and won, but many women were less energetic and assertive.

Not only did the government condone exploitation by employers, it was itself an exploitative employer. Government contracts were given to workhouses in the 1830s and 1840s, and subsequently to prisons, meaning that garments could be made cheaply by captive labour; alternatively, contracts were given to soldiers' wives, who were subsidized by their husbands' wages. This reduced prices to the point where it was impossible for independent seamstresses to compete, although some were forced to try, hence shirts being paid for at a penny apiece. Only those workers capable of high-class work for expensive shops, like Robert Blunt in Charing Cross in the late eighteenth century, or David Lord on Piccadilly and Edward Jackson in Reading a century later, could make anything resembling a living.

Against this background, the numerous charities that tried to help, however well-meaning their members, could make very little impact. That is not to say that some women did not benefit. Several hundred, possibly several thousand, were helped to a greater or lesser extent by charities in the provinces, in Liverpool, in Glasgow, in Dublin and, above all, in London. However, given that there were over 28,000 seamstresses nationwide in 1841 and over 81,000 in 1871, the majority struggled on without assistance. Charity records show how precarious working-class lives were and the way in which illness, bad luck or an unexpected expense could all derail the family economy. The work of a wife and daughter might lift a family out of dire poverty but was never sufficient to support it in any degree of comfort without the addition of a man's wage. Nonetheless, there were families and individuals who knew nothing else. A sympathetic employer or landlord, like the one who allowed Mayhew's two elderly spinsters to go through the winter without paying rent, might enable them to just about survive. Such women lived for months on a diet of bread or oatmeal and weak tea with the very occasional 'relish', while starving women in the countryside stole turnips from the edge of fields. Women, like Mary Ann Stanton in Bluegate Fields, slept on piles of straw on the ground after pawning their beds and shivered through the winter having pawned most of their underwear. All this, they believed, was better than facing the hostile environment of the workhouse and the shame of being there. Like their 'betters', the poor had been conditioned to see poverty as something shameful.

Social investigators, even the comparatively enlightened Beatrice and Sidney Webb, continued to blame the poor for accepting work at starvation wages, failing to realise that the alternative for many was actual starvation. There were always too many desperate people out there for anyone to dare to refuse work, at almost any price, hence the acceptance of poverty rates of pay. Women, in particular, were exhausted and isolated, and the suggestions made by do-gooders that they should cooperate and negotiate for better wages were totally unrealistic.

The political commitment to *laissez-faire*, letting the market find its own level without legislative intervention, was a key factor in maintaining the status quo. It inevitably favoured the employer, the person with bargaining power, at the expense of the worker, who, in an overcrowded and desperate marketplace, had none. However, it was a belief deeply entrenched in the Victorian psyche. Of course, needlewomen were not the only sufferers; nineteenth-century society had created a situation where a significant number of the working poor could not earn enough to keep body and soul together however hard they tried. The reports of the various Children's Employment Commissions that came out between 1842 and 1867, of the numerous women's groups established in the 1880s and 1890s, and of the Select Committee on the Sweating System of 1890, shocked newspaper readers, but did little to dislodge their belief in market forces. Received wisdom decreed that the relationship between employer and employee was sacrosanct.

Individual reports of suicides and starvation disturbed the public, and many tried to help, but few joined the dots and realized that without legislative intervention wages would remain at starvation level in trades that were over-subscribed. Charities were set up and thousands of pounds were donated, but they barely touched the edges of the problem. The liberal élite in the shape of artists, poets, novelists, campaigning journalists and magazines like *Punch* attempted to raise people's awareness, but with little in the way of tangible success.

The first glimmerings of an effect came with the Sweated Industries Exhibition of 1906 which was visited by tens of thousands of people in London and from the provinces. Not only did the public read the case studies in the exhibition brochure and hear speeches, they also encountered a – no doubt carefully-vetted – group of sweated workers. These were real people, showing off their skills, living, breathing and talking to the visitors, and not so very scary after all. It was a game-changer; and the game could change because at last there were other factors in play.

A Liberal minority government under Henry Campbell-Bannerman had taken over in 1905 and was then elected with a large majority in 1906. In 1908 Bannerman was replaced by Herbert Asquith, with David Lloyd George as Chancellor of the Exchequer. The Liberals were committed to social reform and alleviating the problems caused by poverty, and they enacted a range of reforms to aid children, workers and the elderly. Free school meals were introduced in 1906 and school medical inspections in 1907, and after 1912 schoolchildren received free medical treatment. From 1908 children were treated separately from adults by the court system and were sent to Borstals (young offenders' centres) rather than adult prisons. Old age pensions for the over-seventies came in in 1908, subject to various caveats. Labour exchanges to help the poor find work were set up in 1909, and a form of National Insurance to support workers who fell sick was introduced in 1911. The Workmen's Compensation Act was passed in 1906 and acts limiting miners' and shop-workers' hours were passed in 1908 and 1911. It was an impressive record.[4]

Of course, none of these reforms was problem-free; workers and employers alike objected to paying National Insurance contributions, and those contributions covered the workers but not their families and only for twenty-five weeks. Not all employers were cooperative; not all vacancies were notified to the employment exchanges; some local authorities refused to supply free school meals and arrange medical inspections; pensions were only available to people who could actually produce a birth certificate and did not have a prison record. Nonetheless, by 1914 a million over-seventies were receiving the new pensions, and no doubt some of them were seamstresses. The children of seamstress mothers would have benefited from free school meals and medical treatment, and out-of-work needlewomen could have sought work through the new labour exchanges. It was a great deal better than nothing.

A Select Committee on Home Working was set up in 1907 and recommended legislation to regulate wages; in 1909 this led to the establishment of the first trade boards, two of which covered parts of the needle trades. The effect was limited. As we have seen, the boards did not establish a national minimum rate of pay but a local one, what the local industry was 'thought able to bear,' and it preserved the traditional differential between men's and women's wages, but no doubt some needlewomen's lives were improved. However, all these reforms, imperfect though they were in execution, were hugely important as a way of demonstrating the new government's belief that it had a responsibility to its less privileged citizens. Ideologically, it was a massive change. The fear of becoming too old or too ill to work was gradually being removed, though it must still have been a concern for, among others, unmarried seamstresses, few of whom would have been covered by National Insurance because many of them were classed as self-employed.

The First World War provided another stimulus for change. With most men of working age away at the front, opportunities for women increased dramatically, if temporarily, between 1914 and 1918, and as a result the profession of seamstry became less overcrowded, though it remained poorly paid for decades. As late as the 1980s, working for herself, May Verita, in her book, *Tailoring, Twopence an*

Hour, claimed never to have earned more than a pound an hour, for example.[5] Many of the opportunities for women were rolled back when the war was over, but things would never be quite the same again; women had proved what they could do and it would in future be less easy to deny them access to a range of types of work. In addition, the terrible slaughter of men had left gaps in the job market, a large number of older women with no husband and a large number of younger ones with no one to marry. Some members of both groups needed to support themselves and there were jobs available. Girls were no longer forced into seamstry because there were no alternatives.

Nonetheless, although much had changed, it is a mistake to assume that seamstresses' lives all improved radically in the early twentieth century; the best conclusion we can come to is that for the most part they ceased to deteriorate.

Notes

Introduction

1 Devon CRO, 1038M/F/1/204.
2 CEC interviewee 360.
3 CEC interviewee 449.
4 Inder, Pam (2020) *Busks, Basques and Brush-Braid: British dressmaking in the 18th and 19th centuries*. London: Bloomsbury.
5 *Oxford Journal*, 1821.
6 Simonton, Deborah (1998) *A History of European Women's Work: 1700 to the Present*. London: Routledge, 153.
7 See Chapter 6, section headed '"Grinders" and "Sweaters".'

Chapter 1

1 North, Susan (2020) *Sweet and Clean? Bodies and Clothes in Early Modern England*. Oxford: Oxford University Press.
2 Clifford, D.J.H. (ed.) (1990) *The Diaries of Lady Anne Clifford*. Stroud: Alan Sutton, p. 81. No children were born to Lady Anne in 1619–20, but we know she suffered numerous miscarriages which she often did not trouble to record.
3 Vickery, Amanda (1993) 'Women and the World of Goods: A Lancashire Consumer and Her Possessions, 1751–81', in Brewer, John and Porter, Roy (eds.), *Consumption and the World of Goods*. London: Routledge, 198.
4 Crane, Elaine Forman (ed.) (1991–1994), *The Diary of Elizabeth Drinker, 1758–1807*, Vol 2. Boston: North Eastern University Press, Vol. 2, 193.
5 Lady, A (1838) *The Workwoman's Guide*. Reprinted (1975) Doncaster: Bloomfield, 11.
6 North, *Sweet and Clean?*.
7 Ibid., 72.
8 Ibid., 34.
9 Lincs. CRO, 28A/14/8.
10 North, *Sweet and Clean?*, 145–50.
11 Salop CRO, 3614/3/60.
12 Pottle, Frederick (ed.) (1950) *Boswell's London Journal, 1762–1763*. London: Heinemann, 336 and 99.

13 Troide, Lars E. (ed.) (1988) *The Early Journals and Letters of Fanny Burney*, 2 vols. Oxford: Clarendon Press, 154.

14 Quennell, Peter (ed.) (1985) *Memoir of an Eighteenth Century Footman* [John Macdonald]. London: Century, 179–80.

15 Ashcroft, Lorraine (ed.) and Hillman, Anne (transcr.) (1994) *The Rake's Diary: The Journal of George Hilton*. Kendal: Curwen Archives Trust, 30.

16 Pottle (ed.), *Boswell's London Journal*, 272.

17 Smollett, Tobias (1771) *The Expedition of Humphry Clinker*. Project Gutenberg edition. It is an epistolary novel and this edition has no page numbers. This quotation occurs in a letter from J. Melford to Sir Watkin Phillips, dated 24 May.

18 Ibid. Letter from Win Jenkins to Mary Jones, dated 14 October.

19 Pottle (ed.), *Boswell's London Journal*, 176.

20 North, *Sweet and Clean?*, 125.

21 Smollett, *The Expedition of Humphry Clinker*. Letter from J. Melford to Sir Watkin Phillips, dated 3 October.

22 Spufford, Margaret (1984) *The Great Reclothing of Rural England: Petty Chapmen and Their Wares in the Seventeenth Century*. London: Hambledon, 151–235.

23 Derbys. CRO, D517/Box 13/2.

24 Vaisey, David (ed.) (1985) *The Diary of Thomas Turner, 1754–1765*. Oxford: OUP, 17–18.

25 Notts. CRO, DD/1487/1.

26 Leics. and Rutland CRO, 2D31/187.

27 Tankard, Danae (2019) *Clothing in 17th-Century Provincial England*. London: Bloomsbury, 119.

28 Derbys. CRO, D258/29/1/1.

29 Heywood, Thomas (attrib.) (1607) *The Fayre Maid of the Exchange*. London, Act 1, Scene 3. The original version was not divided into acts and scenes. This quotation comes from the 1846 Shakespeare's Library online edition.

30 Spufford, *The Great Reclothing of Rural England*, 151–235.

31 Pepys, Samuel *Diary*. All the quotations from Pepys are from the Project Gutenberg online edition. They are easily traceable by date and so will not subsequently be referenced.

32 Leics. and Rutland CRO, 2D31/187.

33 Lancs. CRO, DDX1096/1.

34 Hatcher, Jane and Woodings, Bob (2018) *Life in Georgian Richmond, North Yorkshire: A Diary and Its Secrets*. Barnsley: Pen and Sword History, 115.

35 Kent CRO, EK/U471/A54.

36 Spufford, *The Great Reclothing of Rural England*, 151–235.

37 Johnston, J.A. (ed.) (1991) *Probate Inventories of Lincoln Citizens, 1661–1714*. Woodbridge: Boydell Press for the Lincoln Record Society, 56–61.

38 Lancs. CRO, L3157.

39 Richardson, Samuel (1740) *Pamela: or, Virtue Rewarded*. London: Everyman (1978), Vol. 1, 7 and 32–3.

40 Macdonald, *Memoirs of an Eighteenth Century Footman*, 177–8.

41 Llewellyn, Sacha (1997) '"Inventory of Her Grace's Things, 1747": The Dress Inventory of Mary Churchill, 2nd Duchess of Montagu', *Costume* 31, 49–67.

42 François-Alexandre de Garsault, *L'Art de la lingère*, 11. Open Library online edition.

43 Leics. and Rutland CRO, 12D43.

44 W. Sussex CRO, PAR384/6/1.

45 Spufford, *The Great Reclothing of Rural England*, 492–7.

46 North, *Sweet and Clean?*, 126.

47 Defoe, Daniel (1665) *A Journal of the Plague Year*. London: Penguin (1966), 22.

48 https://ardhindle.com/pdf/academy-of-armory-1688

49 Victoria and Albert Museum, London, T608.1996.

50 Kent CRO, U120A16.

51 Leics. and Rutland CRO, 6D40/19/56.

52 Wilcox, David (2012) 'The Clothing of a Georgian Banker, Thomas Coutts: A Story of Museum Dispersal', *Costume* 46, no. 1, 17–54.

53 North, *Sweet and Clean?*, 131.

54 Llewellyn, '"Inventory of Her Grace's Things"', 17–54.

55 www.londonlives.org. The Oliver case is: LL ref. t1687 1207-44.

56 *The Workwoman's Guide*, chapter fourteen.

57 Kent CRO, P321/12/8/8.

58 Bucks. CRO, D-X1069/2/104.

59 Née Noel. She was married to Thomas Hill of Tern, a cousin of Sir Rowland Hill, first Baronet of Hawkstone. The Hills' son, Noel, became the first Baron Berwick. Salop CRO, 112/6/35/34.

60 Née Ward. They married on 4 January 1729.

61 E. Sussex CRO, PBT1/10/2869.

62 De Garsault, *L'Art de la lingère*, chapter seven.

63 Crane (ed.), *The Diary of Elizabeth Drinker*, 236.

64 Clark, Gillian (1994) 'Infant Clothing in the Eighteenth Century: A New insight', *Costume* 28, no. 1, 50.

65 Delves Broughton, Mrs Vernon (1887) *Court and Private Life in the Time of Queen Charlotte: Being the Journals of Mrs Papendiek, Assistant Keeper of the Wardrobe and Reader to Her Majesty*, 2 vols. London: Richard Bentley & Son, 28.

66 Ibid., Vol. 1, 221.

67 Salop CRO, MI5777/2.

68 Leics. and Rutland CRO, DG7/Inv 2.

69 Rendell, Mike (2011) *Journal of a Georgian Gentleman: The Life and Times of Richard Hall, 1729–1801*. Brighton: The Book Guild, 246.

70 Kresen Kernow ('Cornwall Centre'), BRA 2508.

71 *Diaries of Lady Anne Clifford*, 263.

72 Cumbria CRO, WD HEE/7/8/A.

Chapter 2

1 Cumbria CRO, Q11/1/181/27.

2 Glaisyer, Natasha (2006) *The Culture of Commerce in England, 1660–1720*. Woodbridge: Boydell Press, Introduction.

3 Humphries, Jane and Wesdorf, Jacob (2015) 'The Wages of Women in England, 1260–1850', *Journal of Economic History* 75, no. 2, 417.

4 Boulton, Jeremy (1996) 'Wage Labour in Seventeenth-Century London', *Economic History Review* 49, no. 2, 268–90.

5 Humphries and Weisdorf, 'The Wages of Women in England', 424.

6 Ibid., 411; and www.londonlives.org.

7 See, for example, the Hawkshead overseers' accounts (Cumbria CRO, WPR83/7/1/11); and those of the overseers of the parish of Rockbourne (Hants. CRO, 39M68/).

8 https://www.johnhearfield.com/History/Breadt.htm.

9 https://www.british-history.ac.uk/office-holders/vol11/, 31–35.

10 Somerset CRO, DD/M1/19/31.

11 https://www.york.ac.uk/depts/maths/histstat/king.html.

12 Spufford, Margaret (2000) 'The Cost of Apparel in Seventeenth-Century England and the Accuracy of Gregory King', *Economic History Review* 53, no. 4, Table 4, 692.

13 London Metropolitan Archives, CLC/313/K/C/010/MS19504/006/031.

14 Derbys. CRO, D258/45/10/46.

15 Johnston (ed.), *Probate Inventories of Lincoln Citizens*, 56–61.

16 North, *Sweet and Clean?*, 201.

17 Spufford, *The Great Reclothing of Rural England*, 151–235.

18 London Metropolitan Archives; and www.londonlives.org, LL ref. GLBAAC100000114.

19 www.londonlives.org., LL ref. GLBAAC100000116.

20 Ibid., LL ref. GLBAAC100000207.

21 'Parish Clothing Books with Names of Children at Nurse', Westminster Archives, LL ref. WCCDBN356000004.

22 London Metropolitan Archives; and www.londonlives.org, LL ref. GLBAAC300000386.

23 www.londonlives.org, LL ref. GLBAAC300000389.

24 Cambs. CRO, P30/1/11.

25 W. Sussex CRO, PAR516/31/1/1-89.

26 Salop CRO, 3365/661/109 and 128.

27 Essex CRO, T/A418/73/10 and T/A418/110/21.

28 Defoe, *A Journal of the Plague Year*, 62.

29 W. Sussex CRO, PAR 384/6/1.

30 Leics. and Rutland CRO, 2D31/187.

31 Clarke, Bridget (2009) 'Clothing the Family of an MP in the 1690s: An Analysis of the Day Book of Edward Clarke of Chipley, Somerset', *Costume* 43, 38–54.

32 Scott-Moncrieff, Robert (ed.) (1911) *The Household Book of Lady Grisell Baillie, 1692–1733*. Edinburgh: Scottish History Society.

33 Wilts. and Swindon CRO, 2664/3/1D/2/1.

34 Gowing, Laura (2022) *Ingenious Trade: Women and Work in Seventeenth-Century London*. Cambridge: Cambridge University Press, 139.

35 Wilts. and Swindon CRO, 2664/3/1D/2/1. 'Colbertine' was a type of French lace, the manufacture of which had been promoted by Colbert, First Minister of State under Louis XIV.

36 London Metropolitan Archives, CLC/313/K/C/010/MS19504/046/17.

37 Ibid., CLC/313/K/C/010/MS19504/043/45.

38 Gowing, *Ingenious Trade*, 40, 170, 251–3.

39 London Metropolitan Archives, CLC/313/K/C/010/MS19504/059/09.

40 Earle, Peter (1998) 'The Female Labour Market in London in the Late Seventeenth and Early Eighteenth Centuries', in Sharpe, Pamela (ed.), *Women's Work: The English Experience, 1650–1914* London: Arnold, 130.

41 Yorkshire Archaeological and Historical Society, DD99/B23/62.

42 Barlow, Jill (2001) *A Calendar of the Registers of Apprentices of the City of Gloucester, 1595–1700* Bristol: Bristol and Gloucestershire Archaeological Society.

43 Gowing, *Ingenious Trade*, 153.

44 Bristol RO, P/StM/OP/4a.

45 Salop CRO, 3365/632/21J.

46 Ibid., P221/L/5/2.

47 Gowing, *Ingenious Trade*, 171–2.

48 Ibid., 199.

49 Ibid., 169–70.

50 Earle, Peter (1998).

51 Herefords. CRO, BG11/11/ series.

52 PRO, PROB11/1551/312.

53 Hants. CRO, 1729A/074.

54 Dorset CRO, P5/9Reg/42C.

55 PRO, PROB11/243/309.

56 PRO, PROB11/1133/46.

57 PRO, PROB11/518/463.

58 PRO, PROB11/1182/291.

59 Norfolk CRO, NCC original will no. 96.

60 Kresen Kernow ('Cornwall Centre'), AP/P/1788.

61 PRO, PROB11/265/161.

62 Cumbria CRO, WPR93/E16/7.

63 E. Sussex CRO, PBT/1/1/42/48.

64 Wilts. and Swindon CRO, P16/200.

Chapter 3

1 Lemire, Beverley (1997) *Dress, Culture and Commerce: The English Clothing Trade before the Factory, 1660–1800.* Basingstoke: Macmillan, 9–41.

2 Spufford, 'The Cost of Apparel', 702.

3 North, *Sweet and Clean?*, 202. The contract was with Richard Aldworth and Richard Wollaston.

4 Lambert, Miles (2006) 'The Consumption of New and Used Ready-made Clothing in Northern England, 1660–1830' PhD thesis, University College, London, 40.

5 Northants. CRO, ASL.PS72.

6 Westminster Archives, 0985.

7 Northants. CRO, ASL PS64, PS69.

8 Ibid., PS84, ASL.267.

9 Ibid., ASL 230-254.

10 Ibid., ASL 237.

11 Ibid., ASL 231.

12 See Chapters 6 and 8.

13 Westminster Archives, 0985.

14 PROB 11/701/86.

15 Lemire, *Dress, Culture and Commerce*, 61–2.

16 Kent CRO, U1590/0128/1.

17 Ibid.

18 Wikipedia, *List of Ships of the Line of the Royal Navy.*

19 PRO, ADM106/435/216.

20 Lambert, 'The Consumption of New and Used Ready-made Clothing', 35.

21 53.101/1a and b.

22 https://www.meg-andrews.com/item-details/Sailors-Slops/8657.

23 PRO, ADM106/608/22.

24 Lambert, 'The Consumption of New and Used Ready-made Clothing', 48–9, writing about the 1620s and 1630s.

25 Ibid., 54.

26 Ibid., 44–6.

27 PRO, ADM106/428/306.

28 PRO, ADM106/410/36.

29 PRO, ADM106/435/129 and ADM106/515/86.

30 PRO, ADM106427/340.

31 Lemire, *Dress, Culture and Commerce*, 45–7.

32 Ibid., 47–8.

33 Spufford, 'The Cost of Apparel', 703.

34 London Metropolitan Archives, CLC313/K/C/009/006/018.

35 Ibid., MS19504/08/75.

36 Ibid., CLC313/K/C/009/016/52.

37 Ibid., CLC/313/K/C/010/19504/053/08.

38 Tankard, *Clothing in 17th-Century Provincial England*, 58

39 Spufford, *The Great Reclothing of Rural England*, 124.

40 Ibid., 56–61.

41 Spufford, 'The Cost of Apparel', 699.

42 Inventory 1704, referenced in Tankard, *Clothing in 17th-Century Provincial England*, 69.

43 Berks. CRO, D/EX1942/8/2.

44 PRO, C 2/ChasI/P68/60.

45 PRO, HCA30/636/5/2.

46 It is not clear where 'Middleborough' was. Middlesbrough in North Yorkshire was little more than a farm and a cluster of cottages as late as 1829 – the port did not develop till the late nineteenth century. Middleborough in Massachusetts was known as 'Nemasket' until the 1660s. Was it perhaps Middelburg in Zeeland?

47 London Metropolitan Archives, CLA 024/06/001/091.

48 Derbys. CRO, D517/Box 13/2.

49 Lambert, 'The Consumption of New and Used Ready-made Clothing', 42.

50 Ibid., 69.

51 Nigel Sleigh-Johnson, 'Aspects of the Tailoring Trade in the City of London in the Late Sixteenth and Earlier Seventeenth Centuries', *Costume* 37, no. 1 (2003): 27.

52 Somerset CRO, DD/SAS/S2062.

53 Lemire, *Dress, Culture and Commerce*, 64.

Chapter 4

1 Weatherill, Lorna (1988) *Consumer Behaviour and Material Culture in Britain, 1660–1760*. London: Routledge.
2 Salop CRO, 112/6/346/83.
3 Lincs. CRO, Misc Wills 0/1970.
4 North, *Sweet and Clean?*, 165.
5 Hants. CRO, 47M81/PK109.
6 Lincs. CRO, 1-MM-9-2.
7 Beds. CRO, X109/1/ series.
8 N. Devon CRO, TD146/A/67/ series; and N. Devon CRO, Leworthy TD146/A/67/6.
9 Herefords. CRO, BG11/11/series.
10 Manchester Cathedral Archives, Mancath/1/3/1/2/1/1/ series.
11 Isle of Wight RO, NBC/3/192.
12 Cambs. CRO, KP25/14/1/29.
13 Hunts. CRO, HP82/14/14.
14 Ibid., KHP 82/14//17.
15 Ibid., HP82/14/25.
16 Cumbria CRO, WPR93/11/6/8.
17 Cambs. CRO, K588/F/23.
18 London Metropolitan Archives, MJ/SP/1732/12/032.
19 Cheshire CRO, DSS1/6/52/1 and 2.
20 Beds CRO, J464.
21 Salop CRO, P176/L/6/27.
22 For a fuller discussion of this, see Spufford, *The Great Reclothing of Rural England*, 151–235.
23 *Falkirk Herald*, 12 November 1846.
24 Nottingham University Archives, PwC591.
25 Notts. CRO, DDST 6/1.
26 Johnston (ed.), *Probate Inventories of Lincoln Citizens*.
27 Salop CRO, 112/3/59.
28 Spufford, *The Great Reclothing of Rural England*, 151–235.
29 Ibid.
30 Cumbria CRO, WDX948/76/4.
31 Ibid., WPR83/7/1/11.
32 Kent CRO, EK/U471/450.
33 Hayden, Peter (1988) 'Records of Clothing Expenditure for the Years 1746–79 Kept by Elizabeth Jervis of Meaford in Staffordshire', *Costume* 22, no. 1, 32–8.
34 Wilts. and Swindon CRO, 2664/2/4B/98.
35 Leics. and Rutland CRO, DE3214/8576/1-.

36 Martha Winterton had two payments, one of £1 10s. 6d. and one of £2 2s. 10d. Betty Gunn was paid 17s. 4d. and £1 6s. 3½d. and Anne Fancourt 5s. 10d. and £1 12s. 10d. Elizabeth Stephenson had three payments of 11s. 6d., 10s. 10d. and 2s. 0d. Bridget Prangnell and Anne Rudham had 5s. 10d. and 4s. 2d., respectively.

37 Birmingham RO, MS3145.

38 W. Sussex CRO, PHA6613, 6635, 7541.

39 Salop CRO, 552/12/775.

40 Wilts. and Swindon CRO, 1178/296 and 394.

41 Bird, Margaret (ed.) (2013) *The Diary of Mary Hardy 1773–1809*, 4 vols. Kingston-upon-Thames: Burnham Press.

42 Cambs. CRO, P129/5/2.

43 Kent CRO, P10/12/B4.

44 Ibid., P39/12/4.

45 Lincs. CRO, 13/2/3/1.

46 Hants. CRO, 39M68/32.

47 Leics. and Rutland CRO, DE175.

48 London Metropolitan Archives, A/FH/B/1/1.

49 Salop CRO, 112/6/35B/97.

50 Berks. CRO, D/ESV/M/F148.

51 Lincs. CRO, NEL/8/13/1-126.

52 PRO, 11-1164-3.

53 W. Sussex CRO, PA 11571.

54 https://www.british-history.ac.uk/office-holders/vol11, 31–5.

55 Lancs. CRO, DDX1096/1 diary transcripts.

Chapter 5

1 Lemire, Beverley (1999) '"In the Hands of Workwomen": English Markets, Cheap Clothing and Female Labour, 1650–1800', *Costume* 33, no. 1, 29.

2 Berks. CRO, D/ESv(M)B1/1.

3 *Stamford Mercury*, 19 April 1739.

4 *Kentish Weekly Post*, 26 May 1739.

5 Lambert, 'The Consumption of New and Used Ready-made Clothing', 91.

6 *Saunders' Newsletter*, 12 March 1799.

7 Ireland at this date had its own currency.

8 *Oxford Journal*, 25 July 1789.

9 *Kentish Gazette*, 13 October 1789.

10 Proceedings of the Old Bailey, 17 September 1800.

11 Lambert, 'The Consumption of New and Used Ready-made Clothing', 95.

12 Wikipedia, *Slop Clothing*.

13 For a fuller discussion of this see Inder, *Busks, Basques and Brush-Braid*, ch. 1.

14 Sanderson, Elizabeth (1996) *Women and Work in Eighteenth-Century Edinburgh* Basingstoke: Palgrave Macmillan, 35.

15 See for example, *Derby Mercury*, 26 July 1781.

16 *Northampton Mercury*, 19 August 1782.

17 Notts. CRO, DD/2103/4/7.

18 Ibid., DD/269/13.

19 *The Spectator*, 9 June 1711.

20 Berks. CRO, D/EX1942/8/2.

21 Cheshire CRO, DSS1/5/119.

22 Bird (ed.), *The Diary of Mary Hardy*, Vol. 1.

23 York RO, MFP/1/22.

24 Manchester Local History Library, MSffD65743.

25 W. Sussex CRO, Par/348/33/1.

26 Manchester Directory.

27 Lemire, *Dress, Culture and Commerce*, 64–71.

28 Ibid.

29 Ibid., 64.

30 Ibid.

31 Dorset CRO, PE/PL/OV/3/228.

32 In N. Devon CRO.

33 Putnam, Tyler R. (2015) 'Joseph Long's Slops: Ready-made Clothing in Early America', *Winterthur Portfolio* 49, no. 2/3, 63–91.

34 Dickens, Charles (1857) *Little Dorrit* London: Bradbury and Evans, Chapter 18.

35 www.londonlives.org. The women were Hetty Davis, Martha Jest, Jane Cockbell, Charlotte Mary Jury, Sarah Forty and Dinah Levy.

36 Pamela Clabburn, 'Parson Woodforde's View of Fashion', *Costume* 5, no. 1 (1971): 19–21.

37 Lincs. CRO, 28A/14/8.

38 Leics. and Rutland CRO, 6D40/19/56.

39 Lancs. CRO, DDX1096/1.

40 National Library of Wales, *Index of Wills*.

41 Lancs. CRO, DDX 1096/1.

42 Salop CRO, 821/50.

43 W. Sussex CRO, MP2699.

44 Leics. and Rutland CRO, Eliza Spurrett's diaries 7D54.

45 Ibid., DE 3730.

46 *Morning Chronicle*, 16 November 1849.

47 See Chapter 8.

48 *Bury and Norwich Post*, 10 March 1847.

49 Leics. and Rutland CRO, Eliza Spurrett's diaries 7D54.

50 Salop CRO, XHIL/838/4/67, 68, 70.

51 Hants. CRO, 132M87.

52 Rousseau, Jean-Jacques (1762) *Émile, ou de l'éducation* Paris: Duchesne, Book 1.

53 Ibid., Book 2.

54 Hants. CRO, 132M87.

55 Wikipedia, quoting *Sketches by Boz*, 1836.

56 *Morning Advertiser*, 13 January 1847, for letter from 'Humanitas' about such caps which were paid for at ninepence a dozen and, according to the letter writer, each required 944 stitches. See p.154 for makers of waterproofs.

Chapter 6

1 Blackburn, Sheila C. (2002) '"Princesses and Sweated-Wage Slaves Go Well Together": Images of British Sweated Workers, 1843–1914', *International Labor and Working-Class History* 61, 24–44.

2 http://www.historyhome.co.uk/peel/economic/sweat.htmhttp://www.historyhome.co.uk/peel/economic/sweat.htm

3 Kent CRO, Gr/AW/4.

4 *Coventry Journal*, 29 May 1858.

5 *Dublin Evening Mail*, 24 November 1856.

6 *East London Observer*, 27 December 1884.

7 *Edinburgh Evening News*, 9 December 1889.

8 *Pall Mall Gazette*, 18 March 1886.

9 *Fife Herald*, 24 November 1842.

10 Children's Employment Commission Report (1843) Vol. X. Reprint, Irish University Press, Introduction.

11 For a wider discussion of this, see Rogers, Helen (1997) '"The Good Are Not Always Powerful, nor the Powerful Always Good": The Politics of Women's Needlework in Mid-Victorian London', *Victorian Studies* 40, no. 4, 589–91.

12 *Evening Mail*, 18 September 1843.

13 *Hereford Journal*, 15 November 1843.

14 *Bell's New Weekly Messenger*, 19 November 1843.

15 *Morning Advertiser*, 26 November 1846.

16 Reported in numerous papers. See, for example, the *St James's Chronicle*, 12 October 1844.

17 *Evening Mail*, 13 February 1850.

18 *Durham Chronicle*, 6 October 1848.

19 *Morning Herald*, 10 July 1844.

20 The *Morning Herald*, 6 May 1844, reported that in the first year the Association had spent some £636 14s. 2d., all raised by subscription, but a mere fraction of what was needed.

21 See, for example, the questioning of the Hon. Secretary, Mr Roper, in *Bell's New Weekly Messenger*, 21 October 1848.

22 *Cheltenham Journal and Gloucestershire Fashionable Weekly Gazette*, 9 January 1843.

23 *Kentish Independent*, 14 December 1843.

24 *Dublin Evening Packet and Correspondent*, 27 December 1843.

25 *Liverpool Mail*, 1 February 1862.

26 *Liverpool Weekly Albion*, 16 January 1875.

27 *Bury and Norwich Post*, 10 March 1847.

28 *Stirling Observer*, 15 December 1859.

29 *Weekly Chronicle* (London), 19 December 1846.

30 *Wiltshire and Gloucestershire Standard*, 1 April 1865

31 *Morning Chronicle*, 23 November 1849, 'Letter XI'. See also https://www.victorianlondon.org/mayhew/mayhew11.htm.

32 Ibid.

33 *London Evening Standard*, 4 August 1848. See also Chapter 9, p.?.

34 *The Advocate, or Irish Industrial Journal*, 17 July 1850.

35 *Morning Chronicle*, 16 November 1849, 'Letter IX'.

36 Ibid.

37 Chimes, Jo (2005) '"Wanted: 1000 Spirited Young Milliners": The Fund for Promoting Female Emigration', in Harris, Beth (ed.), *Famine and Fashion: Needlewomen in the Nineteenth Century* London, Routledge, 229–41.

38 See, for example, *Bell's Life and Sporting Chronicle*, 9 December 1849.

39 *Standard of Freedom*, 29 June 1850.

Chapter 7

1 Walkley, Christina (1981) *The Ghost in the Looking Glass: The Victorian Seamstress* London: Peter Owen.

2 Children's Employment Commission Report (1864) Vol. XIV. reprint, Irish University Press.

3 See, for example, the *Royal Cornwall Gazette*, 8 July 1853.

4 *Leeds Times*, 1 October 1853.

5 Hynes, Tina (1993) 'A Polite Struggle; The Dublin Seamstresses' Campaign, 1869–1872', *Saother* 18, 35–9.

6 Schmiechen, James (1984) *Sweated Industries and Sweated Labour: The London Clothing Trades, 1860–1914*. London: Croom Helm, 25–7.

7 *Western Daily Press*, 15 March 1886.

8 For example, Wikipedia, *The Long Depression* or 'The British Economy in 1870–1914: Industrial Retardation' (ivypanda.com).

9 Gartner, Lloyd P. (2001) *The Jewish Immigrant in England, 1870–1915* London: Vallentine Mitchell.

10 Blackburn, "'Princesses and Sweated-Wage Slaves'", 24–44.

11 This seems to have first been reported on 9 January 1877 in the *Birmingham Daily Mail*. However, it may well have been an urban myth. Former Prime Minister Robert Peel had two daughters, both of whom died *after* 1877, Julia (1821–93) and Eliza (1832–83). However, one of his sisters, Lady Henley, died in 1869, and she was the daughter of the *first* Sir Robert Peel.

12 *Pall Mall Gazette*, 18 July 1884.

13 Quoted in the *Lincolnshire Chronicle*, 4 August 1893.

14 Woodward, Kathleen (1983) *Jipping Street: Childhood in a London Slum* London: Harper & Bros, 1928; reprint, Virago, 120–1.

15 *Wiltshire and Gloucestershire Standard*, 18 June 1850.

16 *Daily News* (London), 7 March 1888.

17 *North Wales Times*, 20 March 1897.

18 Blackburn, "'Princesses and Sweated-Wage Slaves'", 33–5.

19 See, for example, *The Gloucester Citizen*, 25 February 1890.

20 Its annual report appeared in the *Newcastle Courant*, 25 October 1890.

21 *Morning Post*, 11 May 1891.

22 *Telegraph and Courier*, 6 June 1890.

23 Brooks, John Gent (1854) *Memoir of John Gent Brooks, Minister of the Poor in Birmingham*; Haynes, Barry (1991), *Working-Class Life in Victorian Leicester: The Joseph Dare Reports* Leicester: Leicestershire Libraries and Information Service.

24 *Pall Mall Gazette*, 18 March 1886.

25 *Westminster Gazette*, 13 May 1909.

26 Meyer, Lady Adele and Black, Clementina (1909) *The Makers of Our Clothes: A Case for Trade Boards*. London: Duckworth, 129.

27 Ibid., 70.

28 Ibid., 13.

29 Ibid., 13–14.

30 *Cork Constitution*, 24 June 1891.

31 *South Buckinghamshire Standard*, 17 February 1893.

32 *Nottingham Journal*, 29 September 1889.

33 Handbook of the 'Daily News' Sweated Industries Exhibition, compiled by Richard Mudie-Smith (London: Burt & Sons, 1906); available at: https://library.si.edu/digital-library/book/handbookofdailyn00mudi.

34 Thom, Deborah (1988) 'The Bundle of Sticks: Women, Trade Unionists and Collective Organisation before 1918', in Roberts Elizabeth, *Women's Work, 1840–1940* Basingstoke: Macmillan, 272–3.

Chapter 8

1 *Reading Mercury*, 12 March 1842.
2 The FitzHerbert accounts are in Derbys. CRO, 3396/4.
3 'A Lady', *The Workwoman's Guide*, 5.
4 See Chapter 4, Case Study A (iv).
5 Kent CRO, P32112/B/8.
6 *Morning Chronicle*, 16 November 1849.
7 John Rylands Library, Manchester.
8 Northants. CRO, L(C) 505.
9 Devon CRO, 1405M/4/F/3/4/34.
10 K1350/1/2746.
11 Northumb. CRO, NRO 00452/5/5/9.
12 Leics. and Rutland CRO, DE3214/10872.
13 London Metropolitan Archives, A/FHA/29/013/001.
14 Jenkins, Carol (2003) 'Learning Domesticity in Late Victorian England', *Women's History Magazine* 44, 19–24.
15 Notts. CRO, SL156/2/6.
16 *Louth and North Lincolnshire Advertiser*, 15 July 1865.
17 *North Wiltshire Herald*, 27 May 1887.
18 *West Sussex County Times*, 15 May 1880.
19 *Herefordshire Journal*, 15 November 1843.
20 Northumb. CRO, NRO808.3.
21 Salop CRO, 6683/4/173/1-.
22 Berks. CRO, D/EX2670/3/1/3.
23 Advertisements from: *Preston Herald*, 30 June 1875; *Wigan Observer and District Advertiser*, 1 December 1894; *Leicester Daily Post*, 26 March 1891; *Liverpool Mercury*, 4 January 1865; *Ipswich Journal*, 1 January 1870; *Exeter and Plymouth Gazette Daily Telegram*, 22 September 1880; *The Scotsman*, 8 April 1875; *Sport*, 14 August 1886.
24 W. Sussex CRO, ADD MS 38303-38312.
25 John Lewis Archives, 265/14(2).
26 Northants. CRO, ZA6668.
27 Durham CRO, Acc134(D0 RefD/Lu).
28 Powell, Margaret (1968) *Below Stairs*. London: Pan, 31.

29 *Mrs Beeton's Book of Household Management* (1861), 2325.

30 Salop CRO, 1497/1.

31 W. Sussex CRO, PH2313 and 2319.

32 PRO, MH12/16548/431, MH12/489/226, MH12/13909/306 and MH12/1101/315.

33 London Metropolitan Archives, MF/A/004-006.

34 *Morning Post*, 18 January 1855.

35 *Morning Herald*, 21 September 1853.

36 *Edinburgh News and Literary Chronicle*, 23 May 1857.

37 *Illustrated Times*, 16 April 1859.

38 *Hertfordshire Gazette, Agricultural Journal and General Advertiser*, 24 November 1860.

39 *Liverpool Daily Post*, 9 January 1857.

40 *Liverpool Daily Mail*, 21 January 1871.

41 *Shields Daily News*, 16 November 1886.

Chapter 9

1 Alexander, Sally (1983) *Women's Work in Nineteenth-Century London: A Study of the Years 1820–50* London: Journeyman.

2 Cambs. CRO, K1350/1/2106.

3 Ibid., K1350/1/ 312.

4 Ibid., K1350/1/464, K1350/1/493, K1350/1/683, K1350/1/831.

5 Ibid., K1350/1/329.

6 Ibid., K1350/1/141, K1350/1/ 54, K1350/1/50, K1350/1/753, K1350/1/2518, K1350/1/895.

7 Ibid., K1350/1/2510, K1350/1/1665, K1350/1/681 and K1350/1/1070.

8 Ibid., K1350/1/2233.

9 Ibid., K1350/1/391.

10 Ibid., K1350/1/479, K1350/1/636, K1350/1/784, K1350/1/88.

11 Ibid., K1350/1/517.

12 Ibid., K1350/1/1669.

13 Ibid., K1350/1/815.

14 Ibid., K1350/1/1027.

15 Ibid., K1350/1/2524, 2913 and 712.

16 Ibid., K1350/1/714.

17 Ibid., K1350/1/508.

18 My thanks to Jenny Dyer for this information.

19 Jebb, Eglantyne (1906) *Cambridge: A Brief Study in Social Questions* Cambridge: Macmillan & Bowes, p. 202.

20 www.davenapier.co.uk/mayors/haberfield.htm.

21 Details on the front of the application form.

22 Bristol RO, 35717/3a/7.

23 Ibid., 35717/3a/3.

24 Ibid., 35717/3a/4.

25 Ibid., 35717/3a/30.

26 Ibid., 35717/3b/16.

27 Ibid., 35717/3b/15.

28 Ibid., 35717/3b/22.

29 Ibid., 35717/3b/39.

30 Census returns for Stapleton, Glos., 1891.

31 Census returns for Clifton, Glos., 1891.

Chapter 10

1 Heywood (attrib.), The Fayre Maid of the Exchange. 1928 edition, Open Library version. The earlier versions were not divided into acts and scenes.

2 Ibid., Act 1, scene 1.

3 Hood, Thomas (1868) *The Serious Poems of Thomas Hood*, with a Preface by Thomas Hood the Younger London: E. Moxon & Co., Preface.

4 Harris, *Famine and Fashion*, 13–39.

5 Albany Institute of the History of Art.

6 Watts Gallery, Compton, near Guildford, Surrey.

7 Sold in Manchester in 2013, see https://victorianweb.org/painting/daniels/1.html for an image.

8 Yale Center for British Art, Paul Mellon Fund.

9 Johannesburg Art Gallery.

10 Location unknown, see Walkley, *The Ghost in the Looking Glass*, p.77, for an image.

11 Bruce Castle Museum, London.

12 Forbes Magazine collection.

13 Private collection, see Walkley, *The Ghost in the Looking Glass*, 17, for an image.

14 Shipley Art Gallery.

15 Speed Art Museum, Louisville.

16 Yale Center for British Art, Paul Mellon Fund.

17 Private collection. Sold 2008, see https://www.bonhams.com/auctions/15902/lot/32/ for an image.

18 Royal Albert Memorial Museum and Art Gallery, Exeter.

19 Russell-Cotes Art Gallery and Museum, Bournemouth.

20 Altick, Richard (1997) *Punch: The Lively Youth of a British Institution, 1841–1851* Columbus: Ohio State University Press, 17.

21 For a fuller discussion of this, see Laura A. Jones, 'E. Moses and Son: The Tailors Who Pioneered Mass-Market Men's Tailoring?' *Fashion, Style and Popular Culture* 5, no. 1 (2018): 97–115.

22 There is a version of this in Birmingham Museum and Art Gallery.

23 Issue unknown.

24 Stone, Elizabeth (1843) *The Young Milliner* London, 136.

25 Dressmaker, A (1857) [Mary Guignard], *The Unprotected: or, Facts in Dressmaking Life* London: Sampson Low, Son & Co., 83.

26 Dickens, *Little Dorritt*, 93.

27 Ibid., 80.

28 Dickens, *The Chimes*, ch. 3. Project Gutenberg edition.

29 Ch. 4, in ibid.

30 Gaskell, Mrs Elizabeth (1848) *Mary Barton: A Tale of Manchester Life*, 2 vols London: Chapman & Hall, ch. 1. Project Gutenberg edition.

31 Ch. 3, in ibid.

32 Ch. 4, in ibid.

33 Ch. 5, in ibid.

34 Ibid.

35 Gaskell, Mrs Elizabeth (1853) *Ruth*, 3 vols London: Chapman & Hall, ch. 36. Project Gutenberg edition.

Conclusion

1 Lemire, *Dress, Culture and Commerce*, 64.

2 Dzelzainis, Ella (2005) 'Chartism and Gender Politics in Ernest Jones's The Young Milliner', in Harris, Beth (ed.), *Famine and Fashion: Needlewomen in the Nineteenth Century* London: Routledge, 87–97.

3 'Sylvia' (1876) *How to Dress Well on a Shilling a Day*, Home Help Series London: Ward Lock.

4 For a simple description, see Wikipedia, *Liberal Welfare Reforms*, or for more detail, Harris, Bernard (2004) *The Origins of the British Welfare State: Society, State, and Social Welfare in England and Wales, 1800–1945* Basingstoke: Palgrave Macmillan.

5 Verita, May (1995) *Tailoring, Twopence an Hour* London: Excalibur.

Bibliography

Abbreviations

In the text/endnotes: CEC – Children's Employment Commission. CRO – County Record Office (Archives service). RO – Record Office. PRO – Public Record Office. County names will be abbreviated in standard form in the endnotes, e.g. Wilts. for Wiltshire, Yorks. for Yorkshire, etc.
In the bibliography: [n.l] – no location of publication.

Manuscript sources and newspapers

These are all fully referenced in endnotes.

Unpublished theses and dissertations

Foden, F.E. (1961) *A History of Technical Examinations in England, with Special Reference to the Examination Work of the City and Guilds of London Institute,* PhD thesis, University of Reading.

Lambert, Miles (2006) *The Consumption of new and used ready-made clothing in northern England 1660–1830,* PhD thesis, University College, London.

Lane, Penelope (1999) *Women in the Regional Economy of the East Midlands 1700–1830,* PhD thesis, University of Warwick.

Lemire, Beverley (1984) *The British Cotton Industry and Domestic Market, Trade and Fashion in Early Industrial Society 1750–1800*, PhD thesis, Balliol College, Oxford.

Sanderson, Elizabeth (1993) *Women's Work in 18th Century Edinburgh*, PhD thesis, Edinburgh University.

Sleigh-Johnson, N.V. (1989) *The Merchant Taylors' Company of London 1580–1645,* PhD thesis, University of London.

Websites

www.britishnewspaperarchive.co.uk
www.londonlives.org
www.oldbaileyonline.org

Published sources pre-1900

Anon (1738) *The Intriguing Milliners and Attornies' Clerks*. London.

Anon (1811 and 1818) *The Book of Trades or Library of Useful Arts*. London, Tabart. Wiltshire Family History Society reprint, 1977.

A Dressmaker [Mary Guignard] (1857) *The Unprotected, or facts in dressmaking life*. London.

Arthur, T.S. (1872) *Grace Myers' Sewing Machine and Other Stories*. Glasgow, the Scottish Temperance League.

Beeton, Isabella (1859–1861) *Beeton's Book of Household Management*. London, Jonathan Cape [Facsimile].

Brooks, John Gent (1854) *Memoir of John Gent Brooks, Minister of the Poor in Birmingham*. [n.l.].

Brown, Davis and Halse (1857) *The ABC Guide to Haberdashery*. [n.l.].

Campbell, Richard (1747) *The London Tradesman*, [n.l.] [David and Charles reprint 1969].

Children's Employment Commission Reports, Vols X and XIV, 1843 and 1864. Irish University Press reprints.

Cleland, John Cleland (1749) *Fanny Hill*. Numerous editions.

Coyne, J.S. (1852) *Wanted, 1000 Spirited Young Milliners*. London, Thomas Hailes Lacy.

Delves Broughton, Mrs Vernon (ed.) (1887) *Court and Private Life in the Time of Queen Charlotte: Being the Journals of Mrs Papendiek, Assistant Keeper of the Wardrobe and Reader to Her Majesty*, 2 volumes. London, Richard Bentley and Son.

Dickens, Charles (1838–1839) *Nicholas Nickleby*. Numerous editions.

Dickens, Charles, (1844) *The Chimes*. Numerous editions.

Dickens, Charles, (1855–1857) *Little Dorrit*. Numerous editions.

Doggett, C.R. (1874) *Nellie Graham, the Young Dressmaker*. Dorking.

Drury, Robert (1753) *The Rival Milliners*. London.

Eden, Sir Frederick (1797) *The State of the Poor*. [n.l.][Facsimile edition 1966].

Faunthorpe, Rev J.P. (1881) *Household Science Readings in Necessary Knowledge for Girls and Young Women*. London, E. Stanford.

Gaskell, Mrs E. (1848) *Mary Barton*. Numerous editions.

Gaskell, Mrs E. (1851–3) *Cranford*. Numerous editions.

Gaskell, Mrs E. (1853) *Ruth*. Numerous editions.

Godfrey, G.W. (1884) *My Milliner's Bill*. London, Lacey.

Grindrod, R.B. (1845) *The Slaves of the Needle*. London and Manchester, Brittain and Gilpin.

Hammersley, William James (1853) *Christmas Shadows, a Tale of the Poor Needlewomen*, Hartford.

Harrison, J. Stewart (1860) 'The Iceberg' in *Once a Week*. [n.l.]

Haywood, (1741) *Anti-Pamela; or feigned innocence detected*. London.

Heywood, Thomas [attrib.] (1607) *The Fayre Maid of the Exchange*. London.

'Home Industries' (1909). *Journal of the Royal Society of Arts* Vol. 57, No. 2964.

Hood, T. (1863) 'Living – and Dying – by the Needle'. *Englishwoman's Domestic Magazine.*

Hood the younger (1868) *The Serious Poems of Thomas Hood.* London, E. Moxon.

Jerrold, Douglas W. (1825) *The White Milliner.* London, Duncombe.

Jewsbury, Geraldine (1856) *The Sorrows of Gentility* (1856). London.

J.F. (1696) *The Merchant's Warehouse Laid Open; or the Plain Dealing Linen Draper.* London, John Sprint and George Conyers.

Jones, Ernest (1851–1852) *The Young Milliner.* [n.l.].

Keats, Chatterton (1870) *Without a Penny in the World; a Story of the 'Period'.* London.

Marsh, Mrs (1850) *Lettice Arnold.* London, Henry Colburn.

Morton, John (1825) *The Milliners' Holiday.* London, Duncombe edition of the British theatre.

Pepys, Samuel (1660–1669) *Diary.* Numerous editions.

Religious Tract Society (1860) *May Coverley, the young dressmaker.* [n.l.].

Reynolds, G.W.M. (1853) *The Seamstress or the White Slave of England.* London, John Dicks.

Richardson, Samuel (1740) *Pamela.* Numerous editions.

Rowcroft, Charles (1846) *Fanny, the Little Milliner, or the Rich and the Poor.* London.

Smollett, Tobias (1771) *The Expedition of Humphrey Clinker.* Numerous editions.

Spurrett, Eliza. (*c.*1880) *Reminiscences.* Leicester, privately printed.

Stone, Mrs Elizabeth (1843) *The Young Milliner.* London.

Tonna, Charlotte Elizabeth, (1843) *The Wrongs of Women,* London, W.H. Dalton.

Tytler, Sarah (1911) *Girl Neighbours.* London, Blackie.

Needlework manuals and advice about dress

Anon (1808) *The Lady's Oeconomical Assistant, or Art of Cutting Out, and Making the Most Useful Articles of Wearing Apparel, without Waste.* London, John Murray.

De Garsault, Francois A. (1771) *L'Art de la Lingère.* Open Library on-line edition.

Grenfell, Mrs H. (1894) *Under-linen Cutting-out: A Pupil's Manual for Home Study.* London, Longmans.

Haweis, Mrs (1879) *The Art of Dress.* London.

Lady, A. (1838) *The Workwoman's Guide.* (Reprinted Doncaster, Bloomfield 1975).

Levine, Mme (1896) *The Rodmure System of Dresscutting.* Glasgow.

'Sylvia' (1876) *How to Dress Well on a Shilling a Day.* London, Home Help Series.

Willimott, Mrs Thomas (1841) *The Young Woman's Guide.* London.

Published sources post-1900

Adburgham, Alison (1989) *Shops and Shopping: Where and in What Manner the Well-dressed Englishwoman Bought Her Clothes.* London, Allen and Unwin.

Alexander, Lynne M. (1999) 'Creating a Symbol: The Seamstress in Victorian Literature', *Tulsa Studies in Women's Literature* Vol. 18, No. 1, pp. 29–38.

Alexander, Lynne M. (2003) *Women, Work and Representation: Needlewomen in Victorian Art and Literature.* Athens, Ohio University Press.

Alexander, Sally (1983) *Women's Work in 19th Century London, a Study of the Years 1820–1850.* London, Journeyman.

Arnold, Janet (1964) *Patterns of Fashion 1660–1860.* London, Wace and Co.

Arnold, Janet [with additional material by Tiramani, Jenny and Levey, Santina] (2008) *Patterns of Fashion. The cut and construction of linen shirts, smocks, neckwear, headwear and accessories c.1540–1660.* London, Macmillan.

Attfield, J. and Kirkham, P. (1995) *A View from the Interior, Women and Design.* London, Women's Press.

Barker, Hannah (2006) *The Business of Women: Female Entreprise and Urban Development in Northern England.* Oxford, Oxford University Press.

Barlow, Jill (2001) *Calendar of the Registers of Apprentices of the City of Gloucester 1595–1700.* Bristol, Bristol and Gloucestershire Archaeological Society.

Baron, Ava and Klepp, Susan E. (1985) 'If I didn't have my sewing machine . . .' in Jenson, Joan M. (ed.) *A Needle, a Bobbin a Strike, Needlewomen in America*, pp. 20–59. Philadelphia, Temple University Press.

Batchelor, Jennie (2005) *Dress, Distress and Desire.* Basingstoke, Palgrave Macmillan.

Bedfordshire Historical Record Society (1993) *A Bedfordshire Historical Miscellany, Essays in Honour of Patricia Bell.* Bedford, Historical Record Society.

Bell, Lady Florence E.E. (1907) *At the Works, a Study of a Manufacturing Town.* London, Edward Arnold.

Berg, Maxine and Clifford, Helen (1999) *Consumers and Luxury: Consumer Culture in Europe 1650–1850.* Manchester, Manchester University Press.

Bird, M. (ed.) (2013) *The Diaries of Mary Hardy.* 5 volumes. Kingston-upon-Thames, Burnham.

Black, Clementina (ed.) (1915) *Married Women's Work.* London, G.Bell and Sons. (Virago edition, 1983).

Blackburn, Sheila C. (2002) '"Princesses and Sweated-Wage Slaves Go Well Together": Images of British Sweated Workers, 1843–1914', *International Labor and Working-Class History* 61, pp.24–44.

Bosomworth, D. (1991) *The Victorian Catalogue of Household Goods (Silber and Fleming).* London, Studio Editions.

Boulton, Jeremy (1996) 'Wage Labour in Seventeenth-Century London', *The Economic History Review*, New Series, Vol. 49 (2), pp. 268–290.

Brandon, Ruth (1977) *Singer and the History of the Sewing Machine: A Capitalist Romance.* London, Barrie and Jenkins.

Brewer, John and Porter, Roy (eds.) (1993) *Consumption and the World of Goods.* London and New York, Routledge.

Burman, S. (1979) *Fit Work for Women.* Oxford, Croom Helm.

Burnett, John (1994) *Destiny Obscure*. London and New York, Routledge.

Burnette, Joyce (2008) *Gender, Work and Wages in Industrial Revolution Britain*. Cambridge, Cambridge University Press.

Bythell, Duncan (1978) *The Sweated Trades, Outwork in 19th Century Britain*. London, Batsford.

Cadbury and Shann (1907) *Sweating*. London, Headley Bros.

Cherry, Deborah (1983) 'Surveying Seamstresses', *Feminist Art News* 9, pp.27–29.

Chinn, Carl (1988) *They Worked All Their Lives, Women of the Urban Poor in England 1880–1939*. Manchester, Manchester University Press.

Clabburn, Pamela (1971) 'Parson Woodforde's View of Fashion', *Costume* 5, pp. 19–21.

Clabburn, Pamela (1977) 'A Provincial Milliner's Shop in 1785', *Costume* 11, pp. 110–112.

Clark, Alice (1919) *The Working Life of Women in the 17th Century*. London, Routledge. (Frank Cass reprint 1968).

Clark, Gillian (1994) 'Infant Clothing in the 18th Century, a new insight', *Costume* 28, pp. 47–59.

Clarke, Bridget (2009) 'Clothing the Family of an MP in the 1690s', *Costume* 43, pp. 38–54.

Clifford, D.J.H. (ed.) (1990) *The Diaries of Lady Anne Clifford*. Stroud, Alan Sutton.

Cochrane, Laura (2000) 'From the Archives: Women's History in Baker Library's Business Manuscripts Collection', *The Business History Review* Vol. 74 (3), pp. 465–476.

Coffin, Judith (1996) *The Politics of Women's Work: The Paris Garment Trades 1750–1915*. Princeton N.J., Princeton University Press.

Cox, Nancy (2016) *The Complete Tradesman, a Study of Retailing 1550–1820*. London, Routledge.

Crane, Elaine Forman (ed.) (1994) *The Diary of Elizabeth Drinker, the life-cycle of an 18th century woman*. Boston, North Eastern University Press.

Crossick, Geoffrey and Jourdain, Sarge (1999) *Cathedrals of Consumption 1850–1939*. Aldershot, Ashgate.

Crowston, Clare Haru (2001) 'Fabricating Women, the Seamstresses of Old Regime France 1675–1791'. Durham, Duke University Press.

Crowston, Clare Haru (2006) 'Women and Guilds in Early Modern Europe', in Lucanen, Jan et al (eds.) *The Return of the Guilds*. Cambridge, Press Sydicate of the University of Cambridge.

Crowston, Clare (2008) 'Women, gender and guilds in early modern Europe, an overview of recent research', *International Review of Social History*, Vol 53 (Supplement 16), pp. 19–44.

Cunnington, C.W. and P. (1970) *A Handbook of Women's Costume in the 19th Century*. London, Faber and Faber.

Cunnington, C.W. and P. (1972) *A Handbook of English Costume in the 18th Century*. London, Faber and Faber.

Cunnington, C.W. and P. (1972) *A Handbook of English Costume in the 17th Century*. London, Faber and Faber.

Davidoff, Leonora (1973) *The Best Circles*. Oxford, Croom Helm.

Davidoff, Leonora and Hall, Catherine (1987) *Family Fortunes 1780–1850, Men and Women of the English Middle Class*. London, Hutchinson.

Davies, Margaret Llewellyn (1915), *Maternity Letters from Working Women*. Women's Co-operative Guild. [n.l.]. (Virago reprint 1978).

Davies, Margaret Llewellyn (1931), *Life As We Have Known It by Co-operative working women*. [n.l.], (Virago reprint 1977).

Davis, Dorothy (1966) *A History of Shopping*. London, Routledge and Kegan Paul.

Djabri, Susan C. (ed.) (2009) *The Diaries of Sarah Hurst 1759–1762*. Stroud, Amberley.

Dyhouse, Carol (2012) *Girls Growing up in Late Victorian and Edwardian England*. London, Routledge.

Earle, Peter (1989) 'The female labour market in London in the late 17th and early 18th centuries', *Economic History Review*. 2nd series XLII, pp. 328–353.

Edelstein, T.J. (1980) 'They sang The Song of the Shirt; the visual iconography of the seamstress', *Victorian Studies* 23(2), pp. 183–210.

Ehrman, Edwina (2015) *Undressed*. London, V&A Museum.

Ewing, Elizabeth (1987) *Dress & Undress*. London, Batsford.

Fabian Society (1914) *The War, Women and Unemployment*. Pamphlet 178 [n.l.].

Farmer, Tony (2001) 'Setting up Home in Dublin in the 1850s', *Dublin Historical Record*, 54(1), pp. 16–27.

Ferguson, Margaret, Quilligan, Maureen and Vickers, Nancy (eds.) (1986) *Rewriting the Renaissance, the Politics of Sexual Difference in Early Modern Europe*. Chicago, Chicago University Press.

Fernandez, Nancy P. (1987) 'Pattern Diagrams and Fashion Periodicals 1840–1900', *Dress* 13 (1), pp. 5–10.

Finnegan, Frances (1979) *Poverty and Prostitution: A Study of Victorian Prostitutes in York*. Cambridge, Cambridge University Press.

Fischer, D.H. (1996) *The Great Wave, Price Revolutions and the Rhythm of History*. Oxford, Oxford University Press.

Fried, Albert and Elman, Richard (eds.) (1971) *Charles Booth's London*. London, Pelican.

Gartner, Lloyd P. (2001) *The Jewish Immigrant in England 1870–1915*. London, Vallentine Mitchell.

Gazeley, Ian (1989) 'The Cost of Living for Urban Workers in Late Victorian and Edwardian Britain', *Economic History Review* 2nd series XLII(2), pp. 207–221.

Glaisyer, Natasha (2006) *Culture of Commerce in England 1660–1720*. Woodbridge, Boydell.

Godfrey, Frank (1982) *The International History of the Sewing Machine*. London, Hale.

Godley, Andrew (1996) 'Singer in Britain, the Diffusion of Sewing Machine Technology and Its Impact on the Clothing Industry in the United Kingdom 1860–1905', *Textile History* 27(1), pp. 59–76.

Godman, Melina (1991) 'A Georgian Lady's Personal Accounts', *Costume* 25, pp. 21–24.

Goose, Nigel (ed.) (2007) *Women's Work in Industrial England, Regional and Local Perspectives*. Hatfield, Local Population Studies.

Gowing, Laura (2022) *Ingenious Trade, Women and Work in Seventeenth Century London*. Cambridge, Cambridge University Press.

Green, Nancy L. (1996) 'Women and Immigrants in the Sweatshop: Categories of Labor Segmentation Revisited', *Comparative Studies in Society and History* Vol. 38 (3), pp.411–433.

Hall, Catherine (1992) *White, Male and Middle Class*. Cambridge, Polity.

Harris, Bernard (2004) *The origins of the British welfare state: social welfare in England and Wales, 1800–1945*. London, Palgrave.

Harris, Beth, (ed.) (2005) *Famine and Fashioning Needlewomen in the 19th Century*. New York, Ashgate.

Hayden, Peter (1988) 'Records of Clothing Expenditure for the Years 1746–79 Kept by Elizabeth Jervis of Meaford, Staffordshire', *Costume* 22, pp. 32–38.

Haynes, Barrie (1991) Working-Class Life in Victorian Leicester: the Joseph Dare Reports. Leicester, Leicestershire Libraries and Information Services.

Healey, Jonathan (2019) 'Coping with Risk, the First Age of the English Old Poor Law' in Tanimoto, Masayuki and Wong, R.Bin (eds.) *Public Goods Provision in Early Modern Economy*. California, University of California Press.

Higgs, E. (2016) 'Women and Occupations and Work in the Victorian Censuses Revisited', *History Workshop Journal* 81(1), pp. 17–38.

Hill, Bridget (1993) *Eighteenth Century Women, an Anthology*. London and New York, Allen and Unwin.

Hillman, Anne (transcriber) (1994) *The Rake's Diary, George Hilton 1775*. Kendal, Curwen Archives Trust.

Honeyman, Katrina and Goodman, Jordan (1991) 'Women's Work, Gender Conflict, and Labour Markets in Europe, 1500–1900', *The Economic History Review,* New Series, Vol. 44 (4), pp. 602–628.

Horrell, S. and Humphries, J. (1992) 'Old Questions, New Data and Altered Perspectives, the Standard of Living in the British Industrial Revolution', *Journal of Economic History* 52(4), pp. 849–880.

Hudson, Pat and Lee, W. Robert (1990) *Women's Work and the Family Economy in Historical Perspective*. Manchester, Manchester University Press.

Humphries, Jane and Weisdorf, Jacob (2015) 'The Wages of Women in England, 1260–1850'. *The Journal of Economic History*, Vol. 75 (2), pp. 405–447.

Hynes, Tina (1993) 'A polite strategy', *Saother* 18, pp. 35–39.

Inder, Pam and Aldis, Marion (1997) 'Buttons, Braids, Bones and Body Linings, a Staffordshire Lady and her London Dressmaker', *Staffordshire History* 25, pp. 24–51.

Inder, Pam and Aldis, Marion (2002) *Finding Susanna*. Leek, Churnet Valley Books.

Inder, Pam (2017) *The Rag Trade: The People Who Made Our Clothes*. Stroud, Amberley.

Inder, Pam (2018) *Dresses and Dressmaking*. Stroud, Amberley.

Inder, Pam (2020) *Busks, Basques and Brush-braid, British Dressmaking in the 18th and 19th centuries.* London, Bloomsbury.

Jackson, R.V. (1987) 'The Structure of Pay in 19th Century Britain', *Economic History Review*, 2nd series XL (4), pp. 561–570.

Jebb, Eglantyne (1906) *Cambridge, A Brief Study in Social Questions.* Cambridge, Macmillan and Bowes.

Jenkins, Carol (2003) 'Learning Domesticity in Victorian England', *Women's History Magazine* 44, pp. 19–30.

Jenson, Joan M. and Davidson, Sue (eds.)(1984) *A Needle, a Bobbin, a Strike, Women Needleworkers in America.* Philadelphia, Temple University Press.

John, Angela (1985) *Unequal Opportunities, Women's Employment 1800–1919.* Oxford, Blackwell.

Johnson, Barbara (1987) *A Lady of Fashion. Barbara Johnson's Album of Styles and Fabrics.* London, V&A Museum.

Johnston, J.A. (ed.) (1991) *Lincoln Inventories 1661–1714.* Woodbridge, Lincoln Record Society.

Jones, Laura A. (2018) 'E. Moses and Son – the tailors who pioneered mass-marketing men's tailoring?' *Fashion, Style and Popular Culture,* Vol 5 (1), pp. 97–115.

Lambert, Miles (2021) 'Check Shirts, Flannel Jackets, Canvas Trousers: the Trade in Slops from 18th Century Liverpool', *Textile History* 52(1–2), pp. 78–100.

Lancaster, Bill (1995) *The Department Store, a Social History.* Leicester, Leicester University Press.

Lane, Penelope, Raven, Neil and Snell, K.D.M. (2004) *Women, Work and Wages in England 1600–1850.* Woodbridge, Boydell.

Lemire, Beverley (1991) 'Peddling Fashion: Salesmen, Pawnbrokers, Tailors, Thieves and the Second Hand Clothes Trade in England c.1700–1800', *Textile History*, 22 (1), pp. 67–82.

Lemire, Beverley (1994) 'Redressing the History of the Clothing Trade in England: Ready-made Clothing, Guilds and Women Workers 1650–1800', *Dress* 21 (1), pp. 61–74.

Lemire, Beverley (1997) *Dress, Culture and Commerce, the English Clothing Trade before the Factory 1660–1800.* Basingstoke, Macmillan.

Lemire, Beverley (1999) '"In the Hands of Workwomen": English Markets, Cheap Clothing and Female Labour 1650–1800', *Costume* 33, pp. 23–35.

Llewellyn, Sacha (1997) 'Inventory of Her Grace's Things, 1847', *Costume* 31, pp. 49–67.

Mahood, Linda (1990) *The Magdalenes, Prostitution in the 19th Century.* London, Routledge.

McIntosh, Robert (1993) 'Sweated Labour: Female Needleworkers in Industrializing Canada', *Labour / Le Travail* 32, pp. 105–138.

McKendrick, Brewer and Plumb (1982) *The Birth of a Consumer Society, the Commercialisation of 18th Century England.* London, Europa.

Meyer, Lady Adele and Black, Clementina (1909) *The Makers of Our Clothes, a Case for Trade Boards*. London, Duckworth.

Miller, Marla (2003) 'Gender, artisanry and craft tradition in early New England, the view through the eye of a needle', *William and Mary Quarterly* 60 (4), pp.743–766.

Miller, Michael B. (1981) *The Bon Marché, Bourgeois Culture and the Department Store 1869–1920*. London, Allen and Unwin.

Morris, Jenny (1986) *Women Workers and the Sweated Trades*. Aldershot, Gower.

Moss, Michael and Turton, Alison (1989) *A Legend of Retailing: The House of Fraser*. London, Weidenfeld and Nicholson.

Mui, L. and Mui, H. (1989) *Shops and Shopkeeping in 18th Century England*. Montreal, McGill University Press.

Nenadic, Stana (1998) 'Social Shaping of Women's Behaviour in the 19th Century Garment Trades', *Journal of Social History* 31(3), pp. 625–645.

Nolan, Mary (2002) 'Sweated Labor: The Politics of Representation and Reform', *International Labour and Working Class History* 61, pp. 8–12.

North, Susan (2020) *Sweet and Clean; Bodies and Clothes in Early Modern England*. Oxford, Oxford University Press.

Perkin, Joan (1994) *Victorian Women*. London, John Murray.

Pember Reeves, Maud (1913) *Round About a Pound a Week*. London, (1979 Virago edition).

Penney, Norman (ed.) (1920) *The Household Account Book of Sarah Fell of Swarthmore Hall*. Cambridge, Cambridge University Press.

Phillips, Nicola (2006) *Women in Business 1700–1850*. Woodbridge, Boydell.

Pinchbeck, Ivy (1981) *Women Workers and the Industrial Revolution 1750–1850*. London, Virago.

Plant, Marjorie (1948) 'Clothes and the 18th century Scot', *Scottish History Review* XXVII (103), pp.1–24.

Potter, Beatrice (1926) *My Apprenticeship*. London, Longman and Co.

Pottle, Frederick A. (ed.) (1950) *Boswell's London Journal 1762–1763*. London, Heinemann.

Powell, Margaret (1970) *Below Stairs*. London, Pan.

Purvis, June (1989) *Hard Lessons, the Lives and Education of Working Class Women*. Cambridge, Polity.

Putman, Tyler Rudd (2015) 'Joseph Long's Slops: Ready-Made Clothing in Early America', *Winterthur Portfolio* Vol. 49 (2/3), pp. 63–91.

Quennell, Peter (ed.) (1985) *John Macdonald, Memoirs of an 18th Century Footman*. London, Century.

Quennell, Peter (1987) *Mayhew's London*. London, Bracken Books.

Reeves, Maud Pember (1913) *Round about a Pound a Week*. London, Bell. (Virago reprint, 1979).

Rendell, Mike, (2011), *The Journal of a Georgian Gentleman, the life and times of Richard Hall, 1729–1801*. Brighton, The Book Guild.

Ribeiro, Aileen (1984 and 2002) *Dress in 18th Century Europe*. London and New York, Yale.

Richardson, George (1904) *Drapers', Dressmakers' and Milliners' Accounts*. London, The Accountants' Library.

Richmond, Vivienne (2013) *Clothing the Poor in 19th Century England*. Cambridge, Cambridge University Press.

Roberts, Elizabeth (1984) *A Woman's Place, an Oral History of Working Class Women 1890–1940*. Oxford, Blackwell.

Roberts, Elizabeth (1988) *Womens Work 1840–1940*. Basingstoke, Macmillan.

Rogers, Helen (1997) "'The Good Are Not Always Powerful, nor the Powerful Always Good": The Politics of Women's Needlework in Mid-Victorian London', *Victorian Studies* Vol. 40 (4), pp. 589–623.

Rose, Clare (1989) *Children's Clothes*, London, Batsford.

Rothstein, Natalie (ed.) (1984) *Four Hundred Years of Fashion*. London, V&A Museum.

Rowntree, Benjamin Seebohm (1901) *Poverty, A Study of Town Life*. London, Macmillan and Co.

Royden, A. Maud (1916) *Downward Paths, an Inquiry into the Causes Which Contribute to the Making of the Prostitute*. London, G. Bell and Sons.

Sanderson, Elizabeth (1984) *Sweated Industry and Sweated Labour: The London Clothing Trade 1860–1914*. London, Croom Helm.

Sanderson, Elizabeth (1996) *Women and Work in 18th Century Edinburgh*. Basingstoke, Macmillan.

Schmiechen, James (1984) *Sweated Industries and Sweated Labour*. London, Croom Helm.

Scott Moncrieff, R. (ed.) (1911) *The Household Book of Lady Grisell Baillie 1692–1733*. Edinburgh, Scottish History Society.

Sharpe, Pamela (1998) *Women's Work, the English Experience 1650–1914*. London, Arnold.

Shearer, Laura Baker (2002) "'I owe no one a penny": Labor and Female Subjectivity in the Working-Class Diaries of Lizzie Goodenough', *Legacy* Vol. 19 (1), pp. 62–70.

Simonton, Deborah (1998) *A History of European Women's Work 1700 to the Present*. London, Routledge.

Snell, K.D.M. (1985) *Annals of the Labouring Poor*. Cambridge, Cambridge University Press.

Sorge-English, Lynn (2016) *Stays and Body Image in London*. Oxford, Routledge.

Spencer, Elizabeth (2022) 'Clothing the Poor' in Collinge, Peter and Falconi, Louise (eds.) *Providing for the Poor: The Old Poor Law 1750–1834*. London, University of London Press Institute of Historical Research.

Spufford, Margaret (1984) *The Great Reclothing of Rural England: petty chapmen and their wares in the 17th century*. London, Hambledon.

Spufford, Margaret (2000) 'The cost of apparel in 17th century England and the accuracy of Gregory King', *Economic History Review* 53 (4), pp.677–705.

Stewart, Margaret and Hunter, Leslie (1964) *The Needle Is Threaded, the History of an Industry*. London, Heinemann.

Styles, John (1994) 'Clothing the North, the Supply of Non-elite Clothing to the North of England', *Textile History* 25 (2), pp. 139–166.

Styles, John (2007) *The Dress of the People, Everyday Fashion in 18th Century England*. New Haven and London, Yale.

Styles, John and Vickery, Amanda (2006) *Gender, Taste and Material Culture in Britain and North America 1700–1830*. New Haven and London, Yale.

Sweated Trades (1906) Exhibition catalogue. [n.l.].

Tankard, Danae (2019) *Clothing in 17th Century Rural England*. London, Bloomsbury.

Thom, Deborah (1988) 'The Bundle of Sticks' in Roberts, Elizabeth, *Womens Work 1840–1940*. Basingstoke, Macmillan.

Thompson, F.M.L. (ed.) (1990) *The Cambridge Social History of Britain 1750–1950. Vol 2, People and their Environment*. Cambridge, Cambridge University Press.

Tilly, L. and Scott, J. (1978) *Women, Work and Family*. London and New York, Methuen.

Tobin, Shelley, (2000) *Inside Out, a brief history of underwear*. London, National Trust

Trautman, Pat (1979) 'Personal Clothiers: A Demographic Study of Dressmakers, Seamstresses and Tailors 1880–1920', *Dress* 5, pp. 1–13.

Troide, Lars E. (ed.) (1988) *The Early Journals and Letters of Fanny Burney*. Oxford, Clarendon.

Turbin, Carole (1987) 'Beyond Conventional Wisdom', in Groneman, C. and Norton, Mary Beth (eds.), *To Toil the Livelong Day, American Women at Work 1780–1980*. Ithaca, Cornell University Press.

Tyrrell, Alex (2000) 'Samuel Smiles and the Woman Question in Early Victorian Britain', *Journal of British Studies* Vol. 39 (2), pp. 185–216.

Vaisey, David (ed.) (1985) *The Diary of Thomas Turner 1754–1765*. Oxford, Oxford University Press.

Verita, May (1995) *Tailoring, Twopence an Hour*. London, Excalibur.

Vickery, Amanda (1998) *The Gentleman's Daughter, Women's Lives in Georgian England*. New Haven and London, Yale.

Vicunus, Martha (1972) *Suffer and Be Still, Women in the Victorian Age*. Bloomington, Indiana University Press.

Walkley, Christina (1981) 'Charity and the Victorian Needlewoman', *Costume* 14, pp.136–143.

Walkley, Christina (1981) *The Ghost in the Looking Glass*. London, Peter Owens.

Walkowitz, Judith R. (1980) *Prostitution and Victorian Society, Women, Class and the State*. Cambridge, Cambridge University Press.

Weatherill, Lorna (1988) *Consumer Behaviour and Material Culture in England, 1660–1760*. London, Routledge.

Weatherill, Lorna (1991) 'Consumer Behaviour in the Late 17th and Early 18th Centuries', *Textile History*, 22 (2), pp. 297–310.

Wilcox, David (2012) 'The Clothing of a Georgian Banker', *Costume* 46(1), pp.17–54.

Wohl, Anthony S. (1968) 'The bitter cry of outcast London'. *International Review of Social History* 13 (2), pp.189–245.

Yeo, Eileen and Thompson, E.P. (1973) *The Unknown Mayhew*. Harmondsworth, Penguin.

Image Sources

National Portrait Gallery, via Wikimedia, Colour Plate I; National Trust, via Wikimedia, Colour Plate II; Peter McDermott, via Wikimedia, Colour Plate III; Heritage Images, Hulton Fine Art Collection, via Getty, Colour Plate IV; Albany Museum of History and Art (Daderot), via Wikimedia, Colour Plate V; Yale Center for British Art, Paul Mellon Fund via Wikimedia, Colour Plate VI; Sepia Times, Universal Images Group, via Getty, Colour Plate VII; Heritage Images, Hulton Fine Art Collection, via Getty, Colour Plate VIII.

Author's photograph, Figure 9.2; Rob Bendall, via Wikimedia, Figure 8.1; Berkshire Archives, Figure 8.4; Bettmann, via Getty, Figure 7.3; Bettman, via Getty, Figure 8.2; Bloomsbury Publishing, Figure 0.2; British Museum, via Wikimedia, Figure 4.1; British Museum (Heal collection), via Wikimedia, Figure 5.4; British Museum (Banks collection), via Wikimedia, Figure 5.1; British Museum, via Wikimedia, Figure 5.2; Heritage Images, Hulton Fine Art Collection, via Getty, Figure 5.7; Hulton Archive (Stringer) via Getty, Figure 3.1; Hulton Archive (Stringer), via Getty, Figure 6.2; Hulton Archive, via Getty (Print Collection), Figure 9.1; Leicestershire Museums, Figure 5.6; Metropolitan Museum of Art, via Wikimedia, Figure 1.12, Metropolitan Museum of Art, New York, NY, via Wikimedia, Figure 2.1; Museum of London, Figure 3.2; National Library of Ireland (Poole Collection), via Wikimedia, Figure 5.9; Courtesy of Scawby Hall, Nelthorpe Deposit via Lincolnshire Archives, Figure 4.4; Royal Collection, via Wikimedia, Figure 1.6; Royal Collection, via Wikimedia, Figure 1.11; Sepia Times, Universal Images Group, via Getty, Figure 10.1; Shropshire Archives, Figure 8.3; Shropshire Archives (Attingham Collection); Courtesy of the Attingham Estate, Figure 1.9; Shropshire Archives (Attingham Collection), Courtesy of the Attingham Estate, Figure 11.1; Shropshire Archives (Attingham Collection), Courtesy of the Attingham Estate, Figure 4.3; Universal History Archive, Universal Images Group, via Getty, Figure 6.1; Universal History Archive, Universal Images Group, via Getty, Figure 7.2; Universal History Archive, Universal Images Group, via Getty, Figure 10.5; Victoria and Albert Museum, London (Image Collection), Figure 1.2; Victoria and Albert Museum, London (Image Collection), Figure 1.8; Victoria and Albert Museum, London (Image Collection), Figure 5.3; Wikimedia, Figure 1.10; Wikimedia, Figure 1.13; Wikimedia, Figure 4.2; Wikimedia, Figure 5.5; Wikimedia, Figure 5.8; Wiltshire and Swindon History Centre, Figure 2.2; Yale University Art Gallery, via Wikimedia, Figure 1.7.

Illustrations from publications referenced in the captions: Figure 0.1, Figure 1.1, Figure 1.3, Figure 1.4, Figure 1.5, Figure 6.3, Figure 7.1, Figure 7.4, Figure 8.5, Figure 10.2, Figure 10.3, Figure 10.4.

Index

Colour Plate I. Anne Clifford, Countess of Dorset, later Countess of Pembroke and Montgomery, mistress of Appleby, Brough, Brougham, Skipton and Mallerstang castles, by William Larkin, 1618.

Colour Plate II. Mary Barwick, Lady Dutton, by an unknown artist in the style of Godfrey Kneller, *c.* 1678–9. The upper part of her shift is clearly visible.

Colour Plate III. Upland road near Bewcastle, 2012, showing how bleak the landscape still is.

Colour Plate IV. The Mabie children, artist unknown, c. 1852. The boy wears a late version of a skeleton suit; the older girl is wearing pantalettes and both girls are wearing dresses with wide off-the-shoulder necklines. The older girl's white dress is deeply impractical for playing out of doors.

Colour Plate V. *The Song of the Shirt* by John Thomas Peele, 1849. It is typical of many paintings based on Thomas Hood's poem.

Colour Plate VI. *For Only One Short Hour* by Anna Blunden, 1854.

Colour Plate VII. *Lord, Thy Will Be Done*, by Philip Hermogenes Calderon, 1855. It shows a young woman widowed in the Crimean War of 1853–6 and forced to become a seamstress to support herself and her child.

Colour Plate VIII. *The Seamstress*, watercolour, by John Everett Millais, 1860, was an illustration for a story called 'The Iceberg' by J. Stewart Harrison. The story tells of Ben, a sailor, and his girlfriend, Esther. Ben returns from a voyage to discover that Esther has had a baby boy by another man. He abandons her and she is reduced to earning her living as a seamstress.

www.ingramcontent.com/pod-product-compliance
Lightning Source LLC
Chambersburg PA
CBHW071836270326
41929CB00013B/2014